Collins

Teache

EDEXCEL INTERNATIONAL GCSE (9-1) BIOLOGY

Sue Kearsey and Mike Smith

William Collins' dream of knowledge for all began with the publication of his first book in 1819. A self-educated mill worker, he not only enriched millions of lives, but also founded a flourishing publishing house. Today, staying true to this spirit, Collins books are packed with inspiration, innovation and practical expertise. They place you at the centre of a world of possibility and give you exactly what you need to explore it.

Collins. Freedom to teach

Published by Collins
The News Building
1 London Bridge Street
London
SE1 9GF

© HarperCollins*Publishers* Limited 2017

Browse the complete Collins catalogue at:
www.collins.co.uk

10 9 8 7 6 5 4 3 2 1

ISBN 978 0 00 823622 9

British Library Cataloguing in Publication Data

A Catalogue record for this publication is available from the British Library

Original material by Sue Kearsey
New material by Mike Smith
Commissioning Editor: Joanna Ramsay
Development Editor: Rebecca Ramsden
Project manager: Maheswari Pon Saravanan
Project editor: Vicki Litherland
Formatting: Jouve India
Copy editor: Diana Anyakwo
Proofreader: Jan Schubert
Answer checker: Nick Mason
Cover design: Ink-tank
Cover image: Roberto Sorin/Shutterstock
Production: Lauren Crisp
Printed and bound by CPI

Health and Safety: All practicals in this book have been safety checked and the publisher and authors have made every reasonable effort to ensure that the experiments and activities in this book are safe when conducted as instructed. However, the publishers assume no responsibility for any damage or injury caused or sustained while performing the experiments or activities in this book to the full extent permitted by law.

Parents, guardians, and/or teachers should supervise students who undertake the experiments and activities in this book, and carry out full risk assessments before carrying out any practical work.

Acknowledgements

Every effort has been made to trace copyright holders and to obtain their permission for the use of copyright materials. The publishers will gladly receive any information enabling them to rectify any error or omission at the first opportunity.

Contents

Introduction

Welcome to the Collins Edexcel International GCSE Biology Teacher Pack, which has been written by experienced authors and teachers and fully safety checked to help you deliver an effective and successful International GCSE Biology course.

Overview

The **printed book** mirrors the Student Book topics and includes:

- **Activity plans** with resource lists, learning outcomes and objectives, and detailed guidance.
- **Practical activities** including teacher demonstrations and student experiments.
- **Worksheets** for students with instructions to follow and questions to answer.
- **Technician's notes** so practicals can be safely planned and executed.
- **Answers** to all the questions in the Student Book.
- **Scheme of Work** that maps all practical activities and shows at a glance all the topics linked with their learning outcomes and Edexcel specification references.
- Matching chart to the **Biology, Science Double Award** and **Science Single Award** specifications.

Activity plans

The Teacher Pack has been matched topic by topic to the Student Book to allow easy cross referencing between the books. Each topic is introduced with a brief introduction, links to other topics and an overview of the activities in an easy-to-navigate table. Activity plans give guidance on delivering learning episodes that can be combined for longer lessons to give you complete flexibility and control.

Activity plans cover the following:

- **Learning objectives and outcomes** linked to the specification and the student book.
- **Common misconceptions** that students hold which may need addressing.
- **Resources** you will need for activities.
- A detailed pick-up-and-teach **Approach** for differentiated, varied tasks.
- **Demonstration and practical activity** technician's notes so you can easily check you have everything you need.
- **Answers** to all the questions in the Student Book.

Activity plans are supported by **Worksheets, Technician's notes** and all **Answers**.

Worksheets

Worksheets provide engaging activities for students. Those that deal with practical work give step-by-step guidance for students to ensure that they carry out their investigations safely and successfully.

Technician's notes

Detailed **Technician's notes** are provided for every lesson with lists of resources needed for practical activities and/or demonstrations, set-up instructions and safety notes.

For Today's Safety Information, which will need to be checked before setting up any practical activity or demonstration, please refer to your employer's guidelines or visit: www.science.cleapss.org.uk

Technician's notes appear within the lesson plans for your reference.

Answers

Every activity plan in this book includes the **answers** to the associated questions in the Student Book. Answers to the **Exam-style questions** are given at the end of every section.

Scheme of Work

The detailed **Scheme of Work** at the back of this book provides a comprehensive overview of the Edexcel International GCSE course, matching each lesson to the learning outcomes in the specification. It also shows at a glance where the practical activities and demonstrations occur so that you can plan ahead.

Introduction

The specification content is divided into five sections, each containing a number of different topics:

1 The nature and variety of living organisms

2 Structure and functions in living organisms

3 Reproduction and inheritance

4 Ecology and the environment

5 Use of biological resources

When determining the teaching sequence for the course, the following considerations are important:

- There should be a logical progression in the development of concepts and knowledge in order to aid students' understanding.
- The course should have a 'storyline' so that wherever possible the sequence can be easily explained to students. You can achieve this can in different ways for this specification, as some topics on body systems in Sections 2 and 3 are covered in relation to humans and to flowering plants. You might approach this from the view of the systems, as in the order of the specification, or from the view of the organisms by covering all systems relating to humans and then covering plant systems at a different time.
- You should consider carefully how to introduce the more difficult concepts. For example, you should ensure that they are not introduced too early in the course, resulting in demotivation, or put in a sequence where they all come one after another.
- Maintain the emphasis on practical and investigative work throughout the course. Note that the investigative work in Topic 4a involves fieldwork to collect organisms. This may only be practical at certain times of the year, and so should be planned accordingly. However, you should not consider this any earlier than the 3rd term of the first year, in order to ensure that students have sufficient background knowledge to make best use of the investigations.
- You will need to allocate different amounts of teaching time to different topics, depending on levels of difficulty or extent of the content.
- It is important to retain some flexibility so that difficult ideas can be revisited or new ideas applied in different contexts.

Suggested teaching sequence

The sequence is mapped over 5 terms on the assumption that much of the time in the 6th term will be allocated to revision. It also uses the approach of covering the systems topics from the view of the organisms, and places Topic 4a in the 3rd term of the first year to time the fieldwork for a northern hemisphere summer.

Where the course is started early or where the time allocated each week is either generous or limited, adjustments will need to be made.

First year, 1st term

1a Characteristics of living organisms

1b Variety of living organisms

2a Level of organisation

2b Cell structure

2c Biological molecules

2d Movement of substances into and out of cells

2f Respiration

First year, 2nd term

2e Nutrition (humans)

2g Gas exchange (humans)

2h Transport (humans)

2i Excretion (humans)

2j Coordination and response (humans)

First year, 3rd term

3a Reproduction (humans)

4a The organism in the environment

4b Feeding relationships

4c Cycles within ecosystems

4d Human influences on the environment

Second year, 1st term

2e Nutrition (flowering plants)

2g Gas exchange (flowering plants)

2i Excretion (flowering plants)

2h Transport (flowering plants)

2j Coordination and response (flowering plants)

3a Reproduction (flowering plants)

Second year, 2nd term

3b Inheritance

5a Food production

5b Selective breeding

5c Genetic modification (genetic engineering)

5d Cloning

Matching chart to Biology, Science Double Award and Science Single Award

This chart matches the statements in the Edexcel International GCSE Biology, and Science Double and Single Awards to the content of the Student Book. A shaded box in a column indicates that the topic is not needed for Science Double Award or Single Award.

The numbers in the columns correspond to the statement numbers in the specification.

Section 1 The nature and variety of living organisms

Topic	Biology	Science Double Award	Science Single Award	Pages
a) Characteristics of living organisms	1.1	1.1	1.1	10, 11
b) Variety of living organisms	1.2	1.2	1.2	12, 15–22
	1.3	1.3	1.3	20
	1.4	1.4	1.4	12, 18, 21–22

Section 2 Structure and functions in living organisms

Topic	Biology	Science Double Award	Science Single Award	Pages
a) Level of organisation	2.1	2.1	2.1	30–33
b) Cell structure	2.2	2.2	2.2*	36
	2.3	2.3	2.3*	36–38
	2.4	2.4	2.4	36–38
	2.5B			39
	2.6B			40
c) Biological molecules	2.7	2.7	2.7	43–44
	2.8	2.8	2.8	44
	2.9	2.9	2.9	43–47
	2.10	2.10	2.10	48–51
	2.11	2.11	2.11	48–50
	2.12	2.12	2.12	48–51
	2.13	2.13	2.13	48–51
	2.14B			48–51
d) Movement of substances into and out of cells	2.15	2.15	2.15	55–62
	2.16	2.16	2.16	63–65
	2.17	2.17		58– 59, 61–62
e) Nutrition	2.18	2.18	2.18	69–72
	2.19	2.19	2.19	69
	2.20	2.20	2.20	72–73
	2.21	2.21	2.21	70–71
	2.22	2.22		77–78
	2.23	2.23	2.23	74–76
	2.24	2.24		78–85
	2.25	2.25		79–80
	2.26	2.26		82
	2.27	2.27	2.27	84–87
	2.28	2.28		86
	2.29	2.29	2.29	87
	2.30	2.30		89
	2.31	2.31		89
	2.32	2.32		90
	2.33B			83

9

Topic	Biology	Science Double Award	Science Single Award	Pages
f) Respiration	2.34	2.34	2.34	97–102
	2.35	2.35	2.35	98
	2.36	2.36	2.36	102
	2.37	2.37	2.37	99
	2.38	2.38	2.38	101
	2.39	2.39		99
g) Gas exchange	2.40B			55–56, 105–109
	2.41B			106–108
	2.42B			109
	2.43B			109
	2.44B			106
	2.45B			108
	2.46	2.46	2.46	110–114
	2.47	2.47	2.47	111–113
	2.48	2.48	2.48	114
	2.49	2.49		116–119
	2.50	2.50		115
h) Transport	2.51	2.51	2.51	124–125
	2.52	2.52	2.52	125
	2.53	2.53		126
	2.54	2.54		125
	2.55B			127
	2.56B			128
	2.57B			129
	2.58B			130
	2.59	2.59	2.59	131–135
	2.60	2.60	2.60	132
	2.61	2.61	2.61	132–133
	2.62	2.62	2.62	133–134
	2.63B			134
	2.64B			135
	2.65	2.65	2.65	135–139
	2.66	2.66		140–141
	2.67	2.67		141
	2.68	2.68	2.68	137–138
	2.69	2.69	2.69*	57, 136–139
i) Excretion	2.70	2.70		148–149
	2.71	2.71		149
	2.72B			150–153
	2.73B			149
	2.74B			150
	2.75B			151
	2.76B			151
	2.77B			151
	2.78B			152–153
	2.79B			152
j) Coordination and response	2.80	2.80		157–171
	2.81	2.81		167–169
	2.82	2.82		158
	2.83	2.83		157–160
	2.84	2.84		158–159
	2.85	2.85		158–159
	2.86	2.86		160–161
	2.87	2.87		161

Matching chart to Double and Single Awards

Topic	Biology	Science Double Award	Science Single Award	Pages
	2.88	2.88		162
	2.89	2.89		162
	2.90	2.90		166
	2.91	2.91		163–164
	2.92	2.92		164–165
	2.93	2.93		167–168
	2.94	2.94		169–171
	2.95B			171, 205

Section 3 Reproduction and inheritance

Topic	Biology	Science Double Award	Science Single Award	Pages
a) Reproduction	3.1	3.1	3.1	190–191
	3.2	3.2	3.2	192–199, 205–207
	3.3	3.3	3.3	195
	3.4	3.4	3.4*	197–199
	3.5	3.5		199–200
	3.6	3.6		199
	3.7	3.7		201
	3.8	3.8	3.8	202–203
	3.9	3.9		204–205
	3.10B			205
	3.11	3.11		207–208
	3.12	3.12		207
	3.13	3.13	3.13	203
b) Inheritance	3.14	3.14		215
	3.15	3.15	3.15	215
	3.16B			216
	3.17B			216
	3.18B			216–218
	3.19	3.19	3.19	218–220
	3.20	3.20	3.20	220–221
	3.21B			225–226
	3.22	3.22		227
	3.23	3.23	3.23	221–225
	3.24	3.24		228–229
	3.25	3.25	3.25	222–225
	3.26	3.26	3.26	230
	3.27	3.27	3.27	230
	3.28	3.28		231
	3.29	3.29		231
	3.30	3.30		231–232
	3.31	3.31	3.31	233
	3.32	3.32		231
	3.33	3.33	3.33	233–234
	3.34	3.34		234
	3.35B			235
	3.36B			235
	3.37B			235
	3.38	3.38	3.38	236–238
	3.39	3.39		238–239

Edexcel International GCSE Biology Teacher Pack   11   © HarperCollins*Publishers* Ltd 2017

Section 4 Ecology and the environment

Topic	Biology	Science Double Award	Science Single Award	Pages
a) The organism in the environment	4.1	4.1	4.1	256–257
	4.2	4.2	4.2	259–262
	4.3B			263–264
	4.4B			263–264
	4.5	4.5	4.5	258
b) Feeding relationships	4.6	4.6	4.6	268–270
	4.7	4.7	4.7	270–276
	4.8	4.8	4.8	279
	4.9	4.9	4.9	277–278
c) Cycles within ecosystems	4.10	4.10	4.10	283–284
	4.11B			286–288
d) Human influences on the environment	4.12	4.12		294–297
	4.13	4.13		298–299
	4.14	4.14		299–301
	4.15	4.15		299–301
	4.16	4.16		301–302
	4.17	4.17		302–305
	4.18B			305–306

Section 5 Use of biological resources

Topic	Biology	Science Double Award	Science Single Award	Pages
a) Food production	5.1	5.1	5.1	323
	5.2	5.2	5.2	323
	5.3	5.3		323–325
	5.4	5.4		325–329
	5.5	5.5	5.5	329–331
	5.6	5.6	5.6	332
	5.7	5.7		
	5.8	5.8		333–334
	5.9B			335–337
b) Selective breeding	5.10	5.10		342–345
	5.11	5.11		342, 346–347
c) Genetic modification (genetic engineering)	5.12	5.12	5.12	351
	5.13	5.13	5.13	351–352
	5.14	5.14	5.14*	352–353
	5.15	5.15	5.15	354–355
	5.16	5.16	5.16	350–351
d) Cloning	5.17B			359–361
	5.18B			361
	5.19B			362–364
	5.20B			363–364

* refers to a small change to the corresponding specification points from Biology and Science Double Award.

Contents

a) Characteristics of living organisms

b) Variety of living organisms

c) Answers to exam-style questions

Overview of the section

This section introduces a definition of 'living'. The characteristics outlined in Topic 1a are covered separately and in detail in Section 2. They are presented together here to revise previous learning and to highlight that all these characteristics need to function well together at some point in an organism's life.

Topic 1b is a general overview of the classification of organisms, again to introduce the contexts for more detailed work on specific groups of organisms in later sections.

It is very likely that students starting the International GCSE course have had some previous experience of biology. However, they may have had different experiences, and their knowledge and levels of recall may vary considerably. For this reason, it is important for you to spend some time at the beginning of each topic to find out exactly what your students remember from their previous study of biology.

Starting points

The Student Book provides a 'section opener', a double page spread that sets the scene (see pages 8–9). It is structured in this way:

- An overview providing details of the areas of study
- Five questions in an order that relates to the structure of this section
- A list of section contents

The questions are intended to provide a structure for introducing the section.

1. What are the characteristics shared by living organisms?

2. Crystals can grow in size, but does that mean they are alive?

3. We talk of 'feeding' a fire when we add fuel, but does that mean fire is a living thing?

4. Why is it useful to group organisms?

5. What features are the most useful for grouping organisms?

The section opener has two main purposes:

- To acknowledge students' prior learning and to value it
- To provide a benchmark against which future learning can be compared

You may use the five questions or 'starting points' in the Student Book in a number of different ways to introduce the section:

- You could ask students to consider the questions as an introductory homework task.
- Students could divide into groups to share their own ideas and understanding and then report back to the whole class.
- Students could access the internet, with a time limit, to find out the information required.

You could use a spider chart or other form of wall chart to summarise all the ideas of students or groups.

The advantage of recording these initial ideas is that you may retain them for reference as you develop the individual topics. In this way, you may readily acknowledge students' progress in learning.

Introduction

This topic revises and extends knowledge from earlier years on the characteristics of living organisms. The individual characteristics are covered separately in more detail later in the course.

Links to other topics

Sections	Essential background knowledge	Useful links
1 The nature and variety of living organisms		1b Variety of living organisms
2 Structure and functions in living organisms		2e Nutrition 2f Respiration 2h Transport 2i Excretion 2j Coordination and response
3 Reproduction and inheritance		3a Reproduction

Topic overview

B1a.1	The eight characteristics of living organisms
	This sorting activity helps students revise their knowledge from KS3 of the characteristics of living organisms.
B1a.2	Consolidation and summary
	This activity provides a quick recap on the ideas encountered in the topic, as well as time for the students to answer the End of topic questions in the Student Book.

Activity B1a.1 The eight characteristics of living organisms

Specification reference: B1a.1.1

Learning objectives

- Name the eight characteristics shown by living organisms.
- Describe each of the characteristics of living organisms.
- Explain that not all living organisms show every characteristic all of the time.

Learning outcomes

- To revise what 'living' means.
- To identify and give examples of the eight characteristics of living organisms.

Common misconceptions

Your students are likely to have several misconceptions: for example, plants carry out photosynthesis but do not respire; excretion and egestion mean the same thing; breathing and respiration also mean the same. These errors will be dealt with in more detail in later topics. Briefly correct any misconceptions now, but make sure students understand fully when the topic is covered in detail later in the course.

Resources

Student Book pages 10–12

Worksheet B1a.1a The eight characteristics of life

Approach

1. Recap knowledge from earlier years

Introduce the unit by giving students two minutes to write down which characteristics all living organisms show. Then ask students to compare what they have written with another student, to identify what they have the same, and what different.

Take examples from around the class to collate a list of characteristics. Encourage discussion for each new suggestion, before adding anything the class agrees is a characteristic to the list.

2. Identifying characteristics

Give students Worksheet B1a.1a to work on, either individually or in pairs, to help them clarify the eight key characteristics of living organisms. They could either use the cards to create their own list of characteristics, or you could give them the characteristics and ask them to identify which is shown in each example. Students could then add one more plant and one more animal example of their own for each characteristic.

3. Create a mnemonic

Ask students to work on their own or in pairs to create a mnemonic for the initials of the eight characteristics, in whichever order they like.

Answers

Page 11

1. a) Any suitable answers for human, such as:

movement: walking; respiration: combination of oxygen with glucose to release energy, carbon dioxide and water; sensitivity: vision; homeostasis: control of core body temperature; growth: increase in height; reproduction: having a baby; excretion: producing urine; nutrition: eating food.

b) Any suitable answers for a specific animal, such as:

movement: crawling; respiration: combination of oxygen with glucose to release energy, carbon dioxide and water; sensitivity: smell; homeostasis: control of body water content; growth: increase in length; reproduction: producing young; excretion: losing carbon dioxide through respiratory surface; nutrition: eating food.

c) Any suitable answers for a plant, such as:

movement: growing towards light; respiration: combination of oxygen with glucose to release energy, carbon dioxide and water; sensitivity: detecting direction of light; homeostasis: controlling loss of water through stomata by opening and closing them; growth: increase in height; reproduction: producing seeds; excretion: diffusion of waste products out of leaf for photosynthesis (oxygen) and respiration (carbon dioxide); nutrition: taking in nutrients from soil and making glucose by photosynthesis.

2. Movement – to reach the best place to get food or other conditions favourable for growth.

Respiration – to release energy from food that can be used for all life processes.

Sensitivity – to detect changes in the environment.

Homeostasis – to prevent damage being done to cells as a result of changes in the body.

Growth – to increase in size until large/mature enough for reproduction.

Reproduction – to pass genes on to the next generation.

Excretion – to remove harmful substances from the body.

Nutrition – to take in substances needed by the body for growth and reproduction.

Page 12

1. Reproduction

2. Movement – viruses cannot move themselves. Respiration – viruses do not respire. Sensitivity – viruses do not sense or respond to changes in the environment. Homeostasis – viruses do not need to control internal conditions. Growth – viruses do not build new materials within their structure to produce a permanent increase in size. Excretion – viruses do not carry out metabolism, so they do not have waste products to excrete. Nutrition – viruses do not take in food substances for use in respiration or to build new materials.

3. Any suitable argument with justification, such as non-living materials do not reproduce, so viruses must be living.

4. Any suitable argument with justification, such as viruses cannot reproduce independently of other organisms and show just one of the eight characteristics of living organisms, so they cannot be classed as living.

Worksheet B1a.1a The eight characteristics of life

The leaves of some plants track the Sun's movement across the sky during the day. **movement/sensitivity**	At night, a plant gives out carbon dioxide. **respiration**	Humans produce urine every day, which contains waste products from the body, as well as any water that the body doesn't need. **excretion**
The air that you breathe out of your lungs contains more carbon dioxide than the air that you breathed in. **respiration**	Humans give birth to live babies, but birds and reptiles lay eggs from which the young hatch. **reproduction**	During the first year of life a human baby may triple its birth weight. **growth**
A *Mimosa* plant responds to touch by wilting. **sensitivity**	A student runs a 400 m race. **movement**	The green colouring of plant leaves is chlorophyll, which plants use to make food. **nutrition**
A healthy diet includes a good balance of protein, fruit and vegetables. **nutrition**	Flowering plants produce seeds that can be grown to produce new plants. **reproduction**	If you receive a shock, your heart usually starts to beat more quickly. **sensitivity**
Trees add another ring of wood around their trunks each year. **growth**	A house plant in the kitchen grows towards the window. **sensitivity/growth**	A bacterium in ideal conditions can divide into two every 20 minutes. **reproduction**

B1a.1a The eight characteristics of life

Cut out the cards, then sort them into piles to identify which key characteristic of living organisms they are examples of.

Note: Some examples may match more than one characteristic, so try to identify all characteristics that each example matches.

The leaves of some plants track the Sun's movement across the sky during the day.	At night, a plant gives out carbon dioxide.	Humans produce urine every day, which contains waste products from the body, as well as any water that the body doesn't need.
The air that you breathe out of your lungs contains more carbon dioxide than the air that you breathed in.	Humans give birth to live babies, but birds and reptiles lay eggs from which the young hatch.	During the first year of life a human baby may triple its birth weight.
A *Mimosa* plant responds to touch by wilting.	A student runs a 400 m race.	The green colouring of plant leaves is chlorophyll, which plants use to make food.
A healthy diet includes a good balance of protein, fruit and vegetables.	Flowering plants produce seeds that can be grown to produce new plants.	If you receive a shock, your heart usually starts to beat more quickly.
Trees add another ring of wood around their trunks each year.	A house plant in the kitchen grows towards the window.	A bacterium in ideal conditions can divide into two every 20 minutes.

Activity B1a.2 Consolidation and summary

Learning objectives

- To review the learning points of the topic.
- To test understanding through answering questions.

Learning outcomes

- Be familiar with the knowledge and understanding summarised in the End of topic checklist.
- Be able to apply this knowledge and understanding by answering the End of topic questions.

Resources

Student Book pages 13–14

Approach

This activity can be very short, with the main focus on the End of topic questions in the Student Book. You could also ask students to create the clues for a crossword that includes all eight characteristics of living organisms.

Answers

End of topic questions mark scheme

Question	Correct answer	Marks
1	Movement, respiration, sensitivity, homeostasis, growth, reproduction, excretion, nutrition	8
	Any suitable sentence.	1
2	Nutrition and respiration	2
3	Dry mass is the mass of all the materials used to make the cells and tissues of the body.	1
	Water content in the body varies as water is gained and lost so wet mass is not reliable.	1
4	Although crystals can grow they are not alive because they do not show all the other characteristics of living things.	1
5	Animals are not 'more alive' just because they have to move around to get their food, etc. Plants must remain attached to the ground because that is where they get support, water and nutrients.	1
	Both plants and animals show all the life processes, so are equally 'alive'.	1
6	The tree does not move during winter, although the cells may still move.	1
	Respiration and therefore excretion may still occur, but at a very slow rate (as gas exchange continues slowly through the bark).	1
	Movement, reproduction, growth and sensitivity will not take place during winter.	1
	However, as long as the tree has the capacity to return to a state where it can carry out all these processes (when leaves grow, during the rest of the year), it is still alive.	1
	Total:	20

Introduction

This topic revises and extends knowledge from earlier years on the classification of living organisms.

Links to other topics

Sections	Essential background knowledge	Useful links
1 The nature and variety of living organisms	1a Characteristics of living organisms	
2 Structure and functions in living organisms		2b Cell structure 2e Nutrition
4 Ecology and the environment		4b Feeding relationships 4c Cycles within ecosystems
5 Use of biological resources		5a Food production 5c Genetic modification (genetic engineering)

Topic overview

B1b.1	Classifying organisms
	This sorting activity will help students revise their knowledge from earlier years of the classification of living organisms, and extend it to cover the six main groups of classification.
B1b.2	Consolidation and summary
	This activity provides an opportunity for a quick recap on the ideas encountered in the topic as well as time for students to answer the End of topic questions in the Student Book.

Activity B1b.1 Classifying organisms

Specification reference: B1b.1.2, B1b.1.3, B1b.1.4

Learning objectives

- Describe the common features shown by eukaryotic organisms: plants, animals, fungi and protoctists.
- Describe the common features shown by prokaryotic organisms such as bacteria.
- Understand the term *pathogen* and know that pathogens may include fungi, bacteria, protoctists or viruses.

Learning outcomes

- To understand that living organisms can be classified by their features into the following groups: plants, animals, fungi, bacteria, protoctists, viruses.
- To give examples of pathogens from fungi, bacteria, protoctists and viruses.
- To understand that pathogenic organisms cause disease in other organisms.

Common misconceptions

Students are likely to have the general understanding that organisms may be plants (green things with leaves), animals (things that have legs and move) or 'other things' (for which they have no special classification except they are 'not plants or animals'). They may need additional questioning to help them to distinguish fungi from plants, protoctists from animals, and to appreciate that the grouping of some of these organisms has changed over time.

Resources

Student Book pages 15–22

Worksheet B1b.1a Classification

Approach

1. Recap knowledge from earlier years

Introduce the unit by giving students two minutes to write down the key features of plants and animals. Take examples from around the class. For each example, ask why they are a key feature of the group. Encourage discussion to highlight students' different understanding, but do not correct them too much at this stage; this will be clarified in the main activities.

2. Classification

Give students Worksheet B1b.1a, which contains a table of characteristics. Ask students to complete the table to show which groups of organisms have each characteristic. Encourage them to add detail to their responses, rather than just a tick or cross.

Note that if students carry out extended research, they may find examples of organisms that don't fit the standard descriptions. For example, some plants have no chlorophyll, and parasitise other plants to get their food. Students should try to explain why the organisms are still classified as they are.

3. Finding examples

Give students the following names, and ask them to carry out research to find out which group of organisms they each belong to. They should give an argument for each classification they suggest.

Lactobacillus	Plasmodium	Mucor	Anopheles	Zea	Pneumococcus	Saccharomyces
Homo	Vicia	Amoeba				

They should then identify any pathogens in each group.

Answers

Page 16 (top)

1. Multicellular means made of many cells, such as human, plant, etc.

2. The xylem vessels in the stems and leaves are strong, so help to support the plant. Water in the cells, when the cells are turgid, also support the plant as it pushes against the cell walls.

3. Chloroplast.

Page 16 (bottom) – 17

1. a) Nucleus, cytoplasm, cell membrane

   b) Cell wall, large central vacuole, possibly chloroplasts

2. Animals have nervous systems and organs for movement that plants do not have.

3. Animals need to move around to find food, or to find suitable habitats to live in. Plants need to take water and nutrients from the ground, so they need roots in the ground.

Page 18

1. a) Cell walls and central vacuole, cannot move around.

   b) No chloroplasts, may store carbohydrate as glycogen.

2. Saprotrophic nutrition is the digestion of dead material by external digestion, where enzymes are secreted onto the food and the digested food is then absorbed into the body. Animals eat the food (sometimes from living / just killed organisms) and digest the food inside their alimentary canal.

3. Toadstools and mushrooms are the reproductive structures of fungi. The main body of the fungus is the mycelium, the mass of tiny thread-like hyphae, which is often below the surface of the ground.

Page 19

1. Some contain chloroplasts and can photosynthesis as some plant cells do, others do not have chloroplasts and feed on other organisms, so are more like single animal cells.

2. Nucleus, cytoplasm, cell membrane, single-celled.

3. No, because mosquitoes only carry the *Plasmodium* which is the actual cause of the disease.

Page 20

1. Any three from:
   - plant cells have cellulose cell walls, bacterial cells may have a cell wall made of other chemicals
   - plant cells have a nucleus containing chromosomes, bacterial chromosome lies free in cytoplasm
   - bacterial cell may contain one or more plasmids, plant cell has no plasmids
   - plant cells have large vacuole/chloroplasts, bacterial cells do not.

2. Bacteria have no nucleus, they have a cell wall and single chromosome lying free in cytoplasm; protoctists have a nucleus containing the chromosomes, only some have a cell wall, they may contain chloroplasts and are much larger than bacterial cells.

3. Bacterial chromosomes are single; circular; lying free in cytoplasm / not in a nucleus.

Page 22

1. Outer protein coat surrounding genetic material

2. They do not have most of the characteristics of a living cell, and behave like particles until they have infected a cell.

3. Viruses are much smaller than bacteria, ~100 nm (100×10^{-9} m) compared with 2 μm (2×10^{-6} m).

Worksheet B1b.1a

	Food source	Cell wall?	Nucleus in cell?	Carbohydrate store	Single or multicelled?
Plants	make own food using light energy from Sun	yes, cellulose	yes	starch or sucrose	multicelled
Animals	eat other organisms	no	yes	glycogen	multicelled
Fungi	extracellular digestion of dead or living plant or animal tissue	yes, chitin	yes	sometimes glycogen	some single-celled, some multicelled
Protoctists	some have photosynthesis, some feed on living organisms or dead matter	some	yes	–	single
Bacteria	some have photosynthesis, some feed on living organisms or dead matter	yes, variable	no – chromosome lies free in cytoplasm	no	single
Viruses	none	no	no	no	not really a cell

B1b.1a Classification

Use the Student Book and your own research to help you complete the table below to show the key characteristics of each group of organisms.

Add details where you can, rather than just a yes or no answer.

	Food source	Cell wall?	Nucleus in cell?	Carbohydrate store	Single or multicelled?
Plants					
Animals					
Fungi					
Protoctists					
Bacteria					
Viruses					

25

Activity B1b.2 Consolidation and summary

Learning objectives

- To review the learning points of the topic.
- To test understanding through answering questions.

Learning outcomes

- Be familiar with the knowledge and understanding summarised in the End of topic checklist.
- Be able to apply this knowledge and understanding by answering the End of topic questions.

Resources

Student Book pages 23–24

Approach

1. Ten questions

Ask students to work in pairs – one member of the pair is to think of an organism, the other member of the pair has to work out what it is by asking questions to which the answer can only be 'yes' or 'no'. They should use their knowledge of how organisms are classified to help them identify the group to which the organism belongs.

2. End of topic questions

Ask students to answer the End of topic questions in the Student Book.

Answers

End of topic questions mark scheme

Question	Correct answer					Marks
1	viruses, bacteria, protoctists					2
2						20
		Multicellular or single-celled	Key cell structures	Food store	Other distinguishing Features	
	plants	multi	cell wall, large central vacuole, may have chloroplasts, cell membrane, nucleus, cytoplasm	starch or sucrose	may be woody and very tall, such as a tree photosynthesis	
	animals	multi	cell membrane, nucleus, cytoplasm	glycogen (and fat)	move around	
	fungi	multi	cell membrane, nucleus, cytoplasm, cell wall	glycogen	saprotrophic nutrition, mushrooms/ toadstools are reproductive structures main body is mycelium, made of hyphae	

bacteria	single	cell membrane, cytoplasm, free chromosome, cell wall, may have plasmids	–	wide range of form and size	
protoctists	single	cell membrane, nucleus, cytoplasm, may have chloroplasts	–	some more like animal cells, other more like plant cells	
viruses	–	–	–	protein coat containing genetic material that infects other cells so that it can reproduce	

Give 1 mark for each valid point up to a maximum of 20.

3	They both contain cells with typical plant cell features	1
	such as cell wall, large central vacuole and may have chloroplasts.	1
4	It is an animal	1
	because animal cells have no cell wall and do not photosynthesis.	1
5	a) A pathogen is an organism that causes disease in another organism.	1
	b) and c) Example and corresponding disease, any appropriate, such as:	4
	fungi – ringworm in humans causes skin lesions, moulds or rusts in plants	4
	bacteria – *Pneumococcus* causes pneumonia	
	protoctists – *Plasmodium* causes malaria	
	viruses – influenza virus in humans and other animals or HIV in humans, tobacco mosaic virus in plants	
	1 mark for each example and 1 mark for each appropriately linked disease.	
6	They can only reproduce when inside the cell of another organism	1
	and cannot live independently.	1
7 a)	They have characteristics in common with each of the other groups,	1
	so depending on which characteristics are used for grouping, they could be grouped as either animals or plants.	1
7 b)	They are too different from plants and animals to be comfortably grouped together.	1
	For example, they have a cell wall so cannot be animals, but the cell wall is made from a different substance to plant cell walls.	1
	Total:	41

Question	Correct answer	Marks
2 a)	i) A: *Amoeba*	1
	B: *Chlorella*	1
	ii) D: *Pneumococcus*	1
	iii) B: *Chlorella*	1
	iv) C: *Lactobacillus*	1
	D: *Pneumococcus*	1
	v) C: *Lactobacillus*	1
2 b)	i) A: nucleus	1
	B: cell membrane	1
	C: cytoplasm	1
	ii) It has a nucleus / it has mitochondria / it does not have a cell wall.	1
3	Viruses are not cellular / they consist of nucleic acid surrounded by a protein coat.	1
	They cannot live (or at least not for very long) outside the cells/body of an organism / they are parasitic.	1
	They do not have the eight characteristics of living things (MRS H GREN).	1
	Plus, one extra mark for mentioning any of the following:	
	Some viruses **move** but many rely on other organisms to get them inside host cells or transport mechanisms in their host to transport them around	1
	Viruses **reproduce** but they are dependent on being inside a host to do this and it is unlike reproduction in other organisms (it involves a copying of their DNA or RNA and assembling a protein coat around them).	
	They are **sensitive** to their environment in that they can gain entry into their host cells.	
	They do not **grow** in the normal sense (they are assembled); they do not **respire** or **excrete** and do not require **nutrition** / feed; they do not do **homeostasis**	
	So, most scientists do not regard them as living organisms.	
4 a)	Maize (or any other example) – cereal crop	1
	Peas/beans (or any other example) – legume	1
4 b)	Human (or any other example) – mammal	1
	Housefly/mosquito (or any other example) – insect	1
4 c)	i) Nervous system / hormonal or endocrine system	1
	ii) Allow any valid answer, such as leaves turning to face direction of light.	1
	Total:	21

Contents

a) Level of organisation

b) Cell structure

c) Biological molecules

d) Movement of substances into and out of cells

e) Nutrition

f) Respiration

g) Gas exchange

h) Transport

i) Excretion

j) Coordination and response

k) Answers to exam-style questions

Overview of the section

Topics 2e–2j in this section cover many of the major systems in living organisms. The first four topics in the section provide some of the basic building blocks for understanding how the systems are constructed and how they work. Topic 2a describes the general way in which differentiated cells, tissues and organs function together within a multicellular organism. This is followed by topics on basic cell structure and the key biological molecules in organisms, and then a topic that describes how substances enter and leave cells by diffusion, osmosis and active transport. Students should be expected to apply what they have learned in the first four topics to their study of the rest of this section.

Topics 2e–2j cover some of the key characteristics of living organisms described in Topic 1a. The systems and processes that enable living organisms to carry out the characteristics are described in detail for humans and for flowering plants.

Starting points

The Student Book provides a 'section opener', a double page spread which sets the scene for the students (see pages 28–29). It is structured in this way:

- An overview providing details of the areas of study
- Ten questions, structured in the same order as the topics within the section, to provide an opening point for each topic
- A list of section contents.

The questions are intended to provide a structure for introducing the section.

1. How is the body organised so that it can carry out the life processes effectively?

2. What do all cells have in common, and how are some cells different from others?

3. What are the basic molecules of life?

4. How do cell membranes control what can get into and out of the cell?

5. How do plants and humans get the food they need for growth?

6. What is cellular respiration and how do the body systems support it?

7. How are gas exchange surfaces adapted for rapid exchange of gases into and out of the body?

8. How are materials transported around the bodies of plants and humans?

9. What are the waste materials of metabolism and how are they removed from the body?

10. How do plants and humans respond to changes in the environment around them?

The section opener has two main purposes:

- To acknowledge students' prior learning and to value it
- To provide a benchmark against which future learning can be compared

You may use the ten questions or 'starting points' in the Student Book in a number of different ways to introduce the section:

- You could ask students to consider the questions as an introductory homework task.
- Students could divide into groups to share their own ideas and understanding and then report back to the whole class.
- Students could access the internet, with a time limit, to find out the information required.

You could use a spider chart or other wall chart to summarise all the ideas of the students or groups.

The advantage of recording these initial ideas is that you can retain them for reference as you develop the individual topics. In this way, you can readily acknowledge students' progress.

Introduction

This topic revises and extends knowledge from previous work, providing another fundamental building block of knowledge that students should refer to in later work on other topics. It revisits what they already know about the organisation of cells into tissues, organs and organs systems, and adds the role of organelles in cells as another level of organisation.

Links to other topics

Sections	Essential background knowledge	Useful links
1 The nature and variety of living organisms	1a Characteristics of living organisms	
2 Structure and functions in living organisms		2b Cell structure
		2d Movement of substances into and out of cells
		2e Nutrition
		2g Gas exchange
		2h Transport
		2i Excretion
		2j Coordination and response
3 Reproduction and inheritance		3a Reproduction
5 Use of biological resources		5c Genetic modification (genetic engineering)
		5d Cloning

Topic overview

B2a.1	Level of organisation within organisms
	This short activity gives students the opportunity to discover a range of organelles, cells, tissues, organs and organ systems.
B2a.2	Consolidation and summary
	This activity provides an opportunity for a quick recap on the ideas encountered in the topic as well as time for the students to answer the End of topic questions in the Student Book.

Activity B2a.1 Level of organisation within organisms

Specification reference: B2a.2.1

Learning objectives

* Describe the levels of organisation in organisms: organelles, cells, tissues, organs and systems.

Learning outcomes

* Write definitions of the terms organelle, cell, tissue, organ, organ system.
* Explain how the levels of organisation in a body contribute to effective functioning.

Common misconceptions

Students need to bear these definitions in mind when categorising organelles, cells, tissues, organs and organ systems. This will help them to appreciate, for example, that blood is a tissue, and the skin is an organ.

Resources

Student Book pages 30–33

Worksheet B2a.1a Organs of the human body

Approach

1. Introduction

On the board, sketch the lines for a table that has four columns (five equally spaced lines) and room for at least four rows. Add titles to the columns, from left to right: *organ system, organ, tissues, cells.*

Ask students to name the organ systems found in the human body, and add each name to a different row in the first column. They should suggest the names of any organs in each system, tissues in each organ and cells in each tissue.

Alternatively, students could copy the table outline and complete it as far as possible, individually or in pairs. Take examples from around the class and check that there are no errors. Keep the table for the end of this activity, so that students can add further examples from what they have learned.

2. Human organs

Worksheet B2a.1a provides a human body outline on which students can draw the positions of the organs. They should include annotated labels to explain what each organ does.

3. Tissue fact cards

Ask students to carry out research on the tissue (or tissues) of their choice to produce a 'tissue fact file'. They should choose any tissue found in the human body, such as muscular tissue, glandular tissue or epithelial tissue, and draw a large labelled diagram showing the special cells found in the tissue.

They should then add notes, details and facts to fully describe what they have found out, such as what the tissues do, where they are found, and how they are suited to their job. They should present their research in a poster or using presentation software.

32

Answers

Page 31

1. Any two from: nucleus, vacuole, chloroplast

2. a) Any two suitable such as: muscle, nervous, epithelium (lining), blood, bone

   b) Each from a) with suitable adaptations, such as:

   - muscle tissue can contract to move bones or other parts of body

   - nervous tissue can carry electrical impulses

   - epithelium tissue has a smooth surface and may have adaptations such as cilia to move substances across surface

   - blood contains cells that carry oxygen, plasma that carries dissolved food substances, etc.

   - bone tissue is hardened to make strong bones.

3. a) Any two suitable such as: xylem, phloem, epidermal, mesophyll

   b) Each from a) with suitable adaptations, such as:

   - xylem: long tubes through which water moves from roots through stems to other parts of the plant

   - phloem: living cells that transport food around the plant

   - epidermal tissues: in continuous layers across surfaces of plants to prevent pathogens entering

   - mesophyll: packs other tissues to hold them all in place

Page 33

1. Any two suitable such as:

   - heart: pumps blood around body

   - kidneys: remove waste substances from body

   - liver: controls many processes in body

   - brain: coordinates thought, response to stimuli

2. Any two suitable such as:

   - leaf contains cells with chloroplasts for photosynthesis

   - stem contains strengthening tissue in xylem, etc. to support other parts of plant

   - roots have root hair cells where water and dissolved nutrients are absorbed into the plant

3. A body system is a group of organs that work together to carry out the life processes in an organism.

B2a.1a Organs of the human body

Use the outline of the human body below to mark the positions of the major organs including: stomach, small intestine, large intestine, liver, pancreas, heart, lungs and kidneys.

Draw the organs in the right place and try to make them the right size and shape.

Label the organs and add short notes to say what you think each organ does.

Compare your diagram with your neighbour's. What has your neighbour drawn well? What will they need to improve?

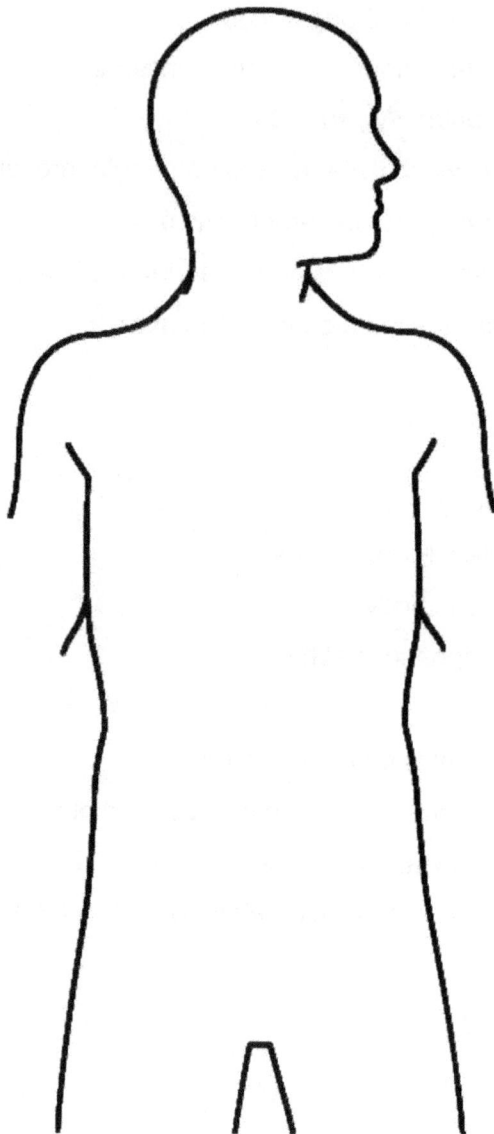

Activity B2a.2 Consolidation and summary

Learning objectives

- To review the learning points of the topic.
- To test understanding through answering questions.

Learning outcomes

- Be familiar with the knowledge and understanding summarised in the End of topic checklist.
- Be able to apply this knowledge and understanding by answering the End of topic questions.

Resources

Student Book pages 34–35

Approach

1. Definitions

Ask students to write definitions that could be used in a printed or web encyclopaedia for the following terms: *organelle*, *cell*, *tissue*, *organ* and *organ system*. They should include one plant and one animal example for each term.

2. End of topic questions

Ask students to answer the End of topic questions in the Student Book.

Answers

End of topic questions mark scheme

Question	Correct answer	Marks
1	system, organ, tissue, cell	3
2 a)	A group of similar cells that carry out a similar function	1
2 b)	Several tissues that are grouped together to carry out a particular function	1
2 c)	Several organs that work together to carry out a particular function	1
3	Any suitable answers, such as:	
	a) palisade cell / root hair cell; xylem tissue / mesophyll tissue; leaf / root	3
	b) muscle cell / nerve cell; muscle tissue / secretory tissue; heart / lungs	3
4	Any three suitable systems, such as:	15

System	Function	Organs in this system	Tissues in these organs	Cells in these tissues
respiratory	gas exchange between body and atmosphere	lungs	epithelial tissue lining tubes and air spaces	epithelial cells
nervous	receives stimuli from surroundings and coordinates responses	brain spinal cord nerves	nervous tissue	nerve cells
circulatory	to carry substances around the body	heart blood vessels	muscle tissue epithelial tissue blood	muscle cells epithelial cells blood cells

Question	Correct answer	Marks
5	epidermis – to cover and protect the outer surfaces of the leaf	1
	palisade tissue – contains cells that photosynthesise	1
	xylem tissue – long tubes that carry water	1
	mesophyll tissue – packing cells that support other tissues	1
	Total:	31

Introduction

In this topic students will learn to recognise the structures found in cells, and to distinguish between structures that are found in both plant and animal cells and those that are only found in plant cells. They will learn how cells can differentiate to become specialised cells with a particular function, and about the advantages and disadvantages of using stem cells in medicine.

Links to other topics

Sections	Essential background knowledge	Useful links
1 The nature and variety of living organisms	1a Characteristics of living organisms	
2 Structure and functions in living organisms	2a Level of organisation	2d Movement of substances into and out of cells 2e Nutrition 2g Gas exchange 2h Transport 2i Excretion 2j Coordination and response
3 Reproduction and inheritance		3a Reproduction 3b Inheritance

Topic overview

B2b.1	**Plant and animal cells**
	This activity gives students an opportunity to develop their microscope skills while studying the similarities and differences between animal cells and plant cells. Differentiation into specialised cells is studied, as well as the medicinal uses of stem cells.
B2b.2	**Consolidation and summary**
	This activity quickly recaps on the ideas encountered in the topic and provides time for the students to answer the End of topic questions in the Student Book.

Activity B2b.1 Plant and animal cells

Specification reference: B2b.2.2; B2b.2.3; B2b.2.4; B2b.2.5**B**; B2b.2.6**B**

Learning objectives

- Describe cell structures, including the nucleus, cytoplasm, cell membrane, cell wall, mitochondria, chloroplasts, ribosomes and vacuole.
- Describe the functions of the nucleus, cytoplasm, cell membrane, cell wall, mitochondria, chloroplasts, ribosomes and vacuole.
- Know the similarities and differences in the structure of plant and animal cells.
- Explain the importance of cell differentiation in the development of specialised cells. **(B)**
- Understand the advantages and disadvantages of using stem cells in medicine. **(B)**

Learning outcomes

- Describe that plant and animal cells have a nucleus, cytoplasm, cell membrane, mitochondria, ribosomes.
- Describe that plant cells also have a cell wall, chloroplasts and often a large central vacuole.
- Describe how each type of cell structure has a specific purpose in the cell.
- Explain how cell differentiation leads to the development of specialised cells. **(B)**
- Describe the advantages and disadvantages of using stem cells in medicine. **(B)**

Common misconceptions

Some students may find it hard to appreciate the very small scale of cells and their components. It helps if they look at a piece of small newsprint or tiny letter drawn with a sharp pencil under the microscope before they look at cells.

Resources

Student Book pages 36–40

Worksheet B2b.1a Using a light microscope

Worksheet B2b.1b Making a microscope slide

Resources for class practicals (see Technician's notes, following)

Approach

1. Introduction

Ask one student to act as 'artist' and draw a reasonably large circle on the board. Other students should then suggest which structures to add to the shape, and how they should be drawn, to create a drawing of a cell. They should also suggest the labelling for each of the structures.

Encourage discussion when students are uncertain or disagree about what should be drawn. (This is likely to happen because you have not specified whether it is a plant or animal cell.)

2. Using a light microscope

If your students are not already familiar with using a light microscope, this activity is a good opportunity to introduce it. Worksheet B2b.1a provides basic instructions on viewing a prepared slide through a light microscope.

You should demonstrate first how to set up and focus a microscope. First focus using the low power objective and then the high power objective, and focus by starting close and then increasing the distance between the objective lens and the slide to avoid the risk of crashing high power objectives into slides. Students may need to be reminded of this several times in order to develop good technique.

Any prepared slide of plant or animal tissue will be suitable, where it is possible to see a simple internal structure in cells. Ideally you should show a labelled diagram or photograph on the board, to help students interpret what they see. Don't offer tissues with complex structure, such as muscle cells – this may confuse students.

Students should draw clearly one or two labelled cells from each slide. Remind them to use a sharp pencil for their drawings, and to draw only what they see even if it is not as clear and obvious as any drawing they have seen.

For more able students, this could lead to discussion about the quality of drawings in text books or on the internet, and the need to see the 'real thing' on a slide to appreciate the limits of a drawing.

3. Making stained slides

Worksheet B2b.1b gives instructions for making stained slides of plant cells (onion) and animal cells (human cheek cells). You may need to demonstrate how to place a cover slip on a slide to avoid trapping air bubbles.

Students often over- or under-stain material, so they may need several attempts to make a slide of each kind. If time is limited, prepare slides in advance to display in case their attempts are unsuccessful.

Before working with their own cheek cells, remind students of safety protocols and make sure pots of disinfectant are available for discarded cotton buds, slides and cover slips.

This practical could be extended to look at cells from other sources, such as banana parenchyma or moss leaf. In each case, students should apply their skills and understanding of cell structure to interpret what they see under the microscope.

4. Functions of cell structures

Use page 36 of the Student Book to introduce the cell structures and functions that students need to learn about. They should make notes on this, and then use their notes to test each other on the functions of the nucleus, cytoplasm, cell membrane, mitochondria, ribosomes, cell wall, chloroplasts and vacuole.

5. Cell differentiation and specialised cells (B)

Use pages 39–40 of the Student Book to introduce the idea that as cells divide, specialised cells are formed by cell differentiation. They should make notes on this, and on some examples of specialised cells. Students could also research, using the internet for example, other examples of specialised cells in more detail and then report back to the rest of the class, in each case explaining how the structure of the specialised cell is linked to its function.

6. Stem cells (B)

Use pages 39–40 of the Student Book to introduce the idea that differentiated cells arise originally from identical stem cells, and that stem cells are found in embryos and also some are found in adults. Ask students to use the internet to research some examples of stem cell use in medicine, explaining also the advantages and disadvantages of uses.

Technician's notes

You will need the following resources for the class practicals.

Be sure to check the latest safety notes on these resources before proceeding.

B2b.1a Using a light microscope

Class practical, per student or pair:

light microscope with low power (such as ×4) and high power (such as ×10) objectives
prepared slides of plant and/or animal tissue in which cell structures are easily visible. Suitable examples are palisade cells in a leaf and squamous epithelial cells (cheek cells).

B2b.1b Making a microscope slide

Class practical, per student or pair:

Cotton buds should be kept in disinfectant for at least 10 minutes after students have used them.

light microscope with low power (×4) and high power (×10) objectives
microscope slides and cover slips
mounted needle or blunt seeker
forceps
pipette, for dropping water onto slide
tap water
methylene blue stain
iodine solution
onion
sharp knife or scalpel and cutting board
clean cotton buds, at least 1 per student
paper towel
pot of disinfectant, such as 1% Virkon

Answers

Page 37

1. a) Drawing should be drawn with thin, clear pencil lines, no crossing out, to show the outline of the cell in the photograph and the central shape.

   b) Diagram should be labelled to show nucleus, cytoplasm and cell membrane.

Page 38

1. a) Chloroplast

   b) (Large) vacuole

   c) Cell wall

Developing investigative skills, page 38

1. a) Place the slide on the microscope stage under a low power objective. Use the stage clips to hold the slide in place. Make sure the light source passes through the slide to the objective (but not focused sunlight). Use the coarse focusing knob to bring the slide into focus as far as possible. Then use the fine focusing knob to get the best focus.

   b) The specimen should always be focused at low power before moving the high power objective into position. Then only the fine focusing knob should be used to focus at high power. This should avoid crashing the objective into the slide, because the high power objective is longer than the low.

   c) Make sure that the sunlight is not shining directly on the mirror, so that the light might be focused through the microscope into the eye, as this can damage the eye.

2. a) Careful drawing with clean pencil lines of white blood cell, labelled to show nucleus, cell membrane (not really visible at this magnification but understood to be at the edge of the cell) and cytoplasm.

   b) Magnification = eyepiece (×4) × objective (×20) = ×80.

3. The cells are animal cells. They don't have features of plant cells, e.g. cell wall, large vacuole.

Page 40

1. Long length so can carry impulses from one place to another; nerve endings to connect to other nerve cells or organs.

2. To reduce the risk of rejection.

B2b.1a Using a light microscope

The light microscope is a very useful tool for biologists. It can be used to look at living specimens and sections of dead material that has been stained with coloured dyes to show the cells more clearly.

In this practical you will practise using a light microscope with a prepared slide.

Apparatus

light microscope with low power and high power objectives

prepared slide

SAFETY INFORMATION

Always focus first using the low power objective and focus by starting close and then increasing the distance between the objective lens and the slide. Then move the high power objective into position, to avoid crashing the objective into the slide.

While working with the high power objective, use the fine focusing knob only.

If using natural light to light the specimen, make sure you do not focus the Sun's rays directly through the objective and eyepiece.

Method

1. Check the magnification of the eyepiece and write it down. Also, check the magnification of the low power and high power objectives and write them down.

2. Place the prepared slide on the microscope stage and hold it firmly with the stage clips. Move it so the specimen on the slide is directly below the eyepiece.

3. Make sure the low power objective is in the lowest position.

4. Look through the eyepiece, and use the coarse focus knob to bring the specimen into focus as best you can. (Note: Practise working with both eyes open, as this will be more comfortable over long periods of working.)

5. Use the fine focus knob to focus clearly on the specimen. You may want to move the slide around a little at this point, to bring the most interesting part of the slide into the middle of the field of view (the area you can see). If so, make sure you refocus with the fine focus knob.

6. Draw the area of interest in your book, using a sharp pencil to make a neat drawing. Try to label what you can see.

7. Choose a part of the slide that you want to look at in more detail and make sure it is in the centre of the field of view and properly focused. Then move the high power objective in to replace the low power.

8. **Use the fine focusing knob only**, to focus the specimen clearly.

9. Draw the area of interest, e.g. one cell, and label it clearly.

10. Before removing the slide from the microscope stage, replace the high power objective with the low power.

11. Calculate the magnification of your drawings by multiplying the magnifying power of the objective with the magnifying power of the eyepiece lens, and add the magnifications to your drawings.

B2b.1b Making a microscope slide

Sometimes in your work you will need to make your own slides. In this practical you will take samples of plant and animal cells to make a slide, and then stain them to show key structures more clearly. You will then use a microscope to look at your slide. If you are not confident when using the microscope, use Worksheet B2b.1a to guide you.

Apparatus

microscope with low and high power objectives

microscope slides and cover slips

mounted needle

forceps

pipette

small beaker of water

methylene blue stain

iodine solution

onion

sharp knife or scalpel

cutting board

clean cotton buds

filter paper or paper towel

pot of disinfectant

eye protection/goggles

SAFETY INFORMATION

Always focus first using the low power objective, and focus by starting close and then increasing the distance between the objective lens and the slide. Then move the high power objective into position, to avoid crashing the objective into the slide.
While working with the high power objective, use the fine focusing knob only. While focusing, start with the objective lens close to the slide and then increase the distance between them to avoid crashing the objective lens into the slide.

If using natural light to light the specimen, make sure you do not focus the Sun's rays directly through the objective and eyepiece.

Handle cover slips with care – they are fragile and have sharp edges.

Only handle slides of your own cheek cells, and place cotton buds and slides into disinfectant when you have finished.

Iodine solution and methylene blue are strong stains. If you spill any on your skin or clothes, then wash it off immediately with water. If you spill any, clean it up before it stains. Wear eye protection when handling the stains.

Method

Plant cells

1. Peel a thick layer from an onion, and find the very fine sheet of cells inside that layer. Use the forceps to carefully remove the sheet of cells, then cut a small piece about 1 cm square. Place this in the middle of a clean microscope slide and add one drop of water to the specimen using a pipette.

2. Place one edge of a cover slip to one side of the specimen and support the opposite edge with a mounted needle. Carefully lower the cover slip over the specimen so that no air bubbles are trapped.

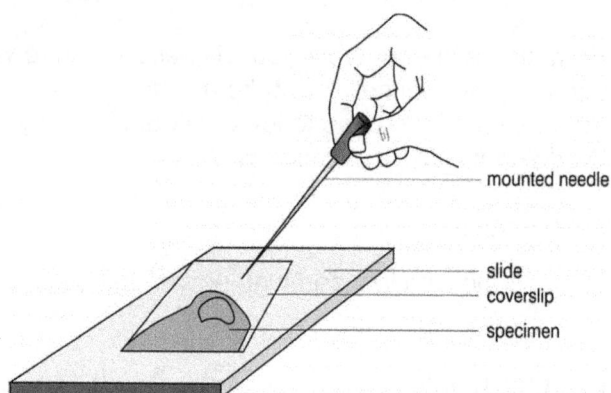

mounted needle
slide
coverslip
specimen

3. Place one drop of iodine solution at one edge of the cover slip. Then use filter paper at the opposite side to draw the stain under the cover slip across the specimen. Use the filter paper to gently blot any excess moisture from the slide.

4. Place the slide on the microscope stage and view it first with a low power objective and then a high power objective. Draw one or two cells from what you can see and label the structures that are visible.

Animal cells

1. Use a clean cotton bud to wipe the inside of your cheek in your mouth.

2. Wipe the cotton bud across the middle of clean microscope slide to cover an area about 1 cm square. **Then put the cotton bud straight into the pot of disinfectant.**

3. Place one drop of methylene blue stain on the smear on the microscope slide, taking care not to touch the smear with the pipette.

4. Place one edge of a cover slip to one side of the specimen and support the opposite edge with a mounted needle. Carefully lower the cover slip over the specimen so that no air bubbles are trapped.

5. Use the filter paper to gently blot any excess moisture from the slide.

6. Place the slide on the microscope stage and view it first with a low power objective and then a high power objective. Draw one or two cells from what you can see and label the structures that are visible.

7. Place the slide and cover slip into the beaker of disinfectant.

Analyse and interpret data

1. Calculate the magnification at low power and high power of your microscope and add those to your drawings.

2. What was the effect of the stain? What did it help you to see more clearly?

3. Compare the structures of the animal cells and plant cells that you looked at. Describe any similarities and any differences.

Activity B2b.2 Consolidation and summary

Learning objectives

- To review the learning points of the topic.
- To test understanding through answering questions.

Learning outcomes

- Be familiar with the knowledge and understanding summarised in the End of topic checklist.
- Be able to apply this knowledge and understanding by answering the End of topic questions.

Resources

Student Book pages 41–42

Approach

1. Labelled cell drawings

Ask students to sketch quickly an animal cell and a plant cell, showing all the key structures and labelling them. They should exchange their drawings with another student and check what has been drawn, identifying any weaknesses. The drawings should be returned and amended to improve them. Then students should add to the labels the function of each structure. Take examples from around the class to make sure students are clear about the functions.

2. End of topic questions

Ask students to answer the End of topic questions in the Student Book.

Answers

End of topic questions mark scheme

Question	Correct answer	Marks
1 a)	The structure that contains the genetic material and controls cell division	1
1 b)	The structure surrounding a cell that controls what enters and leaves the cell	1
1 c)	The material inside the cell that contains the organelles and in which many reactions take place	1
1 d)	The organelles where respiration takes place	1
1 e)	The organelles where protein synthesis takes place	1
2	Table similar to the following, showing the same information: <table><tr><th>Plant cell</th><th>Animal cell</th></tr><tr><td>has a nucleus</td><td>has a nucleus</td></tr><tr><td>surrounded by cell membrane</td><td>surrounded by cell membrane</td></tr><tr><td>surrounded by cellulose cell wall</td><td>no cell wall</td></tr><tr><td>cytoplasm fills cell</td><td>cytoplasm fills cell</td></tr><tr><td>usually large central vacuole</td><td>no large central vacuole</td></tr><tr><td>may contain chloroplasts</td><td>no chloroplasts</td></tr><tr><td>has mitochondria</td><td>has mitochondria</td></tr><tr><td>has ribosomes</td><td>has ribosomes</td></tr></table>	16
3 a)	Animal cells are surrounded by a cell membrane that controls what enters and leaves the cell.	1
3 b)	Some plant cells contain chloroplasts.	1
3 c)	Only plant cells contain a large central vacuole in the middle of the cell.	1
4	As red blood cells have no nucleus, there is nothing to control cell division, so they cannot divide like many other cells to replace damaged cells. So, they have to be replaced with cells from the bone marrow.	2
5	Cells developing into different specialised cells.	1
6	Advantage: can replace damaged or unhealthy cells. Disadvantage: may lead to rejection or other side effects.	2
	Total:	29

Introduction

This topic introduces students to carbohydrates, proteins and lipids, and of what they are made up. Students are introduced to the tests for each of these food groups. The topic then looks at what an enzyme is, how they work and the conditions in which they work best. It is another fundamental building block of knowledge that students should refer to in later work on other topics.

Links to other topics

Sections	Essential background knowledge	Useful links
1 The nature and variety of living organisms		
2 Structure and functions in living organisms		2d Movement of substances into and out of cells 2e Nutrition 2h Transport 2i Excretion
5 Use of biological resources		5a Food production

Topic overview

B2c.1	Food molecules
	This activity introduces students to the structures of carbohydrates, proteins and lipids. This follows with an opportunity to use the tests for starch, glucose, proteins and lipids on different foods.
B2c.2	Enzymes
	This activity gives students several practical opportunities to explore the effects of temperature and pH on the rate of enzyme-catalysed reactions.
B2c.3	Consolidation and summary
	This activity provides an opportunity for a quick recap on the ideas encountered in the topic as well as time for the students to answer the End of topic questions in the Student Book.

Activity B2c.1 Food molecules

Specification reference: B2c.2.7; B2c.2.8; B2c.2.9

Learning objectives

- Identify the chemical elements present in carbohydrates, proteins and lipids (fats and oils).
- Describe the structure of carbohydrates, proteins and lipids, and name the basic units from which they are formed.
- Practical: Investigate food samples for the presence of glucose, starch, protein and fat.

Learning outcomes

- Identify the chemical elements present in carbohydrates, proteins and lipids (fats and oils).
- Describe the carbohydrates starch and glycogen as being large molecules made from simple sugars.
- Describe proteins as being large molecules made from amino acids.
- Describe lipids as being large molecules commonly made from fatty acids and glycerol.
- Describe how to test foods for glucose, starch, protein and fat.

Common misconceptions

Students often confuse the term 'nutrients' with 'food'. Make sure they can distinguish between the two.

Resources

Student Book pages 43–47

Worksheet B2c.1a Practical: Investigate food samples for the presence of glucose, starch, protein and fat

Resources for class practical (see below)

Approach

1. Molecules in food

Write the word *food molecules* in the middle of the board. Ask students to suggest related words that can be added to build a concept map on this topic. They should be able to suggest carbohydrates, proteins and fats from their previous work on nutrition. If not, prompt for these by asking, 'Which are the main food groups in our food?'

Take the opportunity to introduce the word *lipid* to cover fats (lipids that are solid at room temperature, e.g. butter or lard) and oils (lipids that are liquid at room temperature). You could show them examples to reinforce this. Add any other suitable words, but don't extend knowledge at this point.

Keep the concept map for the end of this activity.

2. Basic units

Use the Student Book to introduce the different basic units of the three groups of food molecules. Students could use 'popper beads' or similar to reinforce their understanding of the structure of carbohydrates and proteins, using identical beads for making a 'carbohydrate' and different beads for making a 'protein'. They could suggest a different way of modelling to show how different lipids all contain glycerol but different fatty acids.

3. Food tests

Worksheet B2c.1a gives students the opportunity to use the tests for starch, reducing sugars (glucose), protein and lipids on a range of foods.

4. Consolidation: completing the food molecules concept map

Return to the concept map started at the beginning of this activity, and ask students to suggest further words that could be added to the map using what they have learned in the activity. Encourage discussion among students about which words to add and where best to place them.

Technician's notes

You will need the following resources for the class practical.

Be sure to check the latest safety notes on these resources before proceeding. B2c.1a

Practical: Investigate food samples for the presence of glucose, starch, protein and fat

Include a range of foods, some of which contain glucose (such as sweets, biscuits, cake), some which contain starch (such as pasta, rice, potatoes), some that contain protein (such as egg white, milk, cheese, meat) and some which will contain lipids (such as cream, cheese, cooking oil). If not already liquid, foods may need to be broken down to a paste with a mortar and pestle.

For the test for glucose (reducing sugars) you can use a water bath at 100 °C but it is safer to use water that has just boiled, and put it in an insulated beaker.

Class practical, per group:

samples of foods for testing	test tubes
measuring pipettes	mortar and pestle
white spotting tile	distilled water
hot water from a kettle that has just boiled, beaker and insulation for beaker	heatproof tongs
small spoons or spatulas	eye protection
Benedict's solution *	iodine solution
Biuret reagent (copper sulfate and sodium hydroxide) **	ethanol **

* irritant (skin and eyes)
** highly flammable, harmful if swallowed

Answers

Developing investigative skills, pages 45–46

1. Starting with the 10% concentration solution, remove 1 cm^3 with a pipette and transfer it to a clean test tube. Using a different pipette add 9 cm^3 of distilled water to the test tube and mix. This new solution is now 1% concentration. Repeat the process starting with 1 cm^3 of the 1% solution to produce a 0.1% concentration solution. Repeat the process to produce 0.01% and 0.001% concentrations.

2. Amount and concentration of the Benedict's solution, temperature of the water bath and the time spent eating the solutions.

3. 0.1%, because this was the smallest concentration that showed at least some colour change.

4. Repeat the experiment but this time use a range of concentrations between 0.1% and 0.01%.

Page 47

1. a) Fatty acids and glycerol   b) Simple sugars   c) Amino acids

2. Protein is formed from amino acids, carbohydrates from simple sugars; carbohydrates often made from one kind of simple sugar, proteins from many different kinds of amino acids.

3. a) i) The blue solution would change colour and an orange-red precipitate would form, because glucose is a reducing sugar.

    ii) The solution would not change colour as there is no starch present.

  b) i) There would be no change in colour because sucrose and the starch in wheat flour are not reducing sugars.

    ii) The brown solution would turn blue-black because of the starch in flour.

B2c.1a Practical: Investigate food samples for the presence of glucose, starch, protein and fat

In this activity you will use the tests for glucose, starch, protein and fat on a range of foods to find out which they contain.

Apparatus

samples of foods for testing

measuring pipettes

test tubes

mortar and pestle

distilled water

white spotting tile

hot water (just boiled) from a kettle, beaker and insulation

heatproof test tube holder

small spoons or spatulas

eye protection

Benedict's solution

iodine solution

Biuret reagent (copper sulfate and sodium hydroxide)

ethanol

SAFETY INFORMATION

Wear eye protection.

Be careful using the hot water.

Do not taste foods in a science laboratory.

Benedict's solution and iodine solution are irritants to the skin and eyes.

Ethanol is highly flammable and harmful if swallowed.

Avoid foods that produce known allergies (such as peanuts).

If you spill any of the solutions on your skin, wash it off immediately.

Method

Preparing the food samples

1. Put on eye protection.

2. Use the mortar and pestle to grind up a small amount (about a teaspoonful) of the food, adding drops of distilled water to help produce a thick paste.

3. Place a teaspoonful of the paste into a test tube, then add 4 cm^3 of distilled water and shake or stir to disperse the paste.

4. Prepare all the solid food samples this way. Liquid food samples do not need preparation.

Glucose test

1. Measure 1 cm^3 of the food extract into a clean test tube.

2. Add 1 cm^3 of Benedict's solution and shake to mix the solutions.

3. Using a test tube holder to hold the test tube, place the tube into the insulated hot water and gently shake the solution in the tube to mix it until it reaches near boiling point.

4. If glucose (a reducing sugar) is present, the blue Benedict's solution will turn green, then yellow, and then orange. If there is a large amount of glucose in the solution, a red-brown precipitate may form.

Starch test

1. Place a drop of iodine solution in each of two dimples in a spotting tile.

2. Add a drop or two of a food solution to one dimple.

3. If starch is present in the food solution, the yellow-brown iodine solution will turn blue-black. (Comparing the food dimple with the iodine-only dimple will help you see even a very slight change in colour.)

Protein test

1. Measure 1 cm^3 of the food extract into a clean test tube.

2. Add 1 cm^3 of Biuret reagent and shake to mix the solutions.

3. If protein is present, the pale blue Biuret reagent will turn purple.

Fat test

1. Measure 1 cm^3 of the food extract into a clean test tube.

2. Add 1 cm^3 of ethanol and shake to mix.

3. Let the food extract settle, then pour off some of the ethanol into a test tube containing water. If fat is present, a cloudy white layer will form.

Analyse and interpret data

1. Draw up a table to record the results of the tests for glucose, starch, protein and fat on each of the food samples you analyse, and complete it by adding your results.

2. Use your table to identify which foods contain glucose, starch, protein and fat.

3. Identify any patterns in the results, such as whether all the samples that contain glucose come from plant sources or from animal sources.

Evaluate data and methods

1. Your results are qualitative, which means they only identify the presence or absence of glucose, starch, protein or fat. Suggest how one of the methods could be adapted to produce a quantitative test, where you could compare the amount of one of these substances in different foods.

2. You should also try to find out whether any of the tests are *specific*, i.e. will they give positive results with other substances?

Activity B2c.2 Enzymes

Specification reference: B2c.2.10; B2c.2.11; B2c.2.12; B2c.2.13; B2c.2.14**B**

Learning objectives

- Understand the role of enzymes as biological catalysts in metabolic reactions.
- Understand how temperature changes can affect enzyme function, including changes to the shape of active site.
- Practical: Investigate how enzyme activity can be affected by changes in temperature.
- Understand how enzyme function can be affected by changes in pH altering the active site.
- Practical: Investigate how enzyme activity can be affected by changes in pH. **(B)**

Learning outcomes

- Describe the role of enzymes as catalysing reactions in living cells.
- Describe and explain how temperature and pH affect the rate of enzyme-controlled reactions, including changes to the active site.
- Describe simple experiments to show how enzyme activity is affected by changes in temperature and pH. **(B)**

Common misconceptions

It is important to reinforce the fact that enzymes are proteins, and that all factors that affect proteins will also affect enzymes.

Resources

Student Book pages 48–51

Worksheet B2c.2a Practical: Investigate how enzyme activity can be affected by changes in temperature (1) – Gelatin, enzymes and temperature
Worksheet B2c.2b Practical: Investigate how enzyme activity can be affected by changes in temperature (2) – Trypsin, milk and temperature
Worksheet B2c.2c Practical: Investigate how enzyme activity can be affected by changes in pH **(B)**
Resources for class practicals (see Technician's notes, following)

Approach

1. Introducing catalysts

Ask students if they understand the word *catalyst*. If they do, ask them to explain where they have heard the word and what it means. They may know it from catalytic converters in vehicle exhausts, which are used to trap certain gases, or from their work in chemistry. Explain that enzymes are catalysts found in living cells.

Ask students to suggest what enzymes might do. It doesn't matter if they answer correctly or not; this activity is to help you identify the limits of their knowledge and any misunderstandings they may have developed.

Tell students that humans have over 55 000 different enzymes in their bodies, and that each enzyme controls a different reaction. Give them 5 minutes to work in pairs or small groups to jot down as many reactions that might happen in the human body, or in other living things, as they can think of. (You may need to remind them that a reaction changes reactants into products, so enzymes are not involved in processes such as diffusion and osmosis.)

Take examples from around the class, and make sure these include reactions that they should know from previous years, such as respiration, photosynthesis and the digestion of food molecules.

2. Key features of enzymes

Ask students to use the Student Book to note the key features of enzymes. Their notes should include the fact that they speed up reactions, their specificity and the effects of temperature and pH.

For more able students, explain that enzymes work as a result of shape. Part of the structure of an enzyme matches the shape of the reacting molecule(s). If two molecules join in a reaction (such as when large molecules are built from smaller ones), the enzyme holds them close together, helping the reaction happen more quickly and easily.

If one molecule breaks in a reaction (such as in the digestion of food), the enzyme changes the shape of the molecule so that it breaks apart more quickly and easily. The shape of the enzyme is key to how well it works. If the shape changes, because of increased heat or a change of pH, then the enzyme won't work as well. If the shape is changed too much, the enzyme cannot work at all and is said to be denatured.

To test students' understanding, ask them to sketch a graph of reaction rate for an enzyme that digests food substances in the stomach, where the pH is around 2, and another for an enzyme that digests food substances in the small intestine where the pH is near to 8.

The effect of temperature on the rate of an enzyme-controlled reaction can be investigated using Worksheet B2c.2a or B2c.2b, depending on resources available. The effect of pH on the rate of an enzyme-controlled reaction can be investigated using Worksheet B2c.2c.

3. Consolidation: key points

Give students two minutes to jot down the four most important points they think they have learned about enzymes. They should then spend another minute discussing their points with a partner and selecting the four best points from both sets. Take selections from around the class and encourage discussion to produce a class list of the four key points to remember about enzymes.

Technician's notes

You will need the following resources for the class practicals.

Be sure to check the latest safety notes on these resources before proceeding.

B2c.2a Practical: Investigate how enzyme activity can be affected by changes in temperature (1) Gelatin, enzymes and temperature

This is an investigation into the effect of temperature on an enzyme using exposed and developed black and white film. You may find it difficult to get hold of photographic film. Worksheet B2c.2b is an alternative if you have problems getting hold of black and white film.

Gelatin is digested by a wide range of protease enzymes. For the best results in the time available, it may be worth carrying out some test runs with different enzymes to see which performs best.

Some individuals are allergic to enzymes and proteases will break down the skin's surface. Take great care when preparing the solution for students and wear disposable gloves and eye protection. Use a fume cupboard if preparing solutions from powdered enzymes. At the low concentration used in this experiment, students with an allergy to the enzyme are less likely to have a severe reaction, but gloves and eye protection are still recommended.

Class practical, per group:

5 test tubes	stopwatch or clock
5 water baths set at 20 °C, 30 °C, 40 °C, 50 °C and 60 °C	0.1% protease solution, freshly prepared
lengths of exposed and developed 35 mm black and white film	disposable gloves
scissors	eye protection

B2c.2b Practical: Investigate how enzyme activity can be affected by changes in temperature (2) Trypsin, milk and temperature

This investigation into the effect of temperature on an enzyme uses trypsin and milk. The milk can be fresh pasteurised milk, or made up into solution with water from powdered milk.

Skimmed milk should be used as the fat in milk will prevent the solution from clarifying.

The worksheet suggests a test run, to identify the end-point as effectively as possible in order to generate reliable results.

Students should find that trypsin has an optimum temperature at around 37 °C, similar to the core temperature of the human body.

Some individuals are allergic to enzymes. If you suspect you are allergic, take great care when preparing the solution for students and wear disposable gloves and eye protection. Use a fume cupboard if preparing solutions from powdered enzymes. At the low concentration used in this experiment, students with an allergy to the enzyme are less likely to have a severe reaction, but gloves and eye protection are still recommended.

The time required for this practical can be reduced by giving groups only one or two temperatures from the five, and then collating class results. Additional discussion time will be needed to cover the reliability of shared results.

Class practical, per group:

5 small beakers (or test tubes)
5 water baths set at 20 °C, 30 °C, 40 °C, 50 °C and 60 °C
10% milk solution (use skimmed milk)
stopwatch or clock
2% trypsin solution, freshly prepared
measuring pipettes
disposable gloves
eye protection

B2c.2c Practical: Investigate how enzyme activity can be affected by changes in pH (B)

This practical investigates the effect of pH on amylase using the iodine test for starch to find the point at which all starch is digested. Different amylases have different optimum pHs. Amylase from the pancreas has an optimum between 6.7 and 7.0, but amylase from yeast has an optimum between 4.6 and 5.2. A solution of pancreatin can be substituted for amylase to give the higher result, more appropriate for the human body. The enzyme and starch solutions should be prepared fresh for the lesson.

The time required for this practical can be reduced by giving groups only one or two pHs from the six, and then collating class results. NB, the appropriate five pHs should be provided depending on whether yeast amylase or pancreatin enzymes are used. Additional discussion time will be needed to cover the repeatability of shared results.

The pH/buffer solutions can be made using disodium hydrogenphosphate and citric acid as follows:

pH	Volume of 0.2 mol dm^{-3} Na$_2$HPO$_4$	Volume of 0.1 mol dm^{-3} citric acid
3	20.55	79.45
4	38.55	61.45
5	51.50	48.50
6	63.15	36.85
7	82.35	17.65
8	97.25	2.75

Alternatively, some suppliers provide separate buffer solutions or tablets at the different pHs.

Please note that the activity of some enzymes is affected by the buffer chemicals. You should do a trial reaction with the enzymes to make sure that they are not affected.

Some individuals are allergic to enzymes. If you suspect you are allergic, take great care when preparing the solution for students and wear disposable gloves and eye protection. Use a fume cupboard if preparing solutions from powdered enzymes. At the low concentration used in this experiment, students with an allergy to the enzyme are less likely to have a severe reaction, but gloves and eye protection are still recommended.

Class practical, per group:

5 test tubes and rack
5 different pH solutions
amylase solution
10% starch solution
small measuring syringes or pipettes
0.1 mmol dm^{-3} iodine solution in dropper bottle
stopwatch or clock
marker pen
spotting tile
disposable gloves
eye protection

Answers

Developing investigative skills, page 51

1. Put test tubes containing the protease solution in water baths at each of the temperatures. Place a strip of exposed film in the test tube at 10 °C and time how long it takes for the strip to become clear. Repeat this for each temperature.

2. Temperature on *x*-axis, time on *y*-axis; suitable scales; axes correctly labelled; correct plotting; curved smooth line of best fit.

3. As temperature increases, the time of the reaction decreases and then increases.

4. The reaction initially gets quicker because the enzymes have more energy and move more quickly so collide more frequently with the substrate. Above the optimum temperature, the enzymes start to become denatured as the shape of the active site changes, so there are fewer enzyme-substrate complexes formed.

5. Repeat the experiment but only use temperatures in the range 20–40 °C, e.g. 20, 25, 30, 35, 40 °C.

6. Use the same temperature throughout, e.g. 40 °C, but add acid or alkali to the test tubes to make up a range of pH. Add protease and exposed film to each test tube and time how long it takes for each strip to become clear.

Page 51

1. A chemical that is found in living organisms that speeds up the rate of reactions.

2. Proteins.

3. Without enzymes, the metabolic reactions of a cell would happen too slowly for life processes to continue.

4. As temperature increases, the rate of the reaction will increase, up to a maximum point (the optimum) after which it decreases rapidly as the enzyme is denatured.

B2c.2a Practical: Investigate how enzyme activity can be affected by changes in temperature (1) – Gelatin, enzymes and temperature

Developed black and white negative film consists of a celluloid backing covered with a layer of gelatin. Where the film has been exposed, tiny silver particles in the gelatin turn black. Gelatin is composed mainly of the protein collagen, and is easily digested by enzymes called proteases.

Apparatus

5 test tubes

5 water baths set at 20 °C, 30 °C, 40 °C, 50 °C and 60 °C

lengths of exposed and developed 35 mm black and white film

scissors

stopwatch or clock

protease solution

disposable gloves

eye protection

SAFETY INFORMATION

Wear disposable gloves and eye protection.

Be careful when using the two hottest water baths.

If you accidentally get some enzyme on your skin, wash it off immediately.

Method

1. Put on eye protection and gloves.

2. Cut the film into strips and place one strip in each test tube.

3. Add 10 cm^3 of protease solution to each tube, and place one tube in each water bath at the same time. Start the stopwatch or clock.

4. Every minute, check the films to see if they have cleared. When the gelatin has been digested by the enzyme, the silver grains will fall away from the celluloid backing to leave transparent film. Note down the time taken for each piece of film to clear.

5. Record your results in a suitable table.

Analyse and interpret data

1. Use your results to draw a suitable graph.

2. Draw a conclusion for the effect of temperature on enzymes using your graph.

3. Explain your conclusion using your scientific knowledge about enzymes.

Evaluate data and methods

1. Describe any difficulties you had with this method, and suggest how the method could be improved to reduce their effect.

2. Explain how you could improve the method to find the optimum temperature for this enzyme.

B2c.2b Practical: Investigate how enzyme activity can be affected by changes in temperature (2) – Trypsin, milk and temperature

Milk's white colour is the result of a protein called casein. Trypsin is a protease enzyme that digests (breaks down) casein. When trypsin is added to a solution of milk, the white colour is gradually lost as the casein is digested, and the solution becomes translucent. You can test the effect of temperature on the activity of trypsin by heating it to different temperatures in water baths.

This experiment's end-point can be difficult to work out. It is helpful to do a test run at room temperature, to decide an end-point and to estimate the time needed. One way to measure the translucency of the solution is to carry out the reaction in a flask, so that it can be stood on a piece of white paper with a large mark on it. You can look down through the flask and judge the clarity of the black mark by eye.

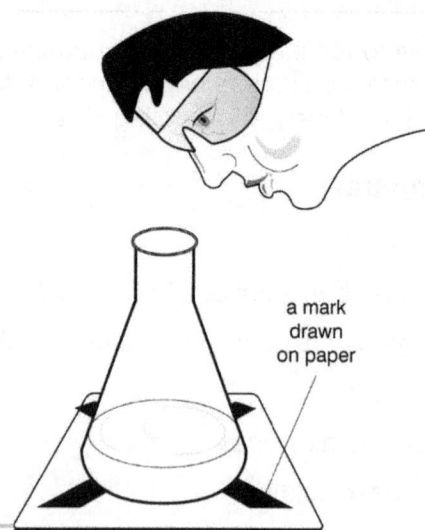

a mark drawn on paper

Apparatus

milk solution

trypsin solution

5 small beakers (or test tubes)

measuring pipettes

stopwatch or clock

disposable gloves

eye protection

5 water baths set at 20 °C, 30 °C, 40 °C, 50 °C and 60 °C

SAFETY INFORMATION

Wear disposable gloves and eye protection.

Be careful when using the two hottest water baths.

If you accidentally get some enzyme on your skin, wash it off immediately.

Method

1. Put on eye protection and gloves.

2. Measure 10 cm^3 milk solution into each small beaker.

3. Add 10 cm^3 of trypsin solution to one beaker, and place the beaker into one of the water baths. Start the stopwatch or clock.

4. Every two minutes check the translucency of the solution in the beaker. When the solution has reached the end-point, record the time.

5. Repeat steps 2 and 3 for each of the other water baths.

6. Record your results in a suitable table.

Analyse and interpret data

1. Use your results to draw a suitable graph.

2. Draw a conclusion for the effect of temperature on enzymes using your graph.

3. Explain your conclusion using your scientific knowledge about enzymes.

Evaluate data and methods

1. Describe any difficulties you had with this method, and suggest how the method could be improved to reduce their effect.

2. Explain how you could improve the method to find the optimum temperature for this enzyme.

B2c.2c Practical: Investigate how enzyme activity can be affected by changes in pH (B)

Amylase is the enzyme that digests starch to simple sugars. Amylase has an optimum pH, and this can be investigated by seeing how long it takes a solution of the enzyme to digest a solution of starch. The end-point can be measured by testing samples of the starch / enzyme solution at regular intervals with iodine solution.

Apparatus

5 test tubes and rack

5 different pH solutions

small measuring syringes or pipettes

amylase solution

starch solution

iodine solution in dropper bottle

spotting tile

stopwatch or clock

marker pen

disposable gloves

eye protection

SAFETY INFORMATION

Wear disposable gloves and eye protection.

If you spill any of the solutions on your skin, wash it off immediately.

Method

1. Put on eye protection and gloves.

2. Use the pen to mark each test tube with a different pH value from those of the pH solutions provided, and place the tubes in the rack.

3. Use the dropper bottle to add a drop of iodine to each dimple in the spotting tile.

4. Measure 2 cm^3 amylase solution into one of the test tubes.

5. Using a clean syringe or pipette, add 1 cm^3 of the appropriate buffer solution to the same tube and swirl gently to mix the solutions.

6. Using a clean syringe or pipette, add 2 cm^3 of the starch solution in to the same tube. Start the stopwatch or clock.

7. After 10 seconds remove a little solution from the test tube and place one drop into one dimple of the spotting tile and squirt the rest back into the test tube. If there is still starch in the solution the iodine solution will turn blue-black. If all the starch has gone, the iodine will remain yellow-orange.

8. Repeat step 7 every 10 seconds until the iodine solution remains yellow-orange. Record this total time and the pH of the solution.

9. Repeat steps 3–8 for each of the other pH solutions, recording the results each time.

10. Draw a suitable table to display your results.

Analyse and interpret data

1. Use your table to draw a suitable graph of your results.

2. Draw a conclusion for the effect of pH on enzymes using your graph.

3. Explain your conclusion using your scientific knowledge about enzymes.

Evaluate data and methods

1. Describe any difficulties you had with this method, and suggest how the method could be improved to reduce their effect.

2. Explain how you could improve the method to find the optimum pH for this enzyme.

Activity B2c.3 Consolidation and summary

Learning objectives

- To review the learning points of the topic.
- To test understanding through answering questions.

Learning outcomes

- Be familiar with the knowledge and understanding summarised in the End of topic checklist.
- Be able to apply this knowledge and understanding by answering the End of topic questions.

Resources

Student Book pages 52–54

Approach

Ask students to answer the End of topic questions in the Student Book.

Answers

End of topic questions mark scheme

Question	Correct answer	Marks
1 a)	They are found in all the basic and most common large molecules of the body,	1
	such as carbohydrates, proteins and lipids.	1
1 b)	To make proteins and other compounds needed in the body	1
2	Three fatty acids	1
	and one glycerol molecule for each lipid that was broken down	1
3	Only lactose and fructose would give a positive result	1
	because they are (reducing) sugars.	1
4 a)	The tests before the experiment show that the bread contained starch but no glucose (reducing sugar).	1
	The tests after the experiment show that the solution contains glucose (reducing sugar) but no starch.	1
4 b)	The starch in the bread has been changed into glucose (reducing sugar). Starch is a large carbohydrate, and glucose is one of the basic units of carbohydrates, so the starch has been digested.	1
	Substance A is an enzyme, such as amylase, that digests carbohydrates.	1
5 a)	Add Biuret solution (copper sulfate and sodium hydroxide).	1
	If protein is present there is a colour change from pale blue to purple.	1
5 b)	Add ethanol and shake.	1
	Pour the ethanol into water.	1
	A cloudy white layer shows lipids are present.	1

Question	Correct answer	Marks
6 a)	The temperature at which an enzyme-controlled reaction is at its fastest rate.	1
6 b)	Sketch should be like the one on page 48 (left) of the Student Book,	1
	labelled to show increasing rate as temperature increases from 0 to optimum because molecules are moving around faster and can interact faster	1
	optimum temperature when reaction is proceeding as quickly as it can	1
	reducing rate of reaction above optimum where heat is causing the enzyme/active site to change shape so it cannot interact with the substrate as well, and eventually is denatured.	1
6 c)	It is most likely to be around 37 °C	1
	because that is the temperature in the core of the human body, including the digestive system where this enzyme is found.	1
6 d)	No, because their optimum pH is acidic	1
	and they will be denatured in non-acidic conditions.	1
	Total:	25

Introduction

This topic covers the areas of diffusion, osmosis and active transport, to help students understand how substances can move into and out of cells. They will need to apply this knowledge later to body systems such as gas exchange, nutrition and excretion.

Note that a number of practical activities are suggested for diffusion and osmosis, and that you may wish to select what can be fitted into your lessons.

Links to other topics

Sections	Essential background knowledge	Useful links
1 The nature and variety of living organisms	1a Characteristics of living organisms	
2 Structure and functions in living organisms	2b Cell structure 2c Biological molecules	2e Nutrition 2g Gas exchange 2h Transport 2i Excretion
3 Reproduction and inheritance		3a Reproduction

Topic overview

B2d.1	**Diffusion**
	This activity introduces students to the concept of diffusion in general, and then to diffusion across partially permeable membranes.
B2d.2	**Osmosis**
	This activity provides students with a range of opportunities to investigate osmosis across partially permeable membranes.
B2d.3	**Active transport**
	This short activity helps students to distinguish active transport from the passive processes of diffusion and osmosis.
B2d.4	**Consolidation and summary**
	This activity provides an opportunity for a quick recap on the ideas encountered in the topic as well as time for the students to answer the End of topic questions in the Student Book.

Activity B2d.1 Diffusion

Specification reference: B2d.2.15; B2d.2.16; B2d.2.17

Learning objectives

- Understand the process of diffusion by which substances move in and out of cells.
- Understand how factors affect the rate of movement of substances into and out of cells, including the effects of surface area to volume ratio, distance, temperature and concentration gradient.
- Practical: Investigate diffusion using non-living systems.

Learning outcomes

- Write a definition of the term *diffusion*.
- Explain how diffusion can occur across cell membranes.
- Describe factors that affect the rate of diffusion across cell membranes.
- Carry out simple experiments to investigate diffusion.

Common misconceptions

Many students confuse the term *diffusion* with simple movement. They think that once diffusion has stopped, the particles have stopped moving too. This can lead to difficulties understanding the process. It is worth reinforcing the point that diffusion is *net movement* by repeating this definition every time you use the word 'diffusion' early on in this work. A video clip or some kinaesthetic work (with the students acting as particles) can also help, as suggested below.

Resources

Student Book pages 55–60

Worksheet B2d.1a Practical: Investigate diffusion using a non-living system (1) – Visking tubing

Worksheet B2d.1b Practical: Investigate diffusion using a non-living system (2) – Temperature and the rate of diffusion

Worksheet B2d.1c Practical: Investigate diffusion using a non-living system (3) – Surface area and the rate of diffusion

Resources for class practicals (see Technician's notes, following)

Approach

1. Introduction to diffusion

Place a crystal of potassium manganate(VII) (potassium permanganate) into a beaker of water and ask students to watch and describe what happens.

SAFETY NOTE: potassium manganate(VII) is oxidising, harmful and dangerous for the environment and should be handled with forceps or disposable gloves. Dispose of the solution carefully to avoid splashes, as the colour stains permanently.

Alternatively spray a small amount of strong perfume at one side of the room and ask students to put their hand up when they smell the perfume.

SAFETY NOTE: if any students suffer from asthma, check beforehand whether they would be affected by spraying perfume into the air.

Ask them to think in terms of particles/molecules and to try and imagine what is happening in the beaker or room. If possible, show them a video clip of Brownian motion (there are many available on the internet). You will need to explain that the dots they see are not molecules, but larger particles (such as dust motes) that are being constantly jiggled by the movement of molecules that are too small to see.

Explain that molecules are always in a state of movement as a result of the energy they have – the greater the temperature, the more heat energy they have and so the more they move (this should reinforce learning in physics).

You can model the effect of the colour or perfume spreading using students as molecules. Choose a small number of students who are wearing similar coloured tops (or provide hats or something to distinguish them from the remaining students) and stand them to one side of the rest of the group.

Within a fairly limited area, ask the students to walk in straight lines, and when they come up against another student or a boundary edge to change direction like billiard balls. After a few minutes, ask your key group of students to raise their hands, so that everyone can see how they have become spread out.

Give students a few minutes to work in pairs or small groups to come up with an explanation for the movement of colour through the solution or perfume across the room. Then ask for a selection of answers from different groups and discuss any differences among them. The key point to get across is that the movement out from the area of high concentration is a result of random movement of particles.

It is also worth asking if any particles of colour/perfume are moving back in the direction of the area of high concentration. As a result of random motion, some will be. However, there will be more molecules moving from the area of greater concentration to the area of lower concentration, and this is what we notice.

When the colour is evenly distributed in the beaker, or the perfume in the air within the room, ask students what happens to the particles. It is essential for them to understand that the movement continues, but that we cannot perceive any change because there is no difference in concentration between areas. Introduce the idea of *net movement*, that is, the sum of movement in different directions, and go on to use this to define the term *diffusion*.

2. Diffusion and cell membranes

In biology, we are most interested in the effect of diffusion within organisms and between organisms and their environment, as a mechanism for getting substances into and out of cells. Worksheet B2d.1a uses Visking tubing as a model for a cell membrane, and acts as a good model for understanding that some molecules (such as glucose) can cross cell membranes easily, and therefore can be redistributed in the system as a result of diffusion, while others (such as starch) cannot.

3. Factors affecting the rate of diffusion

Students need to understand the main factors that affect the rate of diffusion of substances, as they will apply this information later to their understanding of body systems such as gas exchange, nutrition and excretion.

Worksheet B2d.1b gives students the opportunity to plan an experiment into the effect of temperature on the rate of diffusion in a Visking tubing system. Discuss the prediction with them, and if they seem unsure, remind them about the effect of increasing temperature on increasing the energy of molecules. If there is time and their plan is acceptable, students could carry out their plan.

Worksheet B2d.1c gives students the opportunity to investigate the rate of diffusion into agar cubes of different sizes, to explore the effect of surface area to volume ratio on the rate of diffusion.

If students do carry out the practical, you should demonstrate a safe cutting technique for cutting up the cubes of agar.

For the effect of concentration gradient on the rate of diffusion, ask students to draw a cartoon, or develop a model that helps to explain why the rate of diffusion is greater when the concentration gradient is greater. This will provide an opportunity to reinforce what they have learned about diffusion generally.

For the effect of distance on the rate of diffusion, ask students to suggest what would happen to the rate of diffusion in a Visking tubing system if the Visking tubing consisted of several layers, i.e. was thicker overall.

Take time to check students' understanding of the basic principles at this point, as this will underpin a lot of later work.

Technician's notes

You will need the following resources for the class practicals.

Be sure to check the latest safety notes on these resources before proceeding.

B2d.1a Practical: Investigate diffusion using a non-living system (1) – Visking tubing

In this practical, students investigate the diffusion of substances across a partially permeable membrane in a non-living system – Visking tubing.

Students should find that glucose diffuses through the tubing into the water, but not the starch. This is because the glucose molecules are small enough to pass through the holes in the membrane, and are therefore free to diffuse from the region of their higher concentration (inside the tubing) to the area of their lower concentration (water outside the tubing). The starch molecules are too large to move through the holes in the membrane, so are not subject to diffusion.

Note that dry Visking tubing needs to be soaked for a few minutes in water before use. This can be done ahead of the lesson.

Class practical, per group:

glucose solution
starch solution
Visking tubing
sawn-off end of plastic syringe (the plunger end)
elastic band, to attach Visking tubing to syringe end
small beaker
tap water
iodine solution in dropper bottle
spotting tile
boiling tube
pipettes
Benedict's solution*, plus just-boiled water at 100 °C, insulated beaker and heatproof tongs (or Clinistix®)
eye protection

* irritant (skin and eyes)

B2d.1b Practical: Investigate diffusion using a non-living system (2)
Temperature and the rate of diffusion

This practical can be used as a planning exercise or, if time, you may review and approve students' plans to carry out their own. The method is based on the one used in B2d.1a. If students have not had the chance to carry that out, give them the worksheet to help them develop their planned method.

If students carry out their investigation, they should find that the higher the temperature, the faster the rate of diffusion (the sooner that glucose is detected in the water). This is because at a higher temperature a molecule has more energy and so moves faster, increasing the chances of it reaching the membrane and passing through one of the holes to the other side.

The equipment list below contains what students will need. They may suggest other equipment in their plans. Plans should be checked for the equipment suggested, and alternatives offered if some suggestions are not available.

Note that dry Visking tubing needs to be soaked for a few minutes in water before use. This can be done ahead of the lesson.

Class practical, per group:

glucose solution
starch solution
Visking tubing
sawn-off end of plastic syringe (the plunger end)
elastic band, to attach Visking tubing to syringe end
small beaker
tap water
iodine solution in dropper bottle
boiling tube
pipettes
Benedict's solution*, plus just-boiled water at 100 °C, insulated beaker and heatproof tongs (or Clinistix®)
eye protection

* irritant (skin and eyes)

B2d.1c Practical: Investigate diffusion using a non-living system (3)
Surface area and the rate of diffusion

This practical investigates the rate of diffusion of potassium manganate(VII) (potassium permanganate) into agar cubes of different sizes.

The agar cubes can be prepared initially in ice cube trays to give larger cubes than needed. If time is short, or you are concerned about students using sharp knives, the sets of cubes could be prepared ahead of the lesson.

Students should find that the smaller the agar cube, the faster the dye reaches the centre of the cube. This is partly the effect of diffusion distance and partly the result of surface area to volume ratio as smaller cubes have a larger surface area in comparison to volume than larger cubes.

Class practical, per group:

agar blocks, prepared as above
modelling knife or scalpel
ruler
3 small dishes or beakers
0.1 mol dm^{-3} potassium manganate(VII) solution*
disposable gloves or forceps
hand lens
stopwatch or clock
eye protection

* irritant (skin and eyes)

Answers

Developing investigative skills, page 59

1. a) A suitable plan could be: put 5 cm^3 of 1% glucose solution into the Visking tubing; place the Visking tubing into a boiling tube of water that has previously been placed into a water bath at 20 °C and allowed time to reach that temperature; start a stop watch; every 30 seconds use a clean pipette to remove a sample of the water from the boiling tube and test it for glucose using Benedict's solution; repeat this until you get a positive test for glucose; repeat this three times and work out the average mean time taken. Repeat this all again but with the water bath set at temperatures 30 °C, 40 °C, 50 °C, 60 °C.

    b) You should wear eye protection when using liquids such as Benedict's solution. You should also be careful to avoid direct contact with hot water in the water bath.

2. Temperature on *x*-axis, time on *y*-axis; suitable scales; axes correctly labelled, including units; correct plotting; smooth line of best fit.

3. As the temperature increases, the time taken to get a positive test for glucose decreases.

4. As the temperature increases, glucose diffuses more quickly through the Visking tubing.

5. At higher temperatures, the glucose molecules have more kinetic energy and move more quickly, increasing the rate of diffusion.

Page 60

1. Any answer that means the same as the following:

    net movement – the overall direction of movement

    diffusion – the overall movement of particles from an area of higher concentration to an area of lower concentration (in a gas or a solution or across a partially permeable membrane).

2. Passive, because no energy is provided by the cell for it to happen.

3. a) Glucose can but starch cannot.

    b) Only particles that are small enough to pass through the holes in the membrane can diffuse. Larger molecules cannot diffuse through the membrane.

B2d.1a Practical: Investigate diffusion using a non-living system (1) – Visking tubing

Visking tubing is an artificial membrane. Like cell membranes, it is partially permeable so that small molecules will move through it but large molecules will not. We can use Visking tubing to model which molecules can enter cells by diffusion and which cannot.

In this practical, you will use Visking tubing to investigate whether glucose and starch molecules can diffuse through the membrane. If you cannot remember the tests for starch and glucose, revise your work from Worksheet B2c.1a. An alternative to using Benedict's solution to test for glucose are Clinistix®, which change colour in the presence of glucose.

Apparatus

glucose solution | starch solution | Visking tubing
sawn-off end of plastic syringe | elastic band | small beaker
tap water | pipettes | iodine solution in dropper bottle eye
spotting tile | boiling tube | protection

Benedict's solution + just-boiled water at 100 °C, insulated beaker and heatproof tongs, or Clinistix®

SAFETY INFORMATION

Wear eye protection when using iodine solution and Benedict's solution.

If you spill iodine solution on your skin wash it off immediately.

Take care when heating solutions in the hot water for the glucose test.

Do not touch the coloured part of the Clinistix®.

Method

1. Put on eye protection.

2. Tie a tight knot in one end of the Visking tubing and attach the other end to the sawn-off syringe end with an elastic band.

3. Half fill the boiling tube with water.

4. In a small beaker, mix about 5 cm^3 glucose solution with a similar amount of starch solution.

5. Carefully fill the Visking tubing with the starch/glucose mixture, and wash the outside of the tubing with fresh water to remove any spills.

6. Suspend the tubing in the boiling tube of water as shown in the diagram.

7. After 15 minutes, use a pipette to remove some of the water surrounding the Visking tubing in the boiling tube. Test the water for glucose. Record your results.

8. Test some more of the water surrounding the Visking tubing for starch. Record your results.

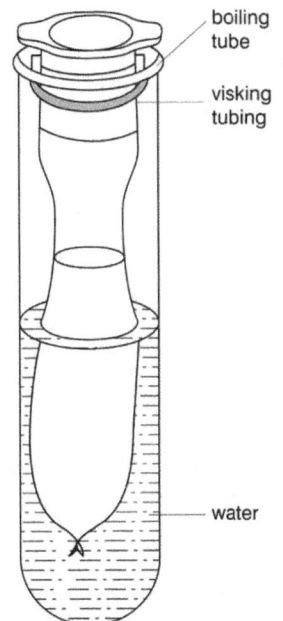

Analyse and interpret data

1. Describe your results.

2. Explain your results using your scientific knowledge about membranes.

3. Explain what your results suggest about the diffusion of glucose and/or starch through partially permeable membranes.

B2d.1b Practical: Investigate diffusion using a non-living system (2) – Temperature and the rate of diffusion

Many factors can affect rate of diffusion, including temperature, concentration gradient, distance and surface area. Using the method in Worksheet B2d.1a, with only glucose solution in the tubing, plan an investigation into the effect of temperature on the rate of diffusion. The apparatus list contains some of the equipment you need, but you may need to add other items.

You will need to consider:

- the range of temperatures you will test

- the number of repeats of each temperature you will use to get reliable results (repeats can most easily be done by sharing results with other groups)

- how frequently you will test each tube to give reliable results of the rate of diffusion

- how you will decide the end-point of each test

- apart from the safety notes below, what other risks should be considered with this method and how they should be handled.

When you have written your plan, show it to your teacher. When your plan has been checked, your teacher will let you know if you can carry out your investigation. If you have been given permission to proceed, below is an example of the apparatus and process you can use to analyse and evaluate your results.

Apparatus

glucose solution	Visking tubing	sawn-off end of plastic syringe
elastic band	small beaker	tap water
boiling tube	pipettes	eye protection

Benedict's solution + boiled water at 100 °C, insulated beaker and heatproof tongs, or Clinistix®

SAFETY INFORMATON

Wear eye protection when using Benedict's solution (irritant for skin and eyes).

Take care when heating solutions in a hot water bath.

Do not touch the coloured part of a Clinistix®.

Prediction

1. Write a prediction for your experiment. Explain your prediction using your scientific knowledge.

Analyse and interpret data

1. Record your results in a suitable table.

2. Identify any anomalous values in repeat experiments and ignoring those, calculate an average time for each temperature.

3. Use your averaged results to draw a suitable graph.

4. Describe any patterns in your results.

5. Explain any patterns in your results using your scientific knowledge.

Evaluate data and methods

1. Describe any problems that you had in carrying out your experiment.

2. Explain how you would adjust the method to avoid these problems as far as possible.

B2d.1c Practical: Investigate diffusion using a non-living system (3) – Surface area and the rate of diffusion

Single-celled organisms can usually exchange all the substances they need with the environment simply through diffusion or osmosis. Larger, multicelled organisms generally need transport systems because of the effect of surface area to volume ratio.

In this practical, you will investigate the effect of surface area to volume ratio on the rate of diffusion of a coloured dye into agar cubes of different sizes.

Apparatus

agar blocks	dilute potassium manganate(VII) solution
modelling knife or scalpel	hand lens
white tile for cutting on	stopwatch or clock
ruler	disposable gloves or forceps
3 small dishes or beakers	eye protection

SAFETY INFORMATION

Wear eye protection and wear gloves or use forceps when removing the cubes.

Avoid contact with potassium(VII) manganate as it stains skin and clothing.

Clean splashes immediately with repeated rinses of tap water.

Method

1. Put on eye protection.

2. Use the knife or scalpel to cut a set of 5 agar cubes that are 2 cm × 2 cm × 2 cm.

3. Prepare a separate set of 5 agar cubes that are 1 cm × 1 cm × 1 cm, and a third set of 5 cubes that are 0.5 cm × 0.5 cm × 0.5 cm.

4. Place each set of cubes in a separate dish or beaker and carefully pour potassium manganate(VII) into each dish to cover the cubes. Note the time (or start a stopwatch/clock).

5. After two minutes, put on disposable gloves or use tongs to remove one cube from each dish and place it on a non-staining surface. Cut each cube in half and use the ruler to measure the distance the dye has penetrated into the cube.

6. Repeat step 4 after 4, 6, 8 and 10 minutes.

7. Record your results in a suitable table.

Analyse and interpret data

1. Calculate the surface area and volume for each size of cube. Use these values to calculate their surface area to volume (SA/V) ratio.

2. Use your SA/V ratios and diffusion results to draw a suitable chart or graph of your results.

3. Describe any patterns you see in your data.

4. Explain the implications of your results for living organisms.

Activity B2d.2 Osmosis

Specification reference: B2d.2.15; B2d.2.16; B2d.2.17

Learning objectives

- Understand the process of osmosis by which substances move into and out of cells.
- Understand how factors affect the rate of movement of substances into and out of cells, including the effects of surface area to volume ratio, distance, temperature and concentration gradient.
- Practical: Investigate osmosis using living and non-living systems.

Learning outcomes

- Write a definition of the term *osmosis*.
- Explain how osmosis can occur across cell membranes.
- Describe factors that affect the rate of osmosis across cell membranes.
- Carry out simple experiments to investigate osmosis.

Common misconceptions

As with diffusion, the important concept to get across is of *net movement*, not just the movement of the water particles.

This topic has the potential to be very confusing because we usually talk in terms of the concentration of solute molecules in a solution, not the concentration of water molecules. If you talk in terms of the concentration of water molecules, then it should be clear to students that osmosis is just diffusion in terms of water molecules. This is particularly important in living systems, as water is essential for life – hence why it is given a special name.

Expect students to be rigorous in their definition of which concentration they are talking about, water or solute, in their discussions and writing.

Resources

Student Book pages 60–64

Worksheet B2d.2a Practical: Investigate osmosis using a non-living system

Worksheet B2d.2b Practical: Investigate osmosis using a living system (1) – Measuring osmosis by change in mass

Worksheet B2d.2c Practical: Investigate osmosis using a living system (2) – Osmosis and change in shape

Resources for class practicals (see Technician's notes, following)

Approach

1. Introduction to osmosis

Before the activity, prepare two eggs by placing the unboiled eggs in vinegar (or other dilute acid) for 3–4 days to dissolve the shell. Then place each egg in a conical flask and cover one egg with a concentrated sugar solution and the other with water. After 24 hours, there should be one shrunken egg that can be removed easily from the flask, and one large 'full' egg that cannot be extracted easily from the flask.

Ensure that the eggs have not passed their best-before date.

Show the eggs to students and explain that the egg is like a large cell, with the membrane surrounding the egg acting as a cell membrane. Ask them to suggest how you produced the difference between the eggs. Remind students that water molecules are small enough to pass through cell membranes. Introduce the term *osmosis* as the special case of diffusion that considers the movement of water molecules across a partially permeable membrane.

Using the definition of diffusion that they learned earlier, ask them to produce a definition for the term *osmosis*. Now you can discuss the need to distinguish between the concentration of solute molecules and concentration of water molecules in a solution when talking or writing about osmosis.

The investigation on Worksheet B2d.2a could be used as a demonstration, or class practical, to help students understand the effect of partially permeable membranes on osmosis and help them to visualise what effect osmosis can have on living cells.

You should demonstrate how to attach the Visking tubing to the glass tubing correctly to minimise the risk of students shattering the glass tubing.

2. Factors affecting osmosis

Worksheets B2d.2b and B2d.2c provide two opportunities for students to investigate the effect of concentration of solution on osmosis in living systems. Worksheet B2d.2b uses a simpler method, and uses change in mass as a method of estimating the amount of gain or loss of water by cells. Worksheet B2d.2c uses the change in curvature of pieces of dandelion stem as a result of differential absorption of water by inner and outer cell layers. It also gives students the opportunity to produce a dilution sequence for the investigation.

Give students opportunities to apply their knowledge of the effect of temperature, distance and surface area to volume ratio on diffusion to their understanding of osmosis. This could be done by simple questioning, or by asking students to draw or describe what happens when cells are placed in solutions of different temperature, when water has to pass through a thicker layer, or the problems for larger organisms that need to take in, or lose, water.

Technician's notes

You will need the following resources for the class practicals.

Be sure to check the latest safety notes on these resources before proceeding.

B2d.2a Practical: Investigate osmosis using a non-living system

This investigation tests understanding of osmosis. It can be carried out as a class demonstration or as a practical by students working in groups. The set-up for the apparatus is shown on Worksheet B2d.2a. The key point is to get students to predict what will happen to the level of liquid in the glass tube after a few hours, and to explain their prediction.

Borosilicate glass tubing should be used as there is less danger of it shattering when students attach the Visking tubing to it.

The equipment will need to be set up and left for a few hours, or preferably overnight, to show a significant change in liquid level.

After this time the level of liquid should have risen in the glass tube. This is because the concentration of water molecules in the starch solution in the Visking tubing is lower than in the water in the beaker, and the starch molecules do not diffuse through the membrane. The net movement of water molecules (osmosis) will be into the Visking tubing, increasing the volume of the solution, so liquid level rises.

Class practical, per group, or for demonstration:

borosilicate glass tube, about 10 cm long, fairly wide bore so that the solution can be pipetted into it
Visking tubing
10% starch solution or other solution of substance that will not diffuse through the Visking tubing
water
beaker or boiling tube
clamp and stand
wire or elastic band to attach tubing to glass tube
pipette
marker pen

B2d.2b Practical: Investigate osmosis using a living system (1)
Measuring osmosis by change in mass

This investigation uses change in mass of tissue samples to measure the effect on osmosis of solutions of different concentration. Any suitable plant tissue can be used, but root vegetables are particularly useful due to their volume. Provide whole vegetables, from which students can cut their own samples. Alternatively take cores from the vegetables as near to the lesson as possible and store them in water.

Any suitable concentrated solution can be used, but choose one that is cheap and safe to handle, such as salt or table sugar. The worksheet suggests the use of a dark-coloured fruit cordial/syrup, as students will be able to see differences in concentration and are less likely to muddle tubes.

The worksheet expects students to carry out the dilutions themselves. Alternatively, these could be prepared ahead of the lesson to save time.

The discs will need to be left in solution for at least two hours to get a significant change in mass. Some students may need help with the calculations in the first step of the analysis on the worksheet.

Students should find that discs gain mass or lose mass (water) depending on how the concentration of cell cytoplasm differs from the solution in which they are placed. Mass loss is as a result of osmosis of water out of the cell when placed in more concentrated solutions, and mass gain is the result of osmosis of water into the cell when placed in more dilute solutions.

Class practical, per group, or for demonstration:

5 boiling tubes and rack
10 cm^3 dark-coloured fruit cordial/syrup
distilled water
glass rod
paper towels
fresh root vegetable, such as potato (see note above)
cork borer
sharp knife
white tile for cutting/boring on
weighing balance, must be capable of weighing to 0.001 g
10 cm^3 measuring cylinder
marker pen

B2d.2c Practical: Investigate osmosis using a living system (2)
Osmosis and change in shape

This investigation links to the Developing investigative skills box on page 62 in the Student Book. It is similar to the previous investigation, but uses a different method of changing stem curvature to show the effects of osmosis. It also gives students an opportunity to create and calculate a dilution sequence.

The plant stalks must be fresh or stored in a dilute salt solution until use (to prevent drying out).

Students should find that the stalks change in curvature as a result of osmosis, and because the outer cells of the stalk cannot absorb water while the inner cells can. The diagram on page 62 of the Student Book shows results from an experiment like this.

Stalks in solutions that are more dilute (have a higher concentration of water molecules) than the cytoplasm in the cells will curve with the outer layer on the inside and inner layer outside. Stalks in solutions that are more concentrated (have a lower concentration of water molecules) than the cytoplasm in the cells will curve with the inner layer on the inside and outer layer outside.
The greater the difference from the concentration of cell cytoplasm, the greater the curvature (although the pressure caused by the cell wall will prevent the curvature in distilled water getting very large).

Class practical, per group:

3 boiling tubes and rack
10 cm^3 0.5 mol dm^{-3} sodium chloride solution
distilled water
glass rod
5 Petri dishes
fresh hollow plant stalks (e.g. dandelion stalks)
sharp knife or scalpel and white tile for cutting on
marker pen

Answers

Developing investigative skills, page 62

1. Plan should include:

- cutting stems with sharp knife/scalpel to give accurate size and reduce damage to cells near the cut
- using a ruler or similar to measure the lengths and widths of the pieces when cutting
- placing cut pieces into water for storage until investigation begins, to prevent cells drying out
- accurate preparation of solutions of different concentrations given in diagram
- quickly placing pieces into each solution so they all have the same time in solution
- ideally, use of several pieces of stem in each solution (two are shown in the diagrams, but more might be better) so that results from different pieces can be averaged to give a more accurate result (since living things can vary).

2. The diagrams show that in solutions of concentration less than 0.25 mol dm^{-3}, the inner cells enlarge and can cause the strips to curve with the outer surface on the inside. In 0.25 mol dm^{-3} there is little change in the strips, and in the most concentrated solution (0.5 mol dm^{-3}), the strips curve more with the outer layer still on the outside.

3. Osmosis results when there is a concentration gradient for water across a partially permeable membrane. In the solutions of concentration less than 0.25 mol dm^{-3}, the inner cells gain water. As the outer cells don't change as much, because of the waxy layer, the increase in turgidity of the inner cells causes the strips to curve with the inner layer on the outer side of the curve. In the most concentrated solution, the inner cells have lost water as a result of osmosis and got smaller, and so the strips have curved even more than they normally do, with the outer layer on the outside.

4. The normal concentration of cell cytoplasm of dandelion cells appears to be about 0.25 mol dm^{-3} because these strips changed least, suggesting there was little osmosis between the cells and solution and so there is little or no concentration gradient between them.

Page 62

1. Any answer that means the same as the following: the net movement of water molecules from a region of their higher concentration to a region of their lower concentration.

2. a) It is a passive movement of molecules as the result of a concentration gradient, moving from where they have a higher concentration to where they have a lower concentration.

   b) Osmosis only considers movement of water molecules, diffusion considers solute molecules. Osmosis always involves movement across a partially permeable membrane, diffusion may or may not involve movement across a membrane.

3. Diagram should show water molecules leaving the red blood cell as a result of osmosis and entering the solution.

Page 64

1. Concentration gradient, distance, temperature and surface area.

2. Any answer that means the same as the following: if there is a greater difference in concentration between two areas then there will be a greater net movement from the area of higher concentration to the area of lower concentration, as there will be more particles moving away from the area of higher concentration than towards it. So rate of diffusion is faster.

3. As size increases, area increases as the square of the length, but volume increases by the cube of the length. This means that volume increases faster than area, so the ratio of surface area to volume must get smaller.

B2d.2a Practical: Investigate osmosis using a non-living system

We can use Visking tubing to investigate the effect of the concentration of a solution on osmosis. This is because water molecules are small enough to pass through the holes in the partially permeable membrane of the tubing. The solute used must be too large to diffuse through the membrane, so in this practical we will use starch.

Apparatus

glass tube

Visking tubing

starch solution

water

beaker or boiling tube

clamp and stand

wire or elastic band to attach tubing to

glass tube pipette

marker pen

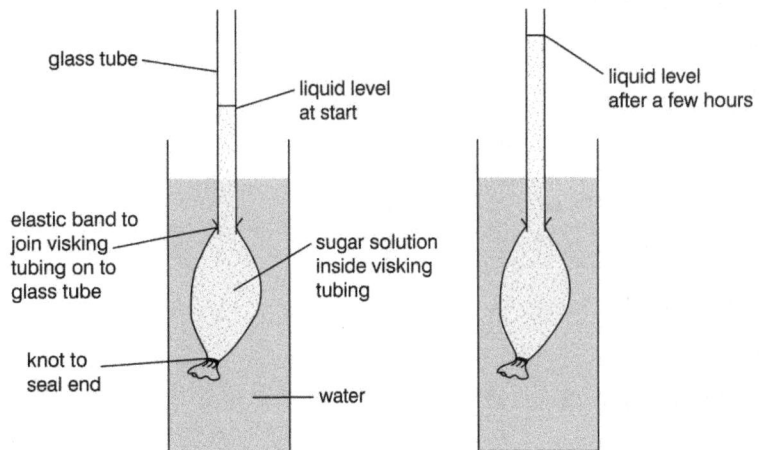

SAFETY INFORMATION

Connect the Visking tubing to the glass tubing in the way that your teacher shows you.

Method

1. Knot one end of the Visking tubing, then attach it to the end of the glass tube using a piece of wire or elastic band. Support the glass tube in a clamp.

2. Use the pipette to carefully add starch solution to the Visking tubing through the glass tube. Keep adding starch solution until about 1 cm is visible in the glass tube. Mark the level of the solution with a marker pen.

3. Wash any spills of starch solution from the outside of the tubing. Then suspend the tubing in a beaker or boiling tube of water, so that the Visking tubing is completely covered in water, as shown in the diagram.

4. Leave the apparatus for several hours or overnight. Then record any difference in the level of solution in the glass tube.

Prediction

1. Write a prediction for this experiment. Explain your prediction using your knowledge of osmosis.

Analyse and interpret data

1. Compare the level of solution before and after the experiment. How did it change?

2. Explain any change using your knowledge of osmosis.

3. Explain the importance of your findings to living organisms.

4. Explain why it was important to use a solution of a substance that cannot diffuse through Visking tubing for this investigation.

B2d.2b Practical: Investigate osmosis using a living system (1) – Measuring osmosis by change in mass

When cells take in water by osmosis, they increase in mass. We can use this to investigate the effect of concentration of solution on osmosis.

Apparatus

5 boiling tubes and rack

fruit cordial/syrup

distilled water

glass rod paper towels

fresh root vegetable, e.g. potato

cork borer

marker pen

sharp knife

white tile for cutting on

balance

10 cm^3 measuring cylinder

SAFETY INFORMATION

Take care with sharp knives.

Method

Preparing solutions of different concentration

1. Pour 5 cm^3 fruit cordial/syrup into the first tube. Label this *full concentration*.

2. Pour 5 cm^3 fruit cordial/syrup into the second tube. Add 5 cm^3 distilled water and stir the solution with a dry glass rod. Label this tube as ½ *concentration*.

3. Pour 5 cm^3 of the ½ concentration solution into an empty tube. Add 5 cm^3 distilled water and stir the solution with a dry glass rod. Label this tube as ¼ *concentration*.

4. Pour 5 cm^3 of the ¼ concentration solution into an empty tube. Add 5 cm^3 distilled water and stir the solution with a dry glass rod. Label this tube as ⅛ *concentration*.

5. Pour 5 cm^3 distilled water into the final empty tube. Label this tube *pure water*.

Preparing the discs

1. Use the cork borer to extract cores from the root. Cut the cores into discs that are about 3 mm deep.

2. When you have five discs, blot them dry on a paper towel and measure their mass on the balance. Record the mass and then place the discs into one of the tubes.

3. Repeat step 7 until all the tubes contain 5 discs.

4. Leave the discs for at least 2 hours. After this time, remove all the discs from one tube, blot them dry on a paper towel, then measure their mass again. Record the results and repeat for the discs from each of the remaining tubes.

Analyse and interpret data

1. For each tube, calculate the change in mass of the discs, and then the percentage change in mass.

2. Draw a suitable graph or chart to display your results.

3. Describe any patterns in your results.

4. Explain any pattern in your results using your knowledge of osmosis.

Evaluate data and methods

1. Describe any problems that you had with your investigation, and explain what could have been done to reduce their effect on the results.

B2d.2c Practical: Investigate osmosis using a living system (2) – Osmosis and change in shape

In some hollow plant stalks the outer cells are unable to take in water because they are covered with a waterproof layer that stops the plant losing water in normal conditions. However, the cells inside the stalk are not protected so they will take in water due to osmosis up to the point when the cell walls prevent further expansion. We can use this difference to investigate osmosis in the cells of pieces of stalk.

Apparatus

3 boiling tubes

0.5 mol dm^{-3} sodium chloride solution

distilled water

glass rod

5 Petri dishes

fresh hollow plant stalks

sharp knife or scalpel

white tile for cutting on

marker pen

SAFETY INFORMATION

Take care with sharp knives.

Wash your hands after handling the dandelion stalks.

Method

Preparing the dilutions

1. Use the marker pen to label the tubes from 1 to 3, and label the Petri dishes from 1 to 5.

2. Measure 5 cm^3 sodium chloride solution into dish 1.

3. Measure 5 cm^3 sodium chloride solution into tube 1. Add 5 cm^3 distilled water and mix with a clean dry glass rod. Measure 5 cm^3 of the solution in tube 1 into tube 2 and pour the rest into dish 2.

4. Add 5 cm^3 distilled water to tube 2 and mix the solution with a clean dry glass rod. Measure 5 cm^3 of the solution in tube 2 into tube 3 and pour the rest into dish 3.

5. Add 5 cm^3 distilled water to tube 3 and mix the solution with a clean dry glass rod. Measure 5 cm^3 of the solution into dish 4.

6. Measure 5 cm^3 distilled water into dish 5.

Preparing the dandelion stalks

1. Cut across a plant stalk to produce a tube about 5 cm long.

2. Cut along the cylinder and open it out to produce a flat sheet.

3. Cut the flat sheet into thin strips, about 3 mm wide along their length.

4. Place two strips into each dish and leave them for about 5 minutes.

5. Note any changes in curvature between the strips. Record your results in words or pictures.

Analyse and interpret data

1. Describe any patterns in your results.

2. Use your knowledge of osmosis to explain any pattern in your results.

Evaluate data and methods

1. Describe any problems that you had with your investigation, and explain what could have been done to reduce their effect on the results.

2. Suggest how the method could be adapted to estimate the concentration of cell cytoplasm in tissue from different plants.

Activity B2d.3 Active transport

Specification reference: B2d.2.15; B2d.2.16

Learning objectives

- Understand the process of active transport by which substances move into and out of cells.
- Understand how factors affect the rate of movement of substances into and out of cells, including the effects of surface area to volume ratio, distance, temperature and concentration gradient.

Learning outcomes

- Write a definition of the term *active transport*.
- Explain how active transport can occur across cell membranes.
- Give examples of active transport in animals and plants.

Common misconceptions

This is an opportunity to reinforce the fact that diffusion and osmosis are passive processes that result from the random movement of molecules, while active transport is the deliberate selection of certain molecules by a cell for transport across the cell membrane.

Resources

Student Book pages 64–65

Approach

1. Why do organisms need active transport?

Show students a plant in a pot and explain that you water the plant every one or two days, but occasionally you add some plant food to the water. Ask them to suggest what would happen if you did not water the plant. Use the discussion of water to revise briefly what students have learned about osmosis.

Then ask what would happen if the plant didn't receive any plant food occasionally. (Make sure students do not confuse 'plant food' which provides some nutrients that plants need for the best rate of growth and 'animal food' without which an animal would soon die of starvation.)

Tell students that the concentration of solutes inside the root cells is greater than the concentration of solutes in the soil water, and ask them to suggest what problems this causes for plants. They should remember from their work on diffusion that the concentration gradient is in the wrong direction for root cells to absorb what they need from soil water by diffusion.

Read through the text in the Student Book and ask students to explain why certain substances move across cell membranes as a result of active transport, and why cells need special carrier proteins in their membranes for this purpose.

Answers

Page 65

1. Active transport is the movement of a substance across a cell membrane against its concentration gradient, using energy.

2. Uptake of nitrate ions by root cells in plants, uptake of glucose from kidney tubules into the blood in animals.

Activity B2d.4 Consolidation and summary

Learning objectives

- To review the learning points of the topic.
- To test understanding through answering questions.

Learning outcomes

- Be familiar with the knowledge and understanding summarised in the End of topic checklist.
- Be able to apply this knowledge and understanding by answering the End of topic questions.

Resources

Student Book pages 66–67

Approach

1. Consolidation of work on movement of substances

Give each student three scraps of paper and ask them to write *diffusion* on one scrap, *osmosis* on another and *active transport* on the third. Then ask a series of questions to which one or more of these words is the answer. For example:

- Which of the processes need energy to happen? (active transport)
- Which of the processes are the result of random movement of molecules? (diffusion and osmosis)
- Which of the processes involves molecules other than water? (diffusion and active transport)

This will help you to identify any weaknesses in learning by individual students.

2. End of topic questions

Ask students to answer the End of topic questions in the Student Book.

Answers

End of topic questions mark scheme

Question	Correct answer				Marks
1	The salt forms a very concentrated solution on the slug's surface				1
	so water leaves its body by osmosis.				1
2					9

	Diffusion	Osmosis	Active transport
active or passive?	passive	passive	active
which molecules move?	only small molecules can pass through partially permeable membrane	water molecules	specific molecules depending on carrier
requires special carrier proteins?	no	no	yes

85

Question	Correct answer	Marks
3 a)	Diffusion	1
3 b)	Neither	1
3 c)	Osmosis	1
4	The larger an organism, the smaller its surface area to volume ratio	1
	and so, though it needs more materials to support the life processes in cells, it would have a relatively smaller surface area over which to absorb/exchange what it needs.	1
	This would slow the rate of diffusion.	1
	Special adaptations, such as alveoli in the lungs, increase the surface area and so increase the rate of diffusion.	1
5 a)	More than	1
5 b)	To provide energy for the active transport of minerals like nitrates into the roots.	1
6 a)	It is a partially permeable membrane like cell membranes are.	1
6 b)	Iodine/potassium iodide to test for starch.	1
	Benedict's test for fructose (because it is a reducing sugar).	1
6 c)	No reaction with the iodine/potassium iodide.	1
	Benedict's test would show a positive reaction (blue colour changes to yellow or orange-red precipitate).	1
6 d)	Fructose is a small molecule and so can diffuse through the membrane,	1
	but starch is too large and cannot pass through.	1
7	The membranes control what enters and what leaves the organelle.	1
	This means that different conditions can be set up in one organelle for a particular process than in a different organelle where something else happens.	1
	This makes it possible for many different processes to go on in one cell at the same time.	1
	Total:	30

Introduction

This section of learning covers photosynthesis, mineral nutrition of plants and human nutrition in terms of the human digestive system.

Links to other topics

Sections	Essential background knowledge	Useful links
1 The nature and variety of living organisms	1a Characteristics of living organisms 1b Variety of living organisms	
2 Structure and functions in living organisms	2a Level of organisation 2b Cell structure 2c Biological molecules 2d Movement of substances into and out of cells	2f Respiration 2g Gas exchange 2h Transport 2i Excretion
3 Reproduction and inheritance		3a Reproduction
4 Ecology and the environment		4b Feeding relationships 4c Cycles within ecosystems
5 Use of biological resources		5a Food production

Topic overview

B2e.1	**Photosynthesis** This activity looks at the process of photosynthesis, including the factors that affect it and the way a leaf is structured to maximise photosynthesis. It provides many opportunities for practical work. You may have to select from the suggestions offered, in order to fit the time and resources available. Some might also be presented as class demonstrations.
B2e.2	**Mineral ions in plants** This short activity explains why plants need mineral ions for healthy growth, and offers a practical to investigate the effect of nitrate and magnesium ions on plant growth. This practical needs at least a month to produce significant results.
B2e.3	**Human nutrition** This activity looks at diet, the structure of the human digestive system and the role of enzymes in digestion. It provides opportunities for research as well as for practical work.
B2e.4	**Consolidation and summary** This activity provides an opportunity for a quick recap on the ideas encountered in the topic as well as time for the students to answer the End of topic questions in the Student Book.

87

Activity B2e.1 Photosynthesis

Specification reference: B2e.2.18; B2e.2.19; B2e.2.20; B2e.2.21; B2e.2.23

Learning objectives

- Understand the process of photosynthesis and its importance in the conversion of light energy to chemical energy.
- Know the word equation and balanced chemical symbol equation for photosynthesis.
- Understand how varying carbon dioxide concentration, light intensity and temperature affect the rate of photosynthesis.
- Describe the structure of the leaf and explain how it is adapted for photosynthesis.
- Practical: Investigate photosynthesis, showing the evolution of oxygen from a water plant, the production of starch and the requirements of light, carbon dioxide and chlorophyll.

Learning outcomes

- Describe photosynthesis, and write word and symbol equations for the process.
- Explain the role of photosynthesis in the nutrition of plants.
- Describe how different factors affect the rate of photosynthesis.
- Explain how the leaf is adapted for photosynthesis.

Common misconceptions

Students may believe that plants need mineral ions in order to grow, because these are often supplied as 'plant food', which they confuse with animal food. Students must understand that plants produce their food in the form of simple carbohydrates from photosynthesis, and that the additional mineral ions are nutrients needed for converting carbohydrates to other biological molecules within cells.

Resources

Student Book pages 68–77

Worksheet B2e.1a Practical: Investigate photosynthesis, showing the production of starch

Worksheet B2e.1b Practical: Investigate photosynthesis, showing the requirement of chlorophyll

Worksheet B2e.1c Practical: Investigate photosynthesis, showing the requirement of carbon dioxide

Worksheet B2e.1d Practical: Investigate photosynthesis, showing the evolution of oxygen from a water plant and the requirement of light

Resources for class practicals (see Technician's notes, following)

Approach

1. Introduction to photosynthesis

Show students a potted plant and give them three minutes to jot down everything they can think of that relates to how the plant gets its food. Take examples from around the class, focusing on the answers that relate to photosynthesis.

Take the opportunity to note any misconceptions that will need to be tackled during the work on this topic.

Use the Student Book to introduce the word and symbol equations for photosynthesis.

2. Investigating photosynthesis

There are four possible practicals for this part of the topic:

- Worksheet B2e.1a explains how to prepare and test a leaf for starch. This method is needed for Worksheets B2e.1b and B2e.1c, so all students should be given the opportunity to do this. If you keep one plant in the dark and test a leaf from that at the end of the students' work, you will be able to show the 'need for light'.

- Worksheet B2e.1b investigates the need for chlorophyll.

- Worksheet B2e.1c investigates the need for carbon dioxide. Note that this might be better done as a demonstration, due to the apparatus used.

  You should put the soda lime into the beakers. You should be wearing eye protection and the material should be dispensed with a spatula or forceps.

- Worksheet B2e.1d provides a method using a water plant to give quantitative data on the effect of light intensity on the rate of photosynthesis. The method assumes that the bubbles produced are all oxygen and of the same size.

  A more accurate method could be to collect and measure the volume of oxygen produced over a fixed time, but this will take longer to produce measurable results. The method could also be adapted by adding different amounts of hydrogen-carbonate indicator to the water to produce quantitative data of the effect of carbon dioxide concentration on the rate of photosynthesis.

If time is limited, different groups of students could carry out different practicals at the same time, and then present their findings to the rest of the class.

You should supervise the pouring of very hot water from kettles to limit the hazard of scalding.

3. Structure of a leaf

If available, ask students to look at prepared slides of transverse sections through a leaf. Alternatively use a digital microscope to display such a slide, or display an example from the internet. Ask students to identify the different tissues in the leaf, and describe how they are adapted to their role in supporting photosynthesis.

4. Consolidation: annotated equation

Ask students to write the word or symbol equation for photosynthesis in the middle of a page of A4. They should then annotate the equation to identify where reactants come from, how the leaf is adapted to supply them as efficiently as possible, and how the different parts of the equation can affect the rate of photosynthesis. They should discuss their annotated equations with a partner to identify how they could improve their notes.

Technician's notes

You will need the following resources for the class practicals.

Be sure to check the latest safety notes on these resources before proceeding.

Please note that the plants need a large amount of daylight to produce starch. If this practical is being carried out in winter, the leaves will need to have several hours of strong, safe illumination to make sure that they have produced some starch.

B2e.1a Practical: Investigate photosynthesis, showing the production of starch

The method described on Worksheet B2e.1a is used on Worksheets B2e.1b and B2e.1c also, so the following applies to all three investigations.

Class practical, per group:

industrial denatured ethanol (IDA) *	forceps
kettle of boiling water	boiling tube
water bath at 90 °C with boiling tube rack	plastic rod or wooden spatula
marker pen	Petri dish
iodine solution in dropper bottle	white tile
large beaker with insulation	eye protection
leaf – best taken from the plant at the start of the practical so that it is fresh	

* highly flammable, harmful if swallowed

B2e.1b Practical: Investigate photosynthesis, showing the requirement of chlorophyll

The plants for this practical need to be destarched. Place them in the dark for about 48 hours, then test a leaf to check that the plants are fully destarched, otherwise this will affect the results.

In addition to the apparatus for B2e.1a, students will need the following.

Class practical, per group:

destarched plant, either with variegated or green leaves
metal foil and paper clip (if green leaves) – students will need a long enough strip of foil to cover both sides of the leaf (if metal foil is not available, black card can be used instead)

B2e.1c Practical: Investigate photosynthesis, showing the requirement of carbon dioxide

The plants for this practical need to be destarched. Place them in the dark for about 48 hours, then test a leaf to check that the plants are fully destarched, otherwise this will affect the results.

In addition to the apparatus for B2e.1a, students will need the following.

Class practical, per group, or per class demonstration:

2 bell jars
2 destarched plants
2 plastic trays, alternatively glass sheets – to create a perfect seal with the bell jar using the jelly/grease
petroleum jelly or silicone grease
small beaker of soda lime *
small beaker containing 10–20 marble chips
dilute hydrochloric acid
safety goggles

* corrosive (skin and eyes)

B2e.1d Practical: Investigate photosynthesis, showing the evolution of oxygen from a water plant and the requirement of light

Prepare the pondweed before the lesson by cutting 10 cm lengths, one for each group. Check that there are no small invertebrates on the plants. *Cabomba* may produce more bubbles than *Elodea* but tends to break apart more easily.

The classroom will need to be darkened for this practical. Students should be reminded how to prepare for this (such as removing all bags etc. from the floor) and how to behave.

If available, a light meter or sensor could be used to measure light intensity directly, instead of recording distance between the light and pondweed.

The voltage of the bulb should not exceed the safety limits of the bench lamp. Low energy bulbs should have some sort of protection so that they do not protrude beyond the protective metal of the bench lamp. Or they can be protected by a plastic or glass screen.

Low energy bulbs contain mercury and so can be hazardous if the bulb is broken.

Teachers should be vigilant while this practical is being carried out because of water being used close to electrical equipment.

LED lights emit a very narrow range of wavelengths of light which might not be absorbed by the plant. Halogen light sources are fine for photosynthesis but they do get hot. A large beaker of tap water placed in front of the light source will absorb the heat.

Class practical, per group:

pondweed, e.g. *Elodea* or *Cabomba* sp.
paper clip
boiling tube containing pond water
beaker of water
metre rule
lamp – ideally low voltage bulb or LED light
stopwatch or clock

Answers

Page 70

1.

$$6CO_2 + 6H_2O \xrightarrow[\text{light energy}]{\text{chlorophyll}} C_6H_{12}O_6 + 6O_2$$

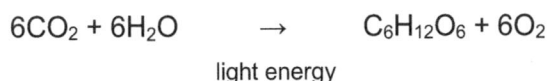

2. CO_2 from air, H_2O from soil water, $C_6H_{12}O_6$ used in cells for respiration or converted to other chemicals for use in cells, O_2 released into air if not needed in respiration.

3. Any four from: as glucose for respiration; converted to sucrose for storage in fruits; converted to starch for storage; converted to cellulose to form cell walls; converted to oils for storage; converted to proteins for growth.

Page 72

1. Thin broad leaves, chlorophyll in cells, veins containing xylem tissue that transports water and mineral ions to the leaves and phloem tissue that takes products of photosynthesis to other parts of the plant, transparent epidermal cells, palisade cells tightly packed in a single layer near top of leaf, stomata to allow gases into and out of leaf, spongy mesophyll layer with air spaces and a large internal surface.

2. A large surface area helps to maximise the rate of diffusion, in this case diffusion of carbon dioxide into cells for photosynthesis and oxygen out of cells so that it can be released into the air.

3. Allows as much light as possible through to the chloroplasts in the palisade cells below.

Developing investigative skills, page 76

1. a) Oxygen is a waste product of photosynthesis. So the rate of production of oxygen is a good estimate of the rate of photosynthesis.

   b) With a glowing splint, because it is oxygen – the splint should relight.

2. a) Line graph should be shown, with distance on x-axis and number of bubbles on y-axis. Smooth line of best fit drawn through the points.

   b) The graph shows that as distance increases the rate of bubble production decreases. This is because light energy is needed for the process of photosynthesis – as light intensity decreases so the rate of photosynthesis decreases.

3. a) A filament light bulb releases heat energy as well as light energy. Heat also affects the rate of reaction, so the closer the lamp was to the plant, the greater the effect of heat on the reactions.

   b) Use a low energy bulb that releases little heat, or place a transparent heat barrier (such as a thin water tank) between the lamp and the plant.

Page 77 (top)

1. Light intensity, carbon dioxide concentration, temperature.

2. As light intensity increases, so rate of photosynthesis increases because more energy is supplied to drive the process.

As carbon dioxide concentration increases, so rate of photosynthesis increases because there is more reactant for the process.

As temperature increases, the rate of photosynthesis increases because the particles in the reaction, including enzymes, are moving faster and bump into each other more. There is a maximum temperature above which the rate of photosynthesis decreases because the enzymes that control the process start to become denatured.

3. The only part of the leaf that can photosynthesise is the green part where there is chlorophyll. So only in the green parts can glucose be produced. Starch is formed from glucose, so it is only formed in the green parts where photosynthesis has taken place.

B2e.1a Practical: Investigate photosynthesis, showing the production of starch

Photosynthesis does not form starch directly. However, it does form simple sugars which are quickly converted to starch in other reactions. So, the production of starch in a leaf can be used as evidence of photosynthesis.

As you learned previously, the test of starch uses iodine solution, which changes from orange-yellow to blue-black in the presence of starch. However, before testing a leaf for starch, we have to remove the green colour of chlorophyll and remove the waxy cuticle so that the iodine solution can penetrate the cells of the leaf. This practical provides the method for preparing and testing leaves for starch, which you can use in other practicals on photosynthesis.

Apparatus

ethanol *

kettle of boiling water

water bath at 90 °C with boiling tube rack

marker pen

iodine solution in dropper bottle

large beaker and insulation material

leaf forceps

boiling tube

plastic rod or spatula

Petri dish

white tile

eye protection

* highly flammable, harmful if swallowed

SAFETY INFORMATION

Do not use open flames (such as a Bunsen burner) when heating ethanol. It is highly flammable and harmful if swallowed.

Wear eye protection when using ethanol or iodine solution.

Take care to avoid scalding with very hot water.

Wash hands thoroughly at the end of the practical.

If you spill iodine solution on your skin, wash it off immediately.

Method

1. Put on eye protection.

2. Pour boiling water into a large insulated beaker.

3. Pick up the leaf by the stalk with the forceps and hold it in the water for about a minute.

4. Remove the leaf from the water with the forceps and place it in a boiling tube. Push the leaf to the bottom of the tube with the plastic rod or spatula. Label the tube with your initials.

Pour enough ethanol into the tube to cover the leaf. Place the tube into the large insulated beaker (or the tube rack in the water bath, if this is being used). The ethanol will boil and remove the chlorophyll.

5. Check the leaf after a few minutes. If there is still green chlorophyll in the leaf, put it back in the tube for a few more minutes.

6. When the leaf has lost all green colour, use forceps to remove the leaf from the tube and rinse it in cold water.

7. Place the leaf on a white tile and place drops of iodine solution to cover the leaf.

8. Where there is any starch in the leaf, a blue-black colour will form.

Analyse and interpret data

1. Explain fully why a leaf turns blue-black after using this method. What does this evidence mean?

2. A plant is left in a dark cupboard for two days. What colour would you expect to see after one of its leaves is tested with iodine solution, yellow-orange or blue-black? Explain your answer.

3. Suggest why a plant should be left in a dark cupboard for two days before carrying out experiments on photosynthesis.

B2e.1b Practical: Investigate photosynthesis, showing the requirement of chlorophyll

You can test the need for chlorophyll in the process of photosynthesis using the method of testing leaves for starch in Worksheet B2e.1a.

You will start with a plant that has been left in a cupboard for two days (to become destarched). You may be given a variegated plant (one that has white and green leaves). The white parts of the leaf contain cells that do not make chlorophyll.

Apparatus

destarched plant, either with variegated or green leaves

metal foil and paper clip (if green leaves)

apparatus from Worksheet B2e.1a

SAFETY INFORMATION

Do not use open flames (such as a Bunsen burner) when heating ethanol. It is highly flammable and harmful if swallowed.

Wear eye protection when using ethanol or iodine solution.

Take care to avoid scalding with very hot water.

Wash hands thoroughly at the end of the practical.

If you spill iodine solution on your skin, wash it off immediately.

Method

1. Choose one leaf on the plant. If the leaf is variegated, draw the green/white markings as carefully as you can.

2. Place the plant in bright light for about 24 hours.

3. Put on eye protection.

4. Remove the leaf from the plant and test for starch using the method on Worksheet B2e.1a.

5. Record your results as a drawing.

Analyse and interpret data

1. Describe your results.

2. Explain your results using your knowledge of photosynthesis.

3. Explain the importance of chlorophyll for plants.

B2e.1c Practical: Investigate photosynthesis, showing the requirement of carbon dioxide

Soda lime is a chemical that absorbs carbon dioxide by reacting with it. It can be used to remove carbon dioxide from the air. Marble chips are a form of calcium carbonate, and react with dilute acid to release carbon dioxide. We can use these chemicals to investigate the role of carbon dioxide in photosynthesis. You can test for starch using the apparatus from Worksheet B2e.1a.

Apparatus

2 bell jars

2 destarched plants

2 plastic trays

small beaker of soda lime (your teacher will put the soda lime in the beaker)

petroleum jelly or silicone grease

small beaker containing 10–20 marble chips

dilute hydrochloric acid

apparatus from Worksheet B2e.1a

eye protection

SAFETY INFORMATION

The soda lime should only be given out by the teacher.

Do not use open flames (such as a Bunsen burner) when heating ethanol. It is highly flammable and harmful if swallowed.

Wear goggles when using soda lime and wear eye protection when using ethanol or iodine solution.

Take care to avoid scalding with very hot water.

Wash hands thoroughly at the end of the practical.

If you spill iodine solution on your skin, wash it off immediately.

Method

1. Put on goggles.

2. With the teacher's help, set up one plant on a plastic tray with the beaker of soda lime beside it.

3. Rub a layer of petroleum jelly or silicone grease around the edge of the bell jar and carefully place the jar over the plant and beaker onto the tray. Press the bell jar down gently so that the jelly/grease forms a good seal between the jar and tray.

4. Pour sufficient acid into the other beaker to just cover the marble chips. Set up the other bell jar with the other plant and the beaker of marble chips and acid on another tray, sealed in the same way with jelly/grease.

5. Leave the plants for about 24 hours. Then test one leaf from each plant for starch using the method on Worksheet B2e.1a. Record your results.

Analyse and interpret data

1. Describe the results from the plant with carbon dioxide (marble chips) and the plant without carbon dioxide (soda lime).

2. Explain any differences in the leaves from the two plants.

3. Use your results to explain the importance of carbon dioxide for photosynthesis.

B2e.1d Practical: Investigate photosynthesis, showing the evolution of oxygen from a water plant and the requirement of light

In the photosynthesis practicals so far, you have investigated the need for various conditions for the process of photosynthesis. To measure changes in the rate of photosynthesis in relation to changes in one of these conditions, we need another method of measuring photosynthesis.

Photosynthesis produces oxygen as a waste product. We can use the rate of oxygen production, in the form of bubbles from a water plant, as a measure of the rate of photosynthesis. In this practical you will investigate the effect of different light intensities on the rate of photosynthesis. The work will need to be carried out in a darkened room.

Apparatus

pondweed

paper clip

boiling tube containing pond water

beaker of water

metre rule

lamp

stopwatch or clock

SAFETY INFORMATION

Cover any cuts with a waterproof plaster.

Make sure the lamp and any electrical equipment does not get wet.

Take care not to touch the lamp; it may get hot.

Wash hands thoroughly after the practical work.

Method

1. Attach a paper clip to the top tip of a fresh sprig of pondweed. Then place the pondweed in a boiling tube of water with the cut end of the stem uppermost. Make sure there is at least 1 cm of water above the end of the pondweed.

2. Place the boiling tube inside a water-filled beaker. This beaker will act as a heat shield.

3. Set up the lamp. Use the ruler to make sure that it is at a set distance away from the pondweed. Record this distance.

4. Look carefully at the cut end of the pondweed. You should be able to see a stream of oxygen bubbles.

5. Leave the pondweed for two minutes, to allow it to adjust to the conditions. Then count the number of bubbles produced in one minute. Record your results.

6. Repeat the count two more times and record those results also.

7. Move the lamp to a different distance from the pondweed. Record this distance and repeat steps 5 and 6.

8. Repeat step 7 for several different distances.

Analyse and interpret data

1. For each distance, calculate the average number of bubbles produced in one minute.

2. Use your averaged results to draw a graph of number of bubbles produced against distance of lamp from the pondweed.

3. Describe the shape of your graph.

4. Explain the shape of your graph using your knowledge of photosynthesis.

Evaluate data and methods

1. Describe any problems you had with this investigation. How do you think they affected your results?

2. Suggest how the method could be adjusted to avoid these problems.

Activity B2e.2 Mineral ions in plants

Specification reference: B2e.2.22

Learning objectives

- Understand that plants require mineral ions for growth, and that magnesium ions are needed for chlorophyll and nitrate ions are needed for amino acids.

Learning outcomes

- Describe the importance of some mineral ions in plant growth.

Common misconceptions

The same misconception may occur as in Topic B2e.1: students may believe that plants need mineral ions in order to grow, because these are often supplied as 'plant food', which they confuse with animal food. Students must understand that plants produce their food in the form of simple carbohydrates from photosynthesis, and that the additional mineral ions are nutrients needed for converting carbohydrates to other biological molecules within cells.

Resources

Student Book pages 77–78

Worksheet B2e.2a Plants and mineral ions

Resources for class practicals (see Technician's notes, following)

Approach

1. Plants need mineral ions

Ask students what plants produce in photosynthesis (glucose/simple sugars/carbohydrates), then ask what other substances are found in plant tissue. If they aren't sure, show them a few examples of foods that we eat that are produced from plants.

From their work on food groups in previous years, they may remember that seeds (and the oils from pressing them) are good sources of lipids, and pulses (such as lentils and beans) are good sources of proteins. They should also be able to offer chlorophyll from their recent work on photosynthesis.

Ask how proteins differ from carbohydrates in terms of the elements from which they are formed. Students should remember that proteins not only contain carbon and hydrogen (as do carbohydrates) but also nitrogen.

Use the Student Book to introduce the idea that plants need a range of mineral ions, to make a range of chemicals and that, without these, growth will be affected.

2. Investigating the need for mineral ions

Worksheet B2e.2a provides a simple method for investigating the need of plants for magnesium ions and nitrate ions using duckweed plants. This will need 4–8 weeks to produce measurable results. Other methods are available on the internet which may take less time but are not as easy to set up.

Note that the jars should be no more than half full of water, so that there is lots of air in the jar for the carbon dioxide needed for photosynthesis.

3. Consolidation: question tag

Ask students to jot down three key facts that they think the class should have learned in this and the last topic on photosynthesis. They should then write a question for each of the facts. Take examples from around the class, and select another student to answer it. If they answer it successfully, they should then read out one of their own questions.

Technician's notes

You will need the following resources for the class practicals.

Be sure to check the latest safety notes on these resources before proceeding.

B2e.2a Plant and mineral ions

Duckweed (*Lemna*), or any other small floating aquatic plant, is suitable for this investigation. Be aware, duckweed is not available from ponds over winter. Select healthy plants for the experiment.

Culture solutions can be bought ready prepared from some suppliers. Alternatively, the recipes for the solutions can be found on CLEAPSS Recipe sheet 66.

There are safety issues if the plants die and start to decompose. You should be alert to this possibility and dispose of decomposing cultures as soon as you notice this. See the CLEAPSS guidance on safe disposal.

Class practical, per group:

duckweed plants
culture solution containing all nutrients
culture solution deficient in nitrate ions
culture solution deficient in magnesium ions
3 beakers or glass jars
plastic film (cling film)
access to light
marker pen

Answers

Page 77 (bottom)

1. Plants make their own foods, and need to convert the carbohydrates made by photosynthesis into other substances, such as proteins, which contain additional elements.

2. a) Limited growth, lack of green colour in leaves.

   b) Lack of green colour in leaves.

3. a) Nitrogen is an essential element for making substances other than carbohydrates, such as amino acids and proteins. Without proteins, the plant cannot make new cells so the plant will not grow well. It is also needed for making chlorophyll, so without nitrogen the plant will not be able to make as much of the green pigment.

   b) Magnesium is needed to make chlorophyll, which is the green substance in plants. Without enough magnesium the plant will lose the green colour and become yellow. Any magnesium in the plant is transported to the new leaves, so that photosynthesis can continue there for making food for growth.

Page 78

1. a) The leaves of the plant with limited nitrogen are paler green / more yellow than those of the plant with a lot of nitrogen.

   b) The plant with plenty of nitrogen is larger, bushier and has more leaves than the plant with limited nitrogen.

2. The leaf cells of the plant with limited nitrogen will contain less chlorophyll because nitrogen is needed to make this substance.

3. The plant with plenty of nitrogen is not only able to make more chlorophyll and therefore photosynthesise more and produce more carbohydrate, it also has sufficient nitrogen to convert some of that glucose into proteins. So it can make more new cells more rapidly than the plant with limited nitrogen, and so grow taller and bushier and produce more leaves.

4. When the crop plants grow, they take in nitrogen as nitrate ions from the soil and use them to make substances such as proteins and chlorophyll in the plant tissues. When the plant is harvested, the nitrogen compounds in the tissues are taken as well. This leaves fewer nitrate ions in the soil for the next crop. With a smaller amount of nitrate ions in the soil, the new crop will not grow as well as the previous crop. Additional nitrate ions, in the form of nitrogen-containing fertilisers, make sure the new crop has sufficient nitrogen for rapid and healthy growth.

B2e.2a Plants and mineral ions

Plants make simple carbohydrates using photosynthesis, but they need mineral ions absorbed from the environment to convert these into all the other substances they need. This practical investigates the need for nitrate ions and magnesium ions in duckweed plants.

Duckweed plants are simple plants that float on the surface of water. When they grow large enough they split off a leaf which becomes a new plant. Rate of growth can be measured by estimating the area of the solution covered by the plants.

Apparatus

duckweed plants

culture solution containing all mineral ions

culture solution deficient in nitrate ions

culture solution deficient in magnesium ions

3 beakers

plastic film

access to light

marker pen

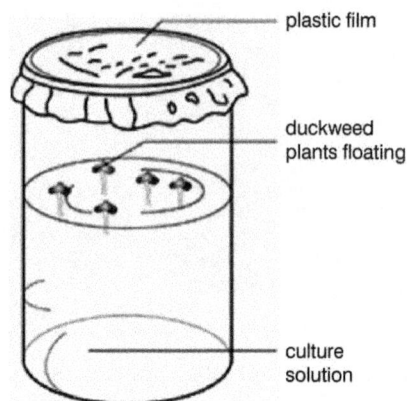

Method adapted from The Nuffield Foundation and Royal Society of Biology's Practical Biology website: www.practicalbiology.org

---

SAFETY INFORMATION

Wash hands thoroughly after handling plants.

Do not remove the covering from the beakers.

Method

1. Label each of the beakers with the pen as follows:
   - complete culture solution
   - minus nitrate
   - minus magnesium

2. Half fill each beaker with the appropriate solution. Beakers should be no more than half full.

3. Select five healthy plants and float them on the top of the solution in one of the beakers, as shown in the diagram. Repeat this for the other two beakers.

4. Cover the top of each beaker with plastic film, and use a sharp point, such as that of a pencil, to make a few air holes in the plastic.

5. Leave the beakers in a bright place for 4–8 weeks.

6. Estimate the coverage of the surface of the solution in each beaker with duckweed.

7. Note any differences between the plants in the three beakers, such as colour or length of root.

8. Record all your results in a suitable table.

Analyse and interpret data

1. Describe any differences between the plants grown in the three solutions.

2. Explain any differences between the plants using your knowledge of plant mineral ions.

Activity B2e.3 Human nutrition

Specification reference: B2e.2.24; B2e.2.25; B2e.2.26; B2e.2.27; B2e.2.28; B2e.2.29; B2e.2.30; B2e.2.31; B2e.2.32; B2e.2.33 **(B)**

Learning objectives

- Understand what is meant by a balanced diet.
- Identify the sources and describe the functions of nutrients in human nutrition.
- Understand how energy requirements vary with activity levels, age and pregnancy.
- Describe the structure and function of organs in the human alimentary canal.
- Understand how food is moved through the gut by peristalsis.
- Understand the role of digestive enzymes.
- Understand that bile is produced by the liver and stored in the gall bladder.
- Understand the role of bile in neutralising stomach acid and emulsifying lipids.
- Understand how the small intestine is adapted for absorption, including the structure of a villus.
- Practical: Investigate the energy content in a food sample. **(B)**

Learning outcomes

- Explain that a balanced diet should include appropriate amounts of carbohydrate, protein, lipid, vitamins, minerals, water and dietary fibre.
- Describe the sources and functions of carbohydrate, protein, lipid (fats and oils), vitamins A, C and D, the mineral ions calcium and iron, water and dietary fibre as components of the diet.
- Describe the structures and functions of organs in the human alimentary canal, including the mouth, oesophagus, stomach, small intestine (duodenum and ileum), large intestine (colon and rectum) and pancreas.
- Describe the role of digestive enzymes, including the digestion of starch to glucose by amylase and maltase; the digestion of proteins to amino acids by proteases; and the digestion of lipids to fatty acids and glycerol by lipases.
- Describe the role of bile indigestion.
- Explain the importance of the structure of a villus.
- Be able to describe an experiment to work out the energy content in a sample of food. **(B)**

Common misconceptions

It is important for students to appreciate that dietary advice is based on an idea of the 'average' person. Such advice is useful as guidance, but everyone is different and has different needs. Be sure to distinguish between the needs of the 'average' population and the needs of the individual.

Resources

Student Book pages 78–90

Worksheet B2e.3a Government health advice

Worksheet B2e.3b Practical: Investigate the energy content in a food sample **(B)**

Worksheet B2e.3c The digestion and absorption of carbohydrates

Resources for class practicals (see Technician's notes, following)

Approach

1. Introduction

Write the words *human alimentary canal* in the middle of the board, and ask students to suggest words to add, and how best to place them, to create a concept map on the topic. They will have covered a wide range of linked topics, including diet and digestion, in their previous work, as well as enzymes in Topic 2c. This will give you an opportunity to assess how much they remember of this earlier work.

2. A healthy diet: nutrients and energy balance

This part of the activity provides opportunities for research work on many diet-related topics. For example, students could find out about:

- the association between obesity and diseases such as diabetes and heart disease – how concerned should we be with our weight?
- the huge market in vitamin pills – do we need them?
- evidence for the role of fibre in preventing bowel cancer, diverticulitis and constipation – why should we eat fibre?
- the increase in cases of rickets in young children in the UK over the past 10 years and its cause – is it preventable?

Be aware of sensitivities in students to ethnic and social differences and to concerns about individual body mass, and treat these with consideration.

Students could carry out their research individually, in pairs or in small groups, according to time and ability. They could use their findings to present a verbal or written report, or create a poster for display.

Alternatively, Worksheet B2e.3a provides a set of questions on government health advice that cover advice on the amount of nutrients and energy we get from our food. The final question might be used as a class activity, to explore what is a healthy diet and how you persuade people to eat healthily.

It may help to discuss some of the terminology and groups they may come across and why they are focused on before starting on this work, such as saturated fats, calories, salt.

3. Practical: Investigate the energy content in a food sample (B)

Worksheet B2e.3b **(B)** gives students an opportunity to measure the energy in different foods. This is a useful practical for discussing the reliability of data, as noted in the Developing investigative skills box on page 79 of the Student Book, and links well to a discussion of energy balance in the diet.

Demonstrate how to skewer a piece of food safely with a needle.

Some students may need help with the calculations in questions 2 and 3 of the analysis and interpretation.

Students should find that foods containing fats release a higher proportion of energy per gram than those consisting mainly of carbohydrates or proteins. However, the weaknesses with this method (loss of large proportion of energy direct to surrounding air and other materials, and incomplete combustion of food before combustion stops), will limit the reliability of their data. You could show them an image of a bomb calorimeter, which is used to avoid most of these problems.

4. The alimentary canal

Learning the structure of the alimentary canal, and which process happens where, is mainly a case of learning the facts. Student Book pages 84–86 provide what students need to know. Consider asking students to use the facts in a way that makes learning more fun, such as asking them to write the 'story' of the digestion of a meal that includes proteins, carbohydrates and fats (such as a pizza), as it passes through the alimentary canal.

5. Enzymes in digestion

Worksheet B2e.3c applies the methods from investigating the movement of molecules through Visking tubing from Topic 2d to the digestion of lactose or sucrose and absorption of glucose. As students should be familiar with these methods, this practical sheet is presented as a planning exercise.

If there is time, and students need opportunity to practise their investigative skills, when you have approved their plans, allow them to carry them out.

6. Consolidation: red, yellow, green notes

Give each student three cards, one red, one yellow and one green. Then ask students questions based on all parts of this activity and ask them to hold up a card depending on how certain they are of the answer: red = not sure, yellow = fairly sure, green = certain.

Suitable questions include:

- Why is fibre important in the diet?
- Why is it important not to eat foods containing more energy than you use during a day?
- What is the problem with a diet that is high in saturated fats?
- In which part of the alimentary canal is food absorbed?
- What are the adaptations of a villus for absorption?

Take examples from those who are holding up a green card. This will help you assess how well students have learned this topic.

Technician's notes

You will need the following resources for the class practicals.

Be sure to check the latest safety notes on these resources before proceeding.

B2e.3b Practical: Investigate the energy content in a food sample (B)

Choose a selection of foods that can be held with tongs or a mounted needle, such as crisps, cheese, bread, biscuits. Ideally, try to select foods that are mainly of one food group, i.e. proteins, carbohydrates, lipids (though the latter is most difficult – cheese is the most suitable here).

NOTE: Tongs are better for brittle materials, whereas a needle is better for rounded materials. Foods containing nuts should not be used because of potential nut allergies. The room should be ventilated thoroughly after this practical, to remove smoke etc.

Class practical, per group:

boiling tubes	heatproof tongs
thermometer	mounted needle
water at room temperature	selection of foods
plastic stirring rod	25 cm^3 measuring cylinder
clamp and stand	weighing balance
Bunsen burner	eye protection

B2e.3c The digestion and absorption of carbohydrates

This is a planning exercise, but students may carry out their planned investigations. If so, the following apparatus will be needed. However, students may suggest other pieces of apparatus (if not available, offer suitable alternatives).

Class practical, per group:

glucose solution
10% milk solution and lactase (β galactosidase) or 10% sucrose solution and invertase
Visking tubing
sawn-off end of plastic syringe (the plunger end)
elastic band, to attach Visking tubing to syringe end
small beaker
tap water
iodine solution in dropper bottle
spotting tile
Benedict's solution*, plus water bath at 100 °C and heatproof tongs (or Clinistix®)
boiling tube
pipettes
eye protection
disposable gloves

* irritant (skin and eyes)

Answers

Page 80

1. More intense sunlight, so likely to make sufficient vitamin D naturally in skin and less dependent on vitamin D in diet.

2. Higher latitude so less intense sunlight means less vitamin D produced in skin, and poor diet would mean increased risk of too little vitamin D in diet.

3. Fish liver oil is formed from liver which is a good source of vitamin D.

4. If diets include more sources of vitamin D, such as fish, eggs, cheese and milk, then the risk of vitamin D deficiency is reduced.

5. Lack of light on the skin means little chance of natural vitamin D production, and a vegetarian diet reduces the amount of vitamin D available in the diet. Vitamin D supplements in the diet can help to avoid the deficiency, but care must be taken not to take too much vitamin D over a long period as high levels in the body can be toxic. So, supplements during the winter may be more advisable than supplements all the time.

Developing investigative skills, page 83

1. a) As the food burns, heat energy is released. The heat energy is transferred to the water molecules in the tube. The temperature in the water rises and is measured by the thermometer.

   b) Care is needed because of the burning food. There should be something below the apparatus that is not flammable (such as a heatproof mat) to catch anything that falls. The burning food should be held on a mounted needle or in tongs, and a heatproof glove used to hold the needle/tongs. The area should be kept clear of anything that is flammable, and there should be good ventilation to remove the fumes of burning.

2. a) Food 57.3 J/g; leaf 8.8 J/g

   b) So that you can compare the amount of energy in each food more easily.

3. Food/crisp.

4. Seeds/nuts/food will provide the animal with more chemical energy than eating leaves.

5. Not all of the heat energy released in burning is transferred to the water molecules, a lot escapes to the surrounding air. An enclosed set of apparatus (calorimeter) would increase the efficiency of transfer to the water molecules.

Page 84

1. Carbohydrates, proteins and lipids.

2. a) USDA: Vegetables and grains. UK: Fruit and vegetables, and bread, rice, potatoes, pasta.

   b) Vitamins, minerals, fibre and carbohydrates.

   c) Foods and drinks high in fat and/or sugar.

   d) To avoid taking in too much energy, which can lead to obesity.

3. Any answers along the lines of: different people need different amounts of energy every day, for example active people need more than people who are seated for much of the day; men have a larger average body mass than women so will need more energy to support that extra tissue; some groups of people need more of a particular group of nutrients than others, for example, pregnant women need additional iron.

4. Food that contains more energy than the body uses is converted into body fat. High levels of body fat cause obesity, which is associated with many health problems.

Page 87

1. Sketch should show the following labels correctly attached to organs shown on the diagram:

- mouth, where food is broken down by physical digestion (chewing) and amylase enzyme starts digestion of starch in food

- oesophagus moves food from mouth to stomach by peristalsis

- stomach, where churning mixes food with protease enzymes and acid to start digestion of protein molecules

- duodenum, where alkaline bile neutralises the acid and enzymes from pancreas help complete digestion of proteins, lipids and carbohydrates

- ileum, where digested food molecules are absorbed into the body

- colon, where water is absorbed from undigested food

- rectum, where faeces is held until it is egested through the anus

- liver, where bile is made

- gall bladder, where bile is stored until needed

- pancreas, where proteases, lipases and amylase are made, which pass to the small intestine

2. Egestion is the removal of undigested food from the alimentary canal – food that has never crossed the intestine wall into the body. Excretion is the removal of waste substances that have been produced inside the body.

3. Waves of contraction of the circular and longitudinal muscles push the food bolus further along the alimentary canal.

Page 89

1. Chemical digestion uses chemicals (enzymes) to help break down large food molecules into smaller ones. Physical digestion is the breaking of large pieces of food into smaller ones, for example by chewing.

2. The digestive enzymes break down food molecules that are too large to cross the wall of the small intestine into smaller ones that can diffuse across cell membranes and so enter the body. If we did not have enzymes, we would not be able to absorb many nutrients from our food.

3. a) Amylase

  b) Maltose

4. a) The acid increases the acidity in the stomach, providing the right conditions for enzymes that digest food in the stomach.

  b) Bile neutralises the acidity of food from the stomach, providing the right conditions for enzymes that digest food in the small intestine. It also emulsifies lipids, providing a larger surface area for lipase enzymes to work on.

Page 90

1. Long length, villi that cover the intestine wall increase the surface area, microvilli on surface of villi cells increase surface area for absorption even further, extensive blood supply removes absorbed food molecules quickly so maintaining a high concentration gradient for diffusion, lacteals in the villi carry absorbed lipid molecules away to the rest of the body.

2. Some foods may be needed quickly by the body; if digested food is not absorbed quickly as food passes along the intestine it may be lost in faeces.

Worksheet B2e.3a

1. Fruit, vegetables, fibre.

2. Fruit and vegetables are key sources of vitamins and minerals in the diet. Fibre is essential for healthy working of peristalsis in the alimentary canal, and prevention of constipation and related problems.

3. Any suitable answers, such as: does not identify which nutrients so cannot tell whether you are ending up with lots of some and not enough of others; does not identify portion size; what if you do not like fruit and/or vegetables, what can you eat instead?

4. It includes all the main food groups, not just fruit and vegetables.

5. About one-third.

6. Any suitable answer, such as: simple visual image easily translated into a meal on a plate, shows balance of food groups in diet, easy to substitute one food in a group for another.

7. Any suitable answers, such as: what if you are not eating a whole meal, does not apply well to snacks; difficult to apply to food eaten over whole day.

8. Energy content; main food groups, i.e. fats, proteins and carbohydrates; saturated fats; sugars; fibre; sodium and salt equivalent.

9. Energy content is the amount of energy in the food, so helps you see what energy you need to use to maintain an energy balance. Fats/lipids are needed but high saturated fat intake is associated with heart disease. Carbohydrates are needed for energy, but having too much as sugar is associated with a risk of diabetes and obesity. Fibre is important for healthy working of alimentary canal. Sodium/salt equivalent is given because high levels in a diet may be a problem for people with heart disease.

10. It shows what proportion of the average daily adult intake of each of the risk food groups are in the food.

11. Any suitable answers, such as: lists of numbers are not easy to make sense of; takes time to add up all the information from all the labels on the foods, who will bother?

12. These are the key elements of food that can cause concern as noted in answer to question 9 (cals = energy) – a simplified way of displaying data from table.

13. It shows you how much you will get of each of the food groups that are of concern, so you can balance it with other foods with lower amounts of those during the rest of the day.

14. Any suitable answers, such as: do the people who need to look at the labelling; does everyone understand percentages; the guideline daily amount is an average, so may not be appropriate advice for everyone.

15. Any suitable answers, such as: lots of different advice so confusing; few people take notice of food advice when eating.

16. Any suitable answers that take into account trying to get a complex message across simply to different groups of people.

B2e.3a Government health advice

In the UK, one of the government health guidelines is '5-a-day'. This is the recommendation for the number of portions of fruit and vegetables that each person should eat. (Portion size obviously differs for different ages.)

1. Which food is this advice aimed at? (Try to include at least three different groups in your answer.)

2. Explain why each of your answers to question 1 are important in the body.

3. What limitations are there with this advice? Try to think of as many limitations as you can.

Look at the 'healthy plate' diagram in the Student Book pages 81 and 82. This is another form of government advice on healthy eating.

4. How does this differ from the '5-a-day' advice?

5. What proportion of the healthy plate does the '5-a-day' match?

6. Why is the 'healthy plate' image useful in showing what we should eat?

7. What limitations can you think of with this image in guiding us on what to eat? Try to think of as many limitations as you can.

Food packaging also has advice on healthy eating.

All packaged foods should have a nutrition advice label, like the one below.

Nutrition				
Typical values (as consumed)	**per 100 g**	**per pack**	**%GDA**	**your GDA***
Energy	541 kJ/128 kcal	2011/476 kcal	24%	2000 kcal
Protein	4.9 g	18.2 g		
Carbohydrates	20.8 g	77.4 g		
of which sugars	1.5 g	5.6 g	6.2%	90 g
Fat	2.8 g	10.4 g	15%	70 g
of which saturates	2.3 g	8.6 g	43%	20 g
Fibre	2.1 g	7.8 g		
Sodium	0.1 g	0.5 g		
Salt equivalent	0.3 g	1.3 g	22%	6 g
*Recommended guideline daily amount for adults (GDA)				

8. What information does this labelling show?

9. Explain as fully as you can why it shows this information.

10. What is useful about this labelling?

11. What limitations are there with this labelling? Try to think of as many limitations as you can.

Another kind of food labelling uses a 'traffic lights' system, with red for high content, orange for medium content and green for low content. The colours are worked out from the proportion of the recommended daily intake for an average adult, as shown by the percentages on the label.

SERVES 2 – HALF PIZZA PROVIDES				
CALS	SUGAR	FAT	SATFAT	SALT
495	9.0 g	18.3 g	9.2 g	2.00 g
25%	10%	26%	46%	33%
MEDIUM	LOW	MEDIUM	HIGH	MEDIUM
(orange)	(green)	(orange)	(red)	(orange)
OF YOUR GUIDELINE DAILY AMOUNT				

12. Why are these particular groups included in the traffic lights system?

13. How is this system helpful?

14. What limitations are there with this labelling? Try to think of as many limitations as you can.

Even with all this advice, there is still concern that many people in developed countries are eating too much of the wrong foods, and so risk diet-related illness later in life.

15. Use your answers to suggest why healthy eating may be difficult.

16. How would you prepare advice on healthy eating for everyone? Explain your answer.

B2e.3b Practical: Investigate the energy content in a food sample (B)

Respiration and combustion both break down food molecules to carbon dioxide and water using oxygen, and then they release energy. So, we can use the combustion of a food to estimate the amount of energy released from a food when it is broken down by respiration.

Apparatus

boiling tubes

thermometer

water at room temperature

plastic stirring rod

clamp and stand

Bunsen burner

heatproof mat

heatproof tongs / mounted needle

selection of foods

measuring cylinder

weighing balance

eye protection

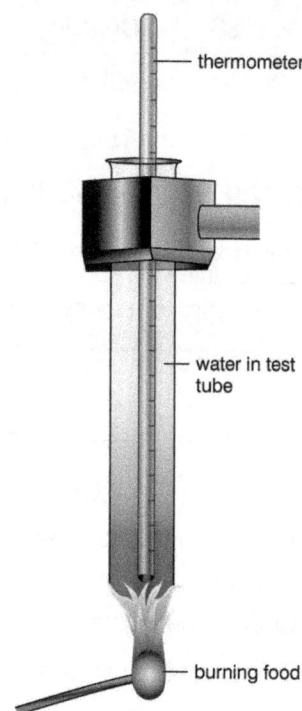

thermometer

water in test tube

burning food

SAFETY INFORMATION

Take care with the Bunsen burner flame.

Always handle foods with heatproof tongs or mounted needle.

Always use a plastic stirring rod to stir the water in the boiling tube.

Foods in a science laboratory are not suitable for eating.

Wear eye protection.

Method

1. Set up the boiling tube in the clamp as shown in the diagram.

2. Carefully measure 10 cm^3 water into the boiling tube and add the thermometer.

3. Leave the apparatus for two minutes and then measure the temperature of the water.

4. Select a small piece of food and use the weighing balance to measure its mass. Record the type of food and its mass.

5. Place the piece of food on the mounted needle or hold with the heatproof tongs. Set light to the food with a Bunsen burner. Immediately place the burning food just under the tube so that the flame covers the bottom of the tube.

6. Hold the food under the tube until it has stopped burning. When it stops burning, attempt to relight it with the Bunsen burner, and continue to use it to heat the water in the tube. When it will no longer relight, immediately measure the temperature of the water, and record this value.

7. Steps 1–6 can be repeated with other foods, or more of the same food. Each time you must start with a fresh tube of water.

Analyse and interpret data

1. Use your results to calculate the temperature rise of the water for each food. Record your results of mass, food and temperature rise in a suitable table.

2. Convert each temperature rise into energy released as follows:

- 4.18 J heat energy raises the temperature of 1 g water by 1 °C
- 1 g water has a volume of 1 cm^3
- so the heat energy in the food (J) = (temperature rise × 10)/4.18

3. Use the heat energy released to calculate the energy per gram of food.

4. Describe your results of heat energy released from each type of food. Can you see any patterns in your results? If so describe them.

5. Explain what your results mean for a healthy diet.

Evaluate data and methods

1. If you took several measurements of the same food, explain any variations.

2. Describe any problems with using this method to measure total energy released.

3. Suggest how the method could be improved to reduce the effect of these problems.

B2e.3c The digestion and absorption of carbohydrates

In Topic 2c (Biological molecules), you were introduced to the use of amylase to digest starch, and in Topic 2d you used an artificial membrane called Visking tubing to model a cell membrane.

1. Plan an investigation, using Visking tubing as a model for the human alimentary canal, to investigate the time taken to digest either lactose or sucrose and the products of digestion being absorbed by the blood.

You will need to consider:

- what apparatus you will need
- the risks associated with the use of any of your suggested apparatus and how you will minimise them
- how you will set up the apparatus
- what you will measure
- how often you will take measurements
- which variables you will need to control and how you will control them
- how you will record your results.

2. Write a plan for your investigation. Worksheets B2c.1a and B2d.1a may help you.

3. When you have completed your plan, give it to your teacher for checking. Your teacher will tell you if you should now carry out your plan. If you have been given permission to proceed, below is an example of the apparatus you can use.

Apparatus

glucose solution	lactose or sucrose solution
Visking tubing	sawn-off end of plastic syringe
elastic band	small beaker
tap water	iodine solution in dropper bottle
spotting tile	boiling tube
pipettes	eye protection
disposable gloves	lactase or invertase

Benedict's solution, plus hot water at 100 °C, insulated beaker and heatproof tongs (or Clinistix®)

SAFETY INFORMATION

Wear eye protection and disposable gloves when using Benedict's solution

as it is an irritant to skin and eyes.

Do not touch the coloured part of a Clinistix®.

Activity B2e.4 Consolidation and summary

Learning objectives

- To review the learning points of the topic.
- To test understanding through answering questions.

Learning outcomes

- Be familiar with the knowledge and understanding summarised in the End of topic checklist.
- Be able to apply this knowledge and understanding by answering End of topic questions.

Resources

Student Book pages 91–96

Approach

Ask students to answer the End of topic questions in the Student Book.

Answers

End of topic questions mark scheme

Question	Correct answer	Marks
1 a)	Photosynthesis is the formation of simple sugars (such as glucose)	1
	from the combination of water and carbon dioxide in the presence of light and chlorophyll.	1
1 b)	Photosynthesis produces simple carbohydrates that the plant then converts to other substances that it needs,	1
	including other carbohydrates (e.g. cellulose for cell walls), proteins, oils.	1
1 c)	Photosynthesis provides the carbohydrates that are converted to all the other substances a plant needs to form new plant tissue. Herbivores get their nutrition from eating plants and carnivores get their nutrition from eating herbivores (or other carnivores that have eaten herbivores). So, all animals ultimately depend on plants for their nutrition.	1
	Photosynthesis provides oxygen which animals need for respiration.	1
2 a)	Ingestion in the mouth, where food enters the alimentary canal	2
2 b)	Digestion in the mouth – physical by teeth, chemical by amylase; stomach – protease enzymes; small intestine – amylase, protease and lipase enzymes produced by the pancreas, also bile from liver via gall bladder to emulsify fats.	2
2 c)	Absorption in small intestine, where digested food molecules can cross the cell membranes of the villi cells and into the blood.	2
2 d)	Egestion through the anus, at the end of the alimentary canal back into the environment.	2

Question	Correct answer	Marks
3	A high concentration gradient and a large surface area to volume ratio maximise the rate of diffusion into and out of cells.	1
	A high concentration gradient for substances needed for photosynthesis is maintained by a thin leaf (so carbon dioxide does not have to travel far from air to chloroplast), and xylem (transporting water from root to leaf).	1
	A high concentration gradient for substances made during photosynthesis is maintained by a thin leaf (for oxygen diffusing out of cells into the air) and phloem (transporting sugars to rest of plant).	1
	The large surface to volume ratio is produced by the leaf being broad and thin, maximising surface area in relation to volume, and by the large internal surface area created by the spongy mesophyll.	1
4 a)	Vitamin A sources: liver, red/orange vegetables, butter, fish oil; needed for healthy vision and skin.	2
	Vitamin C sources: citrus fruit and green vegetables, potatoes; needed for healthy skin and gums and blood vessel linings.	2
	Vitamin D sources: fish, eggs, liver, cheese and milk; needed for strong bones and teeth.	2
4 b)	Calcium sources: milk, eggs; needed for strong bones and teeth, also blood clotting.	2
	Iron sources: red meats, liver and kidneys, leafy green vegetables such as spinach; needed for haemoglobin in red blood cells	2
4 c)	Water source: most foods, but especially fruit; needed in all cells because many reactions take place in watery cytoplasm.	2
4 d)	Fibre source: leafy vegetables such as cabbage, brown rice, wholegrain wheat; needed to keep undigested food in the alimentary canal bulky and soft, helping peristalsis to work efficiently, plus a low-fibre diet may increase the risk of bowel cancer.	2
5 a)	Starch is formed from glucose, which is the product of photosynthesis. If there is no photosynthesis, then no glucose will be produced and so no starch can be produced.	1
5 b)	Place the plant in a dark place	1
	for a couple of days so that the starch in the plant/leaf is all used.	1
	This means any starch in the leaf at the end of the investigation has been produced by photosynthesis during the investigation.	1
6	Physical digestion of food in the mouth breaks food pieces into smaller pieces, which makes them easier to swallow and increases their surface area to volume ratio, making it easier for enzymes to combine with more food molecules more quickly and so speed up the rate of digestion.	1

Question	Correct answer	Marks
7 a)	The surface of the small intestine is covered in villi and the surface of the villi cells are covered in microvilli. These greatly increase the surface area of the small intestine.	1
	As surface area is related to the rate of absorption by passive processes such as osmosis and diffusion, a large surface area means a greater rate of absorption of substances into the body from the small intestine.	1
7 b)	The single layer of cells means there is only a small distance over which substances need to travel to be absorbed into the villi and into the blood vessels that will carry them away to the rest of the body.	1
	As diffusion distance is related to the rate of absorption by passive processes such as osmosis and diffusion, a small distance means a greater rate of absorption of substances into the body from the small intestine.	1
7 c)	The extensive blood supply means that the absorbed substances are rapidly carried away from the villi to other parts of the body, maintaining a steep concentration gradient across the small intestine wall.	1
	A steep concentration gradient will maximise the rate of diffusion and osmosis, and means a greater rate of absorption of substances into the body from the small intestine.	1
8 a)	i) Carbohydrates: cereal, banana, bread, honey/jam, beans, sugars in juices and squash, pasta, fruit, potatoes/rice, bagel, chocolate	1
	ii) Proteins: milk, bacon, eggs, fish/meat, chicken, yoghurt	1
	iii) Lipids: milk, olive/sunflower spread, eggs, (possibly sauce), yoghurt	1
	iv) Vitamins and minerals: dairy for vitamin D and calcium, fish oil for vitamins A and D (if oily fish eaten), vegetables and fruit for vitamin C; green vegetables for iron	1
	v) Fibre: wholegrain cereals, wholegrain bread and vegetables	1
8 b)	Carbohydrates	1
8 c)	They break down easily to glucose for use in respiration to produce energy during training.	1
8 d)	Proteins may be greater	1
	to help with building more muscle.	1
8 e)	It contains too much energy.	1
	Most people do not use this amount of energy during one day. The excess energy in the diet would be laid down as fat in the body, leading to a risk of obesity and related health problems.	1
9 a)	The detail of the shape of the line on the graph is unimportant, as long as it shows an increase in rate from the baseline after sunrise, to a maximum in the afternoon, and a decrease to the baseline at sunset.	2

Question	Correct answer	Marks
9 b)	The increase after sunrise to the maximum should be labelled to indicate that light is a limiting factor (and possibly temperature which will also increase as the sun warms the air and land). At the maximum, light and temperature should be in excess, so carbon dioxide is most likely to limit the rate of photosynthesis. As the rate falls again, the controlling (limiting) factor is most likely to be light.	2
10 a)	As night approaches, the light intensity falls below the level at which it limits the rate of photosynthesis and does not rise again until dawn. Keeping the lights on all night means that photosynthesis continues all night, so more food is made in the leaves and so the plants can grow faster and produce more tomatoes.	1
10 b)	Temperature controls the rate of photosynthesis. So when it gets cold at night, the rate of photosynthesis will drop – closing the windows will help to keep the plants warmer. During the day, if the windows are not open, the temperature may get too high and so limit the rate of photosynthesis by affecting the activity of enzymes involved in the process.	1
10 c)	Adding nutrients to the water makes sure the plants have sufficient nitrate and magnesium to absorb for making chlorophyll and proteins, so maximising the rate of growth of the plants.	1
11 a)	UK is shown as a pie chart, whereas the US is shown as a diagram. Different ways of grouping foods and food types.	1 1
11 b)	Different authorities have different ways of displaying things (or equiv.).	1
11 c)	Student's own answer, with justifications. For example: UK because it is easier to see the proportions of different types of food and examples of the different types of food are given.	2
	Total:	66

Introduction

This topic covers aerobic respiration and anaerobic respiration, and teaches students about the similarities and differences between them.

Links to other topics

Sections	Essential background knowledge	Useful links
1 The nature and variety of living organisms	1a Characteristics of living organisms	
2 Structure and functions in living organisms	2c Biological molecules 2d Movement of substances into and out of cells 2e Nutrition	2g Gas exchange 2h Transport
3 Reproduction and inheritance		3a Reproduction
4 Ecology and the environment		4b Feeding relationships 4c Cycles within ecosystems
5 Use of biological resources		5a Food production

Topic overview

B2f.1	**Respiration**
	This activity gives students opportunities to explore aerobic respiration through practical investigation, or demonstration, and then to investigate why anaerobic respiration is useful for organisms.
B2f.2	**Consolidation and summary**
	This activity provides an opportunity for a quick recap on the ideas encountered in the topic as well as time for the students to answer the End of topic questions in the Student Book.

Activity B2f.1 Respiration

Specification reference: B2f.2.34; B2f.2.35; B2f.2.36; B2f.2.37; B2f.2.38; B2f.2.39

Learning objectives

- Understand how the process of respiration produces ATP in living organisms.
- Know that ATP provides energy for cells.
- Describe the differences between aerobic and anaerobic respiration.
- Know the word equation and the balanced chemical symbol equation for aerobic respiration in living organisms.
- Know the word equation for anaerobic respiration in plants and in animals.
- Practical: Investigate the evolution of carbon dioxide and heat from respiring seeds or other suitable living organisms.

Learning outcomes

- Know that respiration produces ATP in living organisms, which provides energy for cells.
- Understand aerobic respiration uses oxygen from the air to release energy from glucose.
- Write the word and balanced symbol equations for aerobic respiration:

  glucose + oxygen → carbon dioxide + water (+ ATP)

  $C_6H_{12}O_6 + 6O_2 \rightarrow 6CO_2 + 6H_2O$ (+ ATP)
- Describe how anaerobic respiration releases energy from glucose without oxygen.
- In animals, the equation for the reaction is:

  glucose → lactic acid (+ ATP)
- In some plants and fungi, the equation for the reaction is:

  glucose → ethanol + carbon dioxide (+ ATP)

Common misconceptions

In common language, the term *respiration* is used to mean breathing or ventilation. It is important to establish its correct meaning: the release of energy from food molecules within cells.

Anaerobic respiration in animals is often discussed as a 'bad thing' because it produces lactic acid. This is based on the idea that acid is harmful. However, the evidence for this is weak. Many changes happen in muscles during vigorous exercise, including the production of lactate ions (rather than acid, though the understanding of ion production is A level material, not International GCSE). There is no reason to believe that these are what cause the pain in muscles after extreme exercise.

In fact, evidence now shows that, without anaerobic respiration and the production of lactate ions, muscle fatigue (as in the failure of muscles to produce their full effort) would happen even more rapidly than normal. This indicates that anaerobic respiration has an essential part to play in survival (such as when trying to escape from a predator).

Resources

Student Book pages 97–102

Worksheet B2f.1a Practical: Investigate the evolution of carbon dioxide and heat from respiring seeds

Resources for class practicals (see Technician's notes, following)

Approach

1. Introduction

Following on from the last activity on human nutrition, ask students to explain why we need to eat. They should link food to the need for energy for life processes (if not, remind them of Topic 1a). Then ask how energy is released from food. From previous work, they should be able to answer *respiration*.

2. Aerobic respiration

Use the Student Book page 99 to introduce the word and symbol equations for aerobic respiration. Make sure students understand *aerobic* and the need to make this distinction obvious. Ask them to use their knowledge of body systems to explain how each of the reactants is delivered to each cell, and how waste products are removed. Also, ask why it is essential for every cell to carry out aerobic respiration.

3. Investigating aerobic respiration

Worksheet B2f.1a links to the Developing investigative skills box on page 99 of the Student Book, and investigates the release of heat energy by germinating seeds. The practical needs to run for about two days for significant results. If you have limited apparatus, the practical could be presented as a demonstration, with students answering the questions on the practical sheet.

Please note: if you would like to demonstrate aerobic respiration using small animals, the above apparatus is **not suitable**. In that case, please use the following apparatus (shown below). A low suction pump should be used to draw air through the apparatus. Note this experiment should not run for more than 24 hours as the animals will have no food. They should be returned gently to the environment from which they were collected as soon as possible after the end of the experiment.

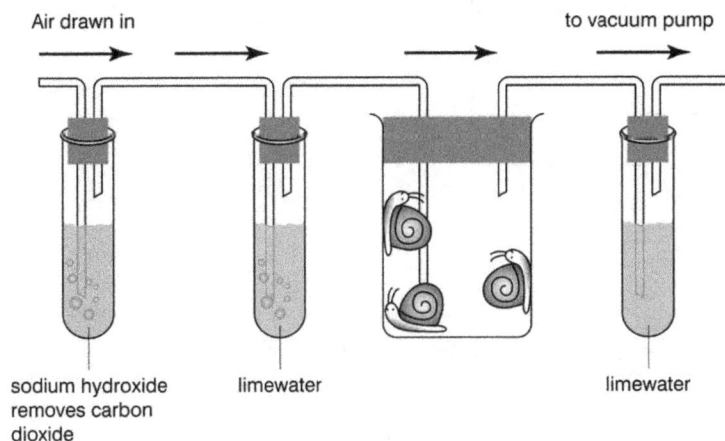

sodium hydroxide removes carbon dioxide   limewater   limewater

Air drawn in   to vacuum pump

4. Anaerobic respiration

Ask students to carry out research into the benefits of anaerobic respiration. This could include the importance of prolonging muscle contraction in conditions of extreme exercise, the need for anaerobic respiration in conditions where oxygen is not available (such as in diving animals that are not adapted to extracting oxygen from water such as seals, inside germinating seeds and in some microorganisms). In each case, students should make clear the survival advantages of anaerobic respiration.

Technician's notes

You will need the following resources for the class practicals.

Be sure to check the latest safety notes on these resources before proceeding.

B2f.1a Practical: Investigate the evolution of carbon dioxide and heat from respiring seeds

Suitable seeds include wheat, barley or dried peas. Soak the seeds in water for 24 hours, then surface-sterilise them in Milton® solution (sodium dichloroisocyanurate solution) before use in the practical. Warn students to use a sterilised spoon to move the seeds into the flask, to reduce risk of infection with microorganisms.

The Thermos flask should also be sterilised with Milton® solution before the practical. Follow the manufacturer's instructions.

Class practical, per group or demonstration:

Thermos flask
bung with 2 holes
thermometer
glass delivery tube (and connectors if suitable tube not available)
boiling tube
hydrogen-carbonate indicator solution or limewater
germinating seeds
sterilised spoon
goggles

Answers

Developing investigative skills, page 99

1. Changes in temperature using the thermometer, release of carbon dioxide which will make the limewater milky.

2. a) The limewater turned milky indicating the release of carbon dioxide. The temperature increased from 15 to 19 °C.

   b) These changes would be expected during cellular respiration because some of the energy released would be heat energy, and both aerobic and anaerobic respiration in plants produce carbon dioxide.

3. You would need to repeat the experiment for the same length of time, with the same apparatus but without the seeds, so that the only difference in the two sets of apparatus was the seeds. Or you could repeat it with seeds that have been boiled to kill them and so stop respiration.

Page 100

1. Inside cells

2. a), b) and c) Glucose (from digested food from alimentary canal via the blood) + oxygen (from air via lungs) → carbon dioxide (excreted through lungs) + water (used in cells or excreted through kidneys) (+ ATP (provides energy for cell processes))

   d) Most water used in cells because the camel is much better than humans at using the water from respiration.

3. Aerobic respiration uses oxygen from the air.

Page 102

1. Aerobic respiration uses oxygen / anaerobic does not. Aerobic respiration releases more ATP/energy than anaerobic. Aerobic produces carbon dioxide and water, but anaerobic produces either lactic acid (animals) or ethanol and carbon dioxide (plants/fungi).

2. During vigorous exercise, they may not be able to get enough oxygen from the blood for all the energy they need for contracting. So, the additional energy comes from anaerobic respiration.

3. Similarities: use glucose as substrate, produce energy, do not need oxygen.
Differences: animals produce lactic acid; plants produce ethanol and carbon dioxide.

4. Inside germinating seeds where the cells may be too deep to get oxygen by diffusion, or where the seed is surrounded by water, which prevents oxygen from the air reaching the seed.

B2f.1a Practical: Investigate the evolution of carbon dioxide and heat from respiring seeds

During respiration, food molecules (such as glucose) are broken down to release energy. Some of this energy is used in reactions within the cell, while some of it is transferred to the surroundings as heat energy. We can measure the heat energy released as evidence of respiration.

Apparatus

Thermos flask

bung with 2 holes

thermometer

glass delivery tube (and connectors if suitable tube not available)

boiling tube

hydrogen-carbonate indicator solution or limewater

germinating seeds

sterilised spoon

goggles

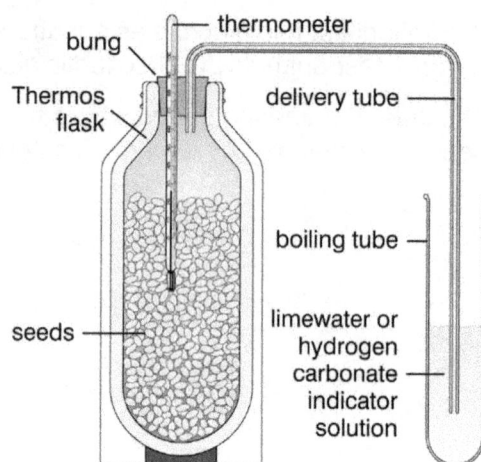

SAFETY INFORMATION
Limewater is a potential irritant.
Wear goggles while handling and wash hands after use.

Method

1. Put on eye protection.

2. Set up the apparatus as shown in the diagram (be sure to use the sterilised spoon to move the seeds into the flask).

3. Allow five minutes for the apparatus to equilibrate, and then note the temperature. Also note the colour of the limewater/indicator.

4. Leave the apparatus for 48 hours, then measure the temperature again and the colour of the limewater/indicator.

Analyse and interpret data

1. Did the temperature change? If so, by how much did it change?

2. Did the limewater/indicator change? If so, how?

3. What do the changes suggest was happening inside the flask? Explain your answer.

Evaluate data and methods

1. Explain why the experiment was carried out using a Thermos flask.

2. Before the seeds were added to the flask they were disinfected to kill microorganisms. Explain why.

3. Could you use this method to reliably compare the rate of respiration in germinating seeds of different species? Explain your answer.

Activity B2f.2 Consolidation and summary

Learning objectives

- To review the learning points of the topic.
- To test understanding through answering questions.

Learning outcomes

- Be familiar with the knowledge and understanding summarised in the End of topic checklist.
- Be able to apply this knowledge and understanding by answering the End of topic questions.

Resources

Student Book pages 103–104

Approach

1. Consolidation: true or false

Ask students to make up three statements that relate to their work on respiration, which are either true or false. They should then write the words *true* and *false* on separate scraps of paper. Select a student to read out one of their statements, and ask the rest of the class to hold up the correct response. Repeat this until you have covered a reasonable range of statements.

2. End of topic questions

Ask students to answer the End of topic questions in the Student Book.

Answers

End of topic questions mark scheme

Question	Correct answer	Marks
1	Reactants: oxygen – enters body through breathing/respiratory system (lungs), travels to cells via circulatory system (blood); glucose – enters body via digestive system (small intestine), travels to cells via circulatory system (blood). Products: carbon dioxide enters circulatory system (blood), excreted through breathing/respiratory system (lungs); water often used in cells or enters circulatory system (blood).	5
2	Any suitable table that shows these facts clearly: <table><tr><td></td><td>**Aerobic respiration**</td><td>**Anaerobic respiration**</td></tr><tr><td>Similarities</td><td colspan="2">Use glucose as reactant Release ATP / energy for cell processes</td></tr><tr><td>Differences</td><td>Always uses oxygen Produces carbon dioxide and water Releases a lot of ATP / energy from each glucose molecule</td><td>Oxygen is not needed Produces either lactic acid (animals) or ethanol and carbon dioxide (plants) Releases a little ATP / energy from each glucose molecule</td></tr></table>	8
3 a)	Tube linked to germinating peas: limewater would have turned milky colour.	1
	Tube linked to the boiled peas: limewater would not have changed.	1
3 b)	The germinating seeds are respiring, breaking down food molecules in aerobic respiration and releasing carbon dioxide as a waste product.	1
	The carbon dioxide turns the limewater milky.	1
	The boiled peas would be dead, so they would not be respiring and no carbon dioxide would be produced.	1
	So the limewater in this apparatus would not change colour.	1
4	At the start the muscles will more probably use the oxygen available for aerobic respiration.	1
	Oxygen levels will drop over time, because the whale cannot breathe air again until it returns to the surface.	1
	During this time, the muscle cells will respire anaerobically, to provide the energy needed for swimming.	1
5 a)	One biscuit lasts one hour, so eight biscuits last eight hours.	1
5 b)	Eight biscuits = c. 1 mole of glucose which releases only c. 150 kJ of energy when respired anaerobically.	1
	If 8 hours aerobically uses c. 2900 kJ of energy, then 150 kJ of energy would last 150/2900 × 8 = 0.4 hours, which is about 25 minutes.	1
5 c)	The time for anaerobic respiration is much less	1
	because the glucose is only partly broken down during anaerobic respiration,	1
	so releasing much less energy,	1
	and more fully broken down during aerobic respiration and so releasing much more energy.	1
	Total:	29

Introduction

This topic applies students' knowledge about diffusion to explain how gases are exchanged between an organism and the environment. The first part of the section looks at the leaf, and gas exchange in plants. The second part looks at gas exchange in humans, including the effect of exercise and the damage caused by smoking.

Links to other topics

Sections	Essential background knowledge	Useful links
1 The nature and variety of living organisms	1a Characteristics of living organisms	
2 Structure and functions in living organisms	2a Level of organisation 2b Cell structure 2d Movement of substances into and out of cells 2e Nutrition 2f Respiration	2h Transport 2i Excretion
4 Ecology and the environment		4b Feeding relationships 4c Cycles within ecosystems 4d Human influences on the environment
5 Use of biological resources		5a Food production

Topic overview

B2g.1	Gas exchange in flowering plants (B)
	This activity gives students an understanding of how changes in light intensity affect the net gas exchange of a plant with the surrounding air, through the use of practical investigation. This is followed by an opportunity for some microscope work to look at the adaptations of leaves for gas exchange.
B2g.2	Gas exchange in humans
	This activity gives students an understanding of how gas exchange takes place in humans. Students look at the effect of exercise on breathing and the effects of smoking.
B2g.3	Consolidation and summary
	This activity provides an opportunity for a quick recap on the ideas encountered in the topic as well as time for the students to answer the End of topic questions in the Student Book.

Activity B2g.1 Gas exchange in flowering plants (B)

Specification reference: B2g.2.40**B**; B2g.2.41**B**; B2g.2.42**B**; B2g.2.43**B**; B2g.2.44**B**; B2g.2.45**B**

Learning objectives

- Understand the role of diffusion in gas exchange. **(B)**
- Understand gas exchange (of carbon dioxide and oxygen) in relation to respiration and photosynthesis. **(B)**
- Understand how the structure of the leaf is adapted for gas exchange. **(B)**
- Describe the role of stomata in gas exchange. **(B)**
- Understand that respiration continues during the day and night, but that the net exchange of carbon dioxide and oxygen depends on the intensity of light. **(B)**
- Practical: Investigate the effect of light on net gas exchange from a leaf, using hydrogen-carbonate indicator. **(B)**

Learning outcomes

- Understand plants exchange gases with the environment to support cellular respiration. **(B)**
- Understand plants also exchange gases with the environment to support photosynthesis. **(B)**
- Explain how the net exchange of oxygen and carbon dioxide between a plant and the environment depends on light intensity. **(B)**
- Describe how the leaf structure is adapted for efficient gas exchange by diffusion. **(B)**
- Describe how stomata allow gases to enter and leave the leaf. **(B)**

Common misconceptions

Many students forget that plants carry out respiration during the day when they are also photosynthesising, because there is a net output of oxygen and net intake of carbon dioxide. Remind them that photosynthesis overshadows the use and release of gases by respiration during daylight, but these become obvious at night when photosynthesis stops.

Resources

Student Book pages 105–109

Worksheet B2g.1a Practical: Investigate the effect of light on net gas exchange from a leaf, using hydrogen-carbonate indicator **(B)**

Worksheet B2g.1b Leaf peels

Resources for class practicals (see Technician's notes, following)

Approach

1. Introduction **(B)**

Explain to students that when hospitals used to allow visitors to bring flowers and plant gifts to patients, the plants and flowers were removed from the ward at night because they affected the quality of the air.

Give students one or two minutes to work in pairs or small groups to think of an explanation for this. They should be able to suggest that at night the plants are adding carbon dioxide to the air and removing oxygen, as a result of respiration, which could leave less oxygen for the patients. (Note: the reason that most hospitals no longer allow plant and flower gifts is not because of this, but mostly because of the number of people who are allergic to pollen.)

2. Net gas exchange (B)

Worksheet B2g.1a gives the method for the investigation in the Developing investigative skills box on page 108 of the Student Book. It allows students to study the effect of light and dark on net gas exchange. If you prefer, you could ask students to use their suggestion for adapting the method to find the compensation point for pondweed from their answers to the Developing investigative skills box. In this case, check students' plans carefully before allowing them to carry them out.

3. The structure of leaves (B)

If not already done in Topic 2e when studying photosynthesis, give students the opportunity to study prepared slides of a transverse section through a leaf, to identify the different cells in the leaf. This could also be done by displaying an image of such a slide using a digital microscope or a suitable image from the internet. Point out to students the stomata, and focus on their role in controlling gas exchange between the leaf and the air surrounding the leaf.

Worksheet B2g.1b gives students an opportunity to create and study leaf peels. It uses clear nail varnish to take an impression of the lower epidermis, and clear sticky tape to hold the peel on a slide.

If clear nail varnish is not available, take an 'oblique leaf peel'. Hold the leaf between the finger and thumb of both hands, with the lower epidermis uppermost. Gently tear the leaf by pulling downwards at an angle with one hand. This should tear the leaf leaving some lower epidermis clear of other tissue.

Cut a small section of the relatively clear epidermis using a sharp scalpel or razor blade, mount it on a slide in a drop of water. Cover with a cover slip and blot away any excess moisture before viewing under the microscope.

Show students how to focus a microscope safely (moving the objective away from the slide). When using microscopes with mirrors, warn students that they must not focus direct sunlight through the microscope.

You will need to explain to students how to use a graticule to estimate the size of objects within the field of view, or they could carry out an estimate based on the field of view at a particular magnification.

If there is limited time they could limit their investigation to comparing the upper and lower epidermal surfaces. This should show that there are more stomata in the lower epidermis than the upper epidermis, though this is not the case for all plant species. This is an adaptation to maximise the light absorbed for photosynthesis and reduce excessive water loss by transpiration (Topic 2h).

If time allows, this investigation could be extended to see how much variation there is between leaves of the same plant (such as between leaves at the top of a bushy plant and leaves that are more shaded), or between leaves of different species.

4. Consolidation: key points (B)

Give students two minutes to jot down the four most important points they think they have learned about gas exchange in plants. They should then spend another minute discussing their points with a partner and selecting the four best points from both sets. Take selections from around the class and encourage discussion to produce a class list of the four key points to remember about gas exchange in plants.

Technician's notes

You will need the following resources for the class practicals.

Be sure to check the latest safety notes on these resources before proceeding.

B2g.1a Practical: Investigate the effect of light on net gas exchange from a leaf,

using hydrogen-carbonate indicator (B)

The pondweed will need thorough washing before the lesson, to remove any small organisms.

The voltage of the bulb should not exceed the safety limits of the bench lamp. Low energy bulbs should have some sort of protection so that they do not protrude beyond the protective metal of the bench lamp. Or they can be protected by a plastic or glass screen.

Low energy bulbs contain mercury and so can be hazardous if the bulb is broken.

Teachers should be vigilant while this practical is being carried out because of water being used close to electrical equipment.

LED lights emit a very narrow range of wavelengths of light which might not be absorbed by the plant. Halogen light sources are fine for photosynthesis but they do get hot. A large beaker of tap water placed in front of the light source will absorb the heat.

The hydrogen-carbonate indicator will need equilibrating with air just before the lesson, by drawing or bubbling air through it for about five minutes.

Class practical, per group or demonstration:

2 small beakers
hydrogen-carbonate indicator
pond water
2 similar-sized pieces of pondweed
access to light (such as windowsill or light bank) and access to dark (such as dark cupboard)
measuring cylinder
marker pen
stop watch or clock
eye protection

B2g.1b Leaf peels

If the suggested extension is carried out, you will need fresh leaves from more than one species of plant. Many plants contain very poisonous chemicals in their leaves. You should check the latest safety notes on suitable plants to use in the classroom (see CLEAPSS website http://www.science.cleapss.org.uk/). When clearing away the practical, be careful of broken cover slips.

Class practical, per group:

leaf, freshly cut from a plant
clear nail varnish
fine forceps or clear sticky tape
2 microscope slides and cover slips
microscope with low power objective and graticule

Answers

Page 107

1. All the time, because they continually need energy for making new substances and other life processes.

2. When the light intensity is high enough / during daylight hours, because photosynthesis needs energy from sunlight.

3. It is the point for a plant when the rate of photosynthesis / oxygen production / carbon dioxide uptake is the same as the rate of respiration / carbon dioxide production / oxygen uptake.

4. From the graph, between the hours of about 9:30 and 14:30 when the rate of photosynthesis exceeds the rate of respiration.

Developing investigative skills, page 108

1. Plan should include:
   - piece of *Elodea* (pondweed) or similar plant in beaker of pond water with added hydrogen-carbonate indicator
   - at least two sets of identical apparatus, for use in different light regimes, or the same apparatus used in different light regimes starting with fresh pond water and indicator each time
   - as soon as apparatus set up, placed in appropriate light regime, including at minimum bright light and dark (such as in dark cupboard)
   - apparatus left for sufficient time (e.g. 20 minutes) without disturbance, to allow for photosynthesis and respiration to have an effect on indicator.

2. a) The colour of the indicator turned from red-orange to purple.

   b) The colour of the indicator turned from red-orange to yellow.

3. The solution was becoming more acidic, because carbon dioxide concentration in the water was increasing. This suggests that the plant was releasing carbon dioxide into the water from respiration.

4. The solution was becoming more alkaline because carbon dioxide was being taken out of the water by the plant for photosynthesis.

5. Respiration is also happening, while photosynthesis is taking place, but no carbon dioxide is added to the solution because the cells use it for photosynthesis.

6. It would mean no carbon dioxide being added or removed from the solution – the plant is at its compensation point.

7. To find the compensation point, you need to have several repeats of the apparatus, and be able to control the light intensity. Then you could find the intensity at which there was no change in colour of the indicator from red-orange, which means the solution remains at the same pH and there is no net uptake or release of carbon dioxide.

Page 109

1. Carbon dioxide is soluble and acidic, so when more gas is being produced, such as during respiration, the solution becomes more acidic. When carbon dioxide is removed from the solution, such as during photosynthesis, the solution becomes less acidic.

2. Sketch should show: thin leaf to maximise area for gas exchange and minimise distance that gases have to diffuse between air and photosynthesising (palisade) cells; spongy mesophyll cells and air spaces connected to air via stomata, to maximise the internal surface area; stomata that control gases moving into and out of leaf.

3. The gas molecules are small and so can diffuse across cell membranes, into and out of cytoplasm and into and out of chloroplasts. The rate of photosynthesis is, in part, controlled by the rate of diffusion of gases between the chloroplasts and air.

B2g.1a Practical: Investigate the effect of light on net gas exchange from a leaf, using hydrogen-carbonate indicator (B)

Hydrogen-carbonate indicator can be used to indicate the acidity or alkalinity of a solution. With normal atmospheric levels of carbon dioxide, it is a red-orange colour. In more acidic solutions, e.g. if there are higher levels of carbon dioxide, it is yellow, and in more alkaline solutions, e.g. if there are lower levels of carbon dioxide, it is purple. We can use hydrogen-carbonate indicator to investigate the net gas exchange in a plant in conditions of different light intensity.

Apparatus

2 small beakers

hydrogen-carbonate indicator

pond water

2 similar-sized pieces of pondweed

access to light (e.g. windowsill or light bank)

access to dark (e.g. dark cupboard)

measuring cylinder

marker pen

stopclock or watch

eye protection

SAFETY INFORMATION
Wash hands after handling pondweed and pond water. Wear eye protection.

Method

1. Label both beakers with your initials using the marker pen.

2. Measure 25 cm^3 pond water into each of the two beakers.

3. Add 1cm^3 equilibrated hydrogen-carbonate solution (this has the same carbon dioxide content as the surrounding air) to each beaker. Note the colour of the two solutions.

4. Add one piece of pondweed to each beaker, and make sure it is fully submerged in the pond water.

5. Place one beaker in an area of bright light and one in a dark place. Start the stop clock or watch.

6. After two minutes, check and record the colour of the solutions in each beaker, without moving them.

7. Repeat step 6 every two minutes, until 10 minutes have passed.

8. Draw up a table to show your results.

Analyse and interpret data

1. Describe your results for the pondweed (a) in the light, and (b) in the dark.

2. Explain the results for each condition, using your knowledge of photosynthesis and respiration.

Evaluate data and methods

1. Explain why the hydrogen-carbonate had to be equilibrated with the surrounding air before use.

2. Before you were given it, the pondweed was washed thoroughly to remove any small organisms. Explain why this was an important preparation for this experiment.

B2g.1b Leaf peels

A leaf peel is a peel of the epidermal layer of a leaf, or of a substance such as clear nail varnish which has been painted onto the leaf surface and left to dry. The varnish takes an impression of the leaf surface and will show the stomata in the epidermal layer.

The leaf peel can then be studied under a light microscope, and an estimate made of the density of stomata in the epidermis using a graticule.

Apparatus

leaf, freshly cut from a plant

clear nail varnish

fine forceps or clear sticky tape

2 microscope slides and cover slips

microscope with low power objective and eyepiece graticule

SAFETY INFORMATION
Cover slips are fragile and have sharp edges, and should be handled carefully.
Keep your hands away from your mouth while carrying out this practical.
Wash your hands thoroughly after handling the leaf.

Method

1. Identify the upper and lower surface of the leaf.

2. Paint a thin layer of nail varnish on to the lower surface of the leaf and leave to dry.

3. Either use the forceps to lift one edge of the varnish layer and carefully peel it away from the leaf, or cover the nail varnish with sticky tape and carefully lift the varnish layer away using the tape.

4. Place the nail varnish on a microscope slide. If using sticky tape, then use the tape to stick the varnish layer in the middle of the slide. Otherwise, hold the varnish layer in place with a cover slip.

5. Place the slide on the microscope stage and focus on the stomata using the low power objective.

6. Use an eyepiece graticule, or microscope's field of view, to estimate the number of stomata in a given area.

7. Repeat steps 2–6, but this time, take a peel of the upper surface of the leaf.

8. Record your results of the number of stomata on the lower and upper surfaces of the leaf.

9. If there is time, repeat this with another leaf from the same plant.

Analyse and interpret data

1. Compare your results of the number of stomata on the upper and lower epidermal surfaces of your leaf, and describe any differences.

2. Try to explain any differences, using your knowledge of leaf structure.

3. If you had time to take peels from other leaves, compare what you found for those with the results from your first leaf, and try to explain any similarities or differences.

Activity B2g.2 Gas exchange in humans

Specification reference: B2g.2.46; B2g.2.47; B2g.2.48; B2g.2.49; B2g.2.50

Learning objectives

- Describe the structure of the human thorax, including the ribs, intercostal muscles, diaphragm, trachea, bronchi, bronchioles, alveoli and pleural membranes.
- Understand the role of the intercostal muscles and the diaphragm in ventilation.
- Explain how alveoli are adapted for gas exchange by diffusion between air in the lungs and blood in capillaries.
- Understand the biological consequences of smoking in relation to the lungs and the circulatory system, including coronary heart disease.
- Practical: Investigate breathing in humans, including the release of carbon dioxide and the effect of exercise.

Learning outcomes

- Know that the human thorax contains the ribs, intercostal muscles, diaphragm, trachea, bronchi, bronchioles, alveoli and pleural membranes.
- Describe how the diaphragm and intercostal membranes are used in ventilation.
- Explain how the alveoli are adapted for efficient exchange of gases by diffusion between the blood and the air in the lungs.
- Understand the damaging effects that smoking has on the lungs and circulatory system.

Common misconceptions

As in Topic 2f Respiration, take the opportunity to reinforce the difference between the terms *breathing (ventilation)* and *respiration* (as in cellular respiration).

Some students think that we breathe in oxygen and breathe out carbon dioxide. Practical B2g.2a demonstrates that there is also carbon dioxide in inhaled air, just far less than in exhaled air.

Resources

Student Book pages 110–119

Worksheet B2g.2a Practical: Investigate breathing in humans – the release of carbon dioxide

Worksheet B2g.2b Practical: Investigate breathing in humans – the effect of exercise

Resources for demonstration and class practicals (see Technician's notes, following)

Approach

1. Introduction

Building on work from the last activity, ask students which gases are involved in respiration. Then ask how they get into and out of the human body. When you receive the response of 'through the lungs', ask students to apply their knowledge of the adaptations of a leaf to gas exchange to consider what adaptations they would expect to find in the lungs for the exchange of gases. They could make a few notes to return to at the end of the lesson.

2. Structure of the human gas exchange system

Use page 110 of the Student Book to introduce the structure of the gas exchange system in humans. This involves a lot of terms, some of which should be familiar but also others that are new. To help with the learning, ask students to create glossary definitions of their own for each of the bold words in the text. They could then test out their definitions on other students to see if they can guess the term correctly.

If available from a butcher, and your LEA or governing body allows (and you are happy to do so), dissect lungs from a sheep to help students understand their three-dimensional structure. Please refer to safety guidelines on the CLEAPSS website. You will need to wear disposable gloves while carrying out the demonstration, and wash down all surfaces, and soak all tools used, in disinfectant (e.g. 1% Virkon) for at least 10 minutes after the demonstration. Wash your hands thoroughly after removing the gloves.

3. Breathing demonstration

Ask students to place their hands on the lower part of their rib cage and to breathe in and out gently. They should note which parts of the lower thorax and abdomen change as they inhale, and again when they exhale. Then ask them to repeat this, taking deep breaths, and to compare how different parts of the lower thorax and abdomen move in gentle and deep breathing.

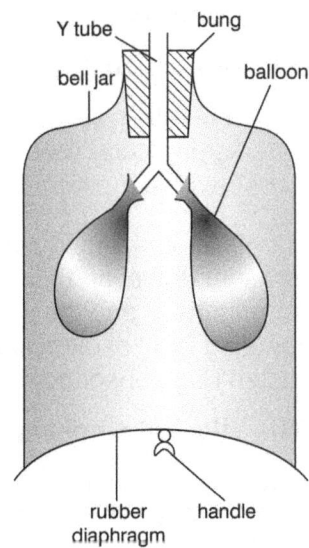

If you have the equipment, use the apparatus on the right to demonstrate the effect of the diaphragm on breathing, by pulling down on the rubber diaphragm (a rubber sheet) and then pushing up on it. Ask students first to describe what they see, then try to explain it. Talk first in simple terms of pulling and pushing. However, with able students, this should be translated into consideration of changing volume and pressure within the jar and within the 'lungs'.

Ask students to compare the model with the real system, and to identify the strengths and weaknesses of the model in explaining how we breathe.

4. Alveoli

If available, allow students to study prepared microscope slides of alveoli, and to draw and label what they see. Alternatively display such a slide using a digital microscope, or a suitable image from the internet, and discuss what is visible with the class.

Focus on the key adaptations that make alveoli well adapted for their role in gas exchange: the thin layer of tissue between the air in the lungs and the capillaries; the large number of capillaries supplying lots of blood; the large number of alveoli providing a large surface area for exchange.

5. The release of carbon dioxide during breathing

Worksheet B2g.2a provides a method for investigating the release of carbon dioxide during breathing, comparing the amounts of carbon dioxide in inhaled and exhaled air. Students count how many breaths it takes for exhaled and inhaled air to turn limewater cloudy, giving an approximation of the relative amounts of carbon dioxide in the two types of air. Note, that it may take quite a while for the inhaled air to turn limewater cloudy, needing about 100 times as many breaths as the exhaled air. Accordingly, students might be encouraged to stop counting for the exhaled air at the first signs of cloudiness.

SAFETY INFORMATION: Clean the mouthpiece with antiseptic solution, or add a new sterilised mouthpiece, for each student.

6. The effect of exercise on breathing

Worksheet B2g.2b provides a method for investigating the effect of exercise on breathing. Students may have produced their own methods when answering questions in the Developing investigative skills box on page 115 of the Student Book. If their plans are suitable, consider allowing them to carry those out instead of using the method on the worksheet. They should, however, complete the questions on the sheet using their own data.

If a spirometer is not available, students can carry out the investigation measuring rate of breathing only. They could also measure heart rate at the same time; this data will be useful for Topic 2h Transport.

SAFETY INFORMATION: Be considerate of students' concerns about exercise. If some students are unable or unwilling to carry out the exercise, pair them with other fit students so that the fit one is the test subject and the other the recorder of results.

Over-exertion may be a hazard, especially for those with some medical conditions. Competitive situations can lead to careless behaviour and accidents.

Students who are exercising should be appropriately dressed, such as in gym kit, and the exercise should take place under supervision. If any student shows signs of difficulty, they should stop exercising immediately and sit quietly until they recover. For further advice on this, consult your PE department.

A suitable form of exercise is doing step-ups on stable equipment. This is much better than students running up stairs.

Mouthpieces should not be shared.

The method gives students the freedom to decide how and when to take measurements, but guides towards a particular way of carrying out the investigation. If class results are to be collated, you may wish to constrain the method so that all students work in the same way.

Students should find that rate and depth of breathing (and heart rate) increase as level of exercise increases. However, there will probably be significant variation between students because of different levels of fitness and the way that students carry out their measurements. A quantitative method for measuring level of exercise would be using exercise equipment, such as a treadmill, which can be adjusted (e.g. for speed).

7. The effect of smoking

Pages 116–117 of the Student Book introduce a number of smoking-related diseases of the breathing and circulatory systems. Students could use this as a basis for a poster on the dangers of smoking, and add other information from their own research from books and the internet to help explain why smoking has these effects.

8. Consolidation: making notes

Ask students to write five bullet point notes for a friend who has missed this work on gas exchange in humans. Give them two minutes to do this, then ask them to compare their notes with a neighbour and select the best five from the two lists. They could then work with another pair to produce the best five points from these. Then take examples from groups and ask students to select the best to create a class list of five key points.

Technician's notes

You will need the following resources for the demonstration and the class practicals.

Be sure to check the latest safety notes on these resources before proceeding.

Structure of the human gas exchange system: demonstration

If available from a butcher, and your LEA or governing body allows (and you are happy to do so), dissect lungs from a sheep to help students understand their three-dimensional structure. You will need to wear disposable gloves while carrying out the demonstration, and wash down all surfaces, and soak all tools used, in disinfectant (e.g. 1% Virkon) for at least 10 minutes after the demonstration. Wash your hands thoroughly after removing the gloves.

lungs
sharp knife or scalpel
dissecting board
disposable gloves
disinfectant such as 1% Virkon for disinfecting all tools and work surfaces

Breathing: demonstration

If you have the equipment, use this apparatus to demonstrate the effect of the diaphragm on breathing.

rubber diaphragm
Y tube
bung
bell jar
2 balloons

B2g.2a Practical: Investigate breathing in humans – the release of carbon dioxide

Apparatus to be set up for each group as shown on the worksheet.

Sterilise mouthpieces using Milton® solution (sodium dichloroisocyanurate) made up according to the manufacturer's instructions. They should be soaked in the solution for at least 30 minutes before use.

Class practical, per group:

2 boiling tubes, 2 bungs, plastic/glass tubing, limewater (set up as shown on the worksheet)
measuring cylinder
nose clip
eye protection

B2g.2b Practical: Investigate breathing in humans – the effect of exercise

If you do not have a commercial spirometer, the following simple apparatus can be constructed. This will not produce as reliable results, as it depends on the student breathing out normally once (rather than breathing in and out using the spirometer), and the tendency will be to breathe out more heavily than normal on each test. However, it may still produce useful results.

Calibrate a two-litre plastic bottle by adding 500 cm^3 of water at a time, and marking the volume on the side of the bottle with a waterproof marker. When the bottle is full of water, invert it into a water trough without allowing any air into the bottle.

Insert a flexible plastic tube into the neck of the bottle and secure the bottle and tube in position. Clean the other end of the tubing with antiseptic solution. Alternatively add a mouthpiece to the end of the tubing that can easily be removed and sterilised after each test. You will need a sterilised one of these for every student who is measured.

Sterilise mouthpieces using Milton® solution (sodium dichloroisocyanurate) made up according to the manufacturer's instructions. They should be soaked in the solution for at least 30 minutes before use.

Class practical, per group:

spirometer (see note above)	nose clip	stopwatch

Answers

Page 111

1. List and functions as follows:

- trachea – carries air from mouth down to lungs
- bronchi – the two large divisions of the trachea as it reaches the lungs, supported with rings of cartilage to prevent collapse during breathing
- bronchioles – the fine tubes in the lungs that carry air to alveoli
- alveoli –have a large surface area and are very thin for efficient diffusion of gases
- pleural membranes – that surround the lungs are involved in ventilation
- ribs and intercostal muscles – protect the lungs but also help expand the volume of the thorax during forced or deep breathing
- diaphragm – muscular sheet below lungs which controls relaxed breathing.

2. Gas exchange is the movement of gases into and out of the cells of the body, or between the lungs and the blood. Ventilation (breathing) is the movement of air into and out of the lungs.

Developing investigative skills, page 115

1. Plan should include:

- several people (because of variation between individuals)
- some form of exercise that can be controlled, so that each individual is exercising as much as the others
- stopwatch to measure number of breaths in a particular time
- spirometer to measure depth of breathing – the people being tested will have to be instructed to breathe normally because forced breaths easily increase volumes
- breathing rate and volume need to be measured immediately after the 2 minutes.

2. Test subjects need to be reasonably fit, so that exercise is not a risk to health, and should be wearing suitable clothing for exercise. Exercise ideally should be carried out in open space or in a gym where the risks of tripping over obstacles is minimised.

3. First check for outliers (errors in measurements), such as the volume of breath for C at rest which seems much higher than the others. Then, ignoring outliers, calculate the average for each factor in the two conditions.

Page 115

1. a) Inhalation: The muscles surrounding the diaphragm contract causing the diaphragm to flatten, pulling downwards; the intercostal muscles contract lifting the ribs out and up; these actions increase the volume of the thorax, causing the volume of the lungs to increase. This decreases the pressure inside the lungs, and so causes air to enter the lungs from outside.

   b) Exhalation: The diaphragm muscle relaxes, and the diaphragm moves upwards; the intercostal muscles relax, so the ribs fall back and down; both actions reduce the volume of the thorax, so reducing the volume of the lungs. This increases the pressure inside the lungs compared with the air outside, so this pushes air out of the lungs.

2. a) Just two: the wall of the alveolus and the wall of the blood capillary.

   b) To ensure that oxygen rapidly diffuses from the area of high concentration, in the alveoli, to the area of low concentration, in the blood.
   (Do not forget that there is also a concentration gradient for carbon dioxide.)

3. Sketch similar to Fig. 2.77 on page 114 of the Student Book, with annotations showing: thin alveolar wall and wall of capillary allows rapid diffusion; high concentration gradients for gases between blood and air in alveolus due to continuous blood flow through capillary and ventilation of alveolus (lungs); large area of contact between capillary and alveolus, maximising area over which diffusion can occur.

Page 119 (top)

1. So it is easier to compare the values, because there will have been different numbers of mothers/babies in each group; makes it easier to see any pattern in the results

2. The chart shows that even some non-smoking mothers had low birthweight babies. However, the proportion goes up as the number of cigarettes per day goes up, and heavy smokers have more than twice the proportion of low birthweight babies as the non-smokers.

3. The conclusion is incorrect, because some babies born to non-smoking women have a low birth weight, so there must be other causes. However, the chart does show that increasing levels of smoking increases the risk of having a low birthweight baby in this sample of women.

A better conclusion would say something like: In this sample, women who smoked a little during pregnancy had an increased risk of having a low birthweight baby, and those that smoked a lot had an even greater risk.

4. This study shows the results for Canadian women only, and there may be other factors in this population that could produce this result. By comparing many studies from different countries, with women who have different lifestyles, it can balance out the effect of other factors. So any remaining relationship between birth weight and smoking becomes more definite and reliable.

5. Carbon monoxide could have this effect, by reducing the amount of oxygen that gets to the fetus's cells. Since oxygen is needed for respiration, if the amount of oxygen is reduced, the rate of respiration will be reduced, which will reduce the rate at which energy is released that can be used for building new cells (growth).

Page 119 (bottom)

1. Bronchitis, respiratory system; emphysema, respiratory system; cancer, any part of the body but mainly respiratory system; stroke / heart attack, circulatory system.

2. Carcinogenic means cancer-causing / a chemical that can cause cells to become cancerous so they grow and divide without stopping.

3. Emphysema is the breaking down of some of the surface of the alveoli. This leaves a smaller area for gas exchange/absorption of oxygen. So the person may not get enough oxygen for activity. Additional oxygen in the gas they breathe can help to get more oxygen into their blood and so to their cells.

4. Small molecules from the smoke, such as nicotine and carbon monoxide, can diffuse into the blood and be carried around to all parts of the body.

B2g.2a Practical: Investigate breathing in humans – the release of carbon dioxide

Respiration uses up oxygen and produces carbon dioxide, so the air we breathe in (inhaled air) is going to be different from the air we breathe out (exhaled air). This investigation compares the relative amounts of carbon dioxide in inhaled and exhaled air. Work in pairs for this investigation, with one of you breathing in and out of the apparatus and the other recording the results.

Apparatus

2 boiling tubes

2 bungs

plastic/ glass tubing

limewater

measuring cylinder

eye protection

nose clip (if available)

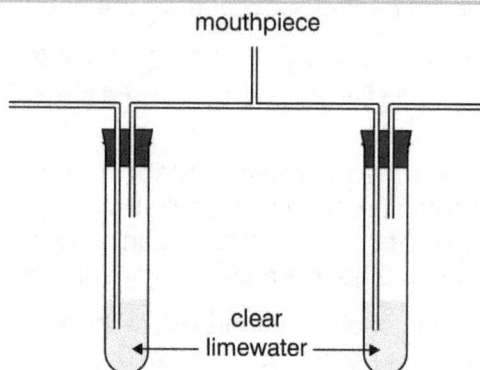

mouthpiece

clear limewater

SAFETY INFORMATION

Only use a mouthpiece if it has been sterilised before you use it.

Wear eye protection.

Breathe gently.

Method

1. Set up the apparatus as shown in the diagram.

2. Add 10 cm^3 of limewater to each boiling tube, making sure that the ends of the longer pieces of tubing in each boiling tube are below the surface of the limewater, and the ends of the shorter pieces of tubing are above the surface.

3. Make sure that the mouthpiece has been cleaned with antiseptic solution.

4. Breathe slowly in and out through the mouthpiece, counting your breaths. Exhaled air bubbles through the limewater in one tube. Inhaled air bubbles through the limewater in the other tube.

5. Count how many breaths it takes for the exhaled air to turn the limewater cloudy. Take note of just how cloudy it is.

6. Count how many breaths it takes in total for the inhaled air to turn the limewater cloudy to the same extent as you noted before.

7. Repeat the experiment with fresh limewater. Repeat several times, with different people.

Analyse and interpret data

1. If you have taken repeat measurements, check first that there are no clearly anomalous values. If there are, try to explain them. Then, ignoring any clearly anomalous values, calculate average values for the number of breaths it took for each type of air to turn the limewater cloudy.

2. Use your results to draw a suitable graph or chart.

3. Describe the shape of your graph or chart, and try to compare the relative amounts of carbon dioxide in inhaled air compared with exhaled air. (Hint: if, for example, one type of air took 10 times the number of breaths to turn limewater cloudy compared with the other type of air, then that means it contains 1/10 the amount of carbon dioxide in each breath.)

4. Compare other students' results with yours. Describe any similarities and differences between the results and try to explain them.

5. Draw a conclusion from your results about the relative amounts of carbon dioxide in inhaled and exhaled air.

Evaluate data and methods

1. If the same student repeated the experiment, suggest explanations for any variation in the results.

2. Describe any problems that you had with your investigation and suggest how the method could be adjusted to reduce the effects of these problems.

B2g.2b Practical: Investigate breathing in humans – the effect of exercise

You will probably have noticed that when you run for a while, or rush up a long flight of stairs, your breathing becomes more rapid and possibly deeper also. But how strongly is breathing affected by exercise? This investigation looks at the effect of different levels of exercise on rate of breathing, and (if a spirometer is available) on depth of breathing. Work in pairs for this investigation, with one of you exercising and the other recording the results.

Apparatus

spirometer and nose clip (if available)

stopwatch

sterilised mouthpiece

SAFETY INFORMATION

Only use a mouthpiece on the spirometer if it has been sterilised before you use it.

If you are exercising, wear appropriate clothing (such as a gym kit) and follow the usual rules of exercise that are used during normal PE lessons.

If at any time you feel uncomfortable during exercise, stop immediately, inform the teacher and sit quietly until you have recovered.

Method

1. Decide what measurements you will take, such as rate or depth of breathing (your teacher may also suggest you measure heart rate), and how you will take them.

- Rate of breathing is usually measured as number of breaths per minute, but you can measure just for half a minute and multiply by two.

- Depth of breathing will be measured using the spirometer. This may measure only one breath, in which case you must try to make it representative of your breathing at the time.

2. Decide what levels of exercise you will test, such as sitting or standing still, after walking, after jogging, after running as fast as possible.

3. Decide how long each level of exercise will be carried out before measurements are taken. For example, you could try a couple of test exercises to see whether one minute is enough, or if two minutes produces higher results.

4. Decide when you will take measurements after the exercise.

5. Decide how long to wait between levels of exercise to allow the body to recover fully before the next test.

6. Decide whether or not you need to do repeat measurements at each level of exercise.

7. Carry out your tests and record your data in a suitable table.

Analyse and interpret data

1. If you have taken repeat measurements, check first that there are no anomalous values. If there are, try to explain them. Then, ignoring anomalous values, calculate average values for each level of exercise.

2. Use your results to draw a suitable graph or chart.

3. Describe the shape of your graph, and try to explain any pattern in your results.

4. If other students have used the same method as you have, compare your graph with theirs. Describe any similarities and differences between the graphs and try to explain them.

5. Draw a conclusion from your results about the effect of exercise on breathing.

Evaluate data and methods

1. Explain fully why the student who was exercising needed to rest between tests.

2. Describe any problems that you had with your investigation and suggest how the method could be adjusted to reduce the effect of these problems.

3. This investigation produced semi-quantitative data (the exercise was described in levels, and the breathing measurements were measured on continuous scales). Suggest how you could adapt the method to make the exercise levels quantitative, so that you could produce a more reliable conclusion.

Activity B2g.3 Consolidation and summary

Learning objectives

- To review the learning points of the topic.
- To test understanding through answering questions.

Learning outcomes

- Be familiar with the knowledge and understanding summarised in the End of topic checklist.
- Be able to apply this knowledge and understanding by answering the End of topic questions.

Resources

Student Book pages 120–123

Approach

Ask students to answer the End of topic questions in the Student Book.

Answers

End of topic questions mark scheme

Question	Correct answer	Marks
1 a)	When the light is switched on, the proportion of oxygen dissolved in the water increases.	1
	This is because more oxygen is released by the plant from photosynthesis than is used in respiration.	1
1 b)	When the light was switched off, the proportion of dissolved oxygen in the water decreased.	1
	This is because no oxygen was being released by the plant from photosynthesis, and the oxygen that was available was being used in respiration.	1
2 a)	Percentage of oxygen is less in exhaled air than inhaled air	1
	because oxygen in the body is used for respiration.	1
2 b)	Percentage of carbon dioxide is greater in exhaled air than inhaled	1
	because the body produces carbon dioxide in respiration.	1
2 c)	Percentage of nitrogen does not change	1
	because it is not used by the body.	1
3 a)	i) The balloons will expand.	1
	This is because pulling down on the rubber diaphragm increases the volume inside the bell jar	1
	which in turn decreases the pressure inside the bell jar	1
	so air will be pushed into the balloons through the pipe from the higher pressure outside.	1
	ii) The balloons will collapse.	1

	This is because the volume inside the bell jar has decreased	1
	increasing the pressure inside the bell jar,	1
	so air will be pushed out of the balloons into the air.	1
3 b)	The ribs and intercostal muscles are not modelled.	1
	During deeper or forced breathing the external muscles contract, pulling the ribs out and upwards increasing the volume of the thorax even further,	1
	and increasing the volume of air entering the lungs.	1
	On exhalation, the muscles relax,	1
	letting the ribs move down and in, reducing the volume of the thorax,	1
	and resulting in a larger outbreath.	1
4	The statement only refers to net production.	1
	During the day, when there is light, the plant photosynthesises as well as respires.	1
	It releases more oxygen from photosynthesis than it uses in respiration, but all the carbon dioxide from respiration is used in photosynthesis.	1
	At night, when it is dark, there is no photosynthesis but respiration continues.	1
	So the plant takes in oxygen and releases carbon dioxide.	1
5 a)	Diffusion is the net movement of molecules from an area of their higher concentration to an area of their lower concentration as a result of random movement.	1
	Gas exchange is process by which oxygen and carbon dioxide move in opposite directions, e.g. between the alveoli and the blood.	1
5 b)	Gas exchange occurs as a result of diffusion of oxygen and carbon dioxide across cell surfaces.	1
	In plants this is in the leaf, in humans it is across the surface of alveoli in the lungs.	1
	For the following, any points up to a max of 3 marks: Tissue adaptations: There is a thin layer of cells between the air and the inside of the organism. This reduces the distance that gases have to pass through cells to get into or out of the body, so the rate of diffusion is as fast as possible.	Max 3 marks: 1
	Organ adaptations: – The surface area where gas exchange occurs (i.e. mesophyll cell surfaces, alveolar walls) is maximised so that diffusion can occur as rapidly as possible.	1
	– The leaf is broad and flat, and has stomata that let air into the leaf, so reducing the distance across which diffusion between the air and leaf cells occurs, which maximises the rate of diffusion of gases across leaf surfaces.	1
	– The lungs have an extensive blood supply that continually transports carbon dioxide from the body cells to the lungs and oxygen from the lungs to the body cells. The continual flow of blood through the capillaries maximises the concentration gradient between alveolar air and blood, which increases the rate of diffusion.	1

Question	Correct answer	Marks
6	Tobacco smoke enters the lungs during smoking, but there is no obvious direct contact with other parts of the body such as the circulation.	1
	We now know that chemicals from smoke, including carbon monoxide, enter the blood vessels in the lungs and are carried around the body.	1
	Some of these chemicals cause narrowing of blood vessels and increased blood pressure,	1
	and others cause cholesterol to build up inside blood vessels, narrowing them further and increasing the risk of blood clots that can block blood vessels.	1
7	The compensation point of a plant is when the rate of photosynthesis and the rate of respiration are equal. This is when the amount of sugar produced from photosynthesis is the same as the amount broken down in respiration.	1
	When the rate of photosynthesis is greater than at the compensation point, more sugars are made.	1
	This means there are more sugars for use for other purposes than the basic level of respiration needed to release energy to keep cells alive.	1
	So the more time that a plant is above the compensation point, the faster it can make new cells and grow.	1
	Total:	44

Introduction

In this section students will learn about the need for transport systems in large multicellular organisms, and then learn about the transport systems in flowering plants and in humans.

Links to other topics

Sections	Essential background knowledge	Useful links
1 The nature and variety of living organisms	1a Characteristics of living organisms	
2 Structure and functions in living organisms	2a Level of organisation 2b Cell structure 2d Movement of substances into and out of cells 2e Nutrition 2f Respiration 2g Gas exchange	2i Excretion 2j Coordination and response
3 Reproduction and inheritance		3a Reproduction
4 Ecology and the environment		4d Human influences on the environment

Topic overview

B2h.1	**Transport in flowering plants**
	This activity explores the tissues involved in transporting materials around a plant, how water is gained through the root hair cells, and lost through evaporation from the leaves (transpiration). There is opportunity to plan and carry out practical work on factors that affect the rate of transpiration from leaves.
B2h.2	**Blood**
	This activity looks at the structure and function of the different components in human blood, including the role of memory cells and vaccination in providing immunity to infection.
B2h.3	**The human circulatory system**
	This activity looks at the structure and function of organs in the human circulatory system, including the heart and blood vessels. It includes some practical work on the effect of exercise on heart rate, and a possible demonstration on the dissection of a heart.
B2h.4	**Consolidation and summary**
	This activity provides an opportunity for a quick recap on the ideas encountered in the topic as well as time for the students to answer the End of topic questions in the Student Book.

Activity B2h.1 Transport in flowering plants

Specification reference: B2h.2.51; B2h.2.52; B2h.2.53; B2h.2.54; B2h.2.55**B**; B2h.2.56**B**; B2h.2.57**B**; B2h.2.58**B**

Learning objectives

- Understand why simple, unicellular organisms can rely on diffusion for movement of substances in and out of the cell.
- Understand the need for a transport system in multicellular organisms.
- Describe the role of phloem in transporting sucrose and amino acids between the leaves and other parts of the plant.
- Describe the role of xylem in transporting water and mineral ions from the roots to other parts of the plant.
- Understand how water is absorbed by root hair cells. **(B)**
- Understand that transpiration is the evaporation of water from the surface of a plant. **(B)**
- Understand how the rate of transpiration is affected by changes in humidity, wind speed, temperature and light intensity. **(B)**
- Practical: Investigate the role of environmental factors in determining the rate of transpiration from a leafy shoot. **(B)**

Learning outcomes

- Understand that large organisms need a transport system to carry materials around the body.
- Describe how xylem tissue transports water and mineral salts from the roots to other parts of the plant.
- Describe how phloem tissue transports sucrose and amino acids around the plant.
- Understand how water enters plants through root hair cells. **(B)**
- Understand that transpiration is the evaporation of water from a leaf, and the rate of transpiration is affected by several environmental conditions. **(B)**

Resources

Student Book pages 124–131

Worksheet B2h.1a Practical: Investigate the role of environmental factors in determining the rate of transpiration from a leafy shoot **(B)**

Resources for class practicals (see below)

Approach

1. Introduction

Remind students of their work with agar cubes, surface area and rate of diffusion from Worksheet B2d.1c, or present this as a prepared demonstration if they did not carry out that practical work.

If possible, show them a picture of a unicellular organism, such as *Paramecium* or *Amoeba*, from a slide or the internet and ask them to apply what they learned from the practical to the diffusion of materials into and out of the unicellular organism. They should then compare this with the problem of getting materials to and from diffusion surfaces and the external environment in larger organisms.

Students can then use page 125 of the Student Book to reinforce what they have discussed about the need for transport systems in larger organisms.

2. Transport through plants: demonstration

If possible, about 24 hours before the lesson a celery stalk with leaves can be prepared (details in Technician's notes, following). After a few days, the leaves should show evidence of red colour in some areas and blue in others. (This can be done with other plants, such as a white chrysanthemum, but the wide stalk of celery makes it particularly suited for this.)

Ask students to suggest why this has happened, and what may be causing the movement of food colour up the stem. A stalk cut across can show how the colour is mainly restricted to the veins (vascular bundles) in the stalk.

3. Transport tissues in plants

Students could use prepared slides of longitudinal and transverse sections of plant roots, stems and leaves to help identify the vascular bundles in the different plant organs. They should use their findings to consider the three-dimensional nature of the transport system in a plant and how far any cell is in a plant from a vascular bundle.

They may need help to distinguish xylem from phloem in the vascular bundles, but they do not need to know any more than their separate roles in transport. Detailed understanding of structure will be covered at A level.

4. Water uptake by roots (B)

Page 127 of the Student Book explains how water enters the root through root hair cells. This is an opportunity to revise and apply the principles of osmosis, and the adaptations of root hair cells to maximise the rate of absorption of water (i.e. large surface area for absorption, maintenance of concentration gradient as water passes across the root by osmosis and is removed from the root by the xylem).

5. Transpiration and the factors that affect it (B)

Worksheet B2h.1a is a planning sheet on the factors that affect the rate of transpiration. It suggests equipment for producing a simple potometer, but a commercial potometer is likely to give better results if set up correctly. (An alternative is to use a mass potometer, with a plant in a pot resting on a balance. Water loss from the leaves is monitored by the overall loss of mass. The pot and soil will need to be covered in plastic to ensure that any water losses are from the leaves alone. This however takes a while to work and monitoring it might need to take place over a week or so to give noticeable results.)

If you have the equipment, then consider allowing students to test their plans once you have checked them for safety and suitability. Otherwise it may need to be a class demonstration. If students carry out their own experiments, the potometers will probably need to be set up for them. Details are given in the Technician's notes below.

Be careful with the possibility of water being spilled close to the electrical fan.

6. Consolidation: transpiration map

Ask students to start by writing the word *transpiration* in the middle of a sheet of paper. They should then add words from what they have learned about transport in plants to produce a concept map on the topic. Allow them five minutes to work on this, then ask them to compare their concept map with that of another student and work together to improve both maps.

Technician's notes

You will need the following resources for the class practical.

Be sure to check the latest safety notes on these resources before proceeding.

Transport through plants: demonstration

Prepare a celery stalk with leaves by cutting the stalk in half from the base to about half way up. Then place one half of the stalk in a large tube of water containing one food colouring, such as red, and the other half in another tube of water containing a different food colour, such as blue.

After a few days, the leaves should show evidence of red colour in some areas and blue in others. (This can be done with other plants, such as chrysanthemum, but the wide stalk of celery makes it particularly suited for this. Make sure the tubes are large enough that they do not dry out before the lesson.)

You could use a sharp knife to cut across the stalk and show how the colour is mainly restricted to the veins (vascular bundles) in the stalk.

B2h.1a Practical: Investigate the role of environmental factors in determining the rate of transpiration from a leafy shoot (B)

To set up a potometer for demonstration or for use by students in an investigation, use the following instructions.

Use woody shoots from a bush or tree that does not have glossy leaves. Assemble the potometer underwater to prevent air bubbles entering the apparatus. (Refer to manufacturer's instructions.) The shoot should also be cut and inserted into the potometer under water.

Allow the leaves to dry before the lesson and allow the plant to adjust to the new conditions. Just before measurement starts, insert an air bubble into the tube as described in the manufacturer's instructions, and adjust its position to sit within the scale.

If students are to carry out their plans from the worksheet, the following apparatus may be needed. However, students may suggest other apparatus. The plans should be checked to make sure that the apparatus suggested is available.

If using lamps, please note the following.

The voltage of the bulb should not exceed the safety limits of the bench lamp. Low energy bulbs should have some sort of protection so that they do not protrude beyond the protective metal of the bench lamp. Or they can be protected by a plastic or glass screen.

Low energy bulbs contain mercury and so can be hazardous if the bulb is broken.

Teachers should be vigilant while this practical is being carried out because of water being used close to electrical equipment.

LED lights emit a very narrow range of wavelengths of light which might not be absorbed by the plant. Halogen light sources are fine for photosynthesis but they do get hot. A large beaker of tap water placed in front of the light source will absorb the heat.

Potometers should be prepared in a different part of the room from the light sources.

Wash hands thoroughly after handling the plants and ventilate the room after the activity.

Class practical, per group or demonstration:

potometer (see note on previous page)	electric fan with several settings
bright light (as light bank or next to bright window)	thermometer
dim and/or dark conditions	access to warm area
light meter or sensor	access to cooler area
a bowl or container large enough to cover the plant cutting with water so that it can be cut under water	
a knife/scalpel/scissors	

Answers

Page 127

1. Over the distance of several cells, diffusion and osmosis work too slowly to supply substances the cell needs to carry out all the life processes as quickly as needed.

2. Xylem tubes carry water and dissolved substances from the roots to other parts of the plant including the leaves.

3. Phloem cells carry dissolved food materials, such as sucrose and amino acids, from the leaves where they are formed to other parts of the plant that use them for life processes or where they will be stored, or from storage regions to growing regions.

Page 128

1. Osmosis

2. Diagram should include annotations like the following, at the appropriate point: soil water has higher concentration of water molecules than cytoplasm of cells in the root; water molecules enter root hair cells by osmosis; water molecules pass from cell to neighbouring cell by osmosis until they reach the xylem.

Developing investigative skills, page 130

1. In each case you would need two potometers set up as identically as possible, or run the investigation twice with the same equipment.

 a) Take measurements at a low temperature, and also at a higher temperature (for example, with a heater nearby, but below 40 °C when damage may start to occur to proteins/enzymes), keeping all other conditions identical.

 b) Take measurements at a low light intensity (such as with curtains/blinds closed), and also at a high light intensity (with curtains/blinds open), keeping all other conditions identical.

 c) Take measurements in still air conditions, and also in windy conditions (such as using a fan), keeping all other conditions identical.

 d) Take measurements in dry air, and also in humid air (such as with humidifier nearby), keeping all other conditions identical.

2. a) Moving air / sunlight with hot / moving air /sunlight so that heat / temperature is the only factor that differs.

 b) Moving air / sunlight compared with moving air / dark cupboard, or still air / sunlight with still air / dark cupboard, so that only the factor of light intensity differs.

 c) Compare still air / sunlight with moving air / sunlight, or compare still air / dark cupboard with moving air / dark cupboard, because light intensity is the same in both and only the factor of wind speed differs.

3. a) The rate of transpiration increases with higher temperature because the bubble moved 5 cm much more quickly (54 seconds for hot / moving air / sunlight compared with 75 seconds with normal / moving air / sunlight).

 b) The rate of transpiration is faster in higher light intensity because the bubble moved 5 cm much more quickly (still: 135 seconds in light compared with 257 seconds in dark; moving air: 75 seconds in light compared with 122 in dark).

 c) The rate of transpiration is faster when wind speed is greater because the bubble moved 5 cm much more quickly (light: 75 seconds in moving air compared with 135 seconds in still air; dark: 122 seconds in moving air compared with 257 seconds in still air).

4. As water is transpired from the leaf, more water is drawn into the leaf from the stem, and more water is then drawn into the stem from the capillary tubing. The bubble moves with the water, so the movement of the bubble indicates how much water has been taken up by the shoot.

5. Apart from a fault in the connection between the shoot and the tubing, some water is used in photosynthesis in the leaves. (But this is usually minimal over the time of the experiment.)

6. The conclusions are based on comparing two results in each case. Carrying out repeats with the same shoot, and with shoots from the same plant, in each set of conditions would make it possible to identify any abnormal results and average variation, to produce more reliable conclusions.

Page 131

1. Diagram should include annotations like the following, at the appropriate point: water molecules evaporate from surfaces of cells into air spaces; water molecules from air spaces move into and out through stomata into the air – diffusion (net movement) from inside leaf to outside; osmosis causes water molecules to move from xylem into neighbouring leaf cells, and then from cell to cell until they reach a photosynthesising cell; transpiration is the evaporation of water from a leaf.

2. Closing stomata reduces diffusion of water molecules out of the leaf. At night, carbon dioxide is not needed for photosynthesis, so keeping stomata open would lose water unnecessarily. (Although some oxygen is needed for respiration, only very small amounts are needed, and this can diffuse in through even almost completely closed stomata.)

3. a) When temperature is higher, water evaporates more easily, and particles move faster, so water molecules will diffuse out of the leaf more quickly.

   b) When air humidity is low, there is a low concentration of water molecules in the air. So far more water molecules will move out of the stomata into the air than are moving from the air into the leaf. This means the rate of transpiration will be faster.

B2h.1a Practical: Investigate the role of environmental factors in determining the rate of transpiration from a leafy shoot (B)

Transpiration is the evaporation of water from the leaf surfaces of a plant. The rate of transpiration from the leaves of a plant shoot can be measured using a potometer.

There are many designs of potometer, but the diagram shows a simple version. A stem is inserted into the apparatus and sealed so that there are no air leaks.

A bubble is introduced to the side arm of the apparatus. The movement of this bubble is used to estimate the amount of water lost by transpiration.

At first the screw clip is left open to allow the shoot to adjust to the new conditions. When the experiment begins, the screw clip is closed and the rate of movement of the bubble over a fixed distance is measured.

The shoot can be exposed to different conditions to test their effect on the rate of transpiration.

1. You are going to plan an investigation, using this apparatus, to test the effect of different factors on the rate of transpiration.

You will need to consider:
- which factors you will test
- how you should set up the apparatus to test each of the factors
- how you will adjust each factor and what you will measure in each test
- which other factors you will need to control and how to control them
- what risks there may be in carrying out your tests and how these can be managed
- how the limitations of the method suggested will affect the conclusions you could draw from any results.

2. Write out your plan for each factor, and make a prediction for each one.

3. Show your plan to your teacher. Your teacher will tell you if you can now carry out your plan. If you have been given permission to proceed, below is an example of the apparatus you can use.

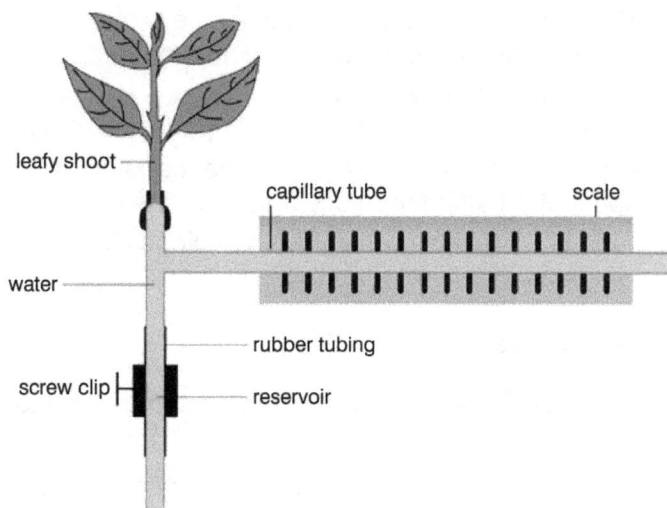

Apparatus

potometer	bright light (as light bank or next to bright window)
dim and/or dark conditions	light meter or sensor
electric fan with several settings	thermometer
access to warm area	access to cooler area

a bowl or container large enough to cover the plant cutting with water so that it can be cut under water

a knife/scalpel/scissors

SAFETY INFORMATION
Wash hands thoroughly at the end of the practical.

Take care with sharp knives/scalpels/scissors.

Activity B2h.2 Blood

Specification reference: B2h.2.59; B2h.2.60; B2h.2.61; B2h.2.62; B2h.2.63**B**; B2h.2.64**B**

Learning objectives

- Describe the composition of the blood: red blood cells, white blood cells, platelets and plasma.
- Understand the role of plasma in the transport of carbon dioxide, digested food, urea, hormones and heat energy.
- Understand how adaptations of red blood cells make them suitable for the transport of oxygen, including shape, the absence of a nucleus and the presence of haemoglobin.
- Understand how the immune system responds to disease using white blood cells, illustrated by phagocytes ingesting pathogens and lymphocytes releasing antibodies specific to the pathogen.
- Understand how vaccination results in the manufacture of memory cells, which enable future antibody production to the pathogen to occur sooner, faster and in greater quantity. **(B)**
- Understand how platelets are involved in blood clotting, which prevents blood loss and the entry of microorganisms. **(B)**

Learning outcomes

- Explain that human blood is formed from plasma carrying red blood cells, white blood cells and platelets.
- Explain how plasma is important in the transport of carbon dioxide, digested food molecules, urea, hormones and heat energy around the body.
- Describe how red blood cells have special adaptations for carrying oxygen, including haemoglobin.
- Understand how white blood cells are part of the immune system that responds to infection by pathogens.
- Understand how vaccination results in the production of memory cells and how they respond to infection. **(B)**
- Understand the role of platelets in blood clotting. **(B)**

Resources

Student Book pages 131–135

Approach

1. Introduction

Give students a minute to jot down three things they remember about blood. Take examples from around the class, and compile a list of remembered facts. Encourage discussion of points that have been mis-remembered, so as not to reinforce these, but don't worry if there is no resolution at this point. Instead, make sure these points are resolved correctly by the end of the lesson.

2. Looking at blood

Use pages 131–134 of the Student Book to introduce the components of blood. If possible, give students the opportunity to study prepared slides of human blood.

Alternatively display such a slide using a digital microscope, or a suitable image from the internet. Ask students to draw examples of each of the different kinds of cell that they can see. This should include red blood cells, and white blood cells if visible. It is unlikely that they will identify platelets, but there may be more than one kind of white blood cell. Ask them to compare the size, structure and number of the different kinds of cell, as well as to describe the functions of the plasma.

Ask students to explain the importance of platelets.

3. Red blood cells

Using the photograph of an electron micrograph of red blood cells on page 132 of the Student Book, ask students to sketch one red blood cell and label it to explain how its structure is adapted to its function.

4. White blood cells and immunity

Using the description of the response of the immune system on pages 133–134 of the Student Book, and any other information they can find, ask students to draw a cartoon to illustrate how phagocytes and lymphocytes respond to pathogens.

Ask students to draw a flow chart or write a story that outlines how vaccination leads to the formation of memory cells, and why this is important in protecting you from infection by that pathogen in the future.

Students could also investigate which infections are commonly prevented by vaccination in childhood and which in later years. They should try to identify any differences they find, and explain them in terms of when you may be infected by the pathogen. For example, measles, mumps and rubella are easily transmitted by air or touch, so easily caught in childhood, hence vaccinations are given to children. Tetanus vaccinations are only given if there is a chance that you have come into contact with the pathogen, through touching infected soil with an open wound.

Note that some pathogens are not commonly vaccinated against because they mutate frequently, so that the memory cells either respond weakly or no longer recognise them. These include flu and cold viruses.

5. Consolidation: crossword clues

Ask students to write clues for a crossword on the structure and function of all the components in blood. They should write at least five clues. Then ask them to test their clues on another student, and to amend the clues if they prove difficult to answer.

Answers

Page 133

1. Haemoglobin binds with oxygen when it is at high concentration such as in the lungs, and releases oxygen when it is at low concentration, such as in respiring tissues where the oxygen has reacted with glucose to produce carbon dioxide and water.

2. Breathing might become more rapid because with each breath the haemoglobin is combining with less oxygen than the body is used to. So it will deliver less oxygen to cells and the body response will be to increase breathing rate and depth.

3. More red blood cells in a given volume of blood means there will be more haemoglobin in that volume. More haemoglobin can combine with more oxygen, so each cm^3 of blood will carry more oxygen and deliver more oxygen to the body cells.

4. Training at high altitude for several weeks will cause the red blood cell count to increase. This will increase the oxygen-carrying capacity of the blood. When the athlete then competes at low altitude, their blood will be delivering more oxygen to their muscle cells than if they had trained at low altitude. So their muscles will be able to work harder aerobically than after low-altitude training.

Page 135

1.

Blood component	Function
plasma	carries dissolved substances, such as carbon dioxide, glucose, urea and hormones; also transfers heat energy from warmer to cooler parts of the body
red blood cells	carry oxygen
white blood cells	protect against infection
platelets	cause blood clots to form when a blood vessel is damaged

2. The biconcave disc shape increases surface area to volume ratio, so rate of diffusion of oxygen into and out of the cell is maximised. Haemoglobin inside the cell binds with oxygen when oxygen concentration is high and releases oxygen when oxygen concentration is low. The cell has no nucleus, so there is as much room as possible for haemoglobin. The cell has a flexible shape so it can squeeze through the smallest capillaries and reach all tissues.

3. Phagocytes engulf pathogens inside the body and destroy them. Lymphocytes produce antibodies that attach to the pathogens, either attracting phagocytes or causing the pathogens to break open and die. This all helps to prevent pathogens causing damage when they infect us.

4. Damage to a blood vessel can create an easy route of infection into the body. So forming a blood clot where there is damage, as quickly as possible, helps to reduce the risk of infection.

Activity B2h.3 The human circulatory system

Specification reference: B2h.2.65; B2h.2.66; B2h.2.67; B2h.2.68; B2h.2.69

Learning objectives

- Describe the structure of the heart and how it functions.
- Explain how the heart rate changes during exercise and under the influence of adrenaline.
- Understand how factors may increase the risk of developing coronary heart disease.
- Understand how the structure of arteries, veins and capillaries relate to their function.
- Understand the general structure of the circulation system, including the blood vessels to and from the heart and lungs, liver and kidneys.

Learning outcomes

- Describe the structure of the heart and be able to link this to its function in pumping blood to the lungs and other parts of the body.
- Understand heart rate is affected by exercise and adrenaline.
- Understand the factors that may increase the risk of coronary heart disease.
- Explain how the structure of arteries, veins and capillaries is related to their different roles in transporting blood around the body.
- Describe the human circulatory system and know that it includes the heart and blood vessels that support all the organs of the body.

Resources

Student Book pages 135–142

Approach

1. Introduction

Remind students of their earlier work on levels of organisation in Topic 2a. Using the circulatory system as an example, ask them to suggest an organ, a tissue and a cell in this system. List correct examples of each on the board and prompt for others that may not be immediately obvious to students.

For example: organ: heart, artery, vein; tissue: blood, muscle in heart and blood vessel walls; cell: red blood cell, white blood cell, muscle cell. You could return to these lists at the end of the activity to see if students can add more examples of each.

2. The circulatory system

Use the diagram on page 136 of the Student Book to introduce the human circulatory system. Point out the distinction between arteries, which carry blood away from the heart, and veins, which carry blood back towards the heart (except the hepatic portal vein).

Discuss the names of different pairs of arteries and veins and how they are named according to the organ they supply: pulmonary for lung, hepatic for liver, renal for kidneys. Give students five minutes to learn as many names as they can, then ask them to close the book and name some blood vessels, such as:

- which vessel carries blood away from the heart to the lungs (aorta)
- which blood vessel carries blood away from the kidneys back towards the heart (renal vein).

If appropriate, include some more difficult questions, such as:

- which artery carries deoxygenated blood (pulmonary artery)
- which vessel links two organs, not including the heart (hepatic portal vein).

3. Structure of blood vessels

If available, students could look at and draw prepared slides of a vein, an artery and a capillary. Alternatively display slides of these using a digital microscope, or use images from the internet. Students should annotate their drawing to show the key features of each type of blood vessel, and explain how each of these features relates to the function of the blood vessel.

Remind students that all these vessels are linked by asking them to describe the route blood might take from the heart through the kidneys and back to the heart. They should include the capillaries within the kidneys between the renal artery and renal veins.

If possible, show students a video clip of blood flowing through capillaries. (You may need to explain that *venules* are small vessels that join capillaries to veins, and *arterioles* are small vessels that join capillaries to arteries.)

4. Heart dissection demonstration

If you are happy to do so, demonstrate to students the dissection of a heart. You will need to wear disposable gloves during the dissection, and afterwards all surfaces and tools that have been in contact with the blood will need disinfecting, such as with 1% Virkon, for at least 10 minutes. Wash your hands thoroughly after finishing the dissection and clearing up.

Start by pointing to where the blood vessels are attached (to the 'top' of the heart). Use a sharp scalpel to cut down through each of the blood vessels into the heart, and then between the right atrium and right ventricle, to open the heart out completely. Please see the Technician's notes below for safety and additional information.

Help students to identify and distinguish the two atria and the two ventricles, looking at differences in the muscle walls. Also point out the valves and 'heart strings' in the ventricles that prevent the valves turning the wrong way when the heart contracts. Discuss how this ensures that blood flow is only one way through the heart.

Students should make notes of the structures and their relationship during the dissection.

5. Increasing heart rate

If students collected data on heart rate while investigating the effect of exercise on breathing on Worksheet B2g.2a, they could analyse this data now. Alternatively, they could repeat the practical to collect data on heart rate at different levels of exercise. The method used in the previous practical will be suitable, and the same safety comments apply.

Ideally students should take repeat measurements at each level of exercise and average their results. Also, if the same method is used by all students, the data could be collated and compared, to identify that different people have different heart rates, but that they all respond to increase in level of exercise with an increased heart rate.

Students should be expected to explain these results in terms of delivering oxygen and glucose (food molecules) for respiration more rapidly to the actively respiring muscle cells which need to release energy for contraction.

Explain that heart rate also changes under the influence of adrenaline. You will come back to this and other effects of adrenaline in Topic 2j Coordination and response.

SAFETY INFORMATION: Be considerate of students' concerns about exercise. If some students are unable or unwilling to carry out the exercise, pair them with other fit students so that the fit one is the test subject and the other the recorder of results.

Over-exertion may be a hazard, especially for those with some medical conditions. Competitive situations can lead to careless behaviour and accidents.

Students who are exercising should be appropriately dressed, such as in gym kit, and the exercise should take place under supervision. If any student shows signs of difficulty, they should stop exercising immediately and sit quietly until they recover. For further advice on this, consult your PE department.

A suitable form of exercise is doing step-ups on stable equipment. This is much better than students running up stairs.

If taking pulse rate in the neck, be careful that blood flow to the brain is not restricted. Please also refer to the CLEAPSS website for full safety information.

6. Coronary heart disease

Remind students that in Topic 2g Gas exchange they have already learnt that smoking increases the risk of coronary heart disease (CHD). Now explain to them that there are also other factors that increase the risk of CHD. Ask students to use page 141 of the Student Book and/or the internet, to research CHD and the various risk factors. They could present their findings as a poster or using presentation software.

7. Consolidation: true or false

Give students two scraps of paper. Ask them to write the word *true* on one piece of paper and *false* on the other. Then give a series of true and false statements on what students have learned from this topic, and ask students to hold up the correct piece of paper each time. Choose the statements to match the ability of the students.

For example:

- The heart has four chambers. (true) (simple form)
- The heart has four chambers, two ventricles at the top and two atria at the bottom. (false) (more challenging).

The responses will help you identify areas that students are still not sure about.

Technician's notes

You will need the following resources for the demonstration.

Be sure to check the latest safety notes on these resources before proceeding.

Heart dissection demonstration

You will need one heart for this demonstration. Ideally the heart should still have the ends of the blood vessels attached – they are best sourced from a butcher with a request to prepare them like this.

Please see also the guidance on the CLEAPSS website (http://www.science.cleapss.org.uk/).

For demonstration:

heart
sharp knife or scalpel
dissecting board
disposable gloves
disinfectant such as 1% Virkon for disinfecting all tools and work surfaces
stopclocks may be needed for heart rate measurement

Answers

Page 138

1. a) Renal arteries.

   b) Aorta.

   c) Hepatic vein.

2. Arteries are large vessels with thick, elastic muscular walls; capillaries are tiny blood vessels with very thin walls that are often only one cell thick; veins are large vessels with thin walls, a large lumen and valves to prevent backflow of blood.

3. The walls stretch as blood enters them, and slowly recoil as the blood flows through, balancing out the pressure so that the change in pressure is reduced.

Page 142

1. Vena cava, right atrium, right ventricle, pulmonary artery, capillaries in the lungs, pulmonary vein, left atrium, left ventricle, aorta.

2. Valves between the ventricles and atria, and at the base of the blood vessels leaving the heart can close to prevent blood moving in the wrong direction.

3. Heart rate increases with increasing level of exercise so that the blood is carried round the body faster and can carry oxygen from the lungs more quickly to the muscle cells, glucose from the alimentary canal (or released from liver cells) to the muscle cells, and carry carbon dioxide from the muscle cells more quickly to the lungs.

Developing investigative skills, page 142

1. a) Allowing exercise to continue for 2 minutes before taking heart rate gives time for the heart rate to adjust to conditions inside the body as a result of the changed level of exercise.

   b) Allowing a long enough time to rest between exercise levels gives the heart time to recover from the previous exercise and conditions inside the body to return to a resting state. So all tests are starting from the same base point.

2. The data shows that heart rate increases from the resting rate to walking, to jogging and finally to running.

3. Heart rate increases as the level of exercise increases.

4. As the level of exercise increases, muscle cells are respiring more quickly. This means they need a faster blood supply to provide the oxygen and glucose that they need more quickly, and to remove waste carbon dioxide more quickly too. The heart rate increases to pump the blood around the body more quickly.

5. The data comes from one subject during one set of tests. The investigation should be repeated several times with the same subject, to check that none of the measurements are anomalous, and to average the results because heart rate varies a lot even in the same person. The investigation should also be repeated with several other test subjects, to make sure the results apply generally and not just to the individual.

Activity B2h.4 Consolidation and summary

Learning objectives

- To review the learning points of the topic.
- To test understanding through answering questions.

Learning outcomes

- Be familiar with the knowledge and understanding summarised in the End of topic checklist.
- Be able to apply this knowledge and understanding by answering the End of topic questions.

Resources

Student Book pages 143–147

Approach

Ask students to answer the End of topic questions in the Student Book.

Answers

End of topic questions mark scheme

Question	Correct answer	Marks
1	The flatworm is very thin, so none of its cells is very far from the surrounding environment.	1
	So diffusion can supply all the substances its cells need fast enough for life processes to continue at a sufficient rate.	1
2 a)	They carry blood that flows from the heart to the body.	1
2 b)	They carry blood that is flowing from body tissues to the heart.	1
2 c)	Blood in the arteries has just left the heart, which generates large pressures when it contracts.	1
	When the heart relaxes and increases in volume it draws in blood from the veins reducing the pressure in them.	1
2 d)	The thick artery walls prevent rupturing when a pulse of blood increases blood pressure.	1
	The muscular and elastic tissue in the walls also allows them to stretch to resist the pulses of high pressure without rupturing and also to recoil to maintain the pressure of blood in the artery and even-out the pulse a bit.	1
2 e)	Veins have a large lumen that allows blood to flow easily back to the heart.	1
	Valves in the vein prevent backflow of the blood.	1
3 a)	The evaporation of water from cell surfaces in the leaf of a plant.	1
3 b)	Xylem vessels in the veins.	1
3 c)	Xylem vessels are long tubes with no cell contents through which water passes easily.	1
	They continue from the root, through the stem to all parts of the plant including the leaves.	1

Question	Correct answer	Marks
3 d)	In transpiration, water evaporates from the leaves of the celery which reduces the concentration of water in the cytoplasm of leaf cells,	1
	so water molecules move out of the xylem in the vascular bundles by osmosis.	1
	This causes a transpiration stream to be set up in the xylem, which draws water up from the base of the stalk.	1
	As the colouring is dissolved in the water, it is carried with the water up the xylem and into the leaves.	1
4 a)	They help in the formation of blood clots	1
	by causing the formation of fibrin where a blood vessel is damaged which traps blood cells to block the damaged area.	1
4 b)	It stops large amounts of blood escaping from the blood vessel	1
	and prevents pathogens getting in the body where they can cause illness.	1
4 c)	It will stop blood reaching cells beyond the clot,	1
	which will prevent cells getting oxygen and sugars needed for respiration,	1
	so the cells may die.	1
4 d)	Aspirin prevents platelets from functioning and producing clots that could cause thrombosis.	1
5	Red blood cells contain haemoglobin, which carries oxygen around the body.	1
	If the red blood cell count is lower than usual, the amount of oxygen that can be carried by the blood will be reduced.	1
	So the rate at which oxygen can be supplied to cells is reduced, so respiration in the cells will be slower.	1
	Respiration releases energy for all cell processes, including activity, so the cells of an anaemic person will not be able to supply energy as quickly as normal and they will feel tired more rapidly.	1
6	Smoking	1
	Lack of exercise	1
	A diet high in fatty foods	1
	Being overweight	1
7	The muscle in the left ventricle wall is much thicker than in the right ventricle wall,	1
	so it can contract more strongly and create a greater pressure.	1
	Blood from the right ventricle goes only to the lungs, where a high pressure would damage the capillaries that flow past the alveoli.	1
	Blood from the left ventricle will eventually travel around the body, through capillaries in organs, before returning to the heart, so a much larger initial pressure is needed to help it move this distance.	1
	Total:	38

Introduction

This section introduces students to a fuller definition of excretion in plants and animals, and then describes the role of the kidneys in the excretion of urine and in osmoregulation.

Links to other topics

Sections	Essential background knowledge	Useful links
1 The nature and variety of living organisms	1a Characteristics of living organisms	
2 Structure and functions in living organisms	2a Level of organisation 2d Movement of substances into and out of cells 2e Nutrition 2f Respiration 2g Gas exchange	2j Coordination and response
4 Ecology and the environment		4c Cycles within ecosystems

Topic overview

B2i.1	**Excretion in organisms** This short activity introduces excretion and its role in plants and animals in removing metabolic waste products from the body.
B2i.2	**Producing urine (B)** This activity looks at the detailed structure of the human kidney and how this relates to the production of urine.
B2i.3	**Osmoregulation (B)** This short activity explores the role of the kidney and the production of ADH in osmoregulation.
B2i.4	**Consolidation and summary** This activity provides an opportunity for a quick recap on the ideas encountered in the topic as well as time for the students to answer the End of topic questions in the Student Book.

Activity B2i.1 Excretion in organisms

Specification reference: B2i.2.70; B2i.2.71; B2i.2.73**B**

Learning objectives

- In plants, understand the origin of carbon dioxide and oxygen as waste products of metabolism and their loss from the stomata of a leaf.
- In humans, know the excretory products of the lungs, kidneys and skin (organs of excretion).
- Describe the structure of the urinary system, including the kidneys, ureters, bladder and urethra. **(B)**

Learning outcomes

- Understand that plants lose excess carbon dioxide and oxygen to the environment through stomata in their leaves.
- Understand that in humans, the organs of excretion are the lungs, kidneys and skin.
- Describe the human urinary system and know that it includes the kidneys, ureters, bladder and urethra. **(B)**

Common misconceptions

The terms *egestion* and *excretion* are commonly confused. Reinforce the fact that substances that are excreted must be produced by metabolic processes in the body.

Some people consider that sweat is not *excreted* but *secreted* onto the skin, as it is produced for specific purposes such as temperature control. This specification does not make this distinction and the term *excretion* is used. It will be developed further in Topic 2j when discussing homeostasis.

Resources

Student Book pages 148–149

Approach

1. Introduction

Show students a plant and give them a minute to discuss in pairs what the plant excretes. If they are not sure of the term, remind them that excretion is one of the eight characteristics of living processes that they learned about in Topic 1a.

After a minute, ask for suggestions. If you get chemicals such as 'perfume' or 'nectar', give hints for the waste products of metabolic reactions that take place in cells. This should result in carbon dioxide (from respiration) and oxygen (from photosynthesis).

Ask students to identify the main organ of excretion in a plant (the leaf).

2. Excretion in humans

Following on from the introduction, ask students what humans excrete and which organs are involved in their excretion. If necessary, reinforce the distinction between excretion and egestion at this point.

Give them two minutes to work in pairs on this, then take answers. They should be able to answer with carbon dioxide (lungs) and urine (kidneys). If not mentioned, suggest sweat from the skin.

3. The human urinary system (B)

Give students a minute to write down all the structures of the urinary system that they can remember and what role each structure plays in the system. Then ask students to compare their list with the text and diagram of the urinary system on page 149 of the Student Book. They should identify any gaps and fill them in using the details in the book. If there were significant gaps in knowledge, give students five minutes in their pairs, taking it in turns to ask questions to reinforce what they have just learned.

4. Consolidation: definition

Ask students to write a definition for a web answers site or encyclopaedia for the term *excretion*, including examples from plants and from humans that clarify the answer. They should compare their definition with another student and work together to improve their definition.

Answers

Page 149

1. Leaf, because this is where the gaseous waste products of photosynthesis and respiration are excreted from the plant into the environment.

2. Lungs – carbon dioxide from respiration excreted from body;

   skin – water and ions excreted from body;

   kidneys – urea and other waste products in excess such as ions and water.

3.

Structure	Function
kidneys	produce urine by filtering waste substances from the blood
ureters	carry urine from kidneys to bladder
bladder	stores urine until it is released to the environment
urethra	short tube linking bladder to environment

Activity B2i.2 Producing urine (B)

Specification reference: B2i.2.72**B**; B2i.2.74**B**; B2i.2.75**B**; B2i.2.76**B**; B2i.2.77**B**; 2i.2.79**B**

Learning objectives

- Understand how the kidney carries out its roles of excretion and osmoregulation. **(B)**
- Describe the structure of a nephron, including the Bowman's capsule and glomerulus, convoluted tubules, loop of Henle and collecting duct. **(B)**
- Describe ultrafiltration in the Bowman's capsule and the composition of the glomerular filtrate. **(B)**
- Understand how water is reabsorbed into the blood from the collecting duct. **(B)**
- Understand why selective reabsorption of glucose occurs at the proximal convoluted tubule. **(B)**
- Understand that urine contains water, urea and ions. **(B)**

Learning outcomes

- Describe the structure of a nephron including a Bowman's capsule, glomerulus, convoluted tubules, loop of Henle and collecting duct. **(B)**
- Describe how ultrafiltration takes place in the Bowman's capsule and glomerulus, producing the glomerular filtrate. **(B)**
- Describe how water is reabsorbed from the kidney tubule in the collecting duct. **(B)**
- Describe how selective reabsorption of glucose occurs in the proximal convoluted tubule. **(B)**
- Understand that excreted urine contains water, urea and salts. **(B)**

Common misconceptions

In order to understand fully how urine is produced in the nephron, students need a good understanding of the processes of diffusion, osmosis and active transport.

Resources

Student Book pages 149–152

Worksheet B2i.2a Kidney dissection

Worksheet B2i.2b Structure of a nephron

Resources for class practical (see Technician's notes, following)

Approach

1. Introduction (B)

Ask students to consider how long they would live if their kidneys didn't work properly, and what the problems would be. Perhaps a student knows someone who has been treated for kidney failure and is willing to describe the problems they had.

If not, explain that kidney failure may happen for many reasons, such as physical damage during an accident or from high blood pressure, or as a result of infection. It is not usually possible to give the patient a new kidney immediately, so they must be treated several times a week to 'clean' their blood. This process is called dialysis. In effect, it passes the blood through an artificial kidney to remove urea and other substances that have accumulated in the blood from metabolic processes. Without treatment, the patient would soon become ill because of the effect of these substances on cells and could die.

Help students to remember the effect of changing pH on enzymes and therefore the effect on the way cells work.

2. Structure of the kidney (B)

Worksheet B2i.2a gives students the opportunity to dissect and identify the main structures in a kidney. Alternatively, this could be done as a class demonstration. Use the diagram of the urinary system on page 150 of the Student Book to help students identify some of the key structures. Explain that they will not be able to see individual nephrons as they are far too small.

Please also refer to the safety guidelines on the CLEAPSS website (http://www.science.cleapss.org.uk/).

3. Producing urine in a nephron (B)

There are many video clips on the internet of the structure of a nephron and how it relates to the production of urine. However, most of these are aimed at a higher level than International GCSE. If you have access to displaying video in class, then take some time to find one that is suitable for your students because the use of models will help their understanding.

Before showing the video clip, ask students to write down five questions that they want to answer from watching it. Discuss those questions and help them to select the five most suitable for the video and for what they need to know. This will help them to focus on the key points that they need to learn.

Be aware that the video may use additional or alternative terms that students do not need to know. Provide a list of alternatives for words that they do need to know, but tell them to ignore the rest.

If you do not have access to the internet or display facilities for video, give students the large diagram of a nephron on Worksheet B2i.2b and ask them to label it fully with the names of the parts and descriptions of what happens in the key parts.

4. Consolidation: true or false (B)

Ask students to write down five statements about the human kidney, some of which are true and some of which are false. Take examples from around the class, asking other students to put up their hands if they think a statement is true.

Help students to clarify their understanding by choosing a student who has the right answer to explain why they made that choice.

Technician's notes

You will need the following resources for the class practical.

Be sure to check the latest safety notes on these resources before proceeding.

B2i.2a Kidney dissection

You will need at least one kidney for each two groups / pair of students. Ideally the kidneys should still have their outer capsule and ureter attached – they are best sourced from a butcher with a request to prepare them like this. If you are concerned about students using sharp knives or scalpels, then present the kidneys already cut in half vertically and ask students to start at step 4 of the instructions on the worksheet.

Please also refer to the safety guidelines on the CLEAPSS website.

Class practical, per group or demonstration:

kidney
sharp knife or scalpel
dissecting board
disposable gloves
disinfectant such as 1% Virkon for disinfecting all tools and work surfaces

Answers

Page 152

1. Blood in glomerulus, nephron (Bowman's capsule, proximal convoluted tubule, loop of Henle, distal convoluted tubule, collecting duct), ureter, bladder, urethra.

2. a) Bowman's capsule (in conjunction with glomerulus of blood capillaries).

   b) Proximal convoluted tubule for most substances, also collecting duct for additional water.

3. a) Glucose.

   b) Active transport.

B2i.2a Kidney dissection

In this dissection, you will get the opportunity to identify some of the key structures in a kidney.

If you have been given a whole kidney, then initially work in pairs until step 4, after which you should work individually.

Apparatus

kidney

sharp knife or scalpel

dissecting board

disposable gloves

disinfectant

SAFETY INFORMATION

Clean any splashes of blood with disinfectant immediately.

Soak all surfaces and equipment that have come into contact with blood for at least 10 minutes with disinfectant at the end of the practical.

Wear disposable gloves during the dissection and wash your hands thoroughly after the practical.

Take care when using the sharp knife or scalpel.

Method

1. Look at the external shape and structure of the kidney, and note the point where the ureter attaches to the kidney. This is also the point where the renal artery and vein attach to the kidney, but it is unlikely that these will still be in place.

2. If the kidney has an outer capsule, note the colour and toughness of the capsule. This helps to protect the kidney from damage from the outside. Use the knife or scalpel to make a small cut in the capsule. Then carefully cut and remove the capsule without damaging the kidney inside.

3. Carefully cut the kidney into two halves vertically.

4. Note where the ureter is attached to the pelvis in the middle of the kidney. The pelvis is the area into which all the collecting ducts drain, delivering urine that will flow down the ureter to the bladder.

5. Note that there are two distinct areas of different shades of red in the kidney. The outer area is the cortex. This is the part of the kidney where the Bowman's capsule and convoluted tubules of each nephron lie. You will not be able to see individual nephrons because they are too small, but you will be able to see that, because these parts of the nephron are well supported by the capillary network and so contain a lot of blood, this area is the brighter red of the two areas.

6. Look at the medulla (think of 'middle' to help you remember which area is which), and note that it is paler than the cortex. This area consists of the loop of Henle and collecting duct from all the nephrons. The collecting ducts end at the inner edge of the medulla and drain into the pelvis. There are blood capillaries in the medulla (which is why it is red) but not as many as in the cortex.

7. Carefully draw the structure of the kidney that you can see, and label it to explain which parts of the nephron occur in which areas.

8. Dispose of the kidney as instructed by your teacher, and thoroughly clean everything that has come into contact with the kidney.

B2i.2b Structure of a nephron

1. Label the diagram fully to identify the different parts of the nephron.

2. Then indicate in which parts of the nephron the following take place:

   a) ultrafiltration

   b) reabsorption of water

   c) selective reabsorption of glucose.

3. Add notes to explain how these processes happen. Remember to include the terms *diffusion*, *osmosis* and *active transport* in your explanations.

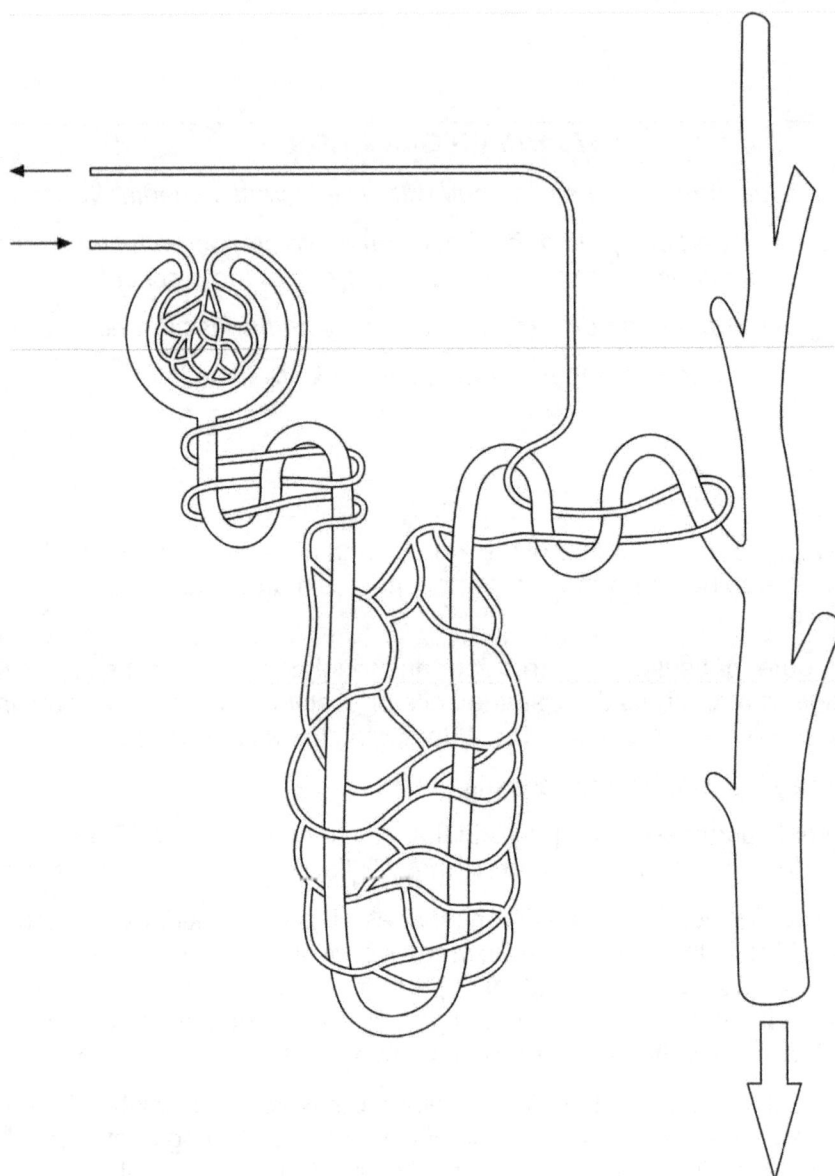

Activity B2i.3 Osmoregulation (B)

Specification reference: B2i.2.72**B**; B2i.2.76**B**; B2i.2.78**B**

Learning objectives

- Understand how the kidney carries out its roles of excretion and osmoregulation. **(B)**
- Understand how water is reabsorbed into the blood from the collecting duct. **(B)**
- Describe the role of ADH in regulating the water content of the blood. **(B)**

Learning outcomes

- Describe the role of the kidneys in osmoregulation. **(B)**
- Understand that water is reabsorbed from the kidney tubule in the collecting duct. **(B)**
- Understand that ADH is the hormone that is involved in regulation of the water content of the blood. **(B)**

Common misconceptions

Note that the role of the kidney is as a filtration/reabsorption system – the waste materials excreted by the kidneys are (mostly) produced elsewhere.

Resources

Student Book pages 152–153

Approach

1. Introduction (B)

Show students two flasks of 'urine', one darker yellow than the other. There should be about twice as much pale 'urine' as dark 'urine'. (These should not be real urine, but prepared using water and different concentrations of yellow food colouring / tea water.) Explain that the darker 'urine' was collected when you were hot and hadn't drunk much, and the pale 'urine' was collected after you had drunk a lot of water.

Ask students to describe the differences between the flasks, and to use their knowledge of the functioning of the nephron to explain any differences. They should link the idea of a well-hydrated body to the production of a large amount of dilute urine.

2. Homeostasis (B)

Ask students why it is important that the body controls its water content. This links to their earlier work on osmosis, from which they should be able to answer that too much water can cause animal cells to swell and burst, and too little water can affect the rate of reactions in cells and so the life processes. If there is time, students could research the effects of dehydration and overhydration on the human body and identify circumstances in which each might happen.

Ask students to write down on one side of a piece of paper 'body water content increases' and on the other side 'body water decreases', and ask them to work in pairs or small groups to work out what happens in each case in order to return body water content to a 'normal' level. (There is no need to understand the mechanism at this point.)

Encourage students to look at this as a continual process of 'too much'→back to normal→overshoot to 'too little'→back to normal→overshoot to 'too much', etc. Explain that this continually returning an internal condition towards a 'normal' point is called *homeostasis*, which will be covered in more detail a little later.

With more able students, introduce the concept of *negative feedback*, where a change in a condition is the cause of the opposite change happening. (Note: they do not need to know this for their exams, but this is useful preparation for A level.)

3. Osmoregulation (B)

Tell students that ADH is the hormone that controls the water content of the blood. Ask students if they can explain what a hormone is. They may not have come across the term, as it will be covered more fully in Topic 2j.

Use the example of ADH to describe a hormone as a chemical substance (ADH) that is released by one organ of the body (in this case the pituitary gland in the brain) and causes cells in another part of the body (in this case the nephrons in the kidney) to change how they are working. A hormone is effectively a chemical message from one part of the body to another.

Students should then annotate their diagrams of the homeostatic control of water content from earlier to show the role of ADH in controlling body water content, using page 153 of the Student Book to help them.

4. Consolidation: crossword clues (B)

Ask students to write crossword clues for key words in this section including *osmoregulation* and *homeostasis*, and if appropriate *ADH, hypothalamus* and *pituitary gland*.

Answers

Page 153

1. Osmoregulation is the control of the concentration of water in the blood.

2. a) ADH

   b) Hypothalamus in brain. (It is later stored and released by the pituitary gland.)

   c) Cells of the collecting ducts in kidneys

3. ADH makes collecting duct walls more permeable to water, so more water is reabsorbed from the filtrate, making more concentrated urine.

Activity B2i.4 Consolidation and summary

Learning objectives

- To review the learning points of the topic.
- To test understanding through answering questions.

Learning outcomes

- Be familiar with the knowledge and understanding summarised in the End of topic checklist.
- Be able to apply this knowledge and understanding by answering the End of topic questions.

Resources

Student Book pages 154–156

Approach

Ask students to answer the End of topic questions in the Student Book.

Answers

End of topic questions mark scheme

Question	Correct answer	Marks
1 a)	Excretion is the removal from the body of waste substances from metabolic reactions in cells.	1
1 b)	i) Carbon dioxide and oxygen through stomata in leaves.	1
	ii) Carbon dioxide in lungs,	1
	sweat (water and salts) from skin,	1
	urea and excess substances in the blood from the kidneys	1
2	The wall of the glomerulus and Bowman's capsule are both very thin (one cell thick)	1
	and have gaps between the cells.	1
	This makes it easier for small molecules to be forced out of the blood and into the nephron to form the filtrate.	1
3 a)	Selective reabsorption is the reabsorption of some molecules more than others.	1
3 b)	i) Glucose is reabsorbed by diffusion and active transport.	1
	ii) Water is reabsorbed by osmosis.	1
3 c)	Much of the glucose reabsorption would stop because active transport requires energy	1
	from respiration in living cells.	1
	Osmosis might continue because it is a passive process.	1
3 d)	Glucose is essential in the body for cellular respiration.	1
	If the kidneys relied just on diffusion for reabsorbing glucose, much would be lost in the urine.	1
	Selective reabsorption takes back into the blood all the glucose that is in the filtrate, so that the body retains as much glucose as possible.	1
4	a) (hot sunny day) when in danger of dehydration.	1
	ADH makes the wall of the collecting duct more permeable	1
	and more water is reabsorbed from the filtrate back into the blood to help prevent dehydration.	1
5	Osmoregulation controls the concentration of water in the blood.	1
	As water moves easily by osmosis, this also controls the concentration of water in all the cells that the blood passes as it circulates round the body.	1
	If water concentration in cells falls too low, this affects reactions in cells and risks damaging the cells.	1
	If water concentration in cells increases too much, there is a risk of the cells bursting as they do not have a cell wall to resist expansion.	1
	Total:	24

Introduction

This topic introduces students to mechanisms of coordination and response in plants and in humans. It begins with the growth responses of plants. This is followed by activities on the human nervous system and hormonal system, with a discussion of the role of these systems in homeostasis.

Links to other topics

Sections	Essential background knowledge	Useful links
1 The nature and variety of living organisms	1a Characteristics of living organisms	
2 Structure and functions in living organisms	2a Level of organisation 2h Transport 2i Excretion	
3 Reproduction and inheritance		3a Reproduction

Topic overview

B2j.1	**Plant tropisms**
	This activity gives students the opportunity to investigate the growth responses of plants to light and gravity.
B2j.2	**Human nervous system**
	In this activity students learn about the structure of the human nervous system, including sense organs, effectors, nerves and the central nervous system. There is practical work on the speed of reaction, which also allows students to investigate the number of repeats on the reliability of an average. Students will also learn about the eye and its function in responding to light, and about reflex responses.
B2j.3	**Homeostasis**
	This activity looks at homeostasis in terms of control of body water content and core temperature. There is a practical opportunity to model the effect of sweat on cooling the body.
B2j.4	**Human hormonal system**
	This activity looks at how responses are controlled by the hormonal system. It also covers the differences between the hormonal and nervous systems.
B2j.5	**Consolidation and summary**
	This activity provides an opportunity for a quick recap on the ideas encountered in the topic as well as time for the students to answer the End of topic questions in the Student Book.

Activity B2j.1 Plant tropisms

Specification reference: B2j.2.80; B2j.2.83; B2j.2.84; B2j.2.85

Learning objectives

- Understand how organisms are able to respond to changes in their environment.
- Understand that plants respond to stimuli.
- Describe the geotropic and phototropic responses of roots and stems.
- Understand the role of auxin in the phototropic response of stems.

Learning outcomes

- Describe how plants respond to stimuli with tropic responses, such as geotropism in response to gravity and phototropism in response to light.
- Explain the role of auxin in the phototropic response of stems.

Common misconceptions

Many people say that 'plants don't move'. What they mean is that plants don't move from place to place as animals may do. There are many examples of plant movement (see Introduction: plant responses, below) as well as the growth responses that cause parts of the plant to change position.

Resources

Student Book pages 157–160

Worksheet B2j.1a Investigating geotropism

Worksheet B2j.1b Investigating phototropism

Resources for class practicals (see Technician's notes, following)

Approach

1. Introduction: plant responses

Ask students if plants move. The answer should be 'yes' from their work on Topic 1a earlier. Then give them two minutes to work in pairs to write down as many examples of plant movement as they can think of. Take examples from around the class.

If possible, play one or more video clips showing plant movement. There are many examples on the internet, such as the closing of a Venus fly trap in response to touch by an insect; leaves tracking the Sun's position; flowers opening and closing in response to light intensity; and the growth of shoots such as brambles or climbing plants. These should quickly dispel any ideas that 'plants don't move'.

Introduce the idea that plants move in response to changes in the environment. Ask students to use the examples they have just seen, and those they listed, to identify the *stimulus* (the change in the environment) and response.

2. Tropisms

Help students to distinguish between plant movements that are the result of growth and those that are not. Explain that movements as a result of growth are called *tropisms*.

If possible, a few days before the lesson, place a potted plant in a dark area with the pot lying on its side, as shown in the diagram. Show students the plant on the base and ask them what may have happened to the plant for it to grow out to the side.

176

After discussion, explain what you did, and tell students that plant growth in response to gravity is called *geotropism* (from *geo*, 'relating to the Earth'). You might also wish to introduce the idea of a *positive* response, towards the stimulus, and a *negative* response, away from the stimulus.

3. Geotropism

Worksheet B2j.1a gives students the opportunity to investigate the geotropic response of the shoot and root of a seedling. Sufficient growth of the root to see the response will take several days; for the shoot, it will take one to two weeks. If there isn't sufficient time, tell students that they will investigate the root response only. They should find the shoot has a negative geotropic response and the root has a positive geotropic response and should interpret these responses in terms of improved chances of survival.

More able students should develop this in terms of natural selection and the evolution of these responses – those plants with genes for these responses will have a greater chance of survival and so of passing on those genes to their offspring.

4. Phototropism

Worksheet B2j.1b gives students the opportunity to carry out the investigation presented in the Developing investigative skills box on page 160 of the Student Book. Note that if you do not have sufficient boxes for all students as described in the instructions, the set-up can be simplified by putting one dish of seedlings in conditions of one-sided light (e.g. a bright windowsill) and the other in the dark (e.g. in a dark cupboard). The investigation will need about a week to produce sufficient growth for measuring results.

Students should find that shoots have a positive phototropic response, growing towards one-sided light. Again, students should interpret these responses in terms of improved chances of survival.

More able students should develop this in terms of natural selection and the evolution of these responses – those plants with genes for these responses will have a greater chance of survival and so of passing on those genes to their offspring.

5. Auxin

Use pages 158–159 of the Student Book to explain the role of auxin in controlling tropisms. Students could be asked to each write down three points about auxins, and then discuss them with a neighbour to decide which are the most important points in explaining tropisms.

6. Consolidation: Zig-zag plant

Ask students to imagine a plant with a zig-zag (Z-shaped) shoot, and to write bullet point notes describing how they could create such a plant without using wires to hold the shoot. They should explain why their method would produce the required result. They should compare their method with another student and work together to produce an improved method from their comparison.

Technician's notes

You will need the following resources for the class practicals.

Be sure to check the latest safety notes on these resources before proceeding.

B2j.1a Investigating geotropism

You may use any suitable seeds that germinate easily and are easy to handle, such as wheat, pea or bean. Soak the seeds for 24 hours in water and then leave to germinate in a warm dark place for several days until the developing roots are about 1 cm long. If signs of decay in the seeds are noted, the seeds and the cotton wool or paper should be disposed of as soon as possible and the container disinfected.

Class practical, per group:

3 germinating seeds with root about 1 cm long (see note above)
Petri dish with lid
3 pins, long mounting pins are best
cotton wool or absorbent paper
scissors
water
marker pen
sticky tape
modelling clay, or other method for stabilising the Petri dish on its side
light-proof box (e.g. cardboard box)

B2j.1b Investigating phototropism

Any suitable seeds that germinate easily and are easy to handle can be used, such as wheat, pea or bean. The seeds will need to be soaked for 24 hours in water and then left to germinate in a warm dark place for several days until the shoots are just beginning to develop.

If the container is set in front of a light bank, it must be one that is designed for continuous illumination. Ordinary bench lamps (that could be knocked over) should not be left on for extended periods of time.

Class practical, per group:

2 small boxes with lids
sharp knife or scissors
black paint and paintbrush, or black paper and sticky tape
2 Petri dishes
absorbent paper
water
germinating seeds (see note above)
access to light, such as windowsill or light bank

Answers

Developing investigative skills, page 160

1. The box should be set up near to a strong light source, so that the light entering the box is clearly one-sided. The seeds should be kept moist, but not wet, during germination and as the seedlings grow. Growth could be measured as angle between tip of shoot and base for quantitative data, or using photographic evidence for qualitative data.

2. The control needs to be set up in exactly the same conditions as the test apparatus, but with light reaching the shoots equally from all directions (e.g. with the top of the box removed and an overhead light).

3. a) The seedlings in the windowed box should have grown so that their tips are heading towards the window. The control shoots should grow straight up.

    b) The seedlings in the windowed box should grow towards the one-sided light (i.e. grow at an angle towards the light) demonstrating positive phototropism, while the control shoots should grow straight up as they receive light equally from all sides.

4. Plants will need to be grown in water so that the roots can be exposed to light (e.g. large bulbs such as hyacinth, grown suspended over water). Then two similar plants will need setting up so one has roots exposed to one-sided light and the other to light all around the roots. Growth over a period of several weeks may be needed to show if the roots in one-sided light grow in a particular direction in relation to the light, compared with the all-around-light roots.

Page 160

1. A tropism is a growth response of a plant to a stimulus.

2. a) Shoots grow towards light.

   b) Roots grow in the direction of the force of gravity.

3. Auxin is produced in the tip of the growing shoot and diffuses down the shoot. Auxin on the bright/light side of the shoot moves across the shoot to the darker side as it diffuses down the shoot. Cells on the dark side of the shoot elongate more than the cells on the light side of the shoot, so the shoot starts to bend as it grows so that the tip is pointing towards the light.

B2j.1a Investigating geotropism

In this investigation you will look at the geotropic response of developing roots, and if there is time, also of shoots.

Apparatus

3 germinating seeds with root about 1 cm long

Petri dish with lid

3 pins

cotton wool or absorbent paper

scissors

water

marker pen

sticky tape

modelling clay

light-proof box (e.g. cardboard box)

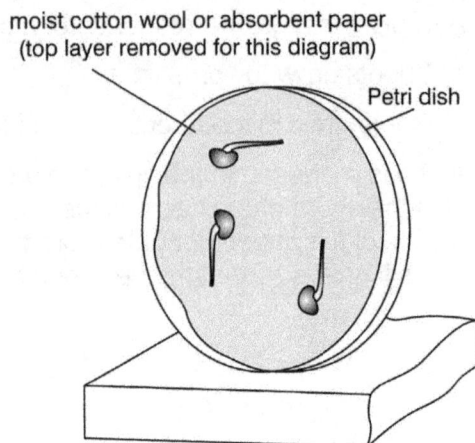
moist cotton wool or absorbent paper (top layer removed for this diagram)

Petri dish

SAFETY INFORMATION
Wash hands after handling seeds.
Take care when using pins to stick seeds onto cotton wool or paper.

Method

1. Use the pen to mark a point on the edge of the Petri dish. This is the reference point.

2. Cut two discs of cotton wool or several discs of absorbent paper to fit snugly within the dish.

3. Fill half of the base of the Petri dish with cotton wool or discs of absorbent paper. Pour on enough water to make the paper or cotton wool wet, leave for a minute then pour off any excess water.

4. Arrange three germinating seeds in the dish so that their roots are pointing in different directions. Carefully and gently attach each germinating seed to the cotton wool / paper using a pin.

5. Gently place another layer of cotton wool, or sufficient layers of absorbent paper, over the seeds to fill the depth of the dish. Replace the lid of the dish.

6. Stand the dish on its edge, with the marked point at the bottom, and use modelling clay to hold the dish in place so that it does not wobble.

7. Place a light-proof box to completely cover the dish.

8. After a few days, carefully remove the lid and the top layer of cotton wool or layers of paper to expose the seeds.

9. Draw the seedlings, making sure you record the relative position of the marked point that indicated the 'down' position.

10. If you are allowed to continue the practical for longer, carefully pour in a little more water, and then pour off the excess without disturbing the seeds. Replace the top layers and lid and stand the dish on its edge again, with the marked point down.

11. Repeat steps 8 and 9 every few days until the shoot has grown at least 1 cm.

Analyse and interpret data

1. Describe your results (a) for the roots and (b) for the shoots if you continued the practical.

2. Explain your results, using your knowledge of tropisms.

3. Explain the survival advantage to a plant of responding to gravity like this.

Evaluate data and methods

1. Covering the seeds with a light-proof box excluded any light. Explain why this is important in this investigation.

B2j.1b Investigating phototropism

In this investigation you will look at the phototropic response of growing shoots.

Apparatus

two small boxes with lids

sharp knife or scissors

black paint and paintbrush, or black paper and sticky tape

2 Petri dishes

absorbent paper

water

germinating seeds

access to light

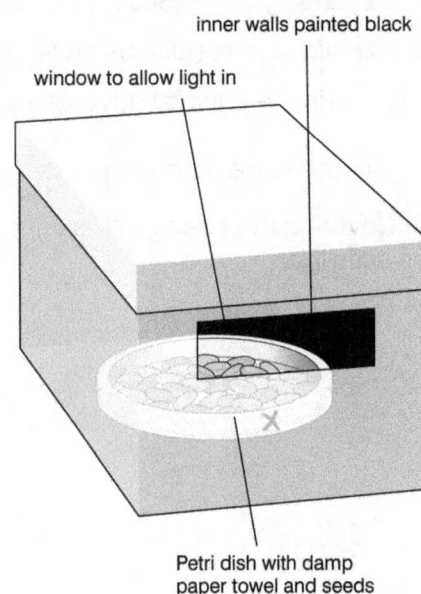

inner walls painted black

window to allow light in

Petri dish with damp paper towel and seeds

SAFETY INFORMATION

Wash hands after handling seeds.

Take care when using the sharp knife or scissors.

Method

1. If available, prepare one box by cutting a window out of one side as shown in the diagram. Either paint the inside of this box with black paint and leave to dry, or line it with black paper.

2. Line the base of each Petri dish with absorbent paper, pour in enough water to wet the paper. Leave the dish for about a minute, then pour off any excess water.

3. Place several seeds gently on the paper in each dish, then place one dish in each box and replace the lids.

4. Place the windowed box near a source of bright light, such as a windowsill or bank of lights.

5. Every couple of days, check that the absorbent paper in both dishes is still moist, but not wet. Add a little more water if needed. The paper should not be wet. If the paper is wet, the seeds may rot.

6. After a week, check the shoots of the seeds to see in which direction they are growing. If there has been insufficient growth for obvious results, continue the investigation for up to another week.

7. Draw the results from both dishes, remembering to indicate the direction of light for those in the windowed box.

Analyse and interpret data

1. Describe your results (a) for the dark box and (b) for the windowed box.

2. Explain your results, using your knowledge of tropisms.

3. Explain the survival advantage to a plant of responding to light like this.

Evaluate data & methods

1. Explain how making the inside of the windowed box black may have improved the response of the seedlings in that box.

Activity B2j.2 Human nervous system

Specification reference: B2j.2.80; B2j.2.82; B2j.2.87; B2j.2.88; B2j.2.89; B2j.2.90; B2j.2.91; B2j.2.92

Learning objectives

- Understand how organisms are able to respond to changes in their environment.
- Understand that a coordinated response requires a stimulus, a receptor and an effector.
- Understand that the central nervous system consists of the brain and spinal cord and is linked to sense organs by nerves.
- Understand that stimulation of receptors in the sense organs sends electrical impulses along nerves into and out of the central nervous system, resulting in rapid responses.
- Understand the role of neurotransmitters at synapses.
- Describe the structure and functioning of a simple reflex arc illustrated by the withdrawal of a finger from a hot object.
- Describe the structure and function of the eye as a receptor.
- Understand the function of the eye in focusing on near and distant objects, and in responding to changes in light intensity.

Learning outcomes

- Know that a coordinated response requires a stimulus, receptor and effector.
- Understand the human central nervous system consists of the brain and spinal cord, which are linked to the sense organs of the body by nerves.
- Describe how stimulation of a sense organ produces electrical impulses in nerves, leading to a rapid response.
- Describe the role of neurotransmitters in a synapse.
- Know that an example of a simple reflex arc is the withdrawing of a finger from a hot object.
- Describe the structure of the eye as an organ specialised for the reception of light stimuli.
- Understand how the eye can change focus between near and far objects, and can respond to changes in light intensity.

Common misconceptions

Many people think that we see with our eyes and hear with our ears. This is incorrect. Our eyes and ears are collectors of information from the environment (receptors), responding to changes in light or sound by sending electrical impulses to the brain through nerves. It is the responses in the brain that produce what we 'see' or 'hear'. For example, a person with perfectly functioning eyes will not 'see' if their optic nerves have been cut as a result of an accident.

Encourage students to talk in terms of 'nerve impulses' not 'messages in the nerves'; otherwise they will lose marks in their exam.

Resources

Student Book pages 160–167

Worksheet B2j.2a Speed of reaction

Worksheet B2j.2b The eye

Resources for class practical (see Technician's notes, following)

Approach

1. Introduction: human senses

Remind students of the concepts of stimulus and response from their work on plant reactions to the environment. Ask them for a few examples of stimulus and response in humans. Extend the discussion to the concepts of *receptors* (sense organs that detect stimuli) and *effectors* (organs that carry out responses). Use the suggested examples and ask students to identify the receptor and effector in each.

Give students three minutes to work individually or in pairs to find an example of responses to as many different kinds of stimuli that they can think of, identifying the sensor and receptor in each case.

Take examples from around the class until you have covered all the sense organs mentioned in the table on page 163 of the Student Book.

2. Structure of the nervous system

Ask students what connects sensors and effectors in the human body – they should be able to give the answer *nerves*. Use page 161 of the Student Book to introduce the nervous system of the human body. Students should be able to identify the role of sense organs, peripheral nerves, the central nervous system and effectors in responding to changes in the environment.

3. Speed of reaction

Worksheet B2j.2a gives students the opportunity to test the speed of their reaction to a stimulus, in this case catching a falling ruler. The method is very simple and quick, so students can easily collect a large number of data for analysis. This makes it particularly useful for looking at the effect of the number of repeats on the reliability of a result, as described on the worksheet.

In addition, if it is possible to collect the class data on a spreadsheet, with additional data on other variables (such as which hand was used to catch (dominant hand or other), gender, athletic achievement, types of computer games played, time of day tested), students can analyse if these variables have any effect on speed of reaction. Allow time before the investigation for students to discuss what might affect speed of reaction, and for them to suggest variables on which to collect data for testing later.

The graph of averages should show that around five or six repeats of an investigation produce an acceptable approximation of an average from a larger number of repeats. This should help students when planning their own investigations where repeat measurements will be needed.

The comparison of speed of reaction with other factors, such as gender, sporting ability, computer game preferences, may or may not show differences. For the more able, introduce the idea of reliability of difference, such as how big a difference is needed for it to be considered a real difference. With students who are good at maths, this is an opportunity to discuss statistical significance and introduce the use of standard error.

Students should not wear open-toed shoes when carrying out the investigation.

4. Reflex responses

Use page 166 of the Student Book to introduce the idea of reflex responses. Students could also research examples using books or the internet. They should be able to explain the response in terms of the reflex arc, so ask them to draw a reflex arc for one of their examples using the diagram of response to touch of a hot object on page 166 of the Student Book.

The response of the pupil to light can be demonstrated easily with a small torch in a dimly lit room. Allow a minute for eyes to adjust to the light conditions, then shine the torch towards the face but from the side (not directly into the eyes). If you have sufficient small mirrors, students could investigate their own response.

SAFETY INFORMATION: A bright light shone into the eye produces an after-image that lingers for several minutes and can be alarming for students. Students with albinism should not have bright lights shone into their eyes.

Discuss the difference between a reflex response and a response that involves a thought, such as the response to catching the ruler on Worksheet B2j.1a. They should identify not only a difference in speed (reflex responses generally being faster) and a difference in purpose (reflex responses are generally ones that protect us from harm, such as the heat/touch reflex and light/pupil reflex).

More able students should explain the evolution of speedy reflex responses in terms of improved chances of survival.

5. Synapses and neurotransmitters

Use page 162 of the Student Book to explain the roles of synapses and neurotransmitters. Students could be asked to produce a flow chart or cartoon sequence to illustrate what happens between a nerve impulse arriving at a synapse and a new impulse leaving.

6. The eye

Students will understand this part of the topic better if they are familiar with using lenses of different kinds. If they have not yet had this opportunity (usually covered in Physics), or do not seem confident in this learning, allow them a little time with a light ray box and convex lenses of different focal lengths to investigate the relationship between focal length and lens shape. They should then be able to apply this to their explanations of the focusing of the eye on near and distant objects.

Worksheet B2j.2b provides two partly completed diagrams of the eye. These can be used in many ways, for example to label the key structures of the eye and the roles they play in allowing us to see, or to draw the light rays from a near or far object and lens shape needed to focus the image properly on the retina.

7. Consolidation: key points

Ask students to make a list of five key points from their work on the human nervous system, for a friend who has missed this work. They should then compare their points with another student and decide on the best five points to cover everything in the work. Take examples from around the class and encourage discussion to produce a class list of the key points on this topic.

Technician's notes

You will need the following resources for the class practical.

Be sure to check the latest safety notes on these resources before proceeding.

B2j.2a Speed of reaction

In this investigation, students will test the speed of their reaction to a stimulus. Each group will need a ruler, at least 50 cm long and made, ideally, of shatterproof plastic or wood.

Answers

Page 165

1. a) The cornea is transparent so light passes through it easily into the eye. The cornea also refracts light to help focus it onto the retina.

   b) The pupil is a hole surrounded by the iris, that controls the amount of light that passes into the eye.

   c) The retina contains the light-sensitive cells that respond to light.

2. As light intensity increases, the pupil gets smaller, reducing the amount of light that can enter the eye. This change happens because the radial muscles in the iris relax and circular muscles contract. As light intensity decreases, the pupil gets larger, increasing the amount of light that can enter the eye. This change happens because the radial muscles in the iris contract and circular muscles relax.

3. Light entering the eye from a near object needs to be refracted more than light from a distant object in order to focus it on the retina. The ciliary muscles contract, which reduces the tension on the ligaments that are attached to the lens. This allows the lens to become thicker and more rounded, which means it refracts light more.

Page 167

1. A reflex response is a simple response of receptor →nerve→spinal cord→nerve→effector, that often does not include the brain. This makes it possible to respond to a stimulus very quickly. Reflex responses are usually important in survival, for example to protect you from holding on to something dangerous, or blinking to protect the eye if something comes toward it.

2. Heat causes the receptor cells in the skin to respond. The receptor cells cause nerve cells (sensory neurones) to send electrical impulses to the spinal cord. The nerve cells pass the electrical impulses to nerve cells in the spinal cord (relay neurones), which pass the electrical impulses to nerve cells in the nerves leading to the arm muscles (motor neurones). These nerve cells pass the electrical impulses to the effector cells i.e. the muscles, which cause the muscle cells to contract and move the hand away from the heat.

186

B2j.2a Speed of reaction

In this investigation you will test the speed of your reaction to a stimulus: a falling ruler. You will use the repeat results to estimate the fewest number of repeats that will give you a reliable answer.

Before you collect any data, consider which factors may affect the results. For example, you may think you respond faster in the morning than in the afternoon. Also consider factors that vary between different people that might affect rate of reaction. As a group or class, decide which factors you wish to test and collect data on these to add to your class or group results.

Apparatus

long ruler (at least 50 cm)

SAFETY INFORMATION
Take care with the falling ruler.
Do not wear open-toed shoes for this practical.

Method

1. Work with a partner. One of you is the test subject and the other is the researcher. Change places halfway through the investigation so that each of you will have your reactions tested.

2. The test subject should stand with their hand in front of them with an open grip in anticipation of catching the ruler. The researcher should hold the ruler just above their open hand, with the 0 cm point on the ruler between their fingers.

3. The researcher should then drop the ruler without warning. The test subject should close their hand as quickly as possible to catch the ruler. The researcher should wait different times before the ruler is dropped, to make it more difficult for the test subject to anticipate when it will fall.

4. Record the point on the ruler where it was caught, to the nearest millimetre. If the ruler is dropped, or caught in a very short distance, disregard that result and repeat the trial.

5. Carry out the test 15 times, and record all valid results.

6. Then change places and repeat steps 2–5.

Analyse and interpret data

1. Using your own results, calculate averages as follows:

   • Take the first two results and calculate and record the average.

   • Take the first three results and calculate and record the average.

Repeat this until you have calculated and recorded the average for all 15 results.

2. Plot your averages on a graph, with number of tries on the x-axis and average values on the y-axis. For a try of one, plot the value of your first result.

3. Describe the shape of your graph and explain what it means.

4. Use your graph to determine the smallest number of repeats that gives a reasonable estimate of the average of all results. Explain how you can apply this finding to other investigations.

5. If possible, collect the final average from all students on a class spreadsheet. Collect data on all the factors discussed and agreed by the class before the investigation.

6. Use the spreadsheet to investigate if there is any link between any of the factors and speed of reaction. For example, if you wish to test the effect of sporting ability, you could calculate an average for each group of students who specialise in a particular sport, and compare it with an average for those who do not play a sport regularly.

Evaluate data and methods

1. Describe any problems that you had with the method, and suggest how you could improve the method to get a more reliable way of measuring speed of reaction.

B2j.2b The eye

Your teacher will explain how you are to use these diagrams.

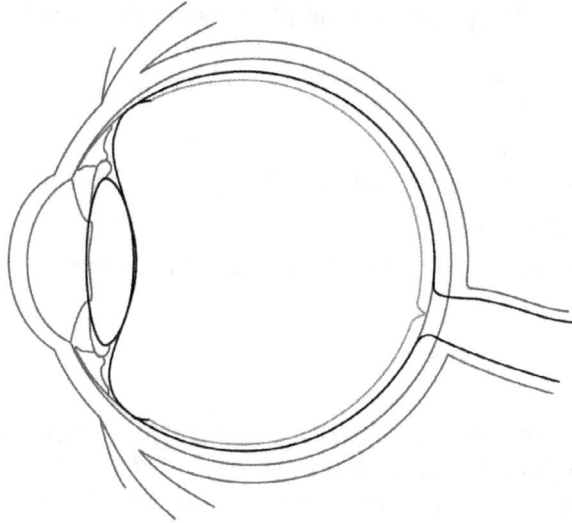

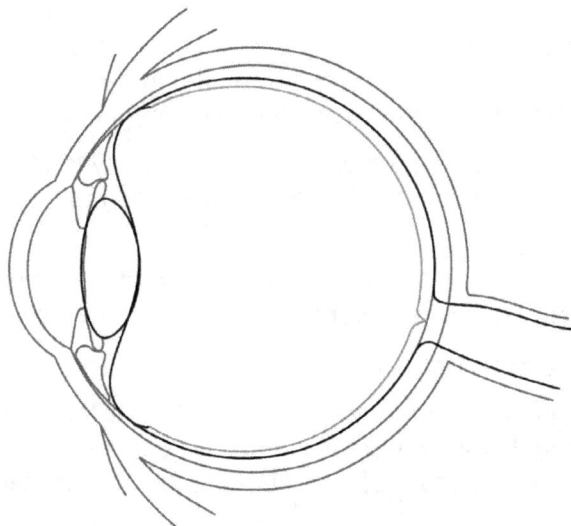

189

Activity B2j.3 Homeostasis

Specification reference: B2j.2.81; B2j2.93

Learning objectives

- Understand that homeostasis is the maintenance of a constant internal environment, and that body water content and body temperature are both examples of homeostasis.
- Describe the role of the skin in temperature regulation, with reference to sweating, vasoconstriction and vasodilation.

Learning outcomes

- Understand that homeostasis is the maintenance of a constant internal environment, such as body water content and body temperature.
- Describe how the skin regulates internal body temperature by sweating, vasoconstriction and vasodilation.

Common misconceptions

When discussing homeostasis, it is important to talk in terms of *core body temperature* rather than just *body temperature*, because temperature varies greatly between different parts of the body. Too much variation in core body temperature (particularly of the brain, heart and liver) is a risk to health.

Resources

Student Book pages 167–169

Worksheet B2j.3a Investigating a model for sweating

Resources for class practical (see Technician's notes, following)

Approach

1. Introduction

Ask students to list all the processes that increase the water content of the body, and those that decrease it. They could do this individually at first and then contribute their ideas to come up with a whole class list. Revise work from Topic 2i on the maintenance of body water content from work on osmoregulation in the kidney. If it was introduced then, remind students of the term *homeostasis*, and ask them to define the word in terms of body water content. If homeostasis was not introduced then, give them the term now and ask them to define it in terms of body water content.

Discuss the definitions and agree a general definition that could apply to other variables inside the body. Remind students of the need for homeostasis by asking what would happen if there were no homeostatic control in the body.

Ask students to suggest other variables in the body that might need to be controlled. They should be able to suggest pH and temperature from their work on enzymes and excretion earlier.

2. Body temperature control demonstration

Choose a student who won't mind the attention. If available, attach a temperature sensor to a fingertip on one hand and then the other hand. If you do not have sensors, use a thermometer (e.g. a temperature strip thermometer). Measure the temperature of both finger tips – they should register similar values.

Show students a large bowl of cold water (around 10 °C) and tell them that the test subject will place one hand in the bowl. Ask them to predict how the skin temperature of the other (dry) hand will change over the following five minutes. It is likely that they will suggest no change since that hand is not in cold water – don't respond to their predictions at this point.

Once you have a prediction from the class, ask the test subject to place the hand without the sensor into the water and leave it for five minutes. Record the change in skin temperature of the other hand. It should go down.

Then ask students to read the section on temperature control in the Student Book (pages 167–168) and to apply what it says about temperature falling too far to what they have seen in the demonstration. They should be able to explain that cold blood returning to the brain from the cold hand triggers a response resulting in general vasoconstriction. This takes warm blood away from the surface of both hands, so the surface of both hands will be cooler.

SAFETY INFORMATION: Allow students to remove their hands from the cold water when they feel uncomfortable. Some students have reduced sensitivity, so do not allow the student to submerge their hands for longer than is sensible (this would need to be tested by the teacher).

3. Investigating a model for sweating

Worksheet B2j.3a provides a method that could be used to produce similar results to those in the Developing investigative skills box on page 169 of the Student Book. It uses wet and dry paper towels surrounding tubes of warm water to model the effect of sweating on heat loss.

Students should find that the tube wrapped in a wet paper towel loses heat more rapidly than the one in the dry paper towel. They should be able to explain this in terms of heat transfer – the water molecules in the paper towel gain heat energy from the tube and evaporate, removing the heat energy more rapidly than the transfer from the 'dry' tube by conduction and convection. This shows that sweating increases the rate of heat loss from a hot body. The water should start at about 50 °C but not higher than this.

4. Homeostasis of body temperature

Remind students of the diagrams they drew in Topic 2i to show the homeostatic control of body water content. Ask them to draw similar diagrams for the control of core body temperature, starting with 'body too hot' on the left side of a blank piece of paper and 'body too cold' on the right side. They should include not only the receptor in their diagrams, but also the effectors and how their responses return the core body temperature to a 'normal' point of around 37 °C.

As before, encourage students to look at this as a continuous process that keeps core body temperature within tight limits. Make sure they are able to explain why keeping core body temperature within tight limits is so important to the body.

5. Consolidation: life in the desert

Tell students that they have been asked to identify the equipment needed for an expedition across a very hot, dry place such as the Sahara Desert. Remind them that as the expedition will constantly be on the move, equipment must be limited to only what is essential for survival.

Give students three minutes in small groups to write down an equipment list, then take examples from each group asking them to justify their choices. Make sure the 'essential' items are associated with the need to control body temperature and body water content.

Technician's notes

You will need the following resources for the class practical.

Be sure to check the latest safety notes on these resources before proceeding.

B2j.3a Investigating a model for sweating

In this investigation students will use a model for sweating to investigate the effect of evaporation on heat loss from a surface.

Class practical, per group:

2 boiling tubes	tube rack or 2 small beakers
hand hot water (about 50 °C)	large pipette (optional)
2 paper towels	2 thermometers or temperature sensors
2 elastic bands	stopwatch or clock

Answers

Page 169

1. Homeostasis is the maintenance of conditions inside the body within limits that allow cells to work efficiently.

2. Control of core body temperature, and control of concentration of water in the blood.

3. Skin blood vessels dilate when the core body temperature is too high. This allows heat energy carried by the blood to reach the skin surface more easily and so be transferred to the environment more rapidly. Skin blood vessels constrict when the core body temperature falls too low. This reduces blood flow to near the skin's surface, so heat energy cannot be transferred as easily to the skin surface and so cannot be transferred to the environment as quickly. This keeps more heat energy within the body.

Developing investigative skills, page 169

1. The hot water in the tube is similar to the heat inside the human body. The wet towel models sweating skin on the surface of the hot body.

2. Another tube set up identically, with hot water, etc. but with a dry paper towel surrounding it.

3. Graph should have time on the x-axis and temperature on the y-axis, with both sets of points drawn on the same axes and clearly labelled. Each set of points should be joined by lines of best fit. There should be a comment about the outlier at 10 minutes of the dry towel.

4. The graph shows that temperature decreased in both tubes over time, but that it decreased faster in the tube surrounded by the wet towel compared with the tube surrounded by the dry towel.

5. Heat transfer from the hot water in the tube to the environment is faster when wrapped in a wet towel compared with a dry towel.

6. Heat energy is transferred from the water in the tube to the water molecules in the towel, increasing their energy and allowing those water molecules to evaporate more quickly. As the water molecules evaporate into the air, they take the energy with them, so the tube cools down.

B2j.3a Investigating a model for sweating

In this investigation you will use a model for sweating to investigate the effect of evaporation on heat loss from a surface.

Apparatus

2 boiling tubes

2 paper towels

tube rack or 2 small beakers

(optional) stopwatch or clock

2 thermometers or temperature sensors

hand hot water (about 50 °C)

2 elastic bands

large pipette

SAFETY INFORMATION
Take care handling hot water.

Method

1. Wrap one boiling tube in a dry paper towel, leaving the top open, and fix it in place with an elastic band.

2. Wet the other paper towel with water, then wrap it around the other tube and fix it in place with the other elastic band. (Or, if it is easier, wrap the paper towel around the tube and then wet it.)

3. Without spilling any water (suggest using a large pipette), carefully fill each tube with the warm water and place it in the rack or a beaker.

4. Place the thermometers or sensors into the water in each tube and leave for one minute.

5. Take the temperature of both tubes and set this as time 0. Record your measurements.

6. Take the temperature of both tubes every two minutes for the next 20 minutes and record your measurements.

7. Draw a suitable table to display your results.

Analyse and interpret data

1. Use your results to draw a suitable graph, displaying both sets of results on the same graph.

2. Draw a curve through each set of points and identify any anomalous values. Try to explain any anomalous values.

3. Describe the curves on your graph and try to explain them using your knowledge of heat transfer and evaporation.

4. Explain the relevance of your results to the effect of sweating on body temperature regulation.

Evaluate data and methods

1. Explain why you did not take measurements from the time that the thermometers or sensors were placed into the water in the tubes.

2. Describe any problems that you had with this practical and suggest how you would change the method to produce more reliable results.

Activity B2j.4 Human hormonal system

Specification reference: B2j.2.86; B2j.2.94; B2j.2.95**B**

Learning objectives

- Describe how nervous and hormonal communication control responses and understand the differences between the two systems.
- Understand the sources, roles and effects of the following hormones: adrenaline, insulin, testosterone, progesterone and oestrogen.
- Understand the sources, roles and effects of the following hormones: ADH, FSH and LH. **(B)**

Learning outcomes

- Describe how, in humans, the nervous system produces rapid responses to stimuli by a particular effector, while the hormonal system usually produces slower responses that last longer and may involve more than one effector
- Understand the sources, roles and effects of adrenaline, insulin, testosterone, progesterone, oestrogen, ADH, FSH and LH.

Common misconceptions

Many students do not appreciate that all cells in the body are exposed to a particular hormone because it is transported in the blood, but that it only exerts its effects on target cells or target organs.

Resources

Student Book pages 169–171

Approach

1. Introduction

Remind students of ADH in Topic 2i as an example of a hormone. Ask them to identify the receptor, control mechanism and effector in this control system.

Give students one minute to think of as many differences as they can between this example and the nervous system's response to a stimulus. Take examples from around the class and encourage discussion to decide which are suitable for recording on the board.

2. Different hormones

Ask students to read pages 169–171 of the Student Book on the different hormones. They should make notes of the name of each hormone, where it is produced, where it has an effect on the body and what that effect is.

Note that in some cases there is more than one effect, and students should identify them all. Students should use their notes to write five questions that they then use to test each other.

3. Comparison between systems

Return to the examples produced in the Introduction and ask students if they can add any further examples of differences between the two systems. The final list should include the following:

- nervous system fast, hormonal system usually slower
- nervous system uses electrical impulses (except for chemical neurotransmitters across synapses); hormonal system uses just chemical signals/hormones

- nervous system usually responds by a small group of effectors (such as muscles), hormonal system may respond in changes in many ways, such as secretion of other chemicals, changes to heart rate, dilation of pupils, uptake of glucose by liver and muscle cells

- nervous system responses don't usually last long, hormonal system responses generally last longer.

Then ask students to identify similarities between the two systems (they both produces changes in the body as a result of changes in the environment). Finally, ask why it is an advantage to have these two different systems in the body.

Answers

Page 171 (top)

1. Homeostasis is the regulation of conditions inside the body so that they remain fairly constant; so the concentration of blood glucose is kept within a narrow range.

2. Insulin is released from the pancreas when blood glucose concentration is high. It causes muscle and liver cells to take in glucose and convert it to glycogen for storage, so that blood glucose concentration falls.

3. The more insulin they inject the more glucose will be taken up by cells, so they have to make sure that blood glucose concentration will not fall too low, because that is dangerous.

4. Exercise needs energy from respiration, and that is supplied by the breakdown of glucose in muscle cells. This will mean that blood glucose concentration falls because the glucose will move down its concentration gradient into the muscle cells. With a lower blood glucose concentration, less insulin is needed in the blood.

Page 171 (bottom)

1. a) A chemical messenger in the body, that produces a change in the activity of some cells.

   b) A gland that secrete hormone.

   c) An organ that contains cells which are affected by hormones.

2.

Hormone	Where produced	Effects
adrenaline	adrenal glands	prepares body for action, e.g. increases heart rate, increases breathing rate, dilates pupils, causes glucose to be released into blood
insulin	pancreas	causes liver and muscle cells to remove glucose from blood
testosterone	testes	produces secondary sexual characteristics in boys and needed for sperm production
progesterone	ovaries	involved in control of menstrual cycle
oestrogen	ovaries	involved in control of menstrual cycle, produces secondary sexual characteristics in girls

Activity B2j.5 Consolidation and summary

Learning objectives

- To review the learning points of the topic.
- To test understanding through answering questions.

Learning outcomes

- Be familiar with the knowledge and understanding summarised in the End of topic checklist.
- Be able to apply this knowledge and understanding by answering the End of topic questions.

Resources

Student Book pages 172–176

Approach

1. Consolidation: traffic lights

Give students three cards, one red, one yellow and one green. Ask a range of questions covering the material in all of Topic 2j and ask them to hold up the red card if they are not sure of the answer, the yellow card if they think they know the right answer, and the green card if they are certain of the answer. Check the latter by asking one or two students who are holding up a green card to give an answer.

2. End of topic questions

Ask students to answer the End of topic questions in the Student Book.

Answers

End of topic questions mark scheme

Question	Correct answer	Marks
1 a)	ii)	1
	The response to light that is brighter in one direction than others is a growth response.	1
1 b)	Positive phototropism means growing towards light.	1
1 c)	If shoots grow towards the light, there is a better chance of the plant receiving more light on its leaves,	1
	so are able to carry out photosynthesis faster and produce more food.	1
1 d)	Positive geotropism means growing in the direction of the force of gravity, that is, down into the Earth.	1
1 e)	Roots that grow down into the soil are more likely to find soil water (and dissolved mineral ions),	1
	and so be able to supply the substances that the plant needs for healthy and rapid growth.	1
2 a)	They allow the body to respond to changes in the environment.	1

2 b)					6

System	Cells of system	Method of transmission	Speed of response
nervous	neurones, receptor cells, effector cells	electrical impulses through neurones, chemical neurotransmitters across synapses	rapid
hormonal	glands, target cells	chemical hormones	slower (but longer-lasting)

2 c)	The nervous system enables the body to respond quickly but for a short time, such as using muscles to move.	1
	The hormonal system enables the body to respond more slowly over a longer time, such as controlling blood glucose concentration,	1
	and also can affect areas in different parts of the body at the same time, as with adrenaline affecting the heart, lungs and eyes.	1
	These different responses enable the body to respond effectively to different stimuli,	1
	and so increase the chances of survival.	1
3 a)	Answers may vary, but should include the following:	
	• eyes sense the direction and speed of the ball	1
	• electrical impulses via nerve cells from the eye to the central nervous system including the brain	1
	• brain identifies best place to stand and how to move the racquet in order to hit the ball	1
	• electrical impulses to muscles in the arm move the racquet into position and then to hit the ball	1
3 b)	No, this is not a reflex action	1
	because the brain is involved, using memories of training in order to give the best response.	1
4 a)	There is no light in the mine, so there is no stimulus	1
	for the light-sensitive receptor cells in the retina.	1
4 b)	The cataract causes light to be refracted in different directions,	1
	so the image produced will not be very clear.	1
4 c)	A long-sighted person cannot focus the light from something nearby clearly on the retina,	1
	and needs additional converging lenses in the spectacles to produce proper focusing for a clear image.	1

Question	Correct answer	Marks
5 a)	Receptor: heat sensors in the skin and receptor cells in the hypothalamus that detect temperature of the blood flowing through them.	2
	Monitoring area: hypothalamus in the brain.	1
	Effectors: sweat glands if too hot; skin blood vessel walls to produce vasoconstriction or vasodilation; muscle cells if too cold to cause shivering.	3
5 b)	Heat energy at the surface of the skin is transferred to the cooler environment by conduction and radiation.	1
	Increased blood flow to the surface of the skin allows heat energy from the blood to be transferred to the skin surface faster than if the blood flow is reduced.	1
5 c)	The core of the body contains the lungs, heart and liver, where many essential reactions take place.	1
	Temperature affects the rate of reactions by affecting the rate of movement of molecules.	1
	Also, if temperature rises too far, enzymes that control reactions can denature.	1
	Slower reactions, due to a core temperature that is either too high or too low, can reduce the ability of the cells to carry out the life processes as quickly as needed for survival.	1
6 a)	Pancreas – liver / muscle tissue – conversion of glucose to glycogen for storage.	3
6 b)	Adrenal glands – heart – increased heart rate.	3
	Total:	50

198 © HarperCollins*Publishers* Ltd 2017

Question	Correct answer	Marks
2 a)	cell membrane	1
	cytoplasm	1
	nucleus	1
	chromosomes	1
	cell wall	1
	cellulose	1
	vacuole	1
	chloroplasts	1
	chlorophyll	1
	photosynthesis	1
2 b)	Ticks in table as shown below. 1 mark for each one correct.	8

Structure	Cell	Tissue	Organ
Blood		✓	
Brain			✓
Liver			✓
Muscle		✓	
Neurone	✓		
Ovum	✓		
Skin			✓
Sperm	✓		

Question	Correct answer	Marks
3 a)	Completed table as shown. 1 mark for each entry.	5

Biological molecule	Units that make up the molecule
Glycogen	glucose
Lipids	fatty acids glycerol
Proteins	amino acids
Starch	glucose

Question	Correct answer	Marks
3 b)	i) Add Benedict's solution to the sample to be tested (in a test tube).	1
	Heat to 95 °C.	1
	A colour change from blue to green to yellow to orange to red-brown / blue to red-brown indicates that glucose/a reducing sugar is present in the sample.	1

Question	Correct answer	Marks
	ii) Add iodine solution to a food sample (on a spotting tile).	1
	A blue-black colour indicates that starch is present in the sample.	1
3 c)	i) stomach protease: about 1.8	1
	small intestine protease 8.0	1
	ii) Enzyme activity depends on the substrate (in this instance, a protein) being able to fit into the shape of the enzyme (the active site of the enzyme).	1
	At pHs other than the optimum, the structure of the enzyme / active site changes,	1
	so the substrate is unable to fit as well.	1
	At a certain point, the structure of the enzyme / active site is changed permanently (it is denatured) and it is no longer able to work.	1
3 d)	stomach	1
	pancreas	1
	small intestine	1
4 a)	+32.2	1
	+21.8	1
	−2.2	1
	−13.5	1
	−19.9	1
	−20.4	1
4 b)	i) Axes drawn with concentration on *x*-axis and average percentage on *y*-axis change	1
	Axes labelled, with units	1
	Points plotted correctly	1
	Points joined appropriately	1
	ii) Student answer from graph:	
	accurate reading of intersection with *x*-axis	1
	correct units ($mol\ dm^{-3}$)	1
	iii) The cell membranes in the cells of the potato cylinders are partially permeable membranes.	1
	In low concentrations of sucrose and distilled water, water moves from where it is in high concentration in the solutions, to where it is in lower concentrations in the potato cells	1
	by osmosis,	1
	so the cylinders increase in mass.	1

Question	Correct answer	Marks
	In high concentrations of sucrose, water is in higher concentration in the potato cells so water moves out of the potato cells by osmosis,	1
	so the potato cylinders decrease in mass.	1
	When the concentrations of water inside the cells and out are equal/in equilibrium, there is no net movement of water.	1
5 a)	A: branch of renal artery / afferent arteriole	1
	B: glomerulus	1
	C: Bowman's capsule	1
	D: proximal convoluted tubule	1
	E: loop of Henle	1
	F: collecting duct	1
	G: distal convoluted tubule	1
	H: branch of renal vein / efferent arteriole	1
5 b)	Amino acids, glucose and ions are forced through the walls of the glomerulus and Bowman's capsule by ultrafiltration.	1
	The proteins remain in the blood as their molecules are too large to be filtered through into the Bowman's capsule.	1
	Amino acids and glucose are selectively reabsorbed along the convoluted tubule.	1
	Ions may be excreted in the urine (or can be reabsorbed into the blood), depending on levels in the body.	1
5 c)	ADH helps the body to conserve water.	1
	If the concentration of water in the blood is too low, ADH (antidiuretic hormone) is released into the blood.	1
	ADH makes the walls of the collecting ducts more permeable to water molecules, so more water moves from the collecting ducts to be returned to the blood.	1
	The urine is more concentrated.	1
	If there is surplus water in the body, the high concentration of water in the blood results in a reduction of ADH production.	1
	The walls of the collecting duct become less permeable to water, and less water is reabsorbed into the blood.	1
	The body produces a larger volume of dilute urine.	1
6 a)	i) As the light intensity increases, the rate of photosynthesis increases,	1
	as light energy is required to drive the process of photosynthesis.	1
	At a certain point, the graph levels off, so any further increase in light intensity will result in no further increase in photosynthesis.	1
	At this point, some other factor must be limiting, for example carbon dioxide, and preventing any further increase.	1

Question	Correct answer	Marks
	ii) Graph drawn with line as shown: 	1
	As carbon dioxide was a factor that was limiting the rate of photosynthesis where the graph levels off, in a higher concentration of carbon dioxide, the graph will continue to a higher point (i.e. a higher rate of photosynthesis) until it again levels off.	1
	At this point, with light and carbon dioxide being available, another factor (e.g. temperature) must be preventing any further increase in the rate of photosynthesis.	1
6 b)	i) Growth in response to the direction of light is called **phototropism**. If the growth is towards light, it is called **positive phototropism**, as shown by plant **shoots**.	1 1 1
	Growth in response to gravity is called **geotropism**. Plant roots are **positively geotropic**. This response helps the plant **roots** to grow **downwards** so the plant can obtain the **water / ions** it needs.	1 2 2
	ii) There is no significant difference between the amount of auxin in the plants kept in the dark or light, or total auxin in plants illuminated on one side,	1
	so light has no effect on the production of auxin.	1
	In the plant illuminated from one side, about 71% of the auxin in the plant is on the dark side,	1
	so as the total auxin was unaffected by light, the auxin must have been redistributed from the light to dark side.	1
7 a)	i) A: cuticle	1
	B: epidermis	1
	C: palisade layer	1
	D: spongy mesophyll	1
	E: guard cell (allow stoma)	1
	ii) Leaves have a large surface area for gas exchange.	1
	Leaves are thin (usually less than 1 mm) so gases are only required to diffuse over small distances.	1
	Stomata regulate the diffusion of gases in and out.	1
	Cells have a moist surface required for the absorption and release of gases.	1
	There are large air spaces between the cells of the spongy mesophyll so that gases can move freely.	1

7 b)	Completed table as shown.			8
		Phloem	**Xylem**	
	Substances transported	Sucrose – 1 mark Amino acids – 1 mark Allow 1 mark for 'products of photosynthesis'	Water – 1 mark Mineral ions – 1 mark	
	Substances are transported from	Leaves / storage regions – 1 mark Allow 'sites where photosynthesis is carried out'	Roots – 1 mark	
	Substances are transported to	Parts of the plant where they are required – 1 mark	Throughout plant – 1 mark	

8 a)	i) Flow chart as shown	1 mark for each box, plus one for labelling the neurones, 6 marks total
8 a)	ii) Neurones in the spinal cord connect with (longitudinal) neurones	1
	at synapses,	1
	which run up the spinal cord to the brain (so that she knows that she has touched the object).	1
8 b)	Hormonal/endocrine system	1
	The response is electrical (and chemical) in the nervous system, and just chemical in the hormonal system.	1
	The response is carried by nerves/neurones in the nervous system, and in the blood in the hormonal system.	1
	The response is very quick in the nervous system, and slower in the hormonal system.	1
9 a)	i) A: right atrium	1
	B: right ventricle	1
	C: left atrium	1
	D: left ventricle	1
	ii) (The walls of the chambers of the heart are muscular.)	
	Contraction of the right atrium pumps blood to the lungs (the pulmonary circulation).	1
	Contraction of the left atrium pumps blood to the whole of the body (the systemic circulation), so blood in the systemic circulation has to be under higher pressure.	1

Question	Correct answer	Marks
9 b)	**i) Red blood cells**: These are packed with haemoglobin	1
	to transport oxygen from the lungs to the body's cells.	1
	ii) White blood cells: (These are for defence.)	
	Phagocytes ingest pathogens / microorganisms / other foreign bodies.	1
	Lymphocytes produce antibodies.	1
	iii) Plasma: Involved in the transport of food, hormones, carbon dioxide, urea.	1
	Involved in the distribution of heat.	1
	iv) Platelets: These are involved in clotting of blood,	1
	which prevents blood loss and the entry of microorganisms.	1
9 c)	The vaccine contains dead or weakened organisms that cause the disease.	1
	Lymphocytes divide and produce the specific antibodies in large numbers.	1
	Antibodies attach to the microorganisms, and the microorganisms are ingested by phagocytes.	1
	Memory cells remain in the blood so that the person can respond quickly / produce antibodies quickly if exposed to the same microorganism.	1
	Total:	143

Contents

Overview of the section

In this section, students will learn about a range of aspects related to reproduction and inheritance. Topic 3a covers the reproductive systems of flowering plants and humans, applying the general principles of systems and processes from Section 2. For plants, this is discussed within the context of pollination, fertilisation and germination. For humans, the structure of the reproductive systems is discussed, before looking at the role of hormones in the menstrual cycle and the development of secondary sexual characteristics.

Topic 3b begins with the structure of DNA and the process of protein synthesis followed by an introduction to genetics through monohybrid inheritance and the inheritance of sex. The topic continues with the production of new cells by mitosis and meiosis, and the role of mutation and inheritance in producing variation within individuals of the same species. The topic concludes with the role of natural selection in the evolution of species.

Starting points

The Student Book provides a 'section opener', a double page spread that sets the scene for the students (see pages 188–189). It is structured in this way:

- An overview providing details of the areas of study

- Ten questions, presented in the same order as key areas of learning within the section, which can be used to introduce each key area

- A list of section contents

The questions are intended to provide a structure for introducing the section.

---

1. How can you produce more plants without using flowers?

2. Why do flowers have to be pollinated before they make seed?

3. Why are some flowers large and brightly coloured and others small and inconspicuous?

4. What do seeds need to help them start growing?

5. How do the structures of the male and female human reproductive system support their function?

6. What controls the menstrual cycle every month?

7. What is DNA and what does it do?

8. How can we predict the inheritance of a characteristic controlled by a gene?

9. Why are there two types of cell division?

10. What is natural selection and how can it bring about evolution?

The section opener has two main purposes:

- To acknowledge students' prior learning and to value it
- To provide a benchmark against which future learning can be compared

You may use the ten questions or 'starting points' in the Student Book in a number of different ways to introduce the section:

- You could ask students to consider the questions as an introductory homework task.

- Students could divide into groups to share their own ideas and understanding and then report back to the whole class.

- Students could access the internet, preferably with a time limit, to find out the information required.

You could use a spider chart or other form of wall chart to summarise the ideas of all the students or groups.

The advantage of recording these initial ideas in this way is that you may retain them for reference as the individual topics are developed. In this way, you may readily acknowledge your students' progress in learning.

Introduction

This topic looks at the differences between asexual and sexual reproduction, and then covers reproduction in flowering plants and human reproduction.

Links to other topics

Sections	Essential background knowledge	Useful links
1 The nature and variety of living organisms	1a Characteristics of living organisms 1b Variety of living organisms	
2 Structure and functions in living organisms	2a Level of organisation 2b Cell structure 2d Movement of substances into and out of cells 2e Nutrition 2g Gas exchange 2h Transport	
3 Reproduction and inheritance		3b Inheritance
5 Use of biological resources		5b Selective breeding 5c Genetic modification (genetic engineering) 5d Cloning

Topic overview

B3a.1	**Sexual and asexual reproduction**
	This short activity looks at the differences between sexual and asexual reproduction, and sets the context for the rest of the work in this topic. It provides practical work on taking cuttings of plants. (Note: The differences between asexual and sexual reproduction are covered further in Topic 3b in the discussion of mitosis and meiosis. Also, growing plants using tissue culture is covered in Topic 5d.)
B3a.2	**Pollination in plants**
	In this activity students will learn how the structure of a flower is adapted to the method of pollination, by wind or by insects. This includes practical work on looking at the structures in a flower.
B3a.3	**Fertilisation and seed formation**
	In this activity, students will learn how the female gamete is fertilised after pollination, and how the structures of the ovule develop into the seed and fruit. There is practical work on dissecting seeds to look at their internal structure.

B3a.4	**Seed germination**
	This activity gives students the opportunity to investigate the conditions in which seeds germinate best, and to find out about the role of food reserves in a seed.
B3a.5	**Human reproductive system**
	This activity introduces the structures and function of the organs of the human male and female reproductive system, and the hormones involved in the development of secondary sexual characteristics.
B3a.6	**Human menstrual cycle**
	In this activity students learn about the roles of hormones in controlling the menstrual cycle.
B3a.7	**Development of the human fetus**
	In this activity students learn about the role of the placenta in supporting the developing embryo, and how the embryo is protected by the amniotic fluid.
B3a.8	**Consolidation and summary**
	This activity provides an opportunity for a quick recap on the ideas encountered in the topic as well as time for the students to answer the End of topic questions in the Student Book.

Activity B3a.1 Sexual and asexual reproduction

Specification reference: B3a.3.1; B3a.3.2; B3a.3.7

Learning objectives

- Understand the differences between sexual and asexual reproduction.
- Understand that fertilisation involves the fusion of a male and female gamete to produce a zygote that undergoes cell division and develops into an embryo.
- Understand that plants can reproduce asexually by natural methods (illustrated by runners) and by artificial methods (illustrated by cuttings).

Learning outcomes

- Explain that sexual reproduction is the production of new individuals by the fertilisation of a female gamete by a male gamete to produce a zygote that develops into an embryo.
- Explain that asexual reproduction is the production of new genetically identical individuals from the body cells of a parent organism.
- Describe natural and artificial methods for producing new individuals in plants by asexual reproduction.

Common misconceptions

Some students confuse *reproduction* and *fertilisation*, which makes it difficult for them to understand asexual reproduction. It is important to establish the right definitions for each term at the start. Also, some students mistakenly think that the key difference between *sexual* and *asexual* reproduction is the number of parents involved.

Resources

Student Book pages 190–192

Worksheet B3a.1a Taking plant cuttings

Resources for class practical (see Technician's notes, following)

Approach

1. Introduction

Write the word *reproduction* in the middle of the board and ask students to suggest related words. Ask how the words should be placed to build a concept map. If students are uncertain or confused, encourage discussion. Consider marking these words with a question mark, so that you may use the map again at the end of the activity to identify what students have learned.

2. Differences

Ask students to use pages 190–192 of the Student Book to make notes about the advantages and disadvantages of the two kinds of reproduction. They could then use their notes to produce questions to test each other.

If there is time and access to books or the internet, students could research other examples of organisms that use asexual reproduction, and try to explain why it is an advantage for them to do so.

3. Taking cuttings

Worksheet B3a.1a gives students the opportunity to take cuttings of a plant. These will need at least three weeks to develop roots, and longer if characteristics are to be measured for comparison. However, these measurements would be useful later for the discussion of the effect of genes and environment on variation in a species for Topic 3b Inheritance.

4. Consolidation: concept map

Return to the concept map started in the introduction. Ask students to resolve any question marks on the diagram. They should also suggest any additional words from this activity and how they should be added to the concept map.

Technician's notes

You will need the following resources for the class practical.

Be sure to check the latest safety notes on these resources before proceeding.

Check the safety information on the container of rooting hormone.

B3a.1a Taking plant cuttings

Many plants are suitable for this investigation, but choose something that grows quickly, such as busy lizzie (*Impatiens*) or pot geranium (*Pelargonium*). You may prefer to give students shoots that have already been cut from the plant for step 3 on the worksheet. If so, these must be cut as late as possible before the lesson and kept with their cut ends in water until the lesson.

Class practical, per group:

healthy mature plant
sharp knife or scalpel
cutting board
rooting hormone
small pot with drainage holes, e.g. yoghurt pot with 3 or 4 holes in the base
compost: use well-draining compost suitable for cuttings
plastic stirring rod
water
large transparent plastic bag and tie

Answers

Page 192

1.

Sexual reproduction	Asexual reproduction
• fusion of male gamete with female gamete • offspring genetically different from parents and from each other • (usually) two parents • slower because male and female need to find each other and mate	• new individuals produced from division of body cell of parent • offspring genetically identical to parent • only one parent • faster because no search for mate

2. Any suitable example that refers to changing environment where genetic variability in offspring increases chance of survival of offspring that are genetically different to parent.

3. Answer should include: summer not long so asexual reproduction increases numbers more rapidly; summer short period, so variability of environment not as big a problem, so genetic variability would not be an advantage; if parent is feeding well on food plant, the offspring from that parent are equally likely to survive and grow well on that food plant, so variability would be a disadvantage.

B3a.1a Taking plant cuttings

Plant growers use the natural ability of plants to produce new plants from parts of an old one by taking cuttings. Cuttings can be taken from stems, leaves or roots. The new plants are produced as a result of asexual reproduction, as they grow from body cells of the parent plant. So, their cells contain the same genes as the parent.

Apparatus

healthy mature plant

sharp knife or scalpel

cutting board

rooting hormone

small pot with drainage holes

compost

plastic stirring rod

water

large transparent plastic bag and tie

SAFETY INFORMATION

Take care when using sharp knives/scalpels.

Wash hands when finished.

Method

1. Fill the pot with compost and gently firm the compost so that it does not completely fill the pot.

2. Water the compost until there is water coming through the drainage holes at the bottom of the pot. Then leave the pot to drain, so that the compost is wet but not waterlogged.

3. Cut a shoot from the plant that has at least four or five leaves. Remove the bottom few leaves to leave at least two leaves. Then cut across the shoot with a sharp knife at right angles to the shoot.

4. Holding the shoot gently but firmly, dip the cut end into the rooting hormone.

5. Use a stirring rod to make a hole in the compost and place the shoot into the hole so that the leaves are clear of the compost. Firm the compost around the shoot to hold it in place.

6. Place the pot in the large plastic bag and use the tie to close the bag.

7. Leave the cuttings in a bright place, such as a windowsill for several weeks until the roots have started to develop. Then remove the plastic bag and water the compost to keep it moist but not waterlogged.

Analyse and interpret data

1. Compare the characteristics of the new plant grown from the cutting with those of the parent plant. Explain any similarities and any differences.

Activity B3a.2 Pollination in plants

Specification reference: B3a.3.3; B3a.3.4

Learning objectives

- Describe the structures of an insect-pollinated and a wind-pollinated flower and explain how each is adapted for pollination.
- Understand that the growth of the pollen tube followed by fertilisation leads to seed and fruit formation.

Learning outcomes

- Describe the structures of an insect-pollinated and a wind-pollinated flower.
- Explain how the structures of an insect-pollinated and a wind-pollinated flower are adapted for pollination.
- Explain how growth of the pollen tube leads to fertilisation, which leads to seed and fruit formation.

Common misconceptions

Many people confuse *pollination* and *fertilisation*. It is important for students to be able to distinguish properly between them.

Resources

Student Book pages 192–197

Worksheet B3a.2a Flower dissection

Resources for class practical (see Technician's notes, following)

Approach

1. Introduction

Give students one minute to write down three important facts about flowers. They should discuss their facts with another student, and choose together their three most important facts. Take examples from the class to cover the biggest possible range of facts. Make sure at least one fact is related to pollination.

Use the opportunity to ask students to distinguish between pollination and fertilisation in plants. If they are not sure, leave this for now but make sure you return to it at the end of the activity.

2. The structure of flowers

If possible, provide flowers from wind-pollinated and insect-pollinated plants for students to dissect. Worksheet B3a.2a will help. Students will also need the diagram of flower structure from page 193 of the Student Book. Consider providing a photocopy of this diagram to avoid damage to the books.

If there is not enough time for students to dissect a flower of each type, then give one half of the class wind-pollinated flowers and the other half insect-pollinated flowers. Allow time for students to present their results to the other half at the end of the practical work.

If practical work is not possible, ask students to research examples on the internet or from books, and to draw one example of each, clearly labelling each diagram to show how it is adapted for its particular mode of pollination.

Students could also research the shapes of pollen grains from different plants, to identify if those from wind-pollinated plants differ from those of insect-pollinated plants.

3. The growth of pollen tubes

The Practical Biology website offers a method for growing pollen tubes, and a range of project ideas to test. The method uses microscope slides that have been thoroughly cleaned before use. Students will then need to use a little more care to keep the liquid drops centred under the microscope objective while the pollen tubes grow.

Note that growing pollen tubes is often unsuccessful, due to age of the pollen, species used and what they are grown in, so the website provides a sequence of timed photographs to show how they develop.

Students could use these to investigate how quickly the tubes grow and how this might relate to the time that elapses between pollination and fertilisation. (Note: conditions in the flower and in the laboratory will vary, so the time taken for a pollen tube to grow in the different conditions may also vary.)

Alternatively, show students a video clip of pollen tube growth, ideally one that shows time passing.

4. Consolidation: drawings

Ask students to sketch a flower with typical features of one type of pollination. They should exchange their sketch with a neighbour. Ask them to identify which type of pollination is involved and then annotate the features that are adaptations for this type of pollination.

Next, they can discuss the sketch with the student who drew it to identify any other features to annotate.

Technician's notes

You will need the following resources for the class practical.

Be sure to check the latest safety notes on these resources before proceeding.

Be aware of students with pollen allergy.

B3a.2a Flower structure

Offer a selection of flowers, some of which are wind-pollinated and some of which are insect-pollinated, but avoid complex 'flowers', such as daises and dandelions, which consist of a large number of true flowers within one flower head.

Class practical, per group:

flowers from plants of different species
sharp knife or scalpel
cutting board
hand lens or magnifying glass
pencil and paper

Answers

Page 195

1. Produces the pollen.

2. In pollen grains.

3. Stigma where pollen grains attach. Style which supports the stigma. Ovary which surrounds and protects the ovule, inside which is the female gamete.

Page 197

1. Wind-pollinated flowers are usually small, no colourful petals, anthers and stigmas hang outside flower, make a lot of lightweight pollen.

2. The lightweight pollen can be carried far in wind, anthers hang outside the flower so pollen is more likely to be caught by wind.

3. Insect-pollinated flowers are often large, brightly coloured, produce nectar and sometimes scent, make small amounts of larger pollen grains.

4. Scent, nectar (as food), large petals with bright colours all help to attract insects to the flower. As the insects feed, they pick up pollen, which is then carried to other flowers.

B3a.2a Flower dissection

Flowers are adapted in different ways to increase the chance of pollination. Some depend on wind and others depend on an animal, such as an insect, to bring pollen to the stigma. In this practical you will dissect flowers to investigate how they are adapted to their method of pollination. If there is time, choose at least one wind-pollinated and one insect-pollinated flower to study.

Apparatus

flowers from plants of different species

sharp knife or scalpel

cutting board

hand lens or magnifying glass

pencil and paper

SAFETY INFORMATION

Take care when using sharp knives/scalpels.

Tell your teacher if you have a pollen allergy.

Method

For each flower that you study, use the following method.

1. Use the hand lens or magnifying glass to look closely at the flower. Using the diagram from page 193 of the Student Book, try to identify the sepals, petals, male parts and female parts of the flower. Note that in some species the flowers only contain one sex.

2. Make annotated outline drawings of your flower to show:

- sepals – number and colour
- petals – number, colour and relative size (large, medium or small).

Also, note if the flower has scent and record this as none, a little, or strongly scented.

3. Use the knife or scalpel to remove the sepals and petals, so that you can see the reproductive parts more clearly. Make annotated drawings of the following:

- stamens – number, relative size and any other distinctive features
- stigmas – number, relative size and any other distinctive features.

4. Remove the stamens and look carefully at the female parts of the flower. Draw and label one carpel. If possible, note the position of the nectaries.

Analyse and interpret data

1. For each flower, identify how it is pollinated and explain how the flower is adapted to improve the chances of it being pollinated.

2. Use your results to compare the adaptations of insect-pollinated and wind-pollinated flowers.

Activity B3a.3 Fertilisation and seed formation

Specification reference: B3a.3.2; B3a.3.4

Learning objectives

- Understand that fertilisation involves the fusion of a male and female gamete to produce a zygote that undergoes cell division and develops into an embryo.
- Understand that the growth of the pollen tube followed by fertilisation leads to seed and fruit formation.

Learning outcomes

- Explain that fertilisation involves the fusion of a male and a female gamete to produce a zygote that undergoes cell division and develops into an embryo.
- Describe how growth of the pollen tube followed by fertilisation leads to seed and fruit formation.

Common misconceptions

See note in Activity B3a.2 about the confusion of *pollination* and *fertilisation*. Students may also confuse the terms *seed* and *fruit*.

Resources

Student Book pages 197–199

Worksheet B3a.3a Looking at seeds

Resources for the class practical (see Technician's notes, following)

Approach

1. Introduction

Remind students of the definition of the term *fertilisation* from Activity B3a.1a, and give them two minutes to make bullet point notes showing the steps from the formation of gametes in the flower up to the fertilisation of a female gamete in a flower. Take examples from around the class to produce, in the correct order, the stages from pollen and egg formation to fertilisation.

2. Forming seeds and fruits

Ask students to use pages 197–199 of the Student Book to identify which parts of the female reproductive structures of a flower become which structures in a seed and its fruit after fertilisation of the female gamete.

They could then investigate the structure of some fruits and seeds using Worksheet B3a.3a or images from books or the internet. (Note: Research may introduce them to terms such as *pome* and *drupe* that describe different kinds of fruits. Explain to students that they are not expected to remember these terms for their exams.)

You may need to remind students that some flowers have only one ovule within an ovary, and so only produce one seed in each fruit (such as a plum), while others have several ovules and so produce several seeds in each fruit (such as apples and beans).

3. Consolidation: which becomes what?

Give students three minutes to write down the key points from this activity for a friend who missed the lesson. Then take examples from around the class to make sure that students are clear about the changes that happen to the different parts of the carpel after fertilisation.

Technician's notes

You will need the following resources for the class practical.

Be sure to check the latest safety notes on these resources before proceeding.

B3a.3a Looking at seeds

Any fruit that is non-toxic and easy to cut open would be suitable. Avoid peanuts and any other nut that may cause allergic reactions.

Suitable seeds for dissection include pea or bean (dicotyledon/two food stores) and maize (monocotyledon/one food store), as these have relatively soft seed coats (testa) if fresh or if soaked in water for a few hours. You could also offer fruits such as apple.

Seeds with hard shells, such as plum, peach or walnut, may need the shell cracking before students can extract the embryo and food stores.

Dried seeds may need soaking in water for several hours to soften the seed coat (testa).

Class practical, per group:

fruits containing seeds
sharp knife or scalpel
blunt forceps
hand lens or magnifying glass

Answers

Page 199

1. Pollination is the transfer of pollen from one flower to another. Fertilisation is the fusion of a male gamete with a female gamete to form a zygote.

2. Pollination (pollen grain lands on stigma); pollen tube grows down through style to ovule; pollen tube delivers male gamete to egg cell; nucleus of male gamete and nucleus of female gamete fuse to form zygote.

3. Female gamete develops into embryo plant; ovule wall forms hard outer shell of seed; ovary forms fruit.

B3a.3a Looking at seeds

In this practical, you will dissect one or more seeds to look at their internal structure. Use your notes from the Student Book to help you identify from which part of the flower each part of the seed developed.

Apparatus

fruits containing seeds

sharp knife or scalpel

blunt forceps

hand lens or magnifying glass

pencil and paper

SAFETY INFORMATION

Take care when handling sharp knives/scalpels.

Do not eat any of the fruits when prepared in a science lab.

Wash your hands thoroughly after the practical.

Method

For each of the fruits you will dissect, use the following method:

1. Draw an outline drawing of the fruit and label any structures you can see, such as the stalk.

2. Carefully cut the fruit in half to show the seed (or seeds) inside.

3. Draw the half of the fruit with the seed (or seeds) in place. Label all the structures you can see, and annotate the labels to describe them (such as soft, tough, hard).

4. Remove one seed and inspect it using the hand lens or magnifying glass. You may be able to see where the embryo lies inside the seed by the shape of the seed coat. Close to this you may be able to see a tiny hole, called the micropyle, which is where the pollen tube entered the ovule. Water enters the seed here before germination.

5. Carefully remove the seed coat from the seed. The seed may contain two large food reserves (cotyledons) or just one. You should also be able to see the plant embryo attached to the food reserve(s). You may be able to distinguish the embryo shoot and embryo root.

bean seed in seed coat

bean seed with seed coat removed

6. Draw the structures you can see inside the seed and label them to explain what they are.

Analyse and interpret data

1. After fertilisation, the ovary becomes the fruit. Use your descriptions of the fruit to explain its role in seed protection and dispersal.

2. After fertilisation, the ovule wall becomes the seed coat. Use your descriptions of the seed coat to explain its role in protecting the seed.

3. After fertilisation, tissue inside the ovule develops into the food stores. Use your descriptions of the cotyledons to explain their role in providing nutrition to the embryo as the seed germinates.

Activity B3a.4 Seed germination

Specification reference: B3a.3.5; B3a.3.6

Learning objectives

- Practical: Investigate the conditions needed for seed germination.
- Understand how germinating seeds utilise food reserves until the seedling can carry out photosynthesis.

Learning outcomes

- Explain that seeds need particular conditions for germination.
- Describe how germinating seeds use their food reserves until the seedling can carry out photosynthesis.

Common misconceptions

Students sometimes confuse the conditions – including light – needed for germination with those needed for photosynthesis. Remind students that many seeds need to be below the surface of the ground (where it is more moist) before they will germinate, and so light cannot be a necessary condition for germination.

Resources

Student Book pages 199–202

Worksheet B3a.4a Practical: Investigate the conditions needed for seed germination

Resources for the class practical (see Technician's notes, following)

Approach

1. Introduction

Remind students of their investigation of seed structure in the last activity, and ask them to explain what the food reserves contain and why they are needed. Students should remember that they are needed to supply the food for respiration, and the materials for new growth, in the early stages of germination when the seed needs to grow but cannot yet photosynthesise. Then ask students what other conditions a plant seed may need for germination. Just take suggestions at this point, without comment, as this will lead into the practical investigation.

2. Investigating the conditions for germination

Worksheet B3a.4a provides a method for investigating the conditions needed for germination, and supports the Developing investigative skills box on page 200 of the Student Book. If students have suggested other possible conditions, add these to the investigation. Note that class results will be analysed, taking averages of repeat tests from groups investigating the same set of conditions. So, the more conditions investigated at the same time, the fewer groups and fewer repeats of a set of conditions will be available for analysis. Seeds do not always germinate successfully, so at least one repeat for each condition (light intensity, moisture level and temperature) is advisable.

It is important to control other variables as far as possible during the investigation. This will mean trying to provide a light place and a dark place at similar temperatures, and a warm place and a cool place with similar light intensity. If any of these are not possible, remove that condition from the investigation.

Students should find that seeds need moisture and warmth to germinate successfully. Seeds in the dark should germinate as successfully as seeds in the light in similar moisture and temperature.

3. Consolidation: definitions

Ask students to write dictionary definitions for the words pollination, fertilisation and germination. Take examples from the class and ask students to vote for the best example for each, justifying their choice.

Technician's notes

You will need the following resources for the class practical.

Be sure to check the latest safety notes on these resources before proceeding.

B3a.4a Practical: Investigate the conditions needed for seed germination

Use seeds that germinate quickly such as *Arabidopsis* or cress. This practical will need to run for at least a week, depending on the seeds used. Students will need a few minutes each day to check the dishes during this period. **Note** that some seeds sold for growing in gardens or at home are treated with fungicide that may cause an allergic response.

Class practical, per group:

20 seeds	access to light
2 Petri dishes	access to dark
2 paper towels	access to bright cold place
light sensor, or temperature sensor or thermometer	marker pen
water	

Answers

Developing investigative skills, page 200

1. a) Set up two identical dishes with same number of seed, treated in exactly the same way for moisture and kept at same temperature, but one placed in bright light and one placed in dark cupboard.
   b) Set up two identical dishes with the same number of seed, placed in bright light, but one has a dry paper towel and other has a paper towel that is kept damp.
   c) Set up two identical dishes with the same number of seed, placed in bright light, treated in exactly the same way for moisture, but one kept cooler than the other (by any reasonable means).

2. Line graph with day on x-axis and total number on x-axis and total number on y-axis, with two lines, one for each temperature clearly labelled.

3. There is no significant difference in the total number of seeds that germinated at the two temperatures, but those at 20 °C germinated more quickly than those at 10 °C. (Seeds that didn't germinate may have failed for many reasons, e.g. dead embryo, and should be ignored in the results.)

4. The seeds germinated more quickly at the higher temperature.

5. Increased temperature increases the rate of action of enzymes that control reactions. So, at the warmer temperature, reactions were carried out faster so that the cells grew faster.

Page 202 (top)

1. The food reserves provide the food needed for respiration, so that cell growth can take place, until photosynthesis supplies food.

2. a) Essential for germination.
   b) Increased temperature (up to the point when enzymes are denatured) increases rate of enzyme action and so growth.

3. Most seeds germinate below the surface of the ground, where there is no light. If they needed light, they would not germinate.

4. Take a piece of existing plant (such as piece of stem, root or shoot) → dip it into rooting hormone mixture → place it in compost → keep moist → after a few weeks, roots will develop.

B3a.4a Practical: Investigate the conditions needed for seed germination

In this practical you will investigate the conditions that seeds need for germination. You will test one set of conditions and your results will contribute to a class analysis. Your teacher will tell you whether you are testing light intensity, temperature, or moisture level.

Apparatus

20 seeds	2 Petri dishes	2 paper towels	marker pen

light sensor, or temperature sensor or thermometer   water

access to light, access to dark, access to bright cold place

SAFETY INFORMATION

Wash hands thoroughly after handling seeds.

Only keep seeds for one week and dispose after this.

Method

1. Use the pen to mark the two dishes on the edge with your initials.

2. Fold a paper towel and fit it neatly into the bottom of one Petri dish. Repeat with the other paper towel and dish.

3. If you are investigating light intensity or temperature, pour sufficient water into each dish to wet the paper towel. Pour off any excess water.

4. If you are investigating moisture level, wet the paper towel in only one dish.

5. Scatter 10 seeds evenly across each dish.

6. If you are investigating temperature, place one dish in a bright, warm place and one in a bright, cold place. Measure the light intensity in each place to make sure the dishes are receiving a similar amount of light.

7. If you are investigating moisture level, place both dishes in the same bright place.

8. If you are investigating light intensity, place one dish in a bright warm place and the other in a dark warm place. Measure the temperature in each place to make sure the dishes are receiving a similar amount of heat.

9. Leave the dishes for up to a week in these positions. Every day, check and record how many seeds have germinated. Also, check that the moist paper towels remain moist, adding a little water if needed.

Analyse and interpret data

1. Gather all the data from the class into a spreadsheet, showing the results for each group separately.

2. Compare the repeat tests for each condition and identify any anomalies. Ignoring any anomalies, calculate an average number of germinated seedlings for each day in repeat dishes.

3. Use your results to draw separate graphs for temperature, moisture and light with days along the x-axis and number of seedlings along the y-axis. Each graph will have two lines.

4. Describe the results shown in each graph, and use your scientific knowledge to explain them.

Evaluate data and methods

1. Describe any problems with this practical, and explain how the method could be improved to reduce their effect.

Activity B3a.5 Human reproductive system

Specification reference: B3a.3.8; B3a.3.13

Learning objectives

- Understand how the structure and function of the male and female reproductive systems are adapted for their functions.
- Understand the roles of oestrogen and testosterone in the development of secondary sexual characteristics.

Learning outcomes

- Explain that the organs, tissues and cells in the male and female human reproductive systems are adapted for their role in reproduction.
- Describe how oestrogen and testosterone control the development of secondary sexual characteristics.

Common misconceptions

Students should be reminded that male sex hormones are also found in women, and female hormones are also found in men. It is the different relative concentrations in the body that produce different effects in men and women.

Resources

Student Book pages 202–203

Worksheet B3a.5a Male reproductive system

Worksheet B3a.5b Female reproductive system

Approach

1. Introduction

Teaching students about human reproduction can be embarrassing for some teachers and for some students. It can be helpful to allow five minutes at the start of the first session for students to let out all their giggles and embarrassment by using common and slang terminology for the various parts of the human reproductive system, and then to start the lesson again as 'scientists' using only the appropriate scientific terminology. However, this may not always be appropriate.

Ask students to give the scientific terms for the organs of the human male reproductive system, and then for the human female reproductive system.

Be aware of continuing embarrassment of any student and manage the class if needed by allowing students to work more individually than in pairs or groups.

2. Human male reproductive system

Ask students to read page 202 of the Student Book on the human male reproductive system. They should make notes on the different organs in the system, and identify as many tissues and cells as they can, explaining the roles they play in reproduction, and how they are adapted for this.

Worksheet B3a.5a gives an outline of the male reproductive system that students can use to answer question 1 in the Questions box on page 202.

3. Human female reproductive system

Ask students to read page 203 of the Student Book on the human female reproductive system. They should make notes on the different organs in the system, and identify as many tissues and cells as they can, explaining the roles they play in reproduction, and how they are adapted for this.

Worksheet B3a.5b gives an outline of the female reproductive system that students can use to answer question 2 in the Questions box on page 203.

4. Secondary sexual characteristics

Remind students of their work in Topic 2j on hormones and ask them to describe what testosterone and oestrogen do in the human body. They should remember that these hormones control the development of secondary sexual characteristics. Explain that secretion of these hormones increases at puberty. Ask students to identify the secondary sexual characteristics and to suggest why they develop at this stage. They should be able to explain that after puberty the body is mature enough for sexual reproduction, and that these characteristics either make sexual reproduction possible or increase attractiveness to the opposite sex so that sexual reproduction is more likely to take place.

5. Consolidation: crossword clues

Ask students to write clues for a crossword on the human reproductive system. They should write clues for at least 10 of the scientific terms that have been used in the lesson. If there is time, they could test their clues out on another student.

Answers

Page 202 (bottom)

1. Sketch as Fig. 3.18 on page 202.

2. and 3. Labels and annotations as follows:

- testes, where sperm (male gametes) produced
- sperm duct, carry sperm to urethra
- prostate gland and seminal vesicles, produce liquid in which sperm swim
- penis, when erect delivers sperm into vagina of female
- urethra, tube that carries sperm from sperm ducts to outside the body.

Page 203

1. Sketch as Fig. 3.19 on page 203.

2. and 3. Labels and annotations as follows:

- ovaries, where egg cells form
- oviducts, carry the eggs to the uterus and where fertilisation by sperm takes place
- uterus, where embryo implants into lining and fetus develops
- cervix, base of uterus where sperm are deposited during sexual intercourse
- vagina, where penis is inserted during sexual intercourse, and along which baby passes as it is born.

B3a.5a Male reproductive system

Add annotated labels to the diagram below to explain the function of each of the organs in the human male reproductive system.

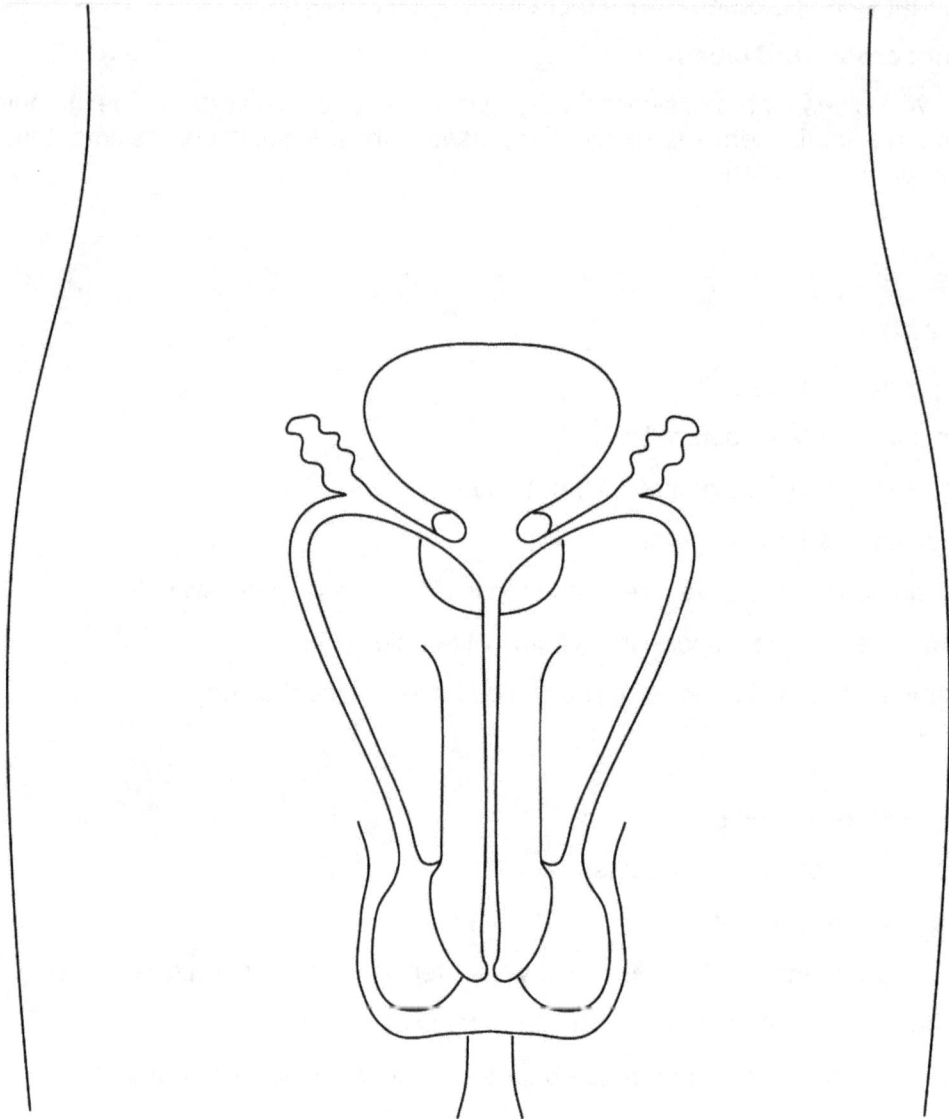

B3a.5b Female reproductive system

Add annotated labels to the diagram below to explain the function of each of the organs in the human female reproductive system.

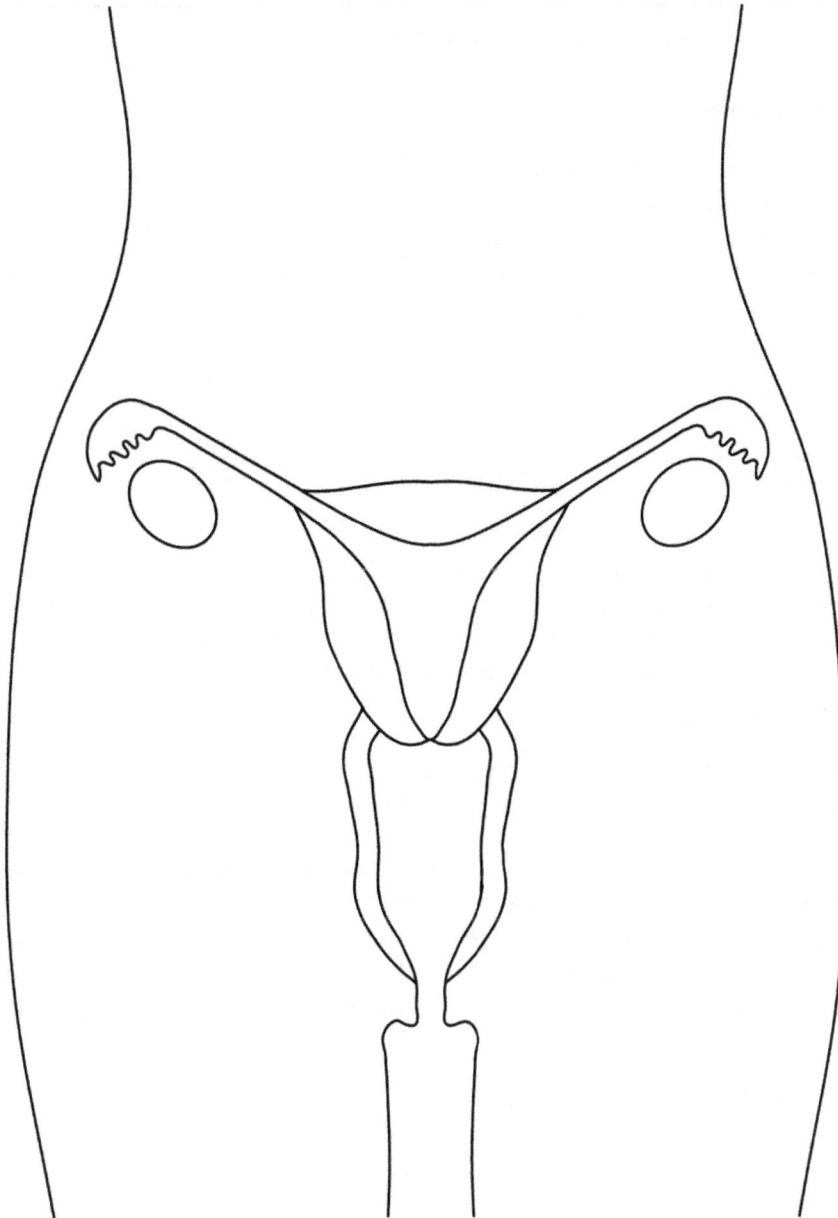

Activity B3a.6 Human menstrual cycle

Specification reference: B3a3.9; B3a3.10**B**

Learning objectives

- Understand the roles of oestrogen and progesterone in the menstrual cycle.
- Understand the roles of FSH and LH in the menstrual cycle. **(B)**

Learning outcomes

- Understand how the hormones oestrogen and progesterone control the menstrual cycle.
- Understand how FSH and LH control the menstrual cycle. **(B)**

Common misconceptions

Materials about the menstrual cycle often refer to the 28-day length of the average cycle and a period (bleed) or menstruation of about five days. It is important to make clear that many women vary from this, with longer or shorter cycles and longer or shorter menstruation, and that this is usually completely normal. If any girl seems concerned about this, she should be advised to speak to her doctor.

Resources

Student Book pages 204–205

Approach

1. Introduction

Revise what students already know about the menstrual cycle by giving them one or two minutes to write down three facts about it. Take examples from around the class and encourage discussion if some of the facts seem confused. Be sensitive to the response of students and allow any students who seem embarrassed to stay out of the discussion unless they wish to join in.

2. Describing the menstrual cycle

Note: if students are preparing for International GCSE Science (Double Award), they will only be examined on the roles of oestrogen and progesterone; however, if they are preparing for International GCSE Biology they also need to learn about the roles of FSH and LH. Ask students to read pages 204–205 of the Student Book on the menstrual cycle and to make notes about the roles of oestrogen and progesterone, and FSH and LH if appropriate, in controlling the cycle. Explain that some videos on the internet are written at too high a level for International GCSE, so they should use their notes to make a storyboard for a video that is more suitable. They could work individually or in pairs to do this. They should research what diagram to use as a basis for this, and write the text that should be voiced at each stage of the video.

3. Consolidation: red, yellow green

Give students three cards, red, yellow and green. Then read out questions about the menstrual cycle, explaining that they should hold up the red card if they are uncertain of the answer, yellow card if they think they know the answer and the green card if they are certain of the answer. Questions could include: Which hormone causes ovulation? Which hormone maintains the thickness of the uterus wall?

Answers

Pages 204–205

1. Characteristics of the body that develop at puberty and prepare the body for sexual reproduction.

2. The shedding of the thickened lining of the uterus and the start of the development of another egg in the ovary.

3. Circle numbered 1 to 28 around the circle;

   a) ovulation at about day 14

   b) menstruation about days 28/0–4

   c) increase in oestrogen about days 8–12, decrease about days 12–14

   d) increase in progesterone about days 14–18, decrease about days 23–28.

Page 205

1. a) and b) FSH: secreted from pituitary gland, target cell egg in ovary; oestrogen: secreted from developing egg in ovary, target cells include cells lining uterus wall and cells in pituitary gland; LH: secreted by pituitary gland, target cells in ovary, causing ovulation; progesterone: secreted by ovary cells, target cells include cells lining uterus wall and cells in pituitary gland (inhibiting FSH and LH secretion).

2. In the blood.

3. a) and b) Sketch should include curves for oestrogen and progesterone as shown in Fig. 3.20 on page 204 plus curves for FSH and LH as shown in Fig. 3.21 on page 205.

   Annotations should indicate:

   • rise in FSH at start due to low levels of progesterone and oestrogen, fall when increasing progesterone inhibits production

   • rise in oestrogen as a result of developing egg, fall in oestrogen after egg ovulated

   • rise in LH due to high oestrogen, fall after progesterone increases and inhibits production

   • rise in progesterone after ovulation, fall at end of cycle if egg not fertilised.

4. The actions happen over a long time, and target cells may be in more than one part of the body. Hormones can control these kinds of responses much more easily than the nervous system.

5. Although each hormone has a different effect, the coordination of all four hormones acts to keep the cycle within limits and produces a repeating pattern.

Activity B3a.7 Development of the human fetus

Specification reference: B3a.3.11; B3a.3.12

Learning objectives

- Describe the role of the placenta in the nutrition of the developing embryo.
- Understand how the developing embryo is protected by amniotic fluid.

Learning outcomes

- Be able to describe the role of the placenta in providing nutrition for the developing embryo.
- Explain how structures in the uterus support the developing embryo.

Common misconceptions

Although the maternal blood and fetal blood are in close proximity in the placenta, they cannot exchange all materials freely – only what can diffuse from the mother to the baby and from the baby to the mother. This prevents some substances, including large blood proteins (such as the Rhesus factor), from passing from one to the other.

Resources

Student Book pages 205–208

Worksheet B3a.7a The placenta

Approach

1. Introduction

Ask students what happens after fertilisation of a human egg. Make sure they understand the terms *zygote* (the fertilised egg), *embryo* (up to the end of the third month of pregnancy), *fetus* (from start of fourth month to end of pregnancy) and *baby* (from birth). Help students to understand how they are different. Encourage them to use the terms appropriately in their work.

Give them one or two minutes to write down bullet point notes about what happens to the developing embryo, and then the fetus. They should be able to suggest cell division, growth and differentiation of cells to produce tissues, organs and systems. They should also recognise that the embryo and fetus are living and therefore carrying out many of the life processes.

2. Developing fetus

If possible, show the students a video of the development of a fetus in the uterus. Note that many videos on the internet are aimed at women who want to know what happens during pregnancy, so they discuss the development in general terms.

Before the video, ask students to suggest a range of questions that they would like to answer from the video, such as when the limbs develop, or when the fetus responds to sound. Discuss the best questions and pause the video at appropriate points for students to write down the answers. If any questions aren't answered by the video, or a video is not available, students could carry out further research to find the answers.

Make sure students find out about the role of the amniotic fluid in protecting the developing embryo and fetus.

3. The placenta

Worksheet B3a.7a provides a diagram of a developing fetus in the uterus. Students can label and annotate this to explain the role of the placenta in supporting the developing fetus. If students are unsure of the needs of the fetus, remind them that it is a living organism and therefore needs to carry out many of the characteristics of living organisms discussed in Topic 1a.

4. Consolidation: video notes

Gives students three minutes to write bullet point notes for a video about the development of the fetus in the uterus, focusing on how the fetus is supported and protected during development. Take examples from around the class to make sure the learning objectives of the lesson are covered.

Answers

Page 208

1. a) The cell produced by the fusion of a male gamete and female gamete.

   b) The dividing ball of cells formed from the zygote, which implants in the uterus wall lining.

   c) Developing baby in the uterus (womb) from the point where the placenta has developed.

2. a) Protects the baby from bumps from the outside world and from wide variation in temperature.

   b) Provides nutrients from mother's blood and carries waste to mother's blood to be excreted; provides a barrier preventing the mother's and baby's blood mixing, so baby isn't harmed by the mother's higher blood pressure, or by pathogens or many harmful chemicals.

3. For the exchange of materials. Substances such as glucose (food molecules), oxygen and other nutrients diffuse from the mother's blood into the fetus's blood, and waste products such as carbon dioxide and urea diffuse from the fetus's blood into the mother's blood. The rate of diffusion is faster over a large surface area and when the distance that needs to be crossed is as short as possible. The placenta provides both of these so that diffusion is as rapid as possible.

B3a.7a The placenta

The diagram shows a developing fetus in the uterus.

1. Label the following in the diagram:

   (a) fetus   (b) placenta   (c) mother's body   (d) umbilical cord   (e) amniotic fluid.

2. Add notes to the labels for placenta, umbilical cord and amniotic fluid to explain what they do.

3. a) Use a coloured pencil to draw arrows and write notes to explain how food molecules and oxygen from the environment reach the cells in the fetus for respiration.

   b) Use a different colour of pencil to explain how waste products of metabolism are excreted from the fetus.

Activity B3a.8 Consolidation and summary

Learning objectives

- To review the learning points of the topic.
- To test understanding through answering questions.

Learning outcomes

- Be familiar with the knowledge and understanding summarised in the End of topic checklist.
- Be able to apply this knowledge and understanding by answering the End of topic questions.

Resources

Student Book pages 209–213

Approach

Ask students to answer the End of topic questions in the Student Book.

Answers

End of topic questions mark scheme

Question	Correct answer	Marks
1 a)	For reproduction	1
1 b)	Anthers	1
1 c)	They contain the male gametes in the pollen grains.	1
1 d)	Wind, because there are no bright petals or colour to attract insects,	1
	and the anthers are held outside the flower so that they catch the wind easily.	1
2 a)	Germination is when the seed begins to swell and break open the seed coat so that the embryo plant can grow.	1
2 b)	Moisture is needed so that the enzymes in the seed can start to work.	1
	Warmth is needed so the enzyme action is as fast as possible.	1
2 c)	Small seeds contain fewer food reserves than large seeds,	1
	so seedlings from small seeds need to start photosynthesising more quickly than those from larger seeds.	1
	If small seeds are planted too deeply, they may run out of energy supplied from their food reserves if they cannot get their leaves to the surface in time.	1
2 d)	If they germinated too late in the year, they would not be able to grow enough before winter	1
	to flower and reproduce before the winter killed them.	1
3 a)	Make less pollen, less waste of pollen as insects more likely to deliver pollen to the flower than random distribution in wind.	1
3 b)	If the insect species die out, the plant will not get pollinated.	1

Question	Correct answer	Marks
4 a)	The sperm cells are made in the testes.	1
4 b)	The egg cells are formed in the ovaries.	1
4 c)	Fertilisation takes place inside one of the oviducts.	1
4 d)	The sperm travels down the sperm duct and mixes with liquids from the prostate gland and seminal vesicles to form semen.	1
	Semen is ejaculated during sexual intercourse and deposited close to the cervix at the top of the vagina.	1
	The egg cell is released from the ovary and travels along the oviduct.	1
	Sperm cells swim to reach the egg cell in the oviduct.	1
5 a)	Oestrogen is secreted by cells around the egg cell.	1
	Just before ovulation, the amount of oestrogen that is secreted drops.	1
	Cells in the ovary then start secreting progesterone, and a little more oestrogen is secreted – these cause an increase in thickness of the uterus lining.	1
	At about 28 days, the amounts of oestrogen and progesterone start to fall, causing the uterus lining to break down and a new egg cell to start developing in the ovary.	1
5 b)	FSH stimulates the development of an egg in the ovary.	1
	LH causes ovulation.	1
6 a)	An organ produced by the fetus that attaches to the lining of the uterus.	1
6 b)	Substances such as oxygen, carbon dioxide and glucose are exchanged between the mother and the developing fetus.	1
6 c)	Diffusion of small molecules.	1
	Osmosis of water.	1
6 d)	It prevents pathogens and large molecules (such as some chemicals) crossing from the mother's blood into the fetus; or, allows the two blood systems to be at different pressures.	1
6 e)	The fetus needs oxygen for respiration, so that its cells may grow well.	1
	It gets that oxygen from its mother's blood via the placenta.	1
	If the mother's blood isn't carrying as much oxygen, then the fetus will get less oxygen and respiration will be carried out more slowly.	1
	This will result in slower growth of the cells in the fetus, so it will be lighter in weight than normal at birth.	1
	Total:	37

Introduction

This topic begins with a look at the structure of DNA and the process of protein synthesis, inheritance in monohybrid crosses and inheritance of sex. This follows with a description of mitosis and meiosis, their roles in growth and reproduction, and their impact on variation in the offspring. The effect of mutations on characteristics is then introduced, and linked to evolution by natural selection through the increase in antibiotic resistance in bacteria.

Links to other topics

Sections	Essential background knowledge	Useful links
1 The nature and variety of living organisms	1a Characteristics of living organisms	
2 Structures and functions in living organisms	2b Cell structure 2c Biological molecules	
3 Reproduction and inheritance	3a Reproduction	
5 Use of biological resources		5b Selective breeding 5c Genetic modification (genetic engineering) 5d Cloning

Topic overview

B3b.1	**The structure of DNA and protein synthesis**
	This activity helps students to understand the relationship between DNA, chromosomes, genes and alleles, and how DNA exerts its effects through the production of proteins.
B3b.2	**Inheriting characteristics**
	This activity begins with practical work on the inheritance of monohybrid characteristics and codominance. Students then learn how to decode the information in a family pedigree. The activity concludes with a discussion of how sex is inherited in humans.
B3b.3	**Cell division**
	This activity helps students understand how cell division by mitosis and meiosis has different outcomes, and how different kinds of cell division have different purposes.
B3b.4	**Variation and mutation**
	Students study the causes of variation in the phenotype as a result of variation in alleles and changes in the environment. This leads to a discussion of mutation as the cause of new alleles, and looks at some of the causes of mutation, including a data analysis exercise to investigate correlation and causation.

B3b.5	**Evolution by natural selection**
	Students learn how genetic variation is acted upon by environmental conditions, leading to natural selection, and how this can lead to evolution in a species. The increase in antibiotic resistance in bacteria is given as an example of evolution by natural selection.
B3b.6	**Consolidation and summary**
	This activity provides an opportunity for a quick recap on the ideas encountered in the topic as well as time for the students to answer the End of topic questions in the Student Book.

234

Activity B3b.1 The structure of DNA and protein synthesis

Specification reference: B3b.3.14; B3b.3.15; B3b.3.16**B**; B3b.3.17**B**; B3b.3.18**B**; B3b.3.19; B3b.3.32

Learning objectives

- Understand that the genome is the entire DNA of an organism and that a gene is a section of a molecule of DNA that codes for a specific protein.
- Understand that the nucleus of a cell contains chromosomes on which genes are located.
- Describe a DNA molecule as two strands coiled to form a double helix, the strands being linked by a series of paired bases: adenine (A) with thymine (T), and cytosine (C) with guanine (G). **(B)**
- Understand that an RNA molecule is single stranded and contains uracil (U) instead of thymine (T). **(B)**
- Describe the stages of protein synthesis including transcription and translation, including the role of mRNA, ribosomes, tRNA, codons and anticodons. **(B)**
- Understand how genes exist in alternative forms called alleles which give rise to differences in inherited characteristics.
- Know that in human cells the diploid number of chromosomes is 46 and the haploid number is 23.

Learning outcomes

- Explain that a nucleus contains chromosomes, on which genes are located.
- Describe a gene as a small portion of DNA coding for a specific protein, and the genome comprises all the DNA of an organism.
- Describe a DNA molecule as two strands coiled to form a double helix, the strands being linked by a series of paired bases: adenine (A) with thymine (T), and cytosine (C) with guanine (G). **(B)**
- Explain that RNA differs from DNA in being single stranded and containing uracil (U) instead of thymine (T). **(B)**
- Describe the stages of protein synthesis i.e. transcription and translation, including the role of mRNA, ribosomes, tRNA, codons and anticodons. **(B)**
- Explain that genes exist in alternative forms called alleles, which give rise to differences in inherited characteristics.
- Explain that human diploid body cells contain 46 chromosomes, and human haploid gamete cells contain 23 chromosomes.

Common misconceptions

Students can find it difficult to make the connection between the concept of genes as molecules and how genes are able to control the development of body characteristics. It will help if you talk about genes that code for proteins which have noticeable effects on characteristics, such as the colour of skin and hair (caused by amount of the protein melanin that is produced).

With more able students, remind them that enzymes are proteins and so coded for by genes – and that enzymes control many of the reactions that happen in the body. Note that the concept 'one gene produces one characteristic' is a highly simplified description of genetically controlled development, but it helps to start with this basic idea (see further discussion in B3b.2).

Confusion can also arise between the terms *gene* and *genome*.

Resources

Student Book pages 214–219

Worksheet B3b.1a The structure of DNA; Worksheet B3b.1b Protein synthesis

Approach

1. Introduction

Write the word *gene* in the middle of the board. Ask students to suggest related words and how to link them to create a concept map for this subject. They should be able to suggest a wide range of links from their previous learning, including cell structure (nucleus), sexual reproduction (inheritance of characteristics) and variation in characteristics.

You could add to the concept map at the end of other activities in Topic 3b to build a full map on inheritance. If so, leave plenty of room around the outside for adding more words.

2. Chromosomes, DNA and genes

Worksheet B3b.1a provides a cut-and-paste activity to help students relate these structures to each other and to their position in the nucleus. This would be a useful opportunity to point out that chromosomes only show their X-shaped form during cell division, and that most of the time they are 'uncondensed' –meaning that they are not coiled tightly and cannot be distinguished from each other. The diagram on page 216 of the Student Book will help less able students.

Students will have difficulty marking a 'gene' on their diagrams. This is to be expected. Take the opportunity to discuss what a gene is (the position on a chromosome of DNA that codes for a protein) and why we need further information to decide how many bases within the DNA strand equate to 'one gene'. Explain to students that different genes are of different lengths, depending on which characteristic they are coding for. Explain that all the genes of an organism make up its genome. Note, only students taking International GCSE Biology need to learn about the double helix structure and base pairing.

3. DNA helix model

If students are having difficulty understanding the idea of a double helix, get them to cut a ladder from an A4 sheet of paper by folding it in half lengthwise and cutting out equal shaped rectangles, leaving about 1 cm between edges and cuts. They should open out the ladder, and add pairs of bases on the 'rungs' using the correct complementary pairs (A/T and C/G). They should then twist the ladder between top and bottom to produce the double helix shape.

4. Protein synthesis

Ask students to read pages 216–218 of the Student Book on RNA and protein synthesis. Explain that RNA is used in the production of proteins using the information coded in DNA. Remind them of their work in Topic 2b Cell structure on the function of ribosomes and explain that ribosomes are made of RNA and that there are two other types of RNA (mRNA and tRNA) also involved in protein synthesis. Remind them also of their work on protein structure from Topic 2c Biological molecules and explain that DNA codes for the sequence of the amino acids in proteins. Ask students to make a list of the similarities and differences between RNA and DNA. Having clarified that, show them a suitable animation of transcription and translation from the internet. Students can then either make their own flow chart or cartoon strip to describe the processes, or annotate the diagram on Worksheet 3.1b.

5. Alleles

Ask students to identify some obvious physical characteristics in humans (not including gender). They should then identify variation in those characteristics. Then ask students, since one gene codes for a characteristic, how is inherited variation produced? They should be able to suggest variations in the genes.

Introduce the term *allele* for these different forms of the same gene, and ask students to consider how many alleles there might be for the genes that code for eye colour or any other inherited characteristic suggested. For some genes, there are only two alleles, but for others there may be many.

Show students the diagram of the human karyotype (ordered chromosome pairs) on page 216 of the Student Book. Explain that it shows the chromosomes from the nucleus of one human cell. Give students a few minutes to work individually or in pairs to answer the following questions. Then take answers from around the class to check that students have the right answers (shown underlined):

- How many chromosomes are there in a human body cell? (23, <u>46</u>, hundreds, thousands)

- How many genes are there in a human body cell? (23, 46, hundreds, <u>thousands</u>)

- What is the largest number of alleles that a gene can have? (1, 2, <u>many</u>)

- What is the largest number of alleles that one cell can have for a gene? (1, <u>2</u>, many)

- How many chromosomes are there in a human gamete (sex cell)? (<u>23</u>, 46, hundreds, thousands)

It is important for students to understand that although a gene may occur in many different forms (alleles), an individual cell can only have a maximum of two different alleles for a particular gene because there are two copies of each gene in each cell.

Link the chromosome number of gametes to the idea that each gamete contains one set of chromosomes (haploid) and therefore one set of genes, and that body cells contain two sets (diploid) as a result of receiving one set from each parent. This will be covered more fully in the activities on meiosis and fertilisation later.

6. Consolidation

Either ask students to suggest words to amend any errors and add any new learning to the concept map created in the introduction, or ask them to produce definitions for an online dictionary for the following terms: *DNA, chromosome, gene, allele, genome, RNA, tRNA, mRNA, codon, anticodon, transcription, translation.*

Answers

Page 219

1. Gene, chromosome, nucleus, cell.

2. a) The shape of the DNA molecule, a twisted ladder shape with two strands joined by pairs of bases.

   b) The 'rungs' of the DNA double helix, which are formed from an AT pair or a GC pair.

3. Different forms of the same gene that code for different variations of the same characteristic, such as different eye colours.

4. RNA is (usually) single stranded and contains the base uracil (U) instead of thymine (T).

5. a) Transcription involves: a DNA gene 'unzips' forming two single strands; one DNA strand acts as a 'template' for the formation of a corresponding strand of mRNA; the bases on the mRNA and DNA form pairs, C with G, A (mRNA) with T (DNA), and U (mRNA) with A (DNA).
   (The mRNA then leaves the nucleus.)

   b) Translation involves: mRNA attaches to a ribosome; every 3 bases on the mRNA is a codon, and matches with a corresponding anticodon on tRNA; tRNA molecules bring amino acids to the ribosome which are joined together to make up proteins; the mRNA base sequence determines the protein amino acid sequence.

B3b.1a The structure of DNA

Cut out the diagrams below. Identify each structure and arrange them in order of their real size, starting with the largest. Paste them into your workbook in this order.

Link the diagrams by indicating which part of the previous diagram the following diagram represents, such as by circling the part it shows and adding an arrow to link them.

Add the following labels at the correct points on the diagrams. You may need to use some of the labels more than once: base, chromosome, gene, DNA, nucleus.

Add any other notes to your diagram to help you remember all the details of the structure of DNA.

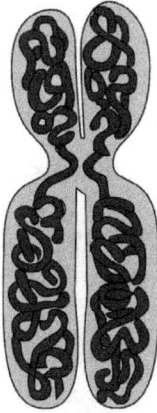

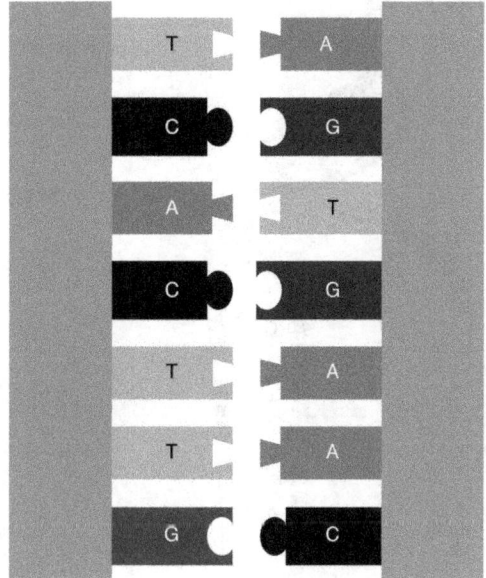

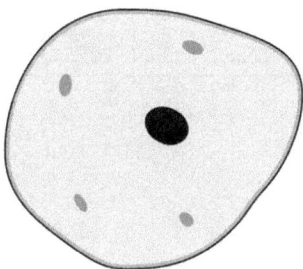

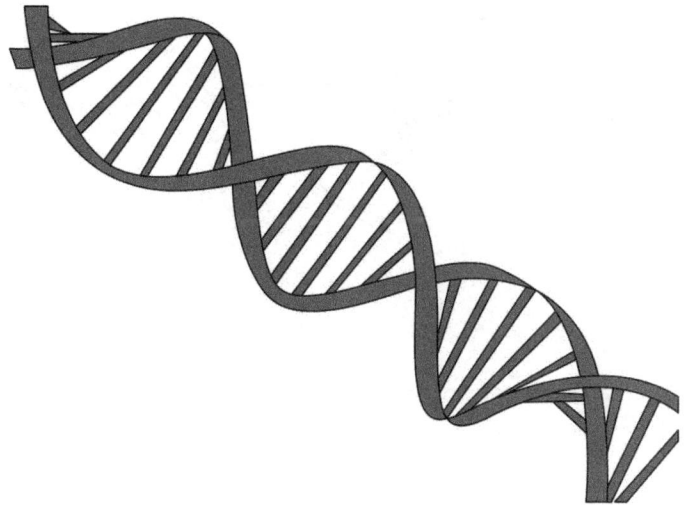

B3b.1b Protein synthesis

1. Label the diagram fully to indicate: nucleus, cytoplasm, DNA, mRNA, tRNA, ribosome, codon, anticodon.

2. Add notes to explain where transcription and translation take place and what happens during these processes.

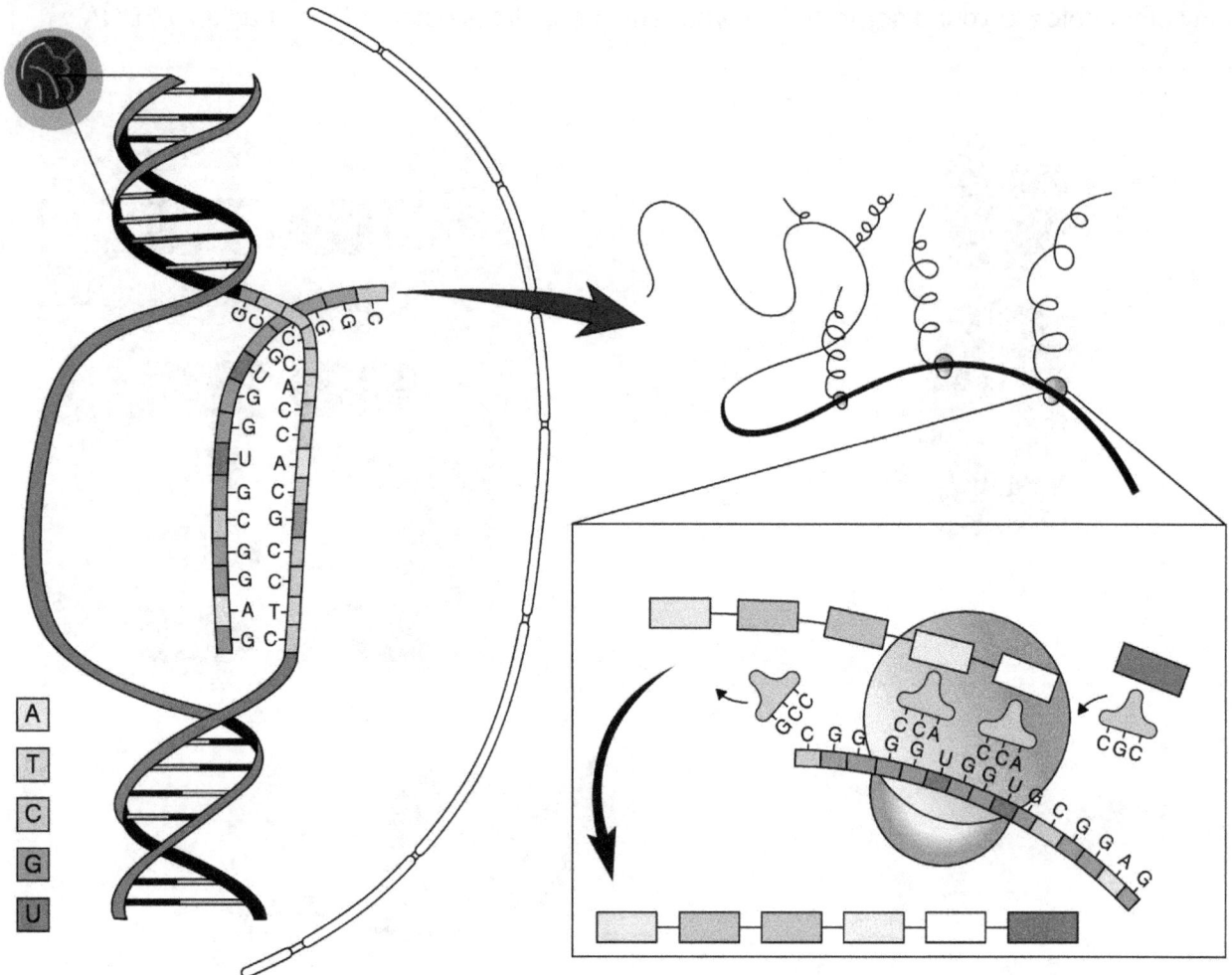

Activity B3b.2 Inheriting characteristics

Specification reference: B3b.3.20; B3b.3.21**B**; B3b.3.22; B3b.3.23; B3b.3.24; B3b.3.25; B3b.3.26; B3b.3.27

Learning objectives

- Understand the meaning of the terms: dominant, recessive, homozygous, heterozygous, phenotype and genotype.
- Understand the meaning of the term codominance. **(B)**
- Understand that most phenotypic features are the result of polygenic inheritance rather than single genes.
- Describe patterns of monohybrid inheritance using a genetic diagram.
- Understand how to interpret family pedigrees.
- Predict probabilities of outcomes from monohybrid crosses.
- Understand how the sex of a person is controlled by one pair of chromosomes, XX in a female and XY in a male.
- Describe the determination of sex of the offspring at fertilisation, using a genetic diagram.

Learning outcomes

- Write a definition for important terms in genetics include: dominant, recessive, homozygous, heterozygous, phenotype, genotype and codominance.
- Understand that most phenotypic features are the result of polygenic inheritance.
- Describe patterns of monohybrid inheritance using genetic diagrams, which can be used to predict probabilities of outcomes.
- Understand how to interpret family pedigrees.
- Describe how the sex of a person is controlled by one pair of chromosomes: XX in a female and XY in a male.
- Describe the determination of the sex of offspring at fertilisation, using a genetic diagram.

Common misconceptions

In humans, females have two identical sex chromosomes, but this is not the case in all animals. In birds and some insects, for example, males have identical sex chromosomes and females have two different sex chromosomes.

Humans are not particularly useful for examples of monohybrid inheritance, as most of our characteristics are controlled by several genes (polygenic). For example, the products of several genes interact to produce eye colour or hair colour. However, students need to understand monohybrid inheritance before moving on at A level to look at more complex examples of genetic inheritance although they should be aware of polygenic effects now, and avoid the common misconception that one gene generally produces one characteristic.

Resources

Student Book pages 219–230

Worksheet B3b.2a Investigating monohybrid inheritance

Resources for class practical (see Technician's notes, following)

Approach

1. Introduction: terminology

Use the diagram on page 220 of the Student Book to introduce the terms *homozygous, heterozygous, dominant allele, recessive allele, genotype* and *phenotype*. Ask students to write their own definitions and to compare with another student's definitions to see if they could be improved.

Test their understanding by telling them that a fictional animal has two alleles for the gene for hair colour. Capital B represents the allele for blue hair and small b represents the allele for white hair. Ask questions such as the following:

- Which letter represents the recessive allele (and how do you know)? (b, lower-case/small letter)
- What is the genotype of a homozygous dominant individual? (BB)
- What is the phenotype of a homozygous recessive individual? (white hair)
- What is the genotype and phenotype of a heterozygous individual? (Bb, blue hair)
- Which allele(s) would be found in the gametes of a homozygous dominant individual? (only B)
- Which allele(s) would be found in the gametes of a heterozygous individual? (some B, some b)

Take answers from around the class to check understanding. Alternatively do this as a red/yellow/green card activity to check how certain all students are of the answers.

2. Investigating monohybrid inheritance

Explain that, while most human phenotypic features are controlled by more than one gene (polygenic), to understand inheritance it's better to begin by trying to understand monohybrid inheritance. Worksheet B3b.2a gives students the opportunity to model monohybrid inheritance using counters or other small objects of two colours to represent the alleles. This supports the Developing investigative skills box on page 224 of the Student Book. It offers four possible crosses for the inheritance for a gene with two alleles. It might help weaker students if you go through the questions as a group or class for the first cross of homozygous dominant and homozygous recessive.

For the practical, students should be able to draw genetic diagrams, either in layout form or as Punnett squares, so some practice in this with the first cross will be helpful. Alternatively, let students use the diagrams on page 222 and 223 of the Student Book for guidance.

Using the genetic diagrams, students should get the following theoretical results:

- homozygous dominant × homozygous recessive: genotype all heterozygous, phenotype all of dominant colour
- heterozygous × heterozygous: genotypes 1 homozygous dominant : 2 heterozygous : 1 homozygous recessive; phenotypes 3 dominant colour : 1 recessive colour
- homozygous dominant × heterozygous: genotypes 1 homozygous dominant : 1 heterozygous; phenotypes all dominant colour
- homozygous recessive × heterozygous: genotypes 1 heterozygous : 1 homozygous recessive; phenotypes 1 dominant colour : 1 recessive colour.

Results can be expressed as ratios, percentages or probabilities. Remind students that ratios are reduced to their simplest form, so 2 : 2 in results above should be reduced to 1 : 1.

3. Mendel and investigating inheritance

Although knowledge of Gregor Mendel's investigations of inheritance in peas is not required for the IGCSE specification, it offers an interesting alternative or extension to the practical work. Students could research how he set up his investigations to make sure they would produce as reliable results as possible, and what results he got from his crosses. They should be expected to explain Mendel's results.

4. Investigating codominance (B)

Students should repeat part of Worksheet B3b.2a, but with the understanding that the two colours of counter represent codominant alleles, so that the heterozygous phenotype shows the effects of both alleles present in the genotype. They should then compare the proportions of each genotype and phenotype in the offspring with those from the same crosses in the previous investigation and explain any differences.

5. Decoding family pedigrees

Ask students to read pages 228–229 of the Student Book on family pedigrees. Work together to check that students follow the deductions made from the diagram. You may need to help them produce genetic diagrams to support the conclusions. Ask students to answer question 3 in the Questions Box on page 223 to check that they fully understand what a pedigree shows. They could then try to produce a family pedigree, including the key, for either a dominant or recessive characteristic. They could test their diagram on another student to make sure they have understood the inheritance correctly.

6. Inheritance of sex

Ask students to compare the photographs of the human X and Y chromosomes on page 230 of the Student Book. Tell students that these chromosomes are the sex chromosomes and link the shape of the chromosomes to the notation of XX for female and XY for male.

Ask students to identify what the gametes from a man and a woman will contain in terms of sex chromosomes. They should realise that the egg cells will all contain one X chromosome, while the sperm may contain one X or one Y chromosome. In fact, there should be equal numbers of X sperm and Y sperm cells produced (but they may not fully understand this until they cover meiosis later in this topic).

From this, they should be able to create their own genetic diagram to show the inheritance of sex in humans. Then ask, if a couple already have two boys, what is the probability that their next child is also a boy. Using their genetic diagrams, students should be able to confirm that this is always 50%.

7. Consolidation: key facts

Either ask students to suggest words to add any new learning to the concept map created in the Introduction of B3b.1, or ask students to write a list of the five most important facts that they have learned about inheritance. They should then compare their list with a neighbour, and agree the five most important facts from the two lists. This could be repeated in fours, and then examples taken from each group to draw up a class list of the five key facts to remember.

Technician's notes

You will need the following resources for the class practical.

Be sure to check the latest safety notes on these resources before proceeding.

B3b.2a Investigating monohybrid inheritance

Class practical, per group:

10 counters each of 2 colours (other small items could be used, such as beads or buttons, as long as they are all identical except for the 2 colours)
two small pots, such as yoghurt pots

Answers

Page 221

1. a) The characteristic is fully expressed in the phenotype even when the organism has only one allele of that form for that gene (heterozygous).

   b) The characteristic is only expressed in the phenotype when both alleles for that gene are of this form and is not expressed in a heterozygote.

   c) Having two identical copies of that allele for a particular gene.

   d) Having different alleles for a particular gene.

2. a) 2

   b) 1

   c) 2

Page 223

1. The inheritance of a characteristic produced by one gene.

2. Genotype (the alleles in the chromosomes) BB, phenotype (what the organism looks like) brown; genotype Bb, phenotype brown (because the brown allele is dominant); genotype bb, phenotype black (because the organism does not have the brown allele).

3. a) Answer may be presented as a full layout diagram or a Punnett square, showing the adult genotypes and phenotypes (male Bb brown and female Bb brown), the possible gametes produced (male B and b, female B and b), genotypes and phenotypes of possible offspring (BB brown, Bb brown, Bb brown, bb black).

   b) This cross produces a theoretical probability of one black rabbit for every three brown rabbits, a ratio of 1:3, probability of 1 in 4 or 0.25 or 25%.

Developing investigative skills, page 224

1. Start with two beakers, containing the same number of beads, but half the beads in each beaker are red and half are blue, because half the gametes will receive the dominant allele during meiosis and the other half will receive the recessive allele. Start with many beads in each pot, well mixed.

For each 'fertilisation' take one bead (gamete) from one beaker, without looking because fertilisation is random. Then take one bead, without looking, from the other beaker. Place the two beads together to represent the genotype of the offspring.

2. There would be 20 red beads and 20 blue beads in each pot because half the gametes will receive one allele from the diploid parent cell and half the gametes will receive the other allele.

3. Genetic diagram or Punnett square, using letters of own choice linked to red and blue beads, such as the following.

R is dominant allele, represented by red bead; r is recessive allele, represented by blue bead.

		gametes	
		R	r
gametes	R	RR	Rr
	r	Rr	rr

Predicted probabilities are 1 RR : 2 Rr : 1 rr for genotypes and 3 dominant : 1 recessive for phenotypes.

4. Actual results are 1 red/red : 2.4 red/blue : 0.6 blue/blue for genotypes and 5.7 dominant : 1 recessive for phenotypes.

5. The actual results vary quite a bit from the predicted results because only a small number of repeats was carried out.

6. If the number of repeats was increased, it is likely that the actual ratios will get closer to the predicted ones.

Page 227 (top)

1. So that, when the plants were bred together, the results in the offspring were not confused by a mix of alleles in one or both of the parents, as both parents would be homozygous.

2. Random variation is possible in the results. So, the larger the sample, the more likely that any random variation will be averaged out.

3. He removed the stamens from every flower, so they could not self-pollinate. He also covered each flower after he had hand-pollinated it, so that other pollen could not get to the stigma.

4. Any characteristic may be used, with alleles appropriately designated with capital letter for dominant and lower-case letter for recessive allele. Parents used should show one with phenotype of dominant allele, homozygous, e.g. BB, and one parent with phenotype of recessive allele, i.e. bb. First cross will produce all individuals with phenotype of dominant allele but heterozygous in genotype, i.e. Bb. Crossing of these individuals will produce characteristic 1 BB : 2 Bb : 1 bb in genotype and 3 dominant characteristic to 1 recessive characteristic in next generation.

5. If Mendel had not been as thorough about his method, then his results would not have been as clear and reliable. So, he would not have been able to have drawn clear and repeatable conclusions about the way characteristics are inherited in pea plants.

Page 227 (bottom) – 228

1. They are polygenic characters, controlled by more than one gene.

2. When both alleles are expressed in the phenotype, and there is no dominance of one allele over the other.

3. a) I^A and I^B.

   b) Only I^o.

   c)

			Father AB	
			Gametes	
			I^A	I^B
Mother O	Gametes	I^o	$I^A I^o$ blood group A	$I^B I^o$ blood group B
		I^o	$I^A I^o$ blood group A	$I^B I^o$ blood group B

   d) There is a 1 : 1 ratio, 0.5 or 50% or a 1 in 2 probability of blood group A and blood group B.

Page 229

1. 3

2. 2

3. 2

4. 'Freckles' are dominant because I has no freckles, but her parents C and D do. I must be homozygous recessive and C and D must both be heterozygous. If having no freckles was dominant then at least one of C and D would have had to have had no freckles.

Page 230

1. XX

2. XY

3. 0.5 or 50% (or 1 in 2), because there is an equal probability that an X sperm or a Y sperm will fertilise the X egg cell.

B3b.2a Investigating monohybrid inheritance

In this investigation, you will model the inheritance of a characteristic controlled by one gene: monohybrid inheritance. You will use coloured counters (or other objects) to represent the alleles for the gene.

Apparatus

10 counters each of 2 colours

two small pots

Method

1. Decide which of the colours will represent the dominant allele, and which represents the recessive allele and write these down. Choose what the alleles code for, such as spotted coat colour and black coat colour in leopards, and write these down.

2. The pots represent the collection of gametes produced by each parent. To start, you will look at a cross between a homozygous dominant parent and a homozygous recessive parent. Since each parent is homozygous, they can only produce gametes containing one type of allele. Place 10 counters of the dominant colour in one pot, and place 10 counters of the recessive colour into the other pot.

3. To carry out a cross, take one counter at random from one pot and one at random from the other pot to produce the genotype of one offspring. Note down the genotype and the phenotype of this offspring.

4. Continue taking one counter from each pot, to represent more crosses from these parents, until you have used all the counters. In each case record the genotype and phenotype of the offspring.

5. Set up the pots again for different crosses. Remember that the gametes of a homozygous individual will all have the same allele. However, for a heterozygous individual half the counters will be of the dominant colour and half of the recessive colour. Try the following crosses, recording the genotypes and phenotypes of each offspring:

   - heterozygous × heterozygous
   - homozygous dominant × heterozygous
   - homozygous recessive × heterozygous.

Analyse and interpret data

1. Use your results to calculate the proportion of different genotypes for each cross, as a ratio, probability or percentage.

2. Use your results to calculate the proportion of different phenotypes for each cross, as a ratio, probability or percentage.

3. Draw a genetic diagram for each of the crosses you carried out. (Remember to identify which letter represents which allele in your diagram.)

4. Calculate the theoretical proportions for each genotype and phenotype for each of the crosses.

5. Compare your practical results with the theoretical values, and explain any differences.

6. Use your answer to question 5 to explain why two heterozygous parents may produce all offspring with the recessive phenotype.

Activity B3b.3 Cell division

Specification reference: B3b.3.28; B3b.3.29; B3b.3.30

Learning objectives

- Understand how division of a diploid cell by mitosis produces two cells that contain identical sets of chromosomes.
- Understand that mitosis occurs during growth, repair, cloning and asexual reproduction.
- Understand how division of a cell by meiosis produces four cells, each with half the number of chromosomes, and that this results in the formation of genetically different haploid gametes.

Learning outcomes

- Explain how division of a diploid cell by mitosis produces two cells that contain identical sets of chromosomes.
- Explain that mitosis occurs during growth, repair, cloning and asexual reproduction.
- Explain that division of a cell by meiosis produces four cells, each with half the number of chromosomes, and that this results in the formation of genetically different haploid gametes.

Common misconceptions

Students commonly confuse mitosis and meiosis because of the similarity of the words. Help them produce their own mnemonics, such as 'miTosis produces Two cells, MEiosis produces gaMEtes'.

Resources

Student Book pages 231–233

Worksheet B3b.3a Mitosis

Worksheet B3b.3b Meiosis

Resources for class practical (see Technician's notes, following)

Approach

1. Introduction

Remind students that one of the characteristics of living organisms is growth, and ask them what needs to happen in a body for it to grow. They should identify cell division as one of the processes needed. Point out that all cells in a body have the same number of chromosomes. Give students a minute or so in pairs or small groups to consider what must happen in a body cell before it can divide to make more body cells. Then take suggestions from around the class. The key point to get from this is that everything in the cell must be duplicated before division, including the chromosomes.

2. Mitosis

Worksheet B3b.3a provides a cut-and-paste task to place the stages of mitosis in the correct order and to annotate them to describe the process. Students could check their layout against the diagram of mitosis on page 231 of the Student Book before pasting the pictures into their workbook. The questions on the worksheet will help students to summarise the key features of the process that they need to learn.

3. Mitosis in action

If possible, show students a video of mitosis in a body cell. Note that many have voice-over that is more suited for A-level, where the stages of mitosis are named. If you use one of these, remind students that they do not need to remember the names of the stages. The key point to take from the video is seeing mitosis as a continuous process rather than a set of fixed stages.

If you are unable to show a video, students could instead look at prepared slides of mitosis in cells of a plant meristem (e.g. root or shoot tip) to identify different stages of mitosis taking place in different cells. They could draw a number of different cells and try to arrange them in the correct order to show mitosis.

4. Meiosis

Worksheet B3b.3b provides a cut-and-paste task to place the stages of meiosis in the correct order and to annotate them to describe the process. The different phases of meiosis are fully muddled in the worksheet. For less able students, you could separate the diagrams for the two main phases before they then put the pictures into the final order.

Students could check their layout against the diagram of meiosis on page 232 of the Student Book before pasting the pictures into their workbook. The questions on the worksheet will help students to summarise the key features of the process that they need to learn.

5. Comparing mitosis and meiosis

You could give students a blank version of the table on page 232 of the Student Book to complete, to summarise the similarities and differences between the two forms to cell division.

6. Consolidation: the right choice

Either ask students to suggest words to add any new learning to the concept map created in the Introduction of B3b.1, or give students two scraps of paper and ask them to write *mitosis* on one scrap and *meiosis* on the other scrap. Then ask questions for which one of these is the answer and ask students to hold up the correct answer each time.

Questions could include:

- Which form of cell division produces four cells?
- Which form of cell division occurs in asexual reproduction?
- Which form of cell division produces haploid cells?

Technician's notes

You will need the following resources for the class practical.

Be sure to check the latest safety notes on these resources before proceeding.

B3b.3a Mitosis

Class practical, per student or group:

light microscope with low and high power objectives
prepared slide of mitosis, such as from root tip squash of onion, stained to show chromosomes

Answers

Page 233

1.

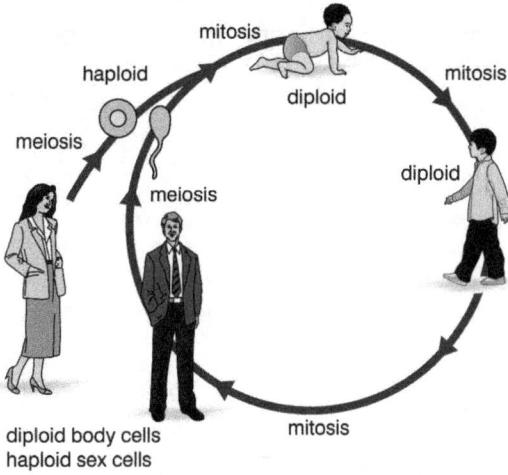

2. Diploid body cell → chromosomes duplicate → chromosomes line up across middle of cell → copies of chromosomes separate and each copy goes to the opposite side of the cell → cell divides in two to produce two identical diploid body cells

3. Diploid body cell → chromosomes duplicate → chromosome pairs line up across middle of cell → one chromosome from each pair moves to opposite sides of the cell → cell divides in two → chromosomes line up across middle of cells → chromosome copies separate and each copy goes to the opposite side of the cells → cells divide in two to form four haploid cells that are not genetically identical

4. Meiosis produces non-identical cells, so there is variety in the gamete cells. When the gamete cells fuse, this will mean that the offspring will vary from each other.

B3b.3a Mitosis

Mitosis is the type of cell division used when body cells divide. The diagrams below, when placed in the correct order, show what happens during mitosis.

1. Cut out the diagrams, arrange them in the correct order, then paste them into your workbook in this order. Annotate each diagram to explain what it shows.

2. Summarise the result of mitotic cell division in terms of:

   a) number of cells produced from one parent cell

   b) how similar or different the daughter cells are from each other and the parent cell.

3. Explain the importance of this kind of cell division in:

   a) growth and repair of body tissue

   b) cloning and asexual reproduction.

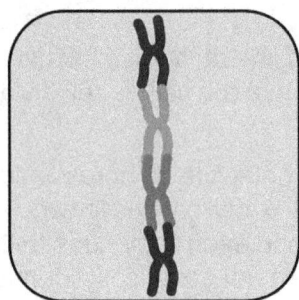
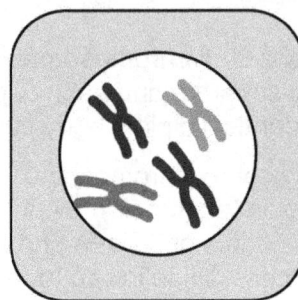

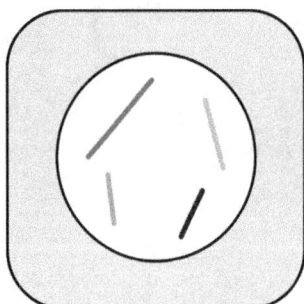
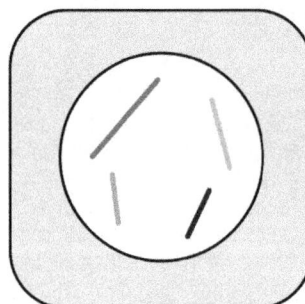

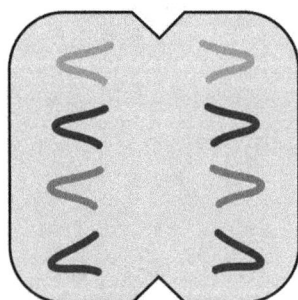
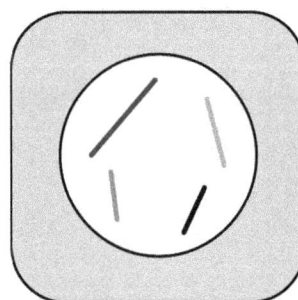

B3b.3b Meiosis

Meiosis is the cell division that produces haploid gametes from diploid body cells. When placed in the correct order, the diagrams show what happens during meiosis.

1. Cut out the diagrams, arrange them in the correct order, then stick them into your workbook in this order. Annotate each diagram to explain what it shows.

2. Summarise the result of mitotic cell division in terms of:

   a) number of cells produced from one parent cell

   b) how similar or different the daughter cells are from each other and the parent cell.

3. Explain the importance of this kind of cell division for sexual reproduction.

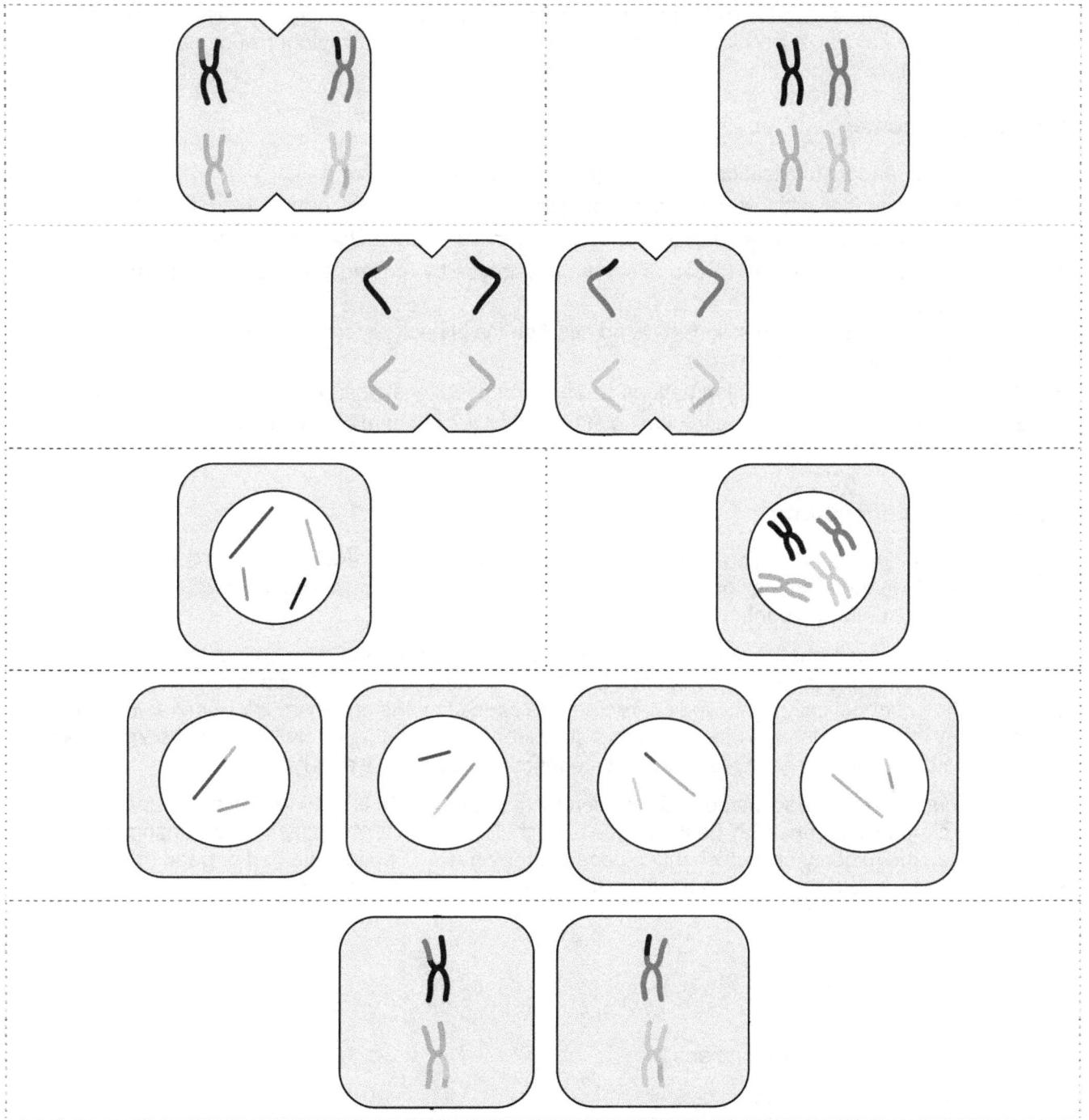

Activity B3b.4 Variation and mutation

Specification reference: B3b.3.31; B3b.3.33; B3b.3.34; B3b.3.35**B** B3b.3.36**B**; B3b.3.37**B**

Learning objectives

- Understand how random fertilisation produces genetic variation of offspring.
- Understand that variation within a species can be genetic, environmental, or a combination of both.
- Understand that mutation is a rare, random change in genetic material that can be inherited.
- Understand how a change in DNA can affect the phenotype by altering the sequence of amino acids in a protein. **(B)**
- Understand how most genetic mutations have no effect on the phenotype, some have a small effect and rarely do they have a significant effect. **(B)**
- Understand that the incidence of mutations can be increased by exposure to ionising radiation (for example gamma rays, X-rays and ultraviolet rays) and some chemical mutagens (for example chemicals in tobacco). **(B)**

Learning outcomes

- Explain that random fertilisation produces genetic variation of offspring.
- Explain that variation within a species can be genetic, environmental, or a combination of both.
- Explain that mutation is a rare, random change in genetic material that can be inherited.
- Describe how a change in DNA can affect the phenotype by altering the sequence of amino acids in a protein. **(B)**
- Explain that most genetic mutations have no effect on the phenotype, some have a small effect and rarely do they have a significant effect. **(B)**
- Describe how the incidence of mutations can be increased by exposure to ionising radiation (for example gamma rays, X-rays and ultraviolet rays) and some chemical mutagens (for example chemicals in tobacco). **(B)**

Common misconceptions

Some students think that variation is either caused by genes or by the environment. It is important that they realise that many examples of variation that are affected by the environment, such as height or weight, have a genetic component too.

Students carrying out further research on genetics may come across the term *epigenetics*. They do not need to understand this term for their exams, but it may be help to explain that this refers to changes in the production of genetically controlled characteristics caused by the environment. For example, this explains why identical twins are often not completely identical even though they have the same genes. This is a rapidly growing area of research that students will learn more about at A level.

The word *mutation* has a bad image and is generally associated with bad things such as cancer. Although a change in a gene may be the cause of such illness, the term applies to any change in a gene. We never see the majority of such changes because they have no noticeable bad or good effect. As students will see in Activity B3b.5, mutation is the source of variation on which natural selection acts and so it is essential for evolution.

Resources

Student Book pages 234–236

Worksheet B3b.4a Variation in humans

Worksheet B3b.4b A cause of skin cancer

Approach

1. Introduction

Give students a few minutes to write down all the variation in phenotypic characteristics that they can see in the students in the class. Take examples, and each time ask what the cause of the variation is. Keep the discussion general and avoid any discussion that focuses on individuals. Try to elicit the two key sources of variation: from genes and from the environment. Then remind students that many examples of variation caused by the environment have a genetic component too.

If students have done work on the inherited and environmental causes of variation in earlier years, you only need to summarise that work here. If students seem unsure of this work, give them the opportunity to investigate it further in the next task. Remind students of their recent work on meiosis and of the variation in gametes produced by this, coupled with the random nature of fertilisation.

2. Variation in human characteristics

Worksheet B3b.4a provides an opportunity to investigate variation in humans, and its causes. If possible, students should enter their data into a spreadsheet and analyse the results on computer. This will make it easier to gather a larger amount of data and so improve the reliability of conclusions. Some students may need help working out how to group the data and to calculate proportions.

Warn students of the risks of drawing conclusions from differences in small amounts of data (due to the effect of random variation). Students who are able in maths could be introduced to the idea of using standard errors on the data, in order to test the significance of any differences.

It is possible that students will not find any significant results, because of small sample sizes. However, the characteristics listed are all known to have some genetic component.

3. Mutations

Use pages 234–235 in the Student Book to introduce mutations. All students should be aware that mutations are random inheritable genetic changes, however, those taking the International GCSE in Biology also need to learn about the factors that increase the incidence of mutation, that most mutations do not affect the phenotype, and those that do, do so by altering the proteins coded for by the mutated genes. Ask students to make notes of the key points and then to test each other on what they have learned by asking questions. If there is access to the internet, students could then research examples of mutations and their effects. Alternatively, they could research evidence for the effect of mutagens on the rate of mutation (e.g. smoking on lung, mouth and throat cancer).

4. The incidence of melanoma

Worksheet B3b.4b provides a graph from Cancer Research UK on the increase in incidence of skin melanoma in the UK between 1975 and 2008. Questions on the sheet ask students to consider the genetic and environmental causes of this increase in mutation. The sheet introduces the terms *correlation* and *cause* to help students identify between the two.

5. Consolidation: true or false

Either ask students to suggest words to add any new learning to the concept map created in the Introduction of B3b.1, or give students two scraps of paper and ask them to write *true* on one scrap and *false* on the other. Then read out statements based on what they should have learned in this activity, some of which are true and some false and ask them to hold up the correct answer.

Statements could include:

- Mutations always cause cancer. (false)
- Height is a characteristic that varies due to genes and the environment. (true)

Technician's notes

No apparatus is needed for the investigation into variation in human characteristics.

Answers

Page 236

1. a) Genes, such as eye colour; environment, such as weight as a result of diet. (Other suitable examples are acceptable.)

   b) Any suitable example showing a combination of genes and environment, such as human height, which depends on genes and a healthy diet to achieve the potential of the genes.

2. A change in the DNA of a gene.

3. Ionising radiation, such as ultraviolet radiation, x-rays or gamma rays; chemical mutagens such as the chemicals in tobacco smoke.

B3b.4a Variation in humans

Some of our characteristics are inherited from our parents, through our genes. Other characteristics are changed by conditions in the environment. Many characteristics are affected by both genes and environment. In this investigation, you will collect data on a number of human characteristics to decide whether or not any variation is inherited or caused by the environment, or both.

Method

1. Choose some of the following characteristics, and draw up a table to record your results. You will need to ask a large number of people, including those who are related, so make sure there is room to record who is related to whom.

Characteristics you could study are:

- hair: naturally straight or curly
- hair: natural colour
- freckles: presence or absence
- tongue: ability to roll the tongue or not
- vision: short-sightedness from childhood or not
- longest finger on hand: first, second or third finger.

There are other characteristics you could include, but remember that some, such as body size and proportion, change with age and so may not be useful for comparing adults and children.

You should also consider how to record variation for each characteristic. For example, if you only have the categories of straight and curly hair, how will you classify hair that is a little wavy?

2. Gather data from as many people as you can, especially from members of the same family.

3. If possible, use a spreadsheet to record your data.

Analyse and interpret data

1. For each characteristic, calculate the proportion of individuals in the whole group who have each variation that you recorded.

2. Taking one family at a time, calculate the proportion of individuals within the family who have each variation of a characteristic. Repeat this for all characteristics and all families.

3. For each characteristic, compare the proportions from families with the proportions of the while group. Describe any differences.

4. If a characteristic is much more or less common in a family group than in the group as a whole, it is possible that the variation is inherited. Looking at your results, can you identify any characteristics that may be inherited?

Evaluate data and methods

1. Explain why you cannot say definitely that any particular characteristic is controlled only by genes or by the environment.

2. Explain why, when researching the cause of variation in a characteristic, scientists usually gather data from thousands of people.

3. In some studies of the causes of variation, scientists only compare data from identical twins. Explain why this helps them produce more reliable conclusions.

B3b.4b A cause of skin cancer

Skin melanoma is an aggressive form of skin cancer. In 2008 it was the sixth most common cause of cancer in men and women in the UK, although many people with this form of skin cancer are successfully treated and live for many years after treatment.

The graph shows the trend in number of people diagnosed with skin melanoma in the UK between 1975 and 2008.

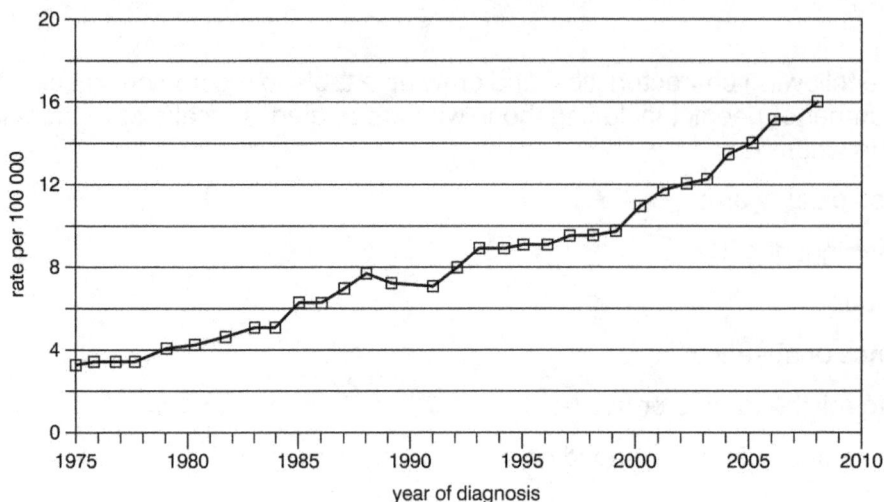

*Data source: Cancer Research UK (http://info.cancerresearchuk.org/cancerstats/types/skin/incidence/)

1. Describe the trend in number of people diagnosed with skin melanoma between 1975 and 2008.

2. Some families show a higher than average rate of developing skin melanoma.

   a) What might this suggest?

   b) Explain, using the graph, why this probably is not the only cause of skin melanoma.

Scientists studying the causes of skin melanoma have shown that the following groups are more likely to be diagnosed with skin melanoma than other groups:

- people with fair skin who do not tan easily
- women (compared with men)
- people who have more money
- people who spend more time in lower latitudes (nearer the Equator).

The relationship between factors, such as skin type and occurrence of melanoma, is known as a *correlation*. This does not mean that one factor *causes* the other. To find a cause, we need to understand why the melanoma starts to form. It is known that UV radiation, from the sun or from using sun beds, is a mutagen that causes cells to change and become cancerous.

3. For each of the groups above, suggest as many reasons as you can why this cause of mutation could produce the correlation.

4. Take one example from your answer to question 3. Describe how you would investigate it to see if was a factor in the changing incidence of skin melanoma. Explain what data you would collect to test this.

Activity B3b.5 Evolution by natural selection

Specification reference: B3b.3.38; B3b.3.39

Learning objectives

- Explain Darwin's theory of evolution by natural selection.
- Understand how resistance to antibiotics can increase in bacterial populations, and appreciate how such an increase can lead to infections being difficult to control.

Learning outcomes

- Describe the process of evolution by means of natural selection.
- Explain how resistance to antibiotics can cause an increase in the size of bacterial populations.

Common misconceptions

One of the most common misconceptions is that the selecting factor somehow causes the variation in the population: for example, that using an antibiotic suddenly makes some bacteria resistant to it. In fact, before the antibiotic was used, there was no way of telling if some bacteria were already resistant or not. As a result of natural variation, some of the bacteria would probably already have been resistant, but it is only since the application of the antibiotic that this has become obvious.

Many people find it difficult to accept that evolution is a random process, caused by random changes in environmental conditions that change the impact of natural selection on the variation in a group of organisms. Instead they think of evolution as a directed 'progress' toward something 'better'. It is important to convey to students the fundamental role of change in environmental conditions in natural selection, so that they realise that evolution is not directed toward a particular goal.

Resources

Student Book pages 236–239

Worksheet B3b.5a A model of natural selection

Resources for class practical (see Technician's notes, following)

Approach

1. Introduction

Give students a minute or two to write down three statements that use the word *evolution* in a way that explains what it means. Take examples from around the class and encourage discussion to try to achieve a definition for the word. Explain that, although evidence for evolution had been known beforehand, it was the scientist Charles Darwin, together with another scientist, Alfred Russel Wallace, who first discovered the process by which evolution happens, i.e. natural selection.

2. Natural selection

Worksheet B3b5.1 gives students an opportunity to model natural selection as a result of 'predation' of coloured sticks on two different colour backgrounds. Note that some students will be tempted to cheat in order to change the results, so be prepared to discount results that do not look reasonable.

Students should find that the colour of stick that most closely matches the colour of the background increases in number over the few generations tested, because the other colour is most obvious. (At some point 'rarity' value of this colour will create a balance of the two colours in the population.)

Students could follow up this practical with research in books or the internet for real-life examples of natural selection, such as the predation of banded snails by thrushes on the Evolution Megalab website.

3. An example of evolution

Ask students to read pages 236–239 of the Student Book on natural selection and the increase of antibiotic resistance in bacteria. Then ask questions such as the following to test understanding:

- Why is the increase in antibiotic resistance in bacteria an example of evolution? (Because the antibiotic is causing a change in characteristics in the population.)

- In terms of natural selection, why is antibiotic resistance increasing so quickly? (This needs an answer that is more than 'We are using lots of antibiotics.') (Because the antibiotic kills a large proportion of the population initially, so only those that are resistant may survive and reproduce.)

- How could antibiotic resistance be reduced? (Any suitable measures, such as: not using antibiotics, but this produces its own problems; killing bacteria by other means such as good hygiene, making sure people complete their course of antibiotics so that the risk of passing on partially-resistant bacteria is minimised, only using antibiotics when really needed.)

4. Consolidation

Either ask students to suggest words to add to the concept map created in the Introduction, or to write at least 10 clues for a crossword on any key word from their work on inheritance. Give them three minutes to do this, then ask them to try their clues out on another student and work together to improve the clues. Take examples from around the class for each key word.

Technician's notes

You will need the following resources for the class practical.

Be sure to check the latest safety notes on these resources before proceeding.

B3b.5a A model of natural selection

The sticks could be cocktail sticks, or any similar short sticks. Alternatively, use rice grains or similar that will absorb colour well.

The sticks should be dyed with food colouring, and should match the colours of the two backgrounds as closely as possible. Avoid using red and green, because of the possibility of colour-blindness in students.

Class practical, per group:

30 sticks each of 2 different colours
2 coloured backgrounds
large pot for mixing up sticks
blunt forceps
stopwatch or clock

Answers

Page 239

1. a) Evolution: change in the characteristics of a species over time.

   b) Natural selection: the influence of the environment on survival and/or reproduction, such that organisms with some characteristics are more successful at producing offspring than others.

2. a) If the individuals in a population are all the same, natural selection will favour (or disadvantage) them all equally.

   b) If individuals with a particular variation of a characteristic have a greater survival advantage, they are more likely to produce offspring that carry their genes, and so their genes will become more common in the next generation.

3. Diagrams should show the following:

person infected with bacteria → bacteria grow in number inside patient → treatment of patient with antibiotics kills off least resistant bacteria but some resistant bacteria survive → some of these bacteria escape into the environment from the patient and infect another person → the same antibiotic cannot be used on that patient as the bacteria are resistant.

B3b.5a A model of natural selection

Natural selection occurs when some individuals in a group are more able to survive and reproduce than others. The factor that makes this possible is called the selection factor. One obvious selection factor is predation, for example predation of snails by birds. Snails that are better camouflaged against the background are less likely to be seen by a bird and therefore less likely to be eaten.

In this practical you are going to investigate the effect of 'predation' on a population of coloured sticks. You will work in pairs, with one student acting as the 'predator' and one as the experimenter.

Apparatus

30 sticks each of 2 different colours

2 coloured backgrounds

large pot for mixing up sticks

blunt forceps

stopwatch or clock

Method

1. The experimenter should place 20 sticks of each colour into the pot and mix them thoroughly.

2. Without the predator looking, the experimenter should scatter the sticks on one of the coloured backgrounds, making sure the sticks do not overlap. They should then start the stopwatch.

3. The predator has 30 seconds to collect as many sticks, one at a time, with the forceps and place them in the empty pot.

4. At the end of one minute, count how many sticks there are of each colour still on the background. Record the number of each colour, and the colour of the background.

5. Empty the pot of sticks that were 'caught' and return the sticks still left on the background to the pot, two of the same colour at a time. For each pair of sticks returned to the pot, add another stick of the same colour. (This models the survivors breeding and producing one 'offspring' of the same colour.)

6. Repeat steps 2–5 two more times, recording the number of each colour of sticks that are left on the background each time.

7. Repeat the investigation with the other colour background.

8. If there is time, swap roles as predator and experimenter.

9. Draw a suitable table to display your results.

Analyse and interpret data

1. Describe your results.

2. Explain your results using what you know about predators and camouflage.

3. Explain what your results suggest about natural selection.

Evaluate data & methods

1. Describe any problems that you had with this practical.

2. Suggest how you could improve the method to reduce these problems as far as possible.

Activity B3b.6 Consolidation and summary

Learning objectives

- To review the learning points of the topic.
- To test understanding through answering questions.

Learning outcomes

- Be familiar with the knowledge and understanding summarised in the End of topic checklist.
- Be able to apply this knowledge and understanding by answering the End of topic questions.

Resources

Student Book pages 240–247

Approach

Ask students to answer the End of topic questions in the Student Book.

Answers

End of topic questions mark scheme

Question	Correct answer	Marks
1	The nucleus in a cell contains the chromosomes, which are made from DNA.	1
	A gene is a short piece of that DNA.	1
2 a)	Using any suitable symbols for wet and dry ear wax, such as E for wet and e for dry, either a layout or a Punnett square including the following information:	

		father's gametes	
		e	e
mother's gametes	E	Ee wet earwax	Ee wet earwax
	e	ee dry earwax	ee dry earwax

	suitable use of letters for alleles	1
	definition of letter for each allele	1
	correct gametes for parents	1
	correct genotypes for offspring	1
	correct phenotypes for offspring	1
2 b)	Predicted genotypes 1 : 1 Ee to ee, 0.5 or 50% or 1 in 2 probability of either outcome.	1
	Predicted phenotypes: 1 : 1 wet to dry, 0.5 or 50% or 1 in 2 probability of either outcome.	1

Question	Correct answer	Marks
2 c)	The chance of inheriting wet or dry earwax is the same at each fertilisation. So it is a 50% chance each time.	1
	Random fertilisation means it could give the same result each time.	1
3	The cross will produce plants that are heterozygous, with one red and one white allele.	1
	If either allele was dominant, then all the offspring would have flowers of the colour that the allele produces.	1
	Instead the flowers show splashes of each colour, suggesting that both alleles are being expressed equally.	1
4 a)	A random change in an allele/gene.	1
4 b)	Ionising radiation.	1
	Mutagenic chemicals.	1
4 c)	Ionising radiation from UV light as a result of overexposure of skin to sunlight.	1
	Because skin is more exposed to this form of radiation than other parts of the body.	1
4 d)	i) Both curves increased	1
	from about 500 new cases to over 2000 new cases for men and around 1500 new cases for women.	1
	ii) Any suitable explanation that refers to increased exposure to stronger sunlight such as: more holidays in tropical regions, people trying to get darker tans.	1
	This increases the risk of overexposure to UV light.	1
5	If there were no meiosis, the chromosome number of the zygote would double each time there was fertilisation.	1
	Meiosis halves the number of chromosomes, and then the full number is restored during fertilisation.	1
6	Asexual reproduction occurs as a result of mitosis of diploid cells.	1
	This form of cell division produces identical diploid cells, so asexual reproduction produces offspring that are genetically identical to the parent.	1
	Sexual reproduction involves gametes that have been produced by meiosis. This form of cell division produces haploid cells that are not genetically identical.	1
	Random fertilisation means that the zygotes produced will vary in their genes, so the offspring will show variation in their characteristics.	1
7	Humans produce few offspring so, as a result of random fertilisation, the variation in offspring may not match the predicted variation from a genetic diagram.	1
	This makes it difficult to identify a dominant or recessive allele through proportion of alleles in the offspring.	1
	A family pedigree shows inheritance over several generations and a wider number of individuals, which makes it easier to see how a particular allele has been passed down.	1
	This makes it easier to tell whether the allele is dominant or recessive.	1

Question	Correct answer	Marks
8	Treatment of person 1 with antibiotic A kills off the less-resistant bacteria, but more-resistant bacteria survive →	1
	the more-resistant bacteria escape to the environment and infect person 2 →	1
	person 2 falls ill, antibiotic A won't control the infection so person 2 is given a different antibiotic (antibiotic B) →	1
	the less-resistant bacteria are killed by antibiotic B but the more-resistant bacteria survive →	1
	these bacteria escape to the environment and infect person 3 →	1
	person 3 falls ill and antibiotics A and B will not have an effect, so they are treated with antibiotic C … and so on.	1
9 a)	RNA is single stranded, rather than double stranded	1
	and contains the base uracil/U rather than thymine (T).	1
9 b)	mRNA forms a copy of the DNA base sequence	1
	and travels out of the nucleus to the ribosomes.	1
	Each tRNA molecule brings an amino acid to the ribosome,	1
	where the anticodon on the tRNA joins with the codon on the mRNA.	1
	The ribosomes are the site of protein synthesis,	1
	they coordinate the bringing of amino acids to form proteins.	1
	Total:	47

Question	Correct answer	Marks
2 a)	Hint: In questions of this type, tell students that they should always have a good look through the family tree, and see what genotypes you can identify, before they even look at the questions.	
	i) Ff (0 marks for this alone – an explanation is required)	
	Father A does not have cystic fibrosis, so must have at least one dominant allele.	1
	But as the son (C) has cystic fibrosis, the father must be Ff (and not FF – if he was FF, there would be no chance of producing a child with cystic fibrosis).	1
	ii) Ff (0 marks for this alone – an explanation is required)	
	Daughter D does not have cystic fibrosis, but must have inherited one cystic fibrosis gene from her mother.	1
	She must be Ff.	1
	iii) Daughter G has cystic fibrosis, so must be ff.	1
	She must have inherited one cystic fibrosis allele from each parent but as both parents E and F do not have cystic fibrosis, both must be Ff.	1
2 b)	A, D, E, F	1
	(none have cystic fibrosis but have one recessive allele)	
3 a)	i) (Codominance is) a condition where both alleles of a gene pair are both expressed.	1
	Neither is dominant over the other.	1
	ii) A red bull and a white cow:	6

		Female – C^WC^W – 1 mark
		possible alleles in eggs
		C^W – 1 mark
Male – C^RC^R – 1 mark	C^R – 1 mark	C^RC^W – 1 mark
possible alleles in sperm		roan cattle – 1 mark

| | Ratio of offspring produced – all roan | 1 |

Question	Correct answer				Marks
	A roan bull and a white cow:			Female – $C^W C^W$ – 1 mark	9
				possible alleles in eggs	
				C^W – 1 mark	
	Male – $C^R C^W$ – 1 mark possible alleles in sperm	C^R – 1 mark		$C^R C^W$ – 1 mark roan cattle – 1 mark	
		C^W – 1 mark		$C^W C^W$ – 1 mark white cattle – 1 mark	
	Ratio of offspring produced – 1 roan: 1 white				1
3 b)	Genetic diagram as below:				
			Mother – $I^B I^O$ possible alleles in eggs		
			I^B	I^O	
	Father – $I^A I^O$ possible alleles in sperm	I^A	$I^A I^B$ Blood group AB	$I^A I^O$ Blood group A	
		I^O	$I^B I^O$ Blood group B	$I^O I^O$ Blood group O	
	correct genotype for father				1
	correct genotype for mother				1
	correct gametes for father				1
	correct gametes for mother				1
	correct genotypes for offspring				1
	correct phenotypes for offspring				1
	There is a 1 in 4, or 0.25 or 25% probability of a child being blood group A.				1
4 a)	gametes				1
	fertilization				1
	two				1
	zygote				1

Question	Correct answer	Marks
4 b)	i) Asexual reproduction:	
	Advantage: only one parent required / large numbers can be produced quickly/because genetically identical, can survive well in conditions suited to them.	1
	Disadvantage: if the environment changes, or there are disease, lack of variation means that they could all die out.	1
	ii) Sexual reproduction:	
	Advantage: genetic information from both parents leads to variety in the offspring, leading to better chances of survival in a changing environment.	1
	Disadvantage: two parents required; in some habitats, for example the desert, it may be difficult for two parents to meet/it takes longer to produce off spring.	1
4 c)	i) A: fallopian tube/oviduct	1
	B: ovary	1
	C: uterus	1
	D: cervix	1
	E: vagina	1
	F: vulva	1
	ii) Oestrogen,	1
	stimulates the repair and thickening of the lining of the uterus.	1
	Progesterone,	1
	maintains the uterus lining.	1
5 a)	A: stigma	1
	B: style	1
	C: ovary	1
	D: carpel	1
	E: anther	1
	F: filament	1
	G: stamen	1
	H: petal	1
	I: ovule	1
	J: sepal	1

Question	Correct answer	Marks
5 b)	i): Petals – small as no need to attract insects,	1
	green or inconspicuous, as no need to attract insects	1
	ii) Stigma – large and feathery / large surface area to collect pollen,	1
	hang down outside the flower to collect pollen	1
	iii) Stamens – large to produce huge numbers of pollen,	1
	hang down outside the flower to release pollen into wind	1
	iv) Pollen grains – large numbers produced (as chances of reaching another flower when carried by the wind are low (lower than if carried by an insect),	1
	light, so as to be carried by the wind.	1
6 a)	Completed table as shown, 1 mark for each correct row.	6

	Mitosis	Meiosis
The chromosome number in each daughter cell is 64.	✓	
The daughter cells are haploid.		✓
Two identical cells are produced.	✓	
The nuclear membrane breaks, and disappears at the beginning, and is reformed at the end of the process.	✓	✓
Some variability occurs in the alleles of parent and daughter chromosomes.		✓
Occurs when new red blood cells are produced in the blood of the horse.		

Question	Correct answer	Marks
6 b)	Meiosis has to take place to produce gametes with half the number of chromosomes	1
	so that on fertilisation, the normal number of chromosomes is restored.	1
	Total:	77

Contents

Overview of the section

This section covers the interaction of living organisms with the environment, including the physical environment and other organisms. Topic 4a starts with definitions of ecological terms that are used in the rest of the section. The topic continues with descriptions of some practical techniques that students may use in their own practical investigations of organisms in the environment.

Topic 4b covers feeding relationships. Students may have been introduced to food chains and food webs in earlier learning. This topic revises this learning and then develops it to describe the use of pyramids of number, biomass and energy, and the transfer of energy along food chains. Topic 4c describes the role of organisms in the large-scale cycling of carbon and nitrogen in the ecosystem.

The final topic, 4d, describes some of the impacts of human activity on ecosystems, including the pollution of air and water and the effects of deforestation.

Starting points

The Student Book provides a 'section opener', a double page spread which sets the scene for the students (see pages 254–255). It is structured in the following way:

- An overview providing details of the areas of study
- Five questions, presented in the same order as key areas of learning within the section, which can be used to introduce each key area
- A list of section contents

The questions are intended to provide a structure for introducing the section.

1. In order to study environments we need to know how abundant organisms are and how they are distributed. How can we do this?

2. There are many species in an ecosystem, but how can we show they are interdependent?

3. What are pyramids of number, biomass and energy and what do they show?

4. The Earth will not run out of carbon and nitrogen, so how are these recycled through living organisms and the environment?

5. Humans are having an ever-increasing effect on the environment, often causing pollution. What kinds of effects are we having and how can we reduce the damage we are causing?

The section opener has two main purposes:

- To acknowledge students' prior learning and to value it
- To provide a benchmark against which future learning can be compared

The five questions or 'starting points' in the Student Book can be used in a number of different ways to introduce the section:

- You could ask students to consider the questions as an introductory homework task.
- Students could divide into groups to share their own ideas and understanding and then report back to the whole class.
- Students could access the internet, preferably with a time limit, to find out the information required.

You could use a spider chart or other form of wall chart to summarise the ideas of all the students or groups.

The advantage of recording these initial ideas in this way is that you may retain them for reference as the individual topics are developed. In this way, you can readily acknowledge students' progress in learning.

Introduction

This topic introduces students to ecology, and gives them opportunities to study the effect of environmental factors on organisms.

Links to other topics

Sections	Essential background knowledge	Useful links
1 The nature and variety of living organisms	1b Variety of living organisms	
2 Structures and functions in living organisms	2e Nutrition	
4 Ecology and the environment		4b Feeding relationships 4c Cycles within ecosystems 4d Human influences on the environment

Topic overview

B4a.1	**Ecology and organisms**
	This short activity starts by introducing students to the terminology used in ecological studies, and follows with opportunities to carry out investigations into the effect of environmental factors on population size, the distribution of organisms in a population, and biodiversity.
B4a.2	**Consolidation and summary**
	This activity provides an opportunity for a quick recap on the ideas encountered in the topic as well as time for the students to answer the End of topic questions in the Student Book.

Activity B4a.1 Ecology and organisms

Specification reference: B4a.4.1; B4a.4.2; B4a.4.3**B**; B4a.4.4**B**; B4a.4.5

Learning objectives

- Understand the terms population, community, habitat and ecosystem.
- Practical: Investigate the population size of an organism in two different areas using quadrats.
- Understand the term biodiversity. **(B)**
- Practical: Investigate the distribution of organisms in their habitats and measure biodiversity using quadrats. **(B)**
- Understand how abiotic and biotic factors affect the population size and distribution of organisms.

Learning outcomes

- Write definitions for the terms *population*, *community*, *habitat*, *ecosystem* and *biodiversity.*
- Describe how to use quadrats to measure the population size of an organism.
- Describe how to use quadrats to measure the distribution of organisms in a habitat, and measure biodiversity. **(B)**
- Explain how abiotic and biotic factors affect the population size and distribution of organisms.

Common misconceptions

Some students will not be familiar with the wide variation of habitats found even in a very small geographical area or single site. Encourage them to consider the wide range of variables at play in the living world and to develop an appreciation that organisms are closely suited to the places that they inhabit.

Resources

Student Book pages 256–264

Worksheet B4a.1a Measuring environmental factors

Worksheet B4a.1b Practical: Investigate the population size of an organism in two different areas using quadrats

Worksheet B4a.1c Practical: Investigate the distribution of organisms in their habitats and measure biodiversity using quadrats **(B)**

Resources for class practicals (see Technician's notes, following)

Approach

1. Introduction

Students should have some understanding of ecological studies from work in earlier years. Give them a minute or so to write down what they remember about *habitats* and *ecosystems*. Then take examples from around the class and encourage discussion to come up with class definitions for the words.

2. Ecology terminology

Ask students to read pages 256–257 of the Student Book on definitions in ecology. Ask them to make notes of the meaning of all the bold words. They should then write a sentence for each word, using it correctly. This may cause some difficulty because some of these words are used in everyday language with slightly different meanings compared to the way we use them in ecology. Students taking the International GCSE in Biology also need to include the term *biodiversity* from page 263 of the Student Book.

Take examples from the class for each word and discuss any apparent variations in meaning. Try to complete each discussion with reinforcement of the definitions given in the glossary in the Student Book.

3. Practical ecology

Practical work in ecology can be both stimulating – because you are working like a real scientist investigating a real question – and frustrating, if the results are too vague to give a clear conclusion. Successful studies depend on choosing a good area to study and suitable factors to investigate.

For a comparison of two areas, choose two places that are quite close to each other but where you can see there is variation in abundance of certain plant species in each area. For a transect, choose a line where there is clear change along the transect of species and growth habit. Where you choose will no doubt depend on access to sites. Make sure you have permission to do so if it is off the school site.

Students do not necessarily need to sample plants. Snails or other minibeasts (small animals such as insects and spiders; arthropods and other invertebrates) are suitable too, as long as their numbers vary between areas with the change in vegetation. If students sample minibeasts, remind them not to remove the animals from the quadrat area. Students should also be reminded to wash their hands thoroughly after completing the sampling.

Suggest that students only focus on one or a small number of species in their study. This avoids sampling taking too long. If you have prior knowledge of the area, you could also suggest which species they should focus on, to help them get satisfactory data for analysis.

Worksheet B4a.1a provides guidance on how to use a range of methods to measure abiotic (physical) factors. Allow time in class before the fieldwork for students to become familiar with apparatus that they have not used before.

Worksheet B4a.1b outlines a method for carrying out random sampling with quadrats. Worksheet B4a.1c outlines a method for sampling with quadrats along a transect. Use the diagrams on pages 259 and 260 of the Student Book to explain how to carry out random sampling and along a transect and how to estimate number and percentage cover in a quadrat.

Work with students to produce a method that will suit the areas that are available for sampling. Remind them of all risk factors and safety procedures for those areas. Then allow them to collect data for investigation as described on the worksheets.

If fieldwork is not possible, consider work in the laboratory, such as the study of brine shrimps, or use the internet to gather data from other studies, such as the distribution of lichen in relation to air pollutants.

3. Consolidation: bullet notes

Give students a few minutes to write down bullet point notes from this activity for a friend who missed the lesson. Take examples of notes from around the class and discuss them to choose the best five notes.

Remember you may need to fill out a risk assessment form. Speak to your employer or to CLEAPSS for more details.

Technician's notes

You will need the following resources for the class practicals.

Be sure to check the latest safety notes on these resources before proceeding.

Check the area to be sampled for hazards, e.g. glass and other debris, animal faeces, toxic plants such as ragwort. Check the label of the soil testing kit for hazards/PPE, precautions required.

B4a.1a Measuring environmental factors

Practical work will need a range of apparatus depending on the work undertaken. The following list suggests some apparatus that might be needed, but you will need to check the plan produced for the fieldwork to see what else might be needed and if all these suggestions are required.

Class practical, per group:

thermometer or temperature probe
maximum–minimum thermometer
sample container or bag
marker pen
trowel
soil testing kit
balance
old tin lid
access to drying oven
light meter or light probe
2 tape measures (30 m)
pegs
table of random numbers or calculator set to produce random numbers
quadrat (with optional grid) – choose a size that is appropriate for the area being surveyed, using a larger square for a larger area
clip board, pencil and paper for recording
keys or identification charts

Answers

Page 258

1. An ecosystem is all the organisms and the environmental factors that interact within an area. Examples include a lake, desert, tropical rainforest, coral reef, or anything similarly large-scale that has reasonably definable boundaries.

2. A habitat is the space in which a species/population of one species lives, such as under a rotting log, in the open water of a pond or lake, or anything of similar scale.

3. Populations of different species that live in different habitats form the community of organisms that live in an ecosystem.

4. Biotic factors are those due to other living organisms, e.g. predation and competition. Abiotic factors are non-living, e.g. temperature and rainfall.

Developing investigative skills, page 261

1. Plan should allow sampling for about one hour on each of the two sites. Each site needs marking with tape measures or some other method, in order to identify positions of quadrats. Students should use random sampling, e.g. with random numbers from a calculator, to place quadrats. Plants within each quadrat should be counted and identified (or characteristics of each species recorded for identification back in the laboratory). Abiotic (physical) factors measured should include light intensity using a light meter. Other factors that might have an effect on abundance should be considered, such as temperature, soil pH, availability of water, presence of other organisms especially grazing animals.

2. Averages: species A south 12.4; species B south 7.0; species A north 5.8; species B north 12.0.

3. There were on average more species A plants on the south side of the hill than on the north side of the hill. Species B plant was, on average, more abundant on the north face of the hill than on the south face of the hill.

4. The abundance of the species varies with the light intensity measured. So light intensity may affect the abundance of these plants, with species A growing better in a habitat where light intensity is high and species B growing better in a habitat where light intensity is lower.

5. a) Moving randomly placed quadrats means that the sampling was not random. This might change the averages and so affect the results and therefore the conclusions that can be drawn.

   b) Taking samples from the top part of each slope might help to avoid the effect of a difference in water availability to the plants.

   c) Light intensity on the two slopes needs to be measured in identical conditions, e.g. at the same time, over the same period (to get an average intensity for the area).

Page 262

1. A square of a specific size, used for defining a sample area.

2. The number of individuals within a given area.

3. Choice might favour some parts of the area over others, such as places where there are no stinging or thorny plants. This may change the results, increasing or decreasing the average for some species, and therefore will change the conclusions that are drawn.

4. It is a quicker method than counting using quadrats.

Page 264

1. How organisms are spread within an area.

2. A sampling line along which quadrats are placed for taking samples.

3. A line transect placed so that it runs from one habitat to another (from a pond edge to a field, or from shade to light under a large tree), can be sampled to show how the factor that is changing (i.e. water availability, or light intensity) affects the distribution of the organisms.

4. A measure of the variety of living things in an area.

5. a) For example, tropical rainforest.

   b) For example, Arctic ice cap.

B4a.1a Measuring environmental factors

During your studies of ecology, you will need to measure some environmental factors, such as some abiotic factors. The details below explain how to do this.

Measuring temperature

Apparatus

thermometer or temperature probe

maximum–minimum thermometer

SAFETY INFORMATION
Take care with delicate equipment.
Avoid holding the thermometer bulb or leaving it in direct sunlight.

Method

1. Let the thermometer or probe adjust to the conditions before recording the temperature.

2. Take temperatures at different sites for the same investigation at similar times, not at different times of day.

3. Use a maximum–minimum thermometer to measure the temperature range at a site.

4. Make a hole in the ground with a peg if measuring soil temperature.

5. Do not leave the thermometer or probe in the ground unattended.

6. Clean your equipment and return it to the classroom.

Measuring soil nutrients

Apparatus

sample container or bag marker pen

trowel

soil testing kit

SAFETY INFORMATION
Take care when taking soil samples – avoid glass, sharp objects and animal waste.
Wash hands thoroughly after handling soil.

Method

1. Use the trowel to take a small soil sample from the site. Avoid sharp objects and other hazardous material.

2. Place the sample in a container or bag and seal it tightly. Mark the container with your name, the date and where the sample was taken.

3. Back in the laboratory, analyse each sample using the soil testing kit. Follow any safety instructions. Do not mix up your samples. Record your findings in a neat table.

4. Dispose of your samples as directed by your teacher.

Measuring soil moisture content

Apparatus

sample container or bag marker pen

trowel balance old tin lid

access to drying oven

SAFETY INFORMATION

Take care when taking soil samples – avoid glass, sharp objects and animal waste.

Wash hands thoroughly after handling soil.

Method

1. Use the trowel to take a small soil sample from the site. Avoid sharp objects and other hazardous material.

2. Place the sample in a container or bag and seal it tightly. Mark the container with your name, the date and where the sample was taken.

3. Back in the laboratory, weigh your sample and place it on an old tin lid or other metal container.

4. Place the sample in the drying oven **set at a warm temperature**.

5. After a day or two take the sample out of the oven. Let it cool.

6. Re-weigh the sample.

7. Calculate how much the mass has reduced. This is the mass of water that has been lost.

8. Using your results, calculate the percentage water content.

9. Dispose of your samples as directed by your teacher.

Measuring light intensity

Apparatus

light meter or light probe

SAFETY INFORMATION
Do not stare directly at the Sun.
Handle the meter with care.

Method

1. Light levels can vary a lot during the day. If you are comparing two sites, you will need to take the readings as near to the same time as possible, with similar levels of cloud cover.

2. Follow the instructions on the light meter. Look carefully to see what units the meter uses.

3. Point the meter in the same direction each time.

4. Take several readings and calculate an average.

5. You can use a light probe to measure the light levels over a longer period. Follow the instructions on the device.

6. Return the instruments carefully to the classroom.

Using data logging probes

Data probes can give you accurate readings and measure conditions over extended periods.

Apparatus

data probes

storage box

SAFETY INFORMATION
Take care with delicate equipment.

Method

1. Follow the instructions that come with the data probe.

2. If you are comparing sites, carry out the same procedure at both sites so that you are comparing like with like.

3. Clean the equipment. Ensure that it is switched off and return it carefully to the classroom.

B4a.1b Practical: Investigate the population size of an organism in two different areas using quadrats

Random sampling with a quadrat

Random sampling is a good way to take quadrat samples of a large open area, because it reduces the risk that you will select particular parts of the area. This means you should produce results that are more representative of the whole area.

Listen carefully to the safety briefing before carrying out fieldwork.

Apparatus

2 tape measures (each 30 m long)

pegs

table of random numbers or calculator set to produce random numbers

quadrat (with optional grid)

clip board, pencil and paper for recording

keys or identification charts

sample containers and trowel

meters or data logging equipment

SAFETY INFORMATION

Always follow safety instructions carefully when carrying out fieldwork.

Method

1. Your teacher will tell you the names of common organisms that you might find – or show you how to find this out using a key or identification chart. Your teacher will tell you whether you are collecting data on all the organisms you find, or if you are investigating the population size of just one particular species.

2. Push a peg into the ground and run out the two tape measures at right angles to each other.

3. Use the random number tables (or a calculator set to display random numbers) to give you two 'coordinates'.

4. Use your 'coordinates' to show you where to place your quadrat. For example, if you are using a 100 cm square quadrat, the numbers 5 and 2 will mean you place one corner of the quadrat parallel to 500 cm (the other corner at 600 cm) on the first tape and parallel to 200 cm on the second tape.

5. Identify and count the organisms that you can see. Alternatively, if your quadrat is divided into a grid, use the grid to estimate the percentage cover. Record all your results.

6. Repeat taking random samples with the quadrat for up to 10 samples.

7. As instructed by your teacher, take a set of measurements of the physical conditions (e.g. temperature, light intensity). Worksheet B4a.1a gives guidance on this. Your teacher may also ask you to take some samples in labelled containers so that they can be analysed back in the lab.

8. To compare two sites, now repeat taking samples using randomly placed quadrats on the second site. Record all your results.

9. Back in the science lab, draw a table to display all your results.

Analyse and interpret data

1. Use your results from one site to calculate the average number of each species in a quadrat.

2. Estimate the population size of each species in the whole area using the following equation:

$$\text{total population size} = \text{average number in a quadrat} \times \frac{\text{total area}}{\text{area of quadrat}}$$

3. Repeat this for the other site that you measured.

4. Compare the population size of each species in the two areas, and record any differences.

5. Compare the differences in population size with the physical factors you measured. Can you suggest any relationship between the physical factors and the differences in population size?

6. Describe how you would test one of the relationships you have suggested to see if it was real.

Evaluate data and methods

1. Describe any problems you had with this method.

2. Suggest changes to the method that would help to reduce the effect of these problems.

B4a.1c Practical: Investigate the distribution of organisms in their habitats and measure biodiversity using quadrats (B)

Sampling along a transect

A transect is a straight line along which quadrat samples are taken. It is usually placed where there is an obvious change in a physical factor (such as light intensity from deep shade to open light, or wave action on a beach) from one end of the transect to the other. It can identify how an organism's distribution varies as a physical factor varies. You can also investigate biodiversity by seeing how many different species, or different types of species, are found in each quadrat along the transect.

Listen carefully to the safety briefing before carrying out fieldwork.

Apparatus

tape measure (30 m long)

quadrat (with optional grid)

keys or identification charts

meters or data logging equipment

pegs

clip board, pencil and paper for recording

sample containers and trowel

SAFETY INFORMATION
Always follow safety instructions carefully when carrying out fieldwork.

Method

1. Your teacher will tell you the names of common organisms that you might find – or show you how to find this out using a key or identification chart.

2. At the start of the transect, push a peg into the ground and run out the tape measure. This should run in a straight line across the area where a physical factor changes.

3. Your teacher will tell you how often to sample along the transect, such as every 2 or 5 metres.

4. Place the quadrat at the first sampling point on the transect and count the number of organisms of each species, or use the grid to estimate percentage cover of each species. Record your results.

5. Repeat step 4 at each sampling point along the transect.

7. As instructed by your teacher, take a set of measurements of the physical conditions at each sampling point (e.g. temperature, light intensity). Worksheet B4a.1a gives guidance on this. Your teacher may also ask you to take some samples in labelled containers so that they can be analysed back in the laboratory.

8. Back in the science laboratory, draw a table to display all your results.

Analyse and interpret data

1. Use your table to display your results of number or percentage cover in a suitable chart or graph, using a separate graph for each species.

2. Also plot on these charts or graphs the physical factors that you measured.

3. Compare the change in number or percentage cover, as well as the biodiversity, with the change in physical factors. Can you suggest any relationship between the physical factors and number or percentage cover for any species, and with the biodiversity?

4. Describe how you would test one of the relationships you have suggested to see if it was real.

Evaluate data and methods

1. Describe any problems you had with this method.

2. Suggest changes to the method that would help to reduce the effect of these problems.

Activity B4a.2 Consolidation and summary

Learning objectives

- To review the learning points of the topic.
- To test understanding through answering questions.

Learning outcomes

- Be familiar with the knowledge and understanding summarised in the End of topic checklist.
- Be able to apply this knowledge and understanding by answering the End of topic questions.

Resources

Student Book pages 265–267

Approach

Ask students to answer the End of topic questions in the Student Book.

Answers

End of topic questions mark scheme

Question	Correct answer	Marks
1 a)	A large unit of the environment including all the organisms that live in it and the physical factors they interact with.	1
1 b)	A small part of the environment in which a population of one species lives.	1
1 c)	All the organisms of one species that live in the same habitat.	1
1 d)	All the populations of organisms, of different species, that live in the same ecosystem.	1
1 e)	Non-living or physical factors, such as temperature or rainfall, that affect the population size or distribution of organisms.	1
1 f)	Factors affecting the population size and distribution of organisms, caused by other organisms, for example through competition or predation.	1
2	Any suitable ecosystem could be used, with appropriate examples, such as for a lake:	
	ecosystem: the lake	1
	habitat: in mid-water or in the mud at the bottom	1
	population: perch swimming in the midwater area of the lake	1
	community: all the organisms living in the lake	1
	abiotic factor: temperature or light intensity	1
	biotic factor: the presence of predator or competitor species.	1

Question	Correct answer	Marks
3	Use quadrats (e.g. 50 × 50 cm square), placed using random coordinates generated by a calculator, on a grid set out by two long measuring tapes on two sides of the garden that meet at a corner. In each quadrat count the number of snails of the species being studied.	1
	Take at least 10 samples, more if time allows. Average the measurements from each quadrat, then multiply the result by 400 to give the population size for the garden.	1
	Random sampling, as large a number of samples as possible and averaging the results will help to give as reliable a value as possible.	1
4	The average number of the plant in 1 quadrat (1 m^2) was 25 ÷ 10 = 2.5.	1
	The field is 200 m^2 so the total number of the plant is 2.5 × 200 = 500.	1
5 a)	Five species – each line of the diagram is one species	1
5 b)	i) Light intensity will not vary across the transect	1
	except when species growing within the creek are submerged by water at high tide.	1
	ii) Time submerged in sea water will vary within the creek	1
	but not beyond the creek where plants are not normally submerged.	1
	iii) Temperature may vary for species submerged by sea water for some part of the day,	1
	but for plants on dry land it may not vary as much.	1
5 c)	Green algae and samphire can grow in the creek,	1
	the rest grow on 'dry' land because the transect was measured from the middle of the creek.	1
5 d)	i) Any suitable explanation, such as: need to be submerged in sea water for part of the day to keep cooler / avoid dehydration; cannot compete with other species; only species that can tolerate submersion in sea water for large part of day.	1
	ii) Any suitable answer that tests the answer in part (i) by experimentation;	1
	with details such as: place pots containing each species submerged in sea water and see how well each grows.	1
5 e)	i) Answer in range 3–4 m, or 5–6 m.	1
	ii) Three species present (in reasonable numbers) at these distances.	1
	Total:	31

Introduction

This topic builds on knowledge of food chains and webs to look at the transfer of substances and energy between organisms and the environment.

Links to other topics

Sections	Essential background knowledge	Useful links
1 The nature and variety of living organisms	1a Characteristics of living organisms 1b Variety of living organisms	
2 Structures and functions in living organisms	2e Nutrition 2f Respiration	
4 Ecology and the environment	4a The organism in the environment	4c Cycles within ecosystems 4d Human influences on the environment
5 Use of biological resources		5a Food production

Topic overview

B4b.1	**Trophic levels and food webs**
	In this activity students build on their knowledge of food chains and food webs from earlier years and consolidate understanding of trophic levels and the transfer of substances and energy along a food chain.
B4b.2	**Using pyramid diagrams**
	This activity gives students an opportunity to create and interpret pyramids of number, biomass and energy.
B4b.3	**Energy losses in food chains**
	In this activity, students will learn to identify energy losses from organisms so they can explain why only a small proportion of the energy in one trophic level is passed to the next.
B4b.4	**Consolidation and summary**
	This activity provides an opportunity for a quick recap on the ideas encountered in the topic as well as time for the students to answer the End of topic questions in the Student Book.

Activity B4b.1 Trophic levels and food webs

Specification reference: B4b.4.6; B4b.4.7; B4b.4.8

Learning objectives

- Understand the names given to different trophic levels, including producers, primary, secondary and tertiary consumers and decomposers.
- Understand the concepts of food chains and food webs.
- Understand the transfer of substances and energy along a food chain.

Learning outcomes

- Identify and explain the names given to the different trophic levels.
- Write definitions for the terms *food chain* and *food web.*
- Explain how substances and energy are transferred along a food chain.

Common misconceptions

If students carry out research on food webs and food chains, they may meet statements such as 'all food webs begin with a plant', and 'all energy for life on Earth comes from the Sun'. Neither of these is completely true. There are many producers other than photosynthesising plants, most of which are bacteria and too small to be noticed, and/or they live in environments that are difficult to explore, such as in mid-ocean ridges or in deep caves. Some of these have unique biochemistry that takes energy from the breakdown of inorganic chemicals to make 'food' rather than using light energy from the Sun. However, it is fair to say that they contribute little to the food chains and food webs that we normally see, but they are often referred to when discussing the origins of life on Earth. Remind students of the dangers of making generalised statements from limited knowledge.

Resources

Student Book pages 268–271

Approach

1. Introduction

Write the words *food chain* and *food web* on the board. Ask students to suggest related words and how they should be linked to create a mind map on the subject. This should help you identify how much they remember from earlier work both in earlier years. The following tasks assume that little has been remembered, and may need adjusting if students have a lot of previous knowledge.

2. Food chains and webs

Ask students to work in pairs and to write down a food chain that they remember. (If they are struggling, give them an example of organisms that could be used to make a food chain, such as fox, grass, rabbit.) They should use their food chain to write a set of 'rules' for drawing a food chain. Take examples from around the class to draw up a set of class rules. They should include the following:

- The chain is set out with the organisms in order of who eats what, usually placing the 'eater' on the right of what they eat.
- An arrow should point from the organism being eaten to the organism that is the 'eater'.

Note the rules above are written in the simplest terms. Students may have a greater understanding and be able to give names for the trophic levels in the chain (if not, do not introduce them yet). They may also explain that the arrows show the direction of transfer of substances (food) and/or energy from organism to organism.

If not, ask them to explain in more detail what the arrows mean. This should elicit 'food', so take this further by asking what food is. From their work on nutrition in Topic 2e and respiration in Topic 2f, they should be able to identify food molecules (such as carbohydrates, lipids and proteins) or individual elements such as carbon and nitrogen, and energy as a result of respiration.

Ask students what information they would need to develop their food chain into a food web. If there is time and access to the internet, they could look for examples of food webs, then choose one and identify as many food chains as possible within it.

3. Trophic levels

Ask students to read pages 268 and 269 of the Student Book about food chains and the naming of trophic levels. They should then annotate one food chain and food web used in the task above, or the diagram of a food web on page 271 of the Student Book, to name the trophic levels.

Alternatively, they could test each other by asking questions, such as:
'Name one primary consumer in the food web.' or, 'Which secondary consumer eats xxx and xxx?'

4. Consolidation: definitions

Give students a few minutes to write notes for a web dictionary to explain food webs and trophic levels. They should include definitions of the key words required for the specification. They should swap their notes with a neighbour to check them and see how they could be improved. They should then swap them back again and make any changes that are needed to improve their notes.

Answers

Page 270

1. Any description that means the same as:

   a) Organism that produces its own food from simpler materials, such as plants making carbohydrates in photosynthesis.

   b) Animal that eats producers, also a herbivore.

   c) Animal that eats primary consumers (grouped with other meat-eaters as a carnivore).

   d) Organism that causes decay of dead material, such as some fungi and bacteria.

2. a) Primary consumers because they eat producers/plants.

   b) Any consumer level above primary consumer because they eat other animals.

   c) Any consumer level because they eat both plant and animal tissue.

3. They feed on dead/decaying tissue and waste materials from all trophic levels. Food chains only show the feeding relationships between living organisms.

Page 271

1. Insectivorous bird, toad, snake, fox or owl.

2. The fox feeds as a secondary consumer on rabbits, rats, mice and seed-eating birds. It also feeds as a tertiary and quaternary consumer on insectivorous birds.

Activity B4b.2 Using pyramid diagrams

Specification reference: B4b.4.7

Learning objectives

- Understand the concepts of pyramids of number, pyramids of biomass and pyramids of energy transfer.

Learning outcomes

- Write definitions for the terms *pyramid of number*, *pyramid of biomass*, *pyramid of energy*.

Common misconceptions

Pyramids of number, biomass and energy sometimes may only have a limited use in contributing to the understanding of the interrelationships of organisms because often many assumptions are taken when collecting the data and using them to construct the diagrams. However, they are a useful introduction to community structure because of their simple form, and when accurate measurements are made by scientists they do significantly increase our understanding of how ecosystems work.

One misconception is thinking that in a pyramid of biomass, smaller organisms, such as insects, must have a smaller biomass than larger organisms, such as insect-eating birds. However, when looking at a pyramid of biomass it is the total biomass of all the organisms at each level that is important, so although they are smaller individually, the total biomass of all the insects is greater than that of all the insect-eating birds.

Resources

Student Book pages 272–276

Worksheet B4b.2a Drawing trophic pyramids

Approach

1. Introduction

Ask students to take a simple food chain from the last activity, such as grass→rabbit→fox, and to think about the number of organisms that would be found in each trophic level in a community of organisms. (For now, take care to choose a chain of organisms that will produce a traditional shape in a pyramid of numbers: that is, avoid something where there are fewer individuals in a lower trophic level than the one above, like lettuce→caterpillars→insect-eating bird.)

Then show them a picture of the plants and animals in an ecosystem, such as the African savannah and ask them to identify the organisms found in this ecosystem (including the plants), and to arrange them into trophic levels. Again, they should consider the number of individuals in each level.

Ask students to comment on what they found in both cases. They should suggest that the number of individuals in each trophic level, for a single food chain or for a community, decreases as you go from producer to top consumer level.

2. Trophic pyramids

Worksheet B4b.2a explains how to construct trophic pyramids, and gives students the opportunity to construct their own pyramids of number and biomass for a food chain, and to comment on the results.

There is a challenge question at the end of the sheet, on the reliability of the results, which could be used as the basis for a class discussion, or for individual or pair work by more able students.

Alternatively, provide an opportunity for students to research numbers and biomass for their own food chain, and give them the rules on the worksheet to construct their pyramids. Gathering data for a pyramid of energy is not recommended, unless it can be carried out by research in books or on the internet.

3. Advantages and disadvantages

Ask students to use pages 272–276 in the Student Book on pyramids of number, biomass and energy and to draw up a table to show the advantages and disadvantages of each.

4. Consolidation: key facts

Ask students to jot down three key facts that they have learned from this activity. They should compare their facts with a neighbour and agree the best three facts from their lists. They could repeat this by comparing with another pair. Take examples from around the class, and agree by class discussion the three most important facts.

Answers

Developing investigative skills, page 274

1. Plants > snails; plants are producers and snails are primary consumers.

2. Plan should include the following:

- method for sampling standard size areas, e.g. quadrat
- counting all individual plants and snails in each area
- repeat samples so that means can be calculated to average out variability.

3. Take several average sized plants. Dry out in warm oven overnight. Measure mass. Repeat drying for a few more hours and measure mass. Repeat until two consecutive masses are the same. Calculate an average mass per plant. Then do the same for several snails and average the mass for one snail.

4. Plants 42, snails 4.

5. Pyramid with two bars centred one on top of other, bottom bar 42 units wide and top bar 4 units wide.

6. Pyramid with two bars centred one on top of the other, bottom bar 1596 units wide and top bar 24 units wide.

7. Both pyramids show the typical shape of the top trophic level being smaller than the lower level. This is because the animals only eat a proportion of the plants.

Page 276

1. a) A diagram showing the total numbers of organisms at each trophic level in a food chain or food web in an area.

    b) A diagram showing the total biomass of organisms at each trophic level in a food chain or food web in an area.

    c) A diagram showing the total energy in the organisms at each trophic level in a food chain or food web in an area.

2. Any suitable example that includes producers, primary consumers and secondary consumers from a reasonable food chain. Count the number of individuals feeding at each level within the same size area. Draw a pyramid of three layers, starting with producers at the bottom and ending with secondary consumers at the top, with the bar for each level drawn to scale.

3. A pyramid of biomass only shows the mass at a particular time in an area. If some trophic levels have a shorter life-span than others, they will be under-represented in the pyramid, which may cause an inverted shape.

B4b.2a Drawing trophic pyramids

Pyramids of number, biomass and energy are drawn according to a particular set of rules. Use the rules to answer the questions below.

Trophic pyramids are drawn to scale, so graph or squared paper will help, and you will need a calculator.

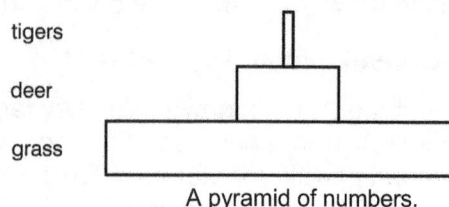

tigers

deer

grass

A pyramid of numbers.

Rules for drawing trophic pyramids

1. Trophic pyramids are always drawn with the producer level at the bottom, and work upwards through the food chain to the top consumer at the top.

2. Start with the largest value for a trophic level (often, but not always, the producer level). Work out a scale that you can use to fit this number within the width of your paper. For example, if the value is 2000 and your diagram can be 10 cm wide, then 1 cm on your scale will be represent the value 200.

3. Use this scale to calculate the relative sizes of the values for the other trophic levels.

4. Mark the maximum line width you can use along the bottom of your paper, and mark the midpoint.

5. Starting with the producer level, mark the width of the scaled value at the bottom of the page. Centre the line on the midpoint of your original line. From this width, create a rectangle to form the first step of the pyramid as shown above. It doesn't matter how high this step is, because the height doesn't represent anything – it just needs to look right on your paper.

6. On the top line of the producer step, mark the width that represents the value for the primary consumer / herbivore level. Make sure this width is centred on the midpoint of the producer step.

7. Draw in a step of the same height as the producer level but using the width you marked out for the primary/consumer herbivore level, so that it sits on top of the producer step.

8. Repeat steps 6 and 7 for each successive trophic level. Label each step with the trophic level or organism that it represents.

A student was studying the food chain: lettuce → caterpillar → thrush in the school vegetable garden. She watched the garden for two hours one day and counted the following numbers of organisms: 56 caterpillars, 4 lettuces, 2 thrushes.

1. Draw a pyramid of number for this food chain, using these values.

2. What do you notice about the shape of this pyramid?

The student then measured the mass of a lettuce and the mass of several caterpillars, and calculated the average mass for one caterpillar. She got the following results: 1 lettuce had a mass of 92 g, and the average mass of 1 caterpillar was 3.9 g. She looked it up and found that the average mass of a thrush is 83 g.

3. Use these values to calculate the total biomass for each trophic level, and then draw a pyramid of biomass for this food chain.

4. What do you notice about the shape of this pyramid?

5. Explain how the student could convert biomass values to energy values to construct a pyramid of energy.

6. Challenge: Comment on the reliability of the values calculated in each pyramid.

Activity B4b.3 Energy losses in food chains

Specification reference: B4b.4.8; B4b.4.9

Learning objectives

- Understand the transfer of energy along a food chain.
- Explain why only about 10% of energy is transferred from one trophic level to the next.

Learning outcomes

- Explain how energy is transferred along a food chain.
- Explain why there are limits to the proportion of energy in one trophic level that is transferred to the next trophic level in a food chain.

Common misconceptions

It is commonly stated, as in the specification, that about 10% of the energy in one trophic level passes to the level above it. This is an extreme simplification. Experimental results show a range in percentage from less than 0.2% to over 20%, depending on the organisms in each trophic level and the ecosystem. Although this produces an average of 'about 10%', the conclusion is doubtful, given that it is an average of a small number of measured values over two orders of magnitude. It is important, though, for students to appreciate that only a very small proportion of the energy in one trophic level passes to the next, and that the rest is passed to the environment either as heat energy or chemical energy.

Resources

Student Book pages 276–279

Worksheet B4b.3a Energy transfer diagrams

Approach

1. Introduction

Remind students of their earlier work on human nutrition in Topic 2e and the energy stored in chemicals in the food. Give them a few minutes working in pairs to identify what happens to that energy. Encourage them to think in types of energy (such as heat energy, chemical energy) as this will tie in with similar work in Physics, and to consider energy gains in the body and energy losses.

Take examples from around the class. Use them to sketch a diagram on the board of energy gains and losses in a human. Avoid commenting at this point, but encourage class discussion to reach agreement. Return to the diagram later in the activity to help revise and confirm ideas.

2. Energy transfer diagrams

Worksheet B4b.3a gives students the opportunity to draw a Sankey diagram to show the energy gains and losses in a leaf. This kind of diagram is commonly used in Physics to show the efficiency of energy transfer in systems. In Biology, the diagram highlights the equivalence of living and non-living systems in terms of energy transfers, something that can easily be missed.

Some students may need help with drawing up the table from the descriptions given. Some may also need help constructing at least the first stages of the diagram.

If there is time and opportunity, students could research the efficiency of transfer of light energy to chemical energy in plant tissue (sometimes called photosynthetic efficiency) for a range of plants. This shows that different kinds of plants (such as crop plants, conifers, broad-leaved plants) can achieve different efficiencies in different conditions (such as in glasshouses under perfect conditions, in wetlands, or in deserts).

3. Comparing energy transfers in plants and animals

Either ask students to produce their own Sankey diagram, or work with them to produce a class diagram, to represent the energy gains and losses for the sheep shown in the diagram on page 277 of the Student Book. For this, they will need to start by calculating the percentage of each value compared with the energy units in the grass eaten by the sheep (not the units produced by the grass).

Encourage students to identify what form the energy is in at each stage (i.e. heat energy or chemical energy) and to annotate their diagram appropriately.

Ask students to compare the diagram for the plant produced from Worksheet B3b.4a and the one created for the sheep, and to comment on any similarities and differences. They should note that the proportion of the energy taken in and converted to living tissue is greater for the sheep than for the plant.

If there is time and opportunity, students could carry out research into the efficiency of energy transfer for different kinds of animals, to investigate the comments about herbivores, carnivores, mammals and birds in the Extension box on page 278 of the Student Book.

4. Consolidation: write a question

Give students five minutes to write a question related to this activity that has a four or five-mark answer. They should also write a mark scheme for their question. They should swap questions with another student and answer the question they have received.

They should then mark their answer using the mark scheme from the other student and comment on any problems with the question or mark scheme and return them to the original student to amend and improve. Take examples of questions from around the class for discussion.

Answers

Page 278

1. Humans eat plant and animal tissue.

2. Wheat grain → human; wheat grain → chicken → human.

3. For wheat grain → human, two steps with wheat at the bottom; for wheat grain → chicken → human, three steps with wheat grain at the bottom and human at the top.

In both pyramids, the steps should get increasingly narrower from the bottom step up the pyramid.

4. As chickens transfer some energy to the environment as heat due to respiration, a smaller proportion of the energy in the wheat is available for humans to eat. This makes this energy transfer less efficient than humans eating the grain directly.

5. a) If we all become vegetarian, then more of the energy in the plants we grow is available to us than if we eat animals that eat the plants.

   b) Humans do not eat grass, so we would need to convert meadows (such as where sheep feed) to crop fields and not all the places where there are meadows will grow crops well. Also, fish are in a food chain that starts with microscopic plankton. Gathering sufficient photosynthetic plankton to eat could take more energy than harvesting the fish that eat them.

Page 279 (top)

1. Light energy from Sun (gain) → some reflected, some passes straight through, some wrong wavelength (losses) → light energy converted to chemical energy during photosynthesis → heat energy transferred to environment from photosynthetic reactions and from respiration (losses) → chemical energy in plant biomass.

2. Chemical energy in food (gain) → chemical energy in undigested food lost as faeces (loss) → chemical energy in absorbed food molecules converted to chemical in waste products such as urea lost in urine (loss) → heat energy from respiration transferred to environment (loss) → chemical energy in animal biomass.

3. Only a proportion of the energy taken in is used to make new biomass, the rest is lost to the environment either as chemical energy or heat energy. That means there is always less energy transferred to the next trophic level than was taken in, so the shape must always be a pyramid.

Page 279 (bottom)

1. Any element found in plant or animal tissue, such as carbon or nitrogen.

2. Both flow in one direction only, but energy is eventually lost to the environment in the form of heat energy whereas substances are retained or recycled back to the start of the chain.

B4b.3a Energy transfer diagrams

We can use diagrams to help us understand the energy gains and losses of non-living systems, such as an electricity-generating power station as shown in this Sankey diagram. The width of each arrow shows the proportion of energy transferred to each process, starting with 100% as the energy gained from fuel on the left. From this we can see that more energy is lost to the environment as heat than reaches houses, offices, etc. as useful electrical energy.

We can use data from living organisms to create similar diagrams of energy gains and losses.

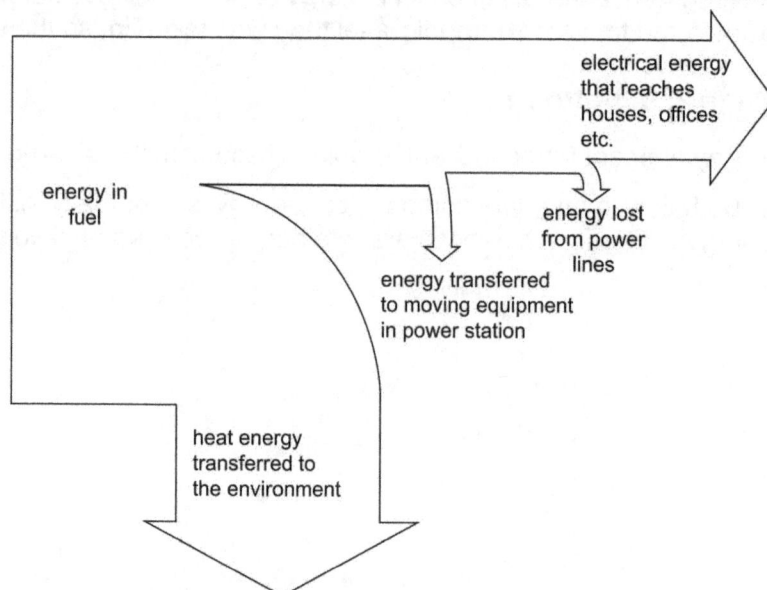

First we need data on the gains and losses of energy by a plant. The energy available to the plant is given the value of 100%, and all the energy transfers are calculated as percentages of this. So, the light energy falling on the plant is given the value 100%.

The transfers for a particular plant are as follows:

- About 53% of the light falling on the plant is of the right wavelength for photosynthesis, the rest passes straight through or is reflected back to the environment.

- Of this 53%, about a third passes straight through because it does not hit a chloroplast, which means about 35% of the original light hits chloroplasts.

- About a quarter of the light energy hitting a chloroplast is not collected by chlorophyll, leaving about 26% of the original light.

- Only about 5% of the original energy is transferred to chemical energy in sugars, the rest is transferred to other chemical reactions and heat energy to the environment from the process of photosynthesis.

- Most of the sugars made by the plant are used for respiration or to make other chemicals in plant tissue, releasing heat energy to the environment from the reactions – the proportion of the original light energy falling on the plant that is transferred to chemical energy in plant tissue is only about 0.5%. This is the energy available to animals that eat the plant.

1. Draw up a table to show the percentage of the original light falling on the plant at each stage, and the method in which energy is lost from the system.

2. Using graph paper, draw a vertical line at the left of the paper to represent 100% and note the scale. Draw a long horizontal line from the top of the vertical line, and a short one from the bottom of the vertical line (about 1/5 of the way across the page, since there are five stages).

3. At the end of the short horizontal line at the bottom, mark vertically the first percentage (i.e. 53% up from the bottom line). Draw a short horizontal line to the right from this point (again about 1/5 of the page width) and draw a curve down from this point and from the original baseline to create an arrow as in the Sankey diagram above. Label this arrow with the method of transfer out of the system (away from the plant).

4. Repeat step 3 with each energy transfer in turn, so that you have four arrows in total pointing down. This will leave the energy transfer to plant tissue as the final horizontal arrow.

5. Comment on the energy transfer efficiency (the proportion of energy that enters the system that is transferred to useful energy at the end of the system – in the plant, this is the energy transferred to plant tissue) for a plant and for a power station.

Activity B4b.4 Consolidation and summary

Learning objectives

- To review the learning points of the topic.
- To test understanding through answering questions.

Learning outcomes

- Be familiar with the knowledge and understanding summarised in the End of topic checklist.
- Be able to apply this knowledge and understanding by answering the End of topic questions.

Resources

Student Book pages 280–282

Approach

Ask students to answer the End of topic questions in the Student Book.

Answers

End of topic questions mark scheme

Question	Correct answer	Marks
1 a)	Carnivore	1
	because it eats animals.	1
1 b)	Primary consumer.	1
1 c)	Organisms in correct order.	1
	Arrows point in right direction.	1
	grass → zebra → lion	
1 d)	Food web showing grass at bottom.	1
	Arrows to zebra, gazelle and wildebeest in middle layer.	1
	Arrows from zebra, gazelle and wildebeest to lions in top.	1
2 a)	Pyramid of three bars drawn to scale,	1
	centred one above the other with producer at bottom and secondary consumer at top,	1
	and lowest bar 5 units wide labelled lettuce or producer, middle bar 40 units wide labelled caterpillar or primary consumer, top bar 2 units wide labelled thrush or secondary consumer.	1
2 b)	There are two kinds of limitation: the pyramid has an inverted shape;	1
	the data are very limited, for example the thrushes feed on insects elsewhere, so the pyramid is not a reliable picture of the community.	1
2 c)	A pyramid of biomass describes the data at one particular time. At one point there were 40 caterpillars and later there were none,	1
	so sampling at different times would give different results.	1
3 a)	The predatory insects would most likely decrease in number, because many would starve for lack of food.	1
		1

Question	Correct answer	Marks
3 b)	The insectivorous birds would also decrease in number,	1
	because many would starve for lack of food.	1
3 c)	The mice may increase in number,	1
	because there might be more food if there are no herbivorous insects.	1
3 d)	The snakes may not change in number,	1
	as they could replace the animals that would be decreasing in number due to the loss of herbivorous insects with mice and seed-eating birds that may be increasing in number.	1
4 a)	Caterpillars,	1
	because they eat the leaves of the tree.	1
4 b)	Because the trees, although bigger in size, are much fewer in number which means that the tree bar is much smaller than the caterpillar bar.	1
4 c)	The caterpillar bar would be much smaller,	1
	because they would have become butterflies and flown away.	1
4 d)	It would have a typical pyramid shape widest at the bottom.	1
	This is because there is a lot of energy in all of the leaves of the tree so the bottom bar would be much wider, and energy is lost at each successive trophic level.	1
5 a)	Of the light energy captured by plants, some is lost immediately as light energy because it is not absorbed by the chlorophyll,	1
	and some is lost as heat energy to the environment through respiration and other chemical reactions.	1
5 b)	Of the chemical energy that enters the primary consumer level, some is lost as chemical energy in undigested food as faeces,	1
	some is lost to the environment as chemical energy in the waste products of reactions, such as urea,	1
	and some is lost as heat energy to the environment through respiration.	1
6	A pyramid of number is relatively easy to collect the data for because it is just counting numbers.	1
	A pyramid of biomass is more difficult,	1
	because you need values for the average biomass of each individual of a species to calculate the biomass for each trophic level, which involves killing and drying the organisms.	1
	A pyramid of energy is even more difficult to produce,	1
	because you have to measure the average energy content of an individual of each species, from which to calculate the energy for each trophic level.	1
	Measuring energy content involves burning the bodies of the dead organisms in a calorimeter.	1
	Total:	41

Introduction

This topic covers the carbon cycle and nitrogen cycle, explaining how these substances cycle between the physical environment and organisms.

Links to other topics

Sections	Essential background knowledge	Useful links
2 Structures and functions in living organisms	2c Biological molecules 2e Nutrition 2f Respiration 2g Gas exchange 2i Excretion	
4 Ecology and the environment	4b Feeding relationships	4d Human influences on the environment
5 Use of biological resources		5a Food production

Topic overview

B4c.1	Carbon cycle
	In this activity students will learn how the processes of respiration, combustion, photosynthesis and decomposition contribute to the carbon cycle.
B4c.2	Nitrogen cycle (B)
	This activity covers the nitrogen cycle, including the role of bacteria.
B4c.3	Consolidation and summary
	This activity provides an opportunity for a quick recap on the ideas encountered in the topic as well as time for the students to answer the End of topic questions in the Student Book.

Activity B4c.1 Carbon cycle

Specification reference: B4c.4.10

Learning objectives

• Describe the stages in the carbon cycle, including respiration, photosynthesis, decomposition and combustion.

Learning outcomes

• Describe stages in the carbon cycle, including respiration, photosynthesis, decomposition and combustion.

Common misconceptions

Combustion rapidly contributes carbon to the atmosphere. This is easier to understand if students are clear that the fossil fuels (particularly coal, oil and natural gas) are formed from the remains of vast quantities of dead plant or animal material deposited over millions of years and changed by geological processes over time. Since plant and animal tissue is rich in carbon, so are fossil fuels. However, combustion of wood does not, on balance, add carbon to the atmosphere as long as new trees are replanted, which take in carbon as they grow.

Resources

Student Book pages 283–286

Worksheet B4c.1a Constructing the carbon cycle

Approach

1. Introduction

Revise work from Topics 2e Nutrition and 2f Respiration by asking students to write down the word equations and (if appropriate for their ability) the balanced symbol equations for photosynthesis and respiration.

If they are not sure, remind them of the practical work they carried out to investigate photosynthesis and respiration, focusing on the measurement of the net release of carbon dioxide using hydrogen-carbonate indicator. Ask them to write down (or give them) the word and balanced symbol equations for burning of fuel (combustion).

Give students a minute or so to compare the equations and write down three key points from the comparison. Take examples from around the class to make sure that students appreciate that combustion and respiration are similar in releasing carbon dioxide, and photosynthesis is opposite in taking in carbon dioxide, and that if the rates of photosynthesis and respiration are the same, then the net release of carbon dioxide to the air is zero.

2. Decomposition

Remind students of the term *decomposer* from their work on trophic levels in Topic 4b Feeding relationships. Ask them to explain what it means, and to give some examples. Introduce the term *decomposition*. Ask students to suggest what it means and what happens when dead plant or animal material decomposes.

If there is time and opportunity, allow students to set up a simple investigation to show whether carbon dioxide is produced or released during decomposition by passing any gases produced through a hydrogen-carbonate indicator. (Safety note: Only use waste vegetable material for this, such as a decaying banana skin or grass, dispose of all material suitably, such as in a compost heap, and clean apparatus and hands thoroughly after touching decaying material.) They should find that the indicator becomes more yellow, as carbon dioxide is released.

Encourage students to make the link between the carbon dioxide released during decay and the respiration of the decomposers as they use the food materials to release energy for growth and reproduction.

3. Constructing the carbon cycle

Worksheet B4c.1a provides cards that students can cut out and use to construct a diagram of the carbon cycle. Explain that the term *carbon store* on the worksheet means something in which carbon is found.

Encourage students to lay out the cards first in what they think is the right arrangement, and then compare their layout with the diagram of the carbon cycle on page 284 of the Student Book before sticking them in their workbook.

For less able students, point out that they will need 3 copies of the word *respiration*. More able students should be encouraged to identify the form of carbon in each of the stores shown in their diagram.

If there is time, students could research in books or on the internet how much carbon there is in each carbon store given on the worksheet.

4. Consolidation: true or false

Give students two scraps of paper and ask them to write *true* on one and *false* on the other. Then read out some statements about the carbon cycle, some of which are true and some false, and ask students to hold up the correct answer each time. Suitable statements include:

- Fossil fuels are formed from dead plant or animal material. (true)
- Carbon is released from living organisms to the air by photosynthesis. (false)

Answers

Pages 285–286

1. a) Respiration releases carbon dioxide into the atmosphere from the breakdown of complex carbon compounds inside organisms.

   b) Photosynthesis is the fixing/conversion of carbon dioxide from the atmosphere into more complex carbon compounds in plant tissue.

   c) Decomposition is the decay/breakdown of dead plant and animal tissue by decomposers, releasing carbon dioxide into the atmosphere during respiration.

2. a) Carbon dioxide.

   b) Complex carbon compounds e.g. starch, cellulose, sucrose.

   c) Complex carbon compounds e.g. as found in oil.

3. Combustion of fossil fuels releases carbon dioxide into the atmosphere from complex carbon compounds where the carbon has been locked away for millions of years. This greatly increases the rate at which carbon dioxide is being returned to the atmosphere.

B4c.1a Constructing the carbon cycle

The boxes below show processes in the carbon cycle in **bold** text, and stores of carbon in normal text.

1. Cut out the boxes and arrange them to form a diagram that describes the carbon cycle. You may need to repeat some of the process names to complete your diagram.

2. When you are sure of the position, stick them into your work book, and complete the diagram by adding arrows to link the boxes correctly.

3. Add any pictures and other annotations to help explain what is happening in the diagram more clearly.

respiration	air in the atmosphere	dead plant and animal material
photosynthesis	plant material	
combustion	animal material	
decomposition	fossil fuels	

Activity B4c.2 Nitrogen cycle (B)

Specification reference: B4c.4.11**B**

Learning objectives

- Describe the stages in the nitrogen cycle, including the roles of nitrogen-fixing bacteria, decomposers, nitrifying bacteria and denitrifying bacteria. **(B)**

Learning outcomes

- Describe the stages in the nitrogen cycle, including the roles of nitrogen-fixing bacteria, decomposers, nitrifying bacteria and denitrifying bacteria. **(B)**

Common misconceptions

Although nitrogen gas forms the majority of air, we tend to ignore it because it is not obviously relevant to living organisms. It is important to get across the essential role of nitrogen-fixing bacteria in converting nitrogen gas to forms that plants can absorb, so that all organisms can get the nitrates they need for life.

Resources

Student Book pages 286–289

Worksheet B4c.2a The nitrogen cycle **(B)**

Approach

1. Introduction (B)

Give students a minute or so to write down everything they know about nitrogen. Take examples from the class to build up a fact list.

If nobody mentions the importance of nitrogen in organisms, remind students of their work on plant and human nutrition in Topic 2e, and the essential role of nitrogen in forming biological molecules such as proteins (and nucleic acids). Ask them to explain what would happen if there wasn't enough nitrogen available to plants and animals.

2. Labelling the nitrogen cycle (B)

Worksheet B4c.2a contains a partially completed diagram of the nitrogen cycle. Explain that they should complete the missing labels for the diagram. Before looking at the Student Book, students could try to add the labels they can in pencil.

Using a large version of the diagram on the board, take suggestions from the class for all labels that do not relate to bacteria. Then ask students to suggest what might fill the remaining gaps. If needed, hint that it is a kind of organism.

Then ask students to read pages 286–287 of the Student Book on the nitrogen cycle and to complete the labelling. They should then write a sentence for each type of bacteria in the cycle to explain what role they play.

3. Root nodule bacteria (B)

If available, give students the opportunity to look at a prepared slide of nitrogen-fixing bacteria (*Rhizobium*) in a nodule of a root of a legume plant. Alternatively, find an image on the internet to show them. Explain that the relationship between the bacteria and the plant is a specialised one called a mutualistic relationship in which each partner benefits.

Ask students to suggest how the bacteria and plant benefit from such a close relationship (bacteria get a protected environment with nutrients in which to grow, the plant gets a good supply of nitrogen directly from the bacteria).

If there is time, students could then research the use of legume crops in plant rotation to maintain soil fertility as an alternative to using fertiliser. (This can be linked back to later from Topic 5c when discussing how genetic modification could improve crop growth.)

4. Consolidation: notes for an essay (B)

Give students the following title for an essay: 'Explain the importance of cycles within ecosystems for living organisms.' Tell them that the essay is worth 10 points, and ask them to work individually or in pairs to prepare a mark scheme for the essay. Give them several minutes to do this, then take examples from around the class and discuss the relative merits of different suggestions.

Answers

Page 288

1. a) Nitrifying bacteria increase the amount of nitrate ions in the soil by converting ammonium ions to nitrite ions and then to nitrate ions.

   b) Nitrogen-fixing bacteria convert atmospheric nitrogen gas directly into a form of nitrogen that plants can use.

   c) Denitrifying bacteria reduce the amount of nitrate ions in soil by converting them to nitrogen gas.

2. Nitrifying bacteria increase the fertility of soils because plants can only take in nitrogen in the form of nitrates dissolved in soil water. Without nitrogen the plants will not grow well, and become stunted.

3. Decomposers break down complex nitrogen compounds in dead plant and animal tissues and animal waste. This releases ammonium ions that nitrifying bacteria convert to nitrate ions that plants need. Without decomposers, the bacteria would have nothing to work on, and the concentration of nitrate ions in the soil would decrease.

Developing investigative skills, page 289

1. Plan should include:

   - growing one plant of each kind in each type of nutrient solution
   - keeping all plants in identical conditions, i.e. same light, temperature and watering, so that other factors that can affect the rate of growth are controlled
   - after several weeks, measure growth of each plant, using some suitable measure of growth, e.g. increase in height.

2. Prediction should suggest that the wheat plant with the nitrogen-containing solution will grow better than the one without, but that there is unlikely to be any difference in the two legume plants.

3. Wheat/all nutrients: $(20.6 - 5.2/5.2) \times 100\% = 296\%$

Wheat/without nitrogen: $(13.6 - 4.8/4.8) \times 100\% = 183\%$

Legume/all nutrients: $(18.1 - 3.6/3.6) \times 100\% = 403\%$

Legume/without nitrogen: $(19.3 - 4.1/4.1) \times 100\% = 371\%$

4. The wheat plant with nitrogen grew much more than the wheat plant without. There is no great difference in growth between the two legume plants.

5. The difference in the wheat plants is because the plant in the solution lacking nitrogen cannot get the nitrogen it needs to make proteins etc. for healthy growth.

6. The lack of difference between the legume plants is because the plant in solution lacking in nitrogen can get the nitrogen it needs for healthy growth from the nitrogen-fixing bacteria in its roots.

7. Plants that contain nitrogen-fixing bacteria can grow as well in conditions when nitrogen is limited as they can when nitrogen is available, but plants without these bacteria grow less well when nitrogen is lacking.

8. This experiment compares two different kinds of plants, so there may be something about the species that causes the difference. It also only compares one plant in each condition, which will not allow for natural variability between individuals. So some of the results may be affected by chance.

9. Growing legumes of the same species, some that are inoculated with bacteria and some without, in conditions with and without nitrogen, and growing a large number in each situation, would get rid of variation between species and allow for averaging to reduce the effect of random variation between individuals.

B4c.2a The nitrogen cycle (B)

Complete the missing labels in this diagram of the nitrogen cycle.

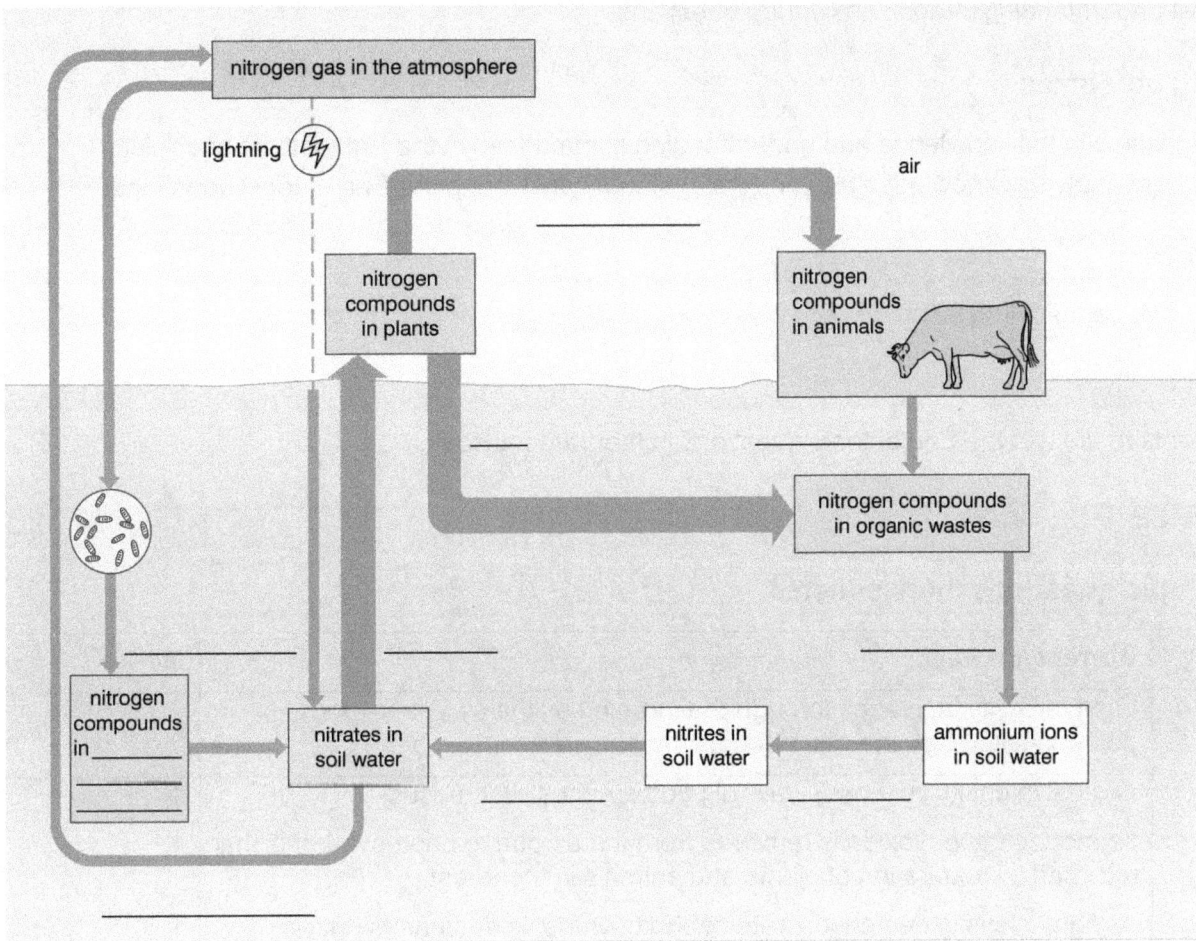

Activity B4c.3 Consolidation and summary

Learning objectives

- To review the learning points of the topic.
- To test understanding through answering questions.

Learning outcomes

- Be familiar with the knowledge and understanding summarised in the End of topic checklist.
- Be able to apply this knowledge and understanding by answering the End of topic questions.

Resources

Student Book pages 290–292

Approach

Ask students to answer the End of topic questions in the Student Book.

Answers

End of topic questions mark scheme

Question	Correct answer	Marks
1 a)	Light intensity increases through the morning as the sun rises, and decreases through the afternoon as the sun sets.	2
1 b)	As light intensity increases, rate of photosynthesis increases	1
	so more carbon dioxide is removed from the air due to photosynthesis than returned by respiration of plants and animals in the forest.	1
	As light intensity decreases, rate of photosynthesis decreases until it stops when it is dark.	1
	So more carbon dioxide is given off into the atmosphere by respiration of all organisms in the forest, than is removed by photosynthesis.	1
2 a)	Nitrifying bacteria need aerobic conditions,	1
	and denitrifying bacteria can grow in anaerobic conditions.	1
	Denitrifying bacteria convert nitrogen compounds in soil to nitrogen gas, which escapes to the atmosphere.	1
2 b)	Plants need nitrogen for healthy growth.	1
	Waterlogged soils have low concentrations of nitrates, so plants will grow poorly without another source of nitrogen.	1
	Digesting animal tissue releases nitrogen compounds that the plants can use for growth.	1

Question	Correct answer	Marks
3 a)	They are broken down by the action of decomposers.	1
	Some of the products of digestion are absorbed by the decomposers and some soak into the ground.	1
3 b)	During the winter it is too cold for decomposer organisms to grow,	1
	so the leaf litter remains on the ground.	1
	In spring, when it gets warm again, the decomposer organisms start to grow and break down the leaf litter.	1
4	Nitrifying and nitrogen-fixing bacteria are essential for adding nitrates to the soil.	1
	Since plants can only take nitrogen in as nitrates from soil water, without these bacteria the nitrate concentration of soil water would drop,	1
	which would reduce the rate of plant growth.	1
	Less plant growth will provide less food for animals,	1
	eventually leading to starvation and death in the community.	1
	Total:	22

Introduction

This topic looks at the effects that human activities are having on ecosystems as a result of air pollution, global warming, eutrophication and deforestation.

Links to other topics

Sections	Essential background knowledge	Useful links
1 The nature and variety of living organisms	1b Variety of living organisms	
2 Structures and functions in living organisms	2e Nutrition 2f Respiration 2g Gas exchange 2h Transport	
4 Ecology and the environment	4c Cycles within ecosystems	
5 Use of biological resources		5a Food production

Topic overview

B4d.1	**Air pollution**
	This activity looks at the effects of sulfur dioxide and carbon monoxide on living organisms.
B4d.2	**The greenhouse effect**
	This activity looks at what greenhouse gases are and their effects. It also looks at the enhanced greenhouse effect.
B4d.3	**Eutrophication**
	Students look at the effects of pollution from sewage and leached minerals from fertiliser and how this can lead to eutrophication. They also look at the effects of eutrophication on aquatic organisms.
B4d.4	**Deforestation (B)**
	This activity looks at the possible consequences of deforestation.
B4d.5	**Consolidation and summary**
	This activity provides an opportunity for a quick recap on the ideas encountered in the topic as well as time for the students to answer the End of topic questions in the Student Book.

Activity B4d.1 Air pollution

Specification reference: B4d.4.12

Learning objectives

- Understand the biological consequences of pollution of air by sulfur dioxide and carbon monoxide.

Learning outcomes

- Describe the biological consequences of pollution of air by sulfur dioxide and by carbon monoxide.

Common misconceptions

Although many people know that carbon monoxide is toxic, they do not realise the effect it can have on the growth of living organisms at lower concentrations. Understanding that carbon monoxide displaces oxygen in red blood cells can help improve understanding.

If students carry out their own research for images showing air pollution, make sure they can distinguish between water vapour (as from air cooling towers of power stations), which is not an air pollutant, and emissions from chimneys that contain pollutant gases such as sulfur dioxide and nitrogen oxides. Many people confuse the two.

Resources

Student Book pages 293–298

Worksheet B4d.1a Acidity and germination

Worksheet B4d.1b The impact of acid rain

Resources for class practical (see Technician's notes, following)

Approach

1. Introduction

Remind students of their work on enzymes and pH in Topic 2c by asking them to sketch a graph of enzyme activity against pH. Take descriptions from around the class, and ask students to explain the relationship. Then revise the effect of bubbling carbon dioxide through a solution of hydrogen-carbonate indicator, and ask them to explain the change. They should appreciate that the carbon dioxide dissolves in the water and acidifies the solution.

2. Acid rain and living organisms

Worksheet B4d.1a lets students investigate the effect of acidity on the germination of seeds, as described in the Developing investigative skills box on pages 296 of the Student Book. This will take at least a week (depending on species used) to produce sufficient results.

If different seeds are available, you could challenge students to amend the simple method before the practical to investigate whether acid rain affects different seeds by different amounts. Also ask them to apply their results to explain how ecosystems may change as a result of acid rain. They will need to consider how many repeats they need to help them get reliable results.

If there is not enough equipment, time or space for all students to set up dishes for every pH, then split the class into groups and give each group a small number of pHs to test. Make sure that a range of pHs are investigated within the whole class.

Depending on the species used, students should find that germination is inhibited at lower pHs, implying that acid rain could damage ecosystems by reducing the success of some plant species. Note that some plant species do better than others at low or high pH, so students may find the opposite result.

3. The impact of acid rain

Ask students to read about acid rain on pages 294–295 in the Student Book and to make notes on the subject. Then give them Worksheet B4d.1b, which has a comprehension and data interpretation exercise on the effect of acid rain in lakes in the US and Canada (data from: http://www.epa.gov.html).

4. Monitoring air pollution

Students could use books or the internet to research the use of organisms as air pollution indicators, such as lichens (some species of which are tolerant of air pollutants such as sulfur dioxide and nitrogen oxides, and some of which cannot grow in those conditions), and blackspot fungus on roses (which is killed in conditions of high air pollution). They should use their findings to prepare a poster or short report on why some organisms are more useful than others as air pollution indicators.

5. Carbon monoxide

Ask students to read page 297 of the Student Book about carbon monoxide. Explain that motor vehicle engines burn fuel least effectively when moving at low speed, particularly when stopping and starting in traffic queues.

Students could carry out further research on carbon monoxide in cities, and how catalytic converters on cars affect the amount of carbon monoxide released. They should then write bullet point notes for a short report to answer the question 'Is carbon monoxide a problem in cities?'

6. Consolidation: air pollution concept map

Give students several minutes to start their own concept maps around the subject of air pollution. Then ask them to compare what they have done with another student and to add anything they have missed to their own map. Take examples from around the class to make sure the key points are included appropriately.

Technician's notes

You will need the following resources for the class practical.

Be sure to check the latest safety notes on these resources before

proceeding. B4d.1a Acidity and germination

The number of each piece of apparatus needed will depend on the number of pHs that each student or group will investigate. **Note:** this practical will need to run for at least a week and students may need a few minutes every day to check the dishes.

Class practical, per student or group:

seeds, ideally of a fast-germinating species such as cress or *Arabidopsis*
solutions of different pHs (see note above)
Petri dishes, 1 per pH investigated
paper towels or other absorbent paper, e.g. filter paper or blotting paper
pipettes, 1 per pH investigated
marker pen
eye protection

The solutions can be produced as follows:

pH	Volume of 0.2 mol dm^{-3} Na$_2$HPO$_4$.2H$_2$O	Volume of 0.1 mol dm^{-3} citric acid
3	20.55	79.45
4	38.55	61.45
5	51.50	48.50
6	63.15	36.85
7	82.35	17.65
8	97.25	2.75

Alternatively, some suppliers provide separate buffer solutions or tablets at the different pHs.

Answers

Developing investigative skills, page 296

1. Plan should include the following:

- description of apparatus, including dishes, seeds, absorbent material such as paper towel (to keep seeds moist), dilute solutions of different pH ranging from a low pH (such as pH 2) to a pH at the high end of the normal range (e.g. pH 8)
- description of how to set up apparatus, with a number of seeds in each dish at each pH
- repeat dishes of each pH (to improve reliability of results)
- description of how seeds are monitored and looked after until germination complete (e.g. over 7 days).

2. Use of solutions of low pH should be handled with care and protective goggles worn to prevent splashes entering the eyes. Spills should be cleaned up immediately.

3. The graph shows that as pH falls, the success rate of germination is reduced, suggesting that germination in wheat seeds is damaged by acidic conditions.

Page 298

1. a) Smoke/emissions from factories contains acidic gases, such as sulfur dioxide, which dissolve in water droplets in clouds that then fall as acid rain.

   b) The clouds containing the acidic water droplets can be blown over great distances away from the industrial areas by wind.

2. Damage direct to delicate tissues in lungs, to soft-skinned organisms such as fish and amphibians, and to single-celled organisms. Indirect damage by changing the acidity of the soil, affecting its fertility due to leaching of minerals, or making poisonous minerals more soluble. As a result of changes in food web other organisms may be affected due to interdependency.

3. Carbon monoxide combines with haemoglobin, replacing the oxygen that it normally carries in the blood. Tissues receive less oxygen for respiration, resulting in damage especially in rapidly growing or respiring tissues.

B4d.1a Acidity and germination

Acid rain can have many effects on living organisms. In this practical you will investigate the effect of acid rain on the germination of seeds.

Apparatus

Petri dishes

seeds

paper towels or other absorbent paper

solutions of different pH pipettes

marker pen

eye protection

SAFETY INFORMATION
If seeds have been coated in antifungal compounds, wash hands thoroughly after touching them.
Wear eye protection.

Method

1. You will need to set up one Petri dish for each pH that you are given. Mark each dish on the side with one of the pHs you will use, and your initials.

2. For each dish, fold a paper towel so that it fits the base of the dish.

3. Using a separate pipette for each pH solution, add enough solution to the paper towel to make it wet but that so all the solution is absorbed. (Seeds need moisture for germination, but wet seeds and seedlings will rot more easily.)

4. Place 10 seeds on the paper in each dish and spread them out as evenly as possible.

5. Place all the dishes in a warm place.

6. Check the dishes each day and add a little more of the correct pH solution if the paper is starting to dry out. Remember not to add too much solution, so that it is all absorbed by the paper.

7. Each day, record the number of seeds germinated in each dish. Repeat this for at least a week.

8. Draw up a table to record your results clearly.

Analyse and interpret data

1. Collect results from other groups. Ignoring any anomalous values, average the results for each pH.

2. Use the averaged results table to draw a suitable chart or graph.

3. Describe any patterns in the results.

4. Use your knowledge of the effect of pH on cells to explain any patterns in the results.

5. Explain what your results suggest about the effect of acid rain on germination of seeds.

Evaluate data and methods

1. Describe any problems that you had with this method and explain how you would change the method to reduce their effect.

B4d.1b The impact of acid rain

Acidic gases emitted from the chimneys of power stations and other industry can cause acid rain. The US Environmental Protection Agency carries out surveys to try to estimate the effect of acid rain on the environment. One survey in 2008 showed that, in over 1000 large lakes, 75% had been made more acidic as a result of acid rain. One of the most acidic lakes was Little Echo Pond near New York which had a pH of 4.2.

Some areas are more sensitive to the effect of acid rain than others, because some soils do not contain as much of the chemicals that can neutralise the acid. In one area, for example, over 90% of the streams were more acidic than they should be.

The lakes surveyed were more acidic all year-round, but some become much more acidic for short periods after snow melt or heavy downpours of rain.

Animal	pH 6.5	pH 6.0	pH 5.5	pH 5.0	pH 4.5	pH 4.0
Trout	▓	▓	▓	▓		
Frog	▓	▓	▓	▓	▓	▓
Salamander	▓	▓	▓	▓		
Mayfly	▓	▓	▓			

The chart shows in grey the acidity that some organisms can tolerate. Not all organisms are as badly affected by acidity as others.

As many of these organisms are linked by feeding relationships (as shown in the food web), even if a species is not directly damaged by the acidity, they may be indirectly affected if their food is killed, or a competitor decreases in number.

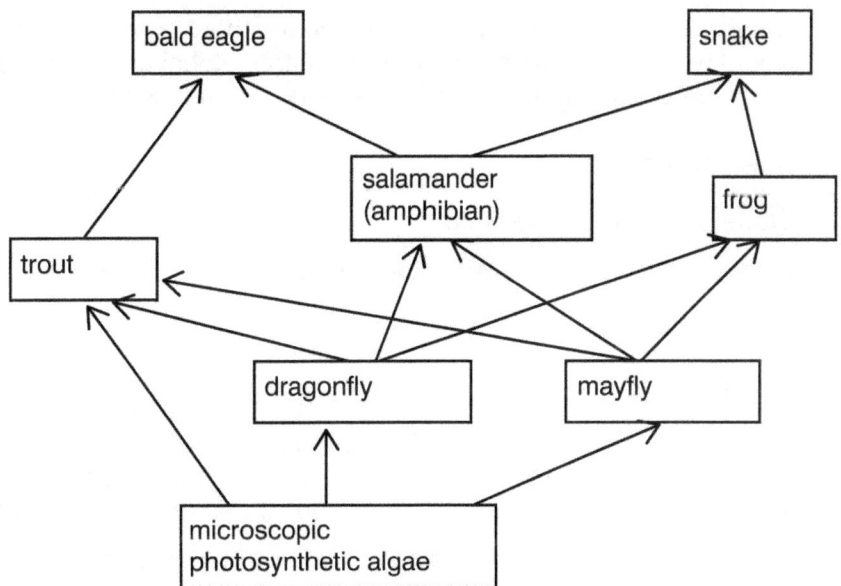

1. What is acid rain and how is it formed?

2. Canada lies north of the USA, and many Canadian lakes that are far from industry also suffer from increased acidity. Explain how this could happen.

3. Explain why some lakes are more affected by acid rain than others. Give as many reasons as you can.

4. Which of the organisms that live in a lake and are shown in the chart is most likely to be affected by acid rain falling in the lake? Explain your answer.

5. Which of the organisms shown in the chart might be found in Little Echo Pond? Explain your answer.

6. Explain why bald eagles might be affected indirectly by acid rain, even though they do not live in lakes.

7. Explain as fully as you can why the governments of the US and European countries have introduced laws to restrict the amount of sulfur dioxide that industry can add to the atmosphere.

Activity B4d.2 The greenhouse effect

Specification reference: B4d.4.13; B4d.4.14; B4d.4.15

Learning objectives

*   Understand that water vapour, carbon dioxide, nitrous oxide, methane and CFCs are greenhouse gases.
*   Understand how human activities contribute to greenhouse gases.
*   Understand how an increase in greenhouse gases results in an enhanced greenhouse effect and that this may lead to global warming and its consequences.

Learning outcomes

*   Name the greenhouse gases and explain how human activities are contributing to their release.
*   Explain how an increase in greenhouse gases may lead to an enhanced greenhouse effect and global warming, and discuss the effects this may have.

Common misconceptions

The terms *greenhouse effect* and *global warming* (as a possible result of an *enhanced* greenhouse effect) are frequently confused, leading to the misconception that the greenhouse effect is a 'bad thing'. It is important for students to distinguish between the terms and to realise that the greenhouse effect is a result of natural processes that make life on Earth possible.

As with any contemporary scientific debate, there is not perfect agreement about the causes of current global warming. Some scientists believe that global warming is due to natural causes. However, the consensus is that global warming is due to human activity. This is the approach used in these materials.

Resources

Student Book pages 298–301

Worksheet B4d.2a Evaluating the evidence

Approach

1. Introduction

Write the words *greenhouse effect* in the middle of the board. Ask students to suggest related words and how to link them to start a mind map. It is likely that students will bring a wide range of ideas – not all of them accurate – from their previous studies and from what they have heard about in the media.

For this task, don't discuss any areas of misunderstanding, but note them for later in the activity.

2. Greenhouse gases

Ask students to read about the greenhouse effect on pages 298–299 of the Student Book. Then ask them to draw up a table naming the five greenhouse gases, how they are formed by natural processes (not appropriate for CFCs) and how they are formed by human activities.

They should then use books or the internet to find out and describe how those activities are changing, so that they can assess the possible future impact of each gas on the enhanced greenhouse effect.

Finally, ask them to suggest how human activities might be changed in order to reduce the rate at which greenhouse gases are being added to the atmosphere.

3. Enhancing the greenhouse effect

Students could use the information in the Student Book and their own research to produce a poster in two parts: one part should be headed 'Why we need the greenhouse effect' and the other part should be headed 'Why we do not need the enhanced greenhouse effect'. The first part should explain how the greenhouse effect happens, and why it is essential for life.

The second part should show critical appreciation of some of the predictions about global warming, such as the likelihood that a predicted change may have the impact suggested.

4. Evaluating the evidence

Worksheet B4d.2a asks students to find graphs of global surface temperature and atmospheric carbon dioxide concentration, in order to discuss cause and correlation, and to evaluate the argument for emissions of carbon dioxide from human activity as a cause for global warming.

Alternatively they could use the graphs on page 300 of the Student Book for the task.

5. Consolidation: concept map revision

Return to the concept map started in the Introduction, and ask students to suggest ways in which it should be added to and amended to clear any confusions or inaccuracies.

Encourage discussion over any areas of weakness and make sure students clearly understand the distinction between the terms *greenhouse effect*, *enhanced greenhouse effect* and *global warming*.

Answers

Page 301

1. The greenhouse effect is a natural process that warms the Earth's surface when greenhouse gases in the atmosphere prevent longer wavelength radiation escaping into space. The enhanced greenhouse effect is the additional warming caused by the addition of greenhouse gases to the atmosphere as a result of human activity.

2. a) Natural, respiration; human, combustion of fossil fuels.

   b) Natural, soil bacteria in the nitrogen cycle; human, addition of nitrogen-containing fertilisers to soil.

   c) Natural, digestion of food in animal guts and decay of waterlogged vegetation; human, increase in herd animals and artificial waterlogged vegetation in rice paddy fields.

3. Any from: increase in number and intensity of storms, more drought, more flooding, change to summer/winter temperatures and precipitation.

Worksheet B4d.2a

1. Make sure students have the standard graphs for this answer, showing a rapid increase in temperature and in carbon dioxide concentration over the past 50 years or so.

2. a) Temperature recently from direct measurements at fixed sites, more distantly some are direct measurements (such as in the UK and US), others are calculated from proxies such as tree ring data and ice core data; carbon dioxide concentration since late 1950s at Mauna Loa, previous to that from bubbles in ice cores.

   b) Using proxies makes assumptions about the relationship between the proxy and the value being calculated, which can reduce the reliability of the calculated value.

3. Graphs should show: gradual rise since c. 1750; an increasingly rapid rise in past 50 years or so.

4. That increasing carbon dioxide in the atmosphere released from human activity is enhancing the greenhouse effect and causing global temperature to rise.

5. Much of the work has been centred on laboratory experiments, and in particular computer modelling.

6. The correlation is very close, and other natural factors have failed to produce good correlations with temperature, so it is becoming increasingly reasonable to accept this cause.

7. Many of the emissions come from industrial processes, or transport. Reducing emissions means persuading people to change what they do, which can be very expensive and difficult to achieve. While there is apparently doubt in the discussion, politicians and industry have used this as an excuse not to face difficult and costly decisions.

B4d.2a Evaluating the evidence

The term *global warming* was first used in the late 1970s, when scientists first suggested a relationship between increased emissions of carbon dioxide from combustion of fossil fuels and an increase in the Earth's average surface temperature. Since then there has been a major debate among scientists, politicians, industry and the general population about whether human activities really do cause increased carbon dioxide emissions and higher temperatures on the Earth, and what we should do to avoid or minimise potential problems caused by global warming.

You are going to look at the evidence for some of this and make your own evaluations.

1. Use books or the internet to find graphs of the following:

  • average global surface temperature over the past 250–400 years

  • average atmospheric carbon dioxide concentration over the past 250–400 years.

You will find graphs that extend beyond this time. However, these vary as the result of many other factors, including the relative positions of the Earth and Sun in the Solar System and global ice ages, and so do not help in the debate about global warming.

2. a) Annotate the graphs you found to explain how those measurements were taken. (Note that different measurements on the same graph may have been gathered in different ways.)

  b) Were all the values measured directly, or have they been calculated from other measurements? If the latter, what assumptions were made in those calculations and how might those assumptions affect the reliability of the calculated values?

3. Compare the graph of surface temperature with that of atmospheric carbon dioxide concentration, and describe any similarities and/or differences.

When two factors vary in a similar way, we say they are *correlated*. Two factors may be correlated for various reasons:

  • factor A is changing and causing factor B to change in a similar way

  • factor B is changing and causing factor A to change in a similar way

  • factor C is changing and causing factors A and B to change in a similar way.

4. What cause is suggested for the correlation between carbon dioxide concentration and temperature? Explain why the cause is changing.

5. It can be very difficult to prove that a correlation has a specific cause. Find out and describe what scientists have done in order to try to prove that the cause you gave in question 4 is real.

6. Given what you have found out, how reasonable do you think it is to say that the cause you gave in question 4 is the fault of human activity?

7. Suggest why politicians and industry have tried very hard to disagree with the scientists about this in the past.

Activity B4d.3 Eutrophication

Specification reference: B4d.4.16; B4d.4.17

Learning objectives

- Understand the biological consequences of pollution of water by sewage.
- Understand the biological consequences of eutrophication caused by leached minerals from fertiliser.

Learning outcomes

- Explain the biological consequences of pollution of water by sewage, including increases in the number of microorganisms causing depletion of oxygen.
- Explain how eutrophication and water pollution can result from fertiliser leaching into water.

Common misconceptions

The term *eutrophication* is commonly misunderstood. This is easiest to resolve by looking at the source of the word: *eutrophic* means 'well-nourished'. Eutrophication is simply the addition of nutrients to an ecosystem, typically a water system. Whether this leads to pollution depends on the ecosystem, the organisms within it and the amount of nutrients added to it.

Eutrophication is a natural process in water systems such as ponds and lakes, as nutrients are brought in by streams and rivers. However, the most rapid eutrophication occurs as the result of human activity, such as run-off of fertilisers or dumping of sewage.

Resources

Student Book pages 301–305

Worksheet B4d.3a Monitoring water pollution

Resources for demonstration (see Technician's notes, following)

Approach

1. Introduction

Remind students of their work on minerals and plant growth from Topic 2e Nutrition by showing them a plant. Ask what effect adding plant fertiliser to the water given to the plant will have on growth, and why it would have this effect. Students should remember that plants need nutrients from soil water, such as nitrogen and magnesium, to convert sugars produced from photosynthesis into other essential molecules in plant tissue.

If possible, show students a photo from the internet of large-scale algal growth, such as off the coast of China just before the Olympics in 2008, and ask what they think might have caused it.

2. Describing eutrophication and its effects

Ask students to read about sewage pollution and eutrophication on pages 301–305 in the Student Book, and to make notes. Then ask them to imagine that they work for a water protection agency, such as the Environment Agency in the UK, which has responsibility for maintaining the quality of water in rivers, canals and lakes.

They should produce a bullet point list for people who add substances to water systems, including industry, farmers and waste water treatment plants, on how they can ensure that what they add to the water system has little impact on the environment.

3. Measuring dissolved oxygen in water: demonstration

If you have an oxygen sensor that will measure dissolved oxygen concentration in water, then set up the following as a demonstration for students. You will also need several tall glass containers, pond/stream water from a source that is not naturally high in nutrients, and soluble plant 'food'. (Safety note: always wash your hands thoroughly after touching pond/stream water and fully cover and cuts, etc. Also take care not to slip into the pond.)

Gently add pond water to each container, so that it is nearly full. The water should contain microscopic pond organisms, including algae, and look a little green/murky and not completely clear. Label each of the containers to indicate the number of drops of plant 'food' you will add.

One container should have no addition, and the container with the most drops should be given about twice the amount recommended by the manufacturer.

Add the drops to each container and gently mix them into the water with a long stick. Allow the contents to settle. Then, using the oxygen sensor, measure the dissolved oxygen concentration at the bottom of each container.

Ask students to predict what will happen to the oxygen concentration over a week and to explain their predictions.

Leave the containers in a sunny place, without disturbance, and measure the oxygen concentration at the bottom of each container every day for a week.

Students should then analyse the results and check whether their predictions were correct. They should explain the importance of their results for the eutrophication of natural water systems.

4. Monitoring water pollution

Worksheet B4d.3a provides information on monitoring water pollution using indicator organisms, such as mayfly nymphs and bloodworms. It would be helpful to provide students with images of some of the organisms mentioned on the sheet, or allow students access to the internet to find their own images.

5. Consolidation: notes for a friend

Ask students to write bullet point notes for a friend who missed this activity, to summarise what they need to learn. Take examples from around the class and encourage discussion to select the five key points of the activity.

Technician's notes

You will need the following resources for the class demonstration.

Be sure to check the latest safety notes on these resources before proceeding.

Measuring dissolved oxygen in water: demonstration

Take the water sample from a pond or stream where nutrient level is not high. Exclude any large animals, but microscopic animals such as water fleas can be included.

Water samples can be returned to their source after the investigation only if suitably diluted to reduce the concentration of added nutrients to a minimum. This is better in flowing water, where natural dilution will occur more easily, than in a pond.

tall glass containers
pond or stream water to fill containers
marker pen
long stick for mixing
oxygen sensor and recording equipment
soluble plant 'food' (as used for houseplants or garden crops)

Answers

Page 304

1. The addition of nutrients to water.

2. Runoff of fertiliser into water as a result of heavy rainfall, leaching of soluble nutrients in fertiliser through soil into water systems.

3. Sewage added to water → adds nutrients to water = eutrophication → plant growth rate increases → increase in dead plant material → increase in microorganisms → respiration by microorganisms increases removing dissolved oxygen from water → less dissolved oxygen for other organisms which die = water pollution.

Page 305

1. They are decomposers.

2. Because the microorganisms are aerobic. If conditions became anaerobic, then other microorganisms would grow and the materials in the liquid would not be broken down in the same way. Some of these anaerobic microorganisms might be pathogenic which would make the water more dangerous for release into water systems.

3. The microorganisms digest the organic molecules in the sewage, causing them to break down into smaller inorganic molecules such as carbon dioxide and nitrate ions.

4. The microorganisms that produce methane are anaerobic.

5. Dried sludge still contains large amounts of organic nitrogen. When this is added to fields, it is broken down by bacteria to release inorganic nitrogen in a form that crop plants can absorb. The plants use these for making proteins and other nitrogen-containing organic molecules, so the sludge improves crop growth.

6. The chlorine kills any microorganisms left in the water, so that none are added to the water system.

7. The BOD of sewage is high because microorganisms can use the nutrients in it to grow and multiply rapidly. So respiration rate is high and the amount of oxygen taken from the water by the microorganisms is high. The BOD of treated water is low because the nutrients in sewage have been broken down to a form that does not encourage growth, or absorbed by the microorganisms in the treatment beds and used for their growth.

B4d.3a Monitoring water pollution

Different aquatic organisms (that live in water) can tolerate different amounts of dissolved oxygen in the water. For example, the larvae of many species of mayfly can only survive in water with very high levels of oxygen, while many species of worm can survive in water with low levels of oxygen.

In the UK, this fact is used in a scoring system, which uses the organisms present in the water to assess the level of oxygen in the water and therefore the level of pollution in the water. This is called the BMWP (Biological Monitoring Working Party) system. Organisms that need the highest levels of dissolved oxygen are given a score of 10, and those that need the lowest are scored as 1.

Samples are taken in a stream by 'kick sampling', where the bottom surface of the stream is agitated by kicking gently for a particular length of time, and anything that is disturbed is caught downstream in a fine net. The organisms that have been caught are identified and scored according to the BMWP system, and the total score for the stream is calculated from all the different kinds of organism present.

1. Explain why aquatic organisms need oxygen dissolved in the water.

2. Suggest why different aquatic organisms can tolerate different amounts of dissolved oxygen in the water.

3. Explain why dissolved oxygen concentration can be used as a measure of water pollution.

4. Dragonfly larvae are scored as 8 on the BMWP system, and leeches as 4. Which of these organisms would be found in more polluted water? Explain your answer.

5. Dissolved oxygen concentration of water can be measured directly using an oxygen sensor. Suggest any advantages of using a sensor rather than sampling organisms.

6. Many water authorities in the UK use the BMWP system rather than oxygen sampling to monitor the long-term quality of the water in rivers and lakes in their region. Suggest why this gives a better result.

7. Explain how the kick sampling method could be used to identify the source of pollution along a stretch of river through a water authority's region.

Activity B4d.4 Deforestation (B)

Specification reference: B4d.4.18**B**

Learning objectives

- Understand the effects of deforestation, including leaching, soil erosion, disturbance of evapotranspiration and the carbon cycle, and the balance of atmospheric gases. **(B)**

Learning outcomes

- Describe the effects of deforestation, including leaching, soil erosion, disturbance of evapotranspiration, and the balance of atmospheric oxygen and carbon dioxide. **(B)**

Resources

Student Book pages 305–306

Worksheet B4d.4a Effects of deforestation **(B)**

Approach

1. Introduction (B)

Ask students to imagine that a small local wood is about to be cleared to make space for some new building. Give them a few minutes, working individually or in pairs, to write down all the effects of this on the environment that they can think of.

Take examples from around the class and discuss any suggestions that might appear to conflict in order to identify a resolution.

2. Reasons for large-scale deforestation (B)

Give students access to the internet or to books to research an area of large-scale deforestation, such as the Amazon Basin or parts of Indonesia and Malaysia. They should try to find answers to the following questions:

- Why is the deforestation taking place? What will replace the forest?
- Who will benefit from what happens after the deforestation?
- Are there any people who will not benefit from the deforestation? Explain your answer.
- Is anything being done to minimise the impact of the deforestation on the environment? If so, what, and how will it help?
- Is there anything that people outside the area could do to help minimise the impact of deforestation within the area? (Note: the answer to this should highlight the role of global trade in creating markets for products from these areas, and indicate that it's not just a local issue.)

3. Effects of deforestation (B)

Worksheet B4d.4a provides a set of cards with words relating to various aspects of deforestation and life processes. Students could use these in different ways, for example:

- to start a concept map on the topic, and then add words and annotations of their own
- to link aspects of deforestation to living processes, to help explain the impact of deforestation on the environment
- to organise ideas to use as the basis of a poster on the subject.

Students could first read pages 305–306 on deforestation in the Student Book. Then explain to students how they should use the cards.

4. Consolidation: crossword clues (B)

Ask students to write 10 clues for a crossword on human influences on the environment, covering all of the last four activities. They could swap their clues with a neighbour to try them out, and comment on any clues that were not clear. They should then try to improve any weak clues. Take examples from around the class, to cover all the key words of the last four activities.

Answers

Page 306

1. a) Deforestation: the destruction / cutting down of large areas of forest and woodland.

   b) Soil erosion: the washing away of soil by heavy rainfall.

   c) Leaching: when soluble nutrients dissolve in soil water and soak away deep into the ground.

2. a) Trees no longer take up water from the ground and release it to the atmosphere through transpiration, however water can now evaporate more easily from exposed soil, which can affect the moisture in the air above the forest and so rainfall.

   b) Soil erosion because there are no tree roots to hold the soil, and increased leaching because there are few plant roots to absorb the nutrients, both remove soluble mineral nutrients from the soil, which will reduce the rate of plant growth.

   c) Burning or rotting of trees releases the carbon stored in the wood as carbon dioxide to the atmosphere at a much faster rate than normal, plus trees are no longer taking in carbon dioxide through photosynthesis, increasing atmosphere carbon dioxide.

B4d.4a Effects of deforestation (B)

The cards below include words related to deforestation and some of the effects that it can have.

Cut out the cards and use them as instructed by your teacher.

leaching	growth	nitrogen cycle
carbon cycle	respiration	atmospheric oxygen concentration
combustion	nutrients	soil erosion
rainfall	global climate change	atmospheric carbon dioxide concentration
photosynthesis	evapotranspiration	enhanced greenhouse effect
local climate	transpiration	decrease in biodiversity

Activity B4d.5 Consolidation and summary

Learning objectives

- To review the learning points of the topic.
- To test understanding through answering questions.

Learning outcomes

- Be familiar with the knowledge and understanding summarised in the End of topic checklist.
- Be able to apply this knowledge and understanding by answering the End of topic questions.

Resources

Student Book pages 307–310

Approach

Ask students to answer the End of topic questions in the Student Book.

Answers

End of topic questions mark scheme

Question	Correct answer	Marks
1 a)	Pollution is the harming of the environment by the addition of substances.	1
1 b)	Burning of fossil fuels in industries/power stations;	1
	burning of petrol/diesel in vehicle engines.	1
1 c)	Sulfur dioxide dissolves in water droplets in clouds to form sulfuric acid.	1
	When precipitation/rain falls from the clouds, it contains the sulfuric acid, making it more acidic than normal.	1
1 d)	Sketch like the diagram on page 294 of the Student Book showing sulfur dioxide gas emissions from chimneys / traffic rising into air	1
	dissolving in clouds to form acidic water droplets and clouds being blown far from the region of emission,	1
	and acid rain falling on a distant region.	1
1 e)	As a gas it can damage breathing surfaces.	1
	As acid rain, it can acidify land and water and damage organisms that come into contact with it.	1
2 a)	To increase crop growth	1
2 b)	Some of the fertiliser will not be used by the plants, and so it will escape into the water system / nearby streams or rivers.	1
2 c)	Fertiliser in the water will increase the nutrients so plants and algae will grow faster.	1
	This will cover the surface of the water, blocking light from reaching plants deeper in the water.	1
	Plants lower down will die, which will increase the number of microorganisms in the water as they decay the plants.	1
	Respiration of the microorganisms removes oxygen from the water, decreasing the oxygen available for other organisms that might die.	1

Question	Correct answer	Marks
2 d)	If farmers only add enough fertiliser to the soil as the plants can absorb, then this will reduce the amount of run-off and leaching of minerals into the streams and rivers around the fields.	1
	This will reduce the amount of eutrophication of the water and reduce the risk of depletion of dissolved oxygen in the water.	1
3 a)	The oxygen is used by the microorganisms in the water	1
	for respiration.	1
3 b)	Polluted water would use more oxygen	1
	because it contains a greater number of microorganisms.	1
3 c)	Worms	1
	because they can survive better in conditions of low oxygen as the result of water pollution.	1
3 d)	It means the organism has characteristics that enable it to survive and reproduce well in that habitat.	1
3 e)	The organisms have to live in the water all the time, so they will show the condition of the water over a long period.	1
	Sampling for oxygen demand only gives a result for the time that the water was sampled, and it may change from one period to another.	1
4 a)	To clear the land for building or growing crops / keeping herd animals,	1
	and to use the timber for construction and woodwork.	1
4 b)	Large-scale deforestation destroys many habitats for plants and for animals.	1
	This means that the organisms that used to live there are unlikely to be able to live there any longer.	1
	Other organisms that are better adapted to the new conditions will move in.	1
4 c)	After deforestation, mineral nutrients that were locked up in the trees are lost or released.	1
	Soil erosion and leaching removes dissolved minerals from the layers of the soil where plant roots can reach, so the soil loses fertility.	1
	This means that new plants cannot grow as quickly as they did before the area was deforested.	1
5	Evidence from measurements show that the Earth's surface temperature is increasing at a faster rate than ever before.	1
	Carbon dioxide concentration in the air is also increasing, probably as a result of human activities, as are other greenhouse gases.	1
	An increase in these gases in the atmosphere could cause an enhanced greenhouse effect leading to global warming.	1
	Total:	38

Question	Correct answer	Marks
2 a)	i) Brazil: 43.9	1
	Colombia: 46.7	1
	French Guiana: 10.0	1
	Peru: 45.3	1
	Suriname: 9.2	1
	Venezuela: 47.7	1
	ii) greatest: Venezuela	1
	least: Suriname	1
	iii) Two of the following: timber / agriculture / crop plantations / grazing area for cattle / mining	1 mark for each – 2 marks maximum
2 b)	**Leaching:** nutrients are lost from the habitat as without tree roots to absorb them and lock them away they are washed away when it rains.	2
	Soil erosion: without the protective cover of trees and other vegetation, rain washes away the soil.	1
	Evapotranspiration: trees would normally take up water from the ground and release it to the atmosphere through the process of transpiration,	1
	with deforestation, less water ends up in the atmosphere and there is a decrease in rainfall,	1
	owing to the lack of trees, the soil is less able to cope when it rains heavily, and run off from the soil increases.	1
	Atmospheric oxygen and carbon dioxide: trees take up carbon dioxide for photosynthesis and form a major carbon store.	1
	They release oxygen into the air.	1
	As trees are felled, then burned or left to rot, the carbon is released as carbon dioxide.	1
	This rapidly increases the atmospheric carbon dioxide in proportion to the oxygen.	1
3 a)	i) microscopic algae	1
	brown seaweed	1
	ii) topshell	1
	limpet	1
	periwinkle	1
	iii) crab	1
	dog whelk	1
	gull	1

Question	Correct answer	Marks
3 b)	From the Sun's energy falling on a leaf, plants only convert a maximum of 1–2% of this light energy into chemical energy in biomass.	1
	Energy is lost as it is transferred from one trophic level to the next	1
	through respiration, excretion, egestion (undigested food) and heat.	1
	The rate of transfer from one level to another is only 5-20% (depending on the organisms involved).	1
	Although an organism at the next level eats a large number of organisms of the level below, length is limited by the energy remaining at higher trophic levels.	1
3 c)	i) Feed on brown seaweed,	1
	obtain protection/shelter from brown seaweed or any sensible suggestion.	1
	ii) Place a transect line, e.g. a tape measure down the seashore,	1
	starting at high water and extending down the shore,	1
	at intervals of 10 m,	1
	put a quadrat of suitable area, e.g. 0.5 × 0.5 m, on the line,	1
	count the numbers of periwinkles in the quadrat,	1
	repeat across the beach at that distance,	1
	calculate the mean number of periwinkles per m^2 for each distance.	1
4 a)	i) **Carbon dioxide** from the atmosphere is converted to complex carbon	1
	compounds in **plants** by the process of **photosynthesis**. This is often	2
	called carbon **fixation**.	1
	Plants are then often eaten by **animals**, which build up their own complex carbon compounds.	1
	The process of **respiration**, in both plants and animals, returns some of	1
	this carbon back to the atmosphere as **carbon dioxide**.	1
	When organisms die, their bodies decay because of the action of **decomposers**. Some of the complex carbon compounds are taken into	1
	the bodies of these organisms, where some may be converted to carbon dioxide during their **respiration**.	1
	ii) Combustion.	1
4 b)	A: nitrogen-fixing	1
	B: decomposers	1
	C: denitrifying	1
	D: nitrifying	1

Question	Correct answer	Marks
5 a)	i) Sewage concentration shows a steady increase from 2006 to part way through 2009, then the increase accelerated.	1
	The oxygen concentration was stable from 2006 to 2007, showed a sharp decrease through to 2009, then the rate of decrease slowed down towards 2010.	1
	ii) Because of its organic content,	1
	sewage is fed upon / used for the respiration of bacteria / microorganisms in the water.	1
	The bacteria/microorganisms use oxygen for respiration, so this is removed from the water.	1
5 b)	Trout are most sensitive to low oxygen concentration,	1
	and their population in the river dies first.	1
	Perch show a steady decrease, but then their population decreases rapidly as the oxygen reaches a certain level.	1
	Some perch are tolerant of low oxygen concentrations, so their population does not completely die out.	1
	Carp are most tolerant of low oxygen concentrations and their numbers increase as oxygen concentrations fall.	1
	As oxygen concentrations reach a certain level, carp numbers start to level off.	1
	Total:	67

Contents

Overview of the section

This section looks at some of the ways in which humans manipulate organisms and the environment to provide what we need. Topic 5a starts with the use of chemicals, including fertilisers and pesticides, and enclosed environments to maximise the yield of crop plants. This is followed by a discussion of some of the ways we use microorganisms to produce food, including the use of fermenters to culture microorganisms on a large scale. The topic finishes with a description of factors that need to be controlled in fish farming in order to maximise yield.

The last three topics look at ways in which we manipulate organisms, and some of the advantages and disadvantages of these techniques. Topic 5b covers selective breeding, Topic 5c looks at genetic modification and Topic 5d covers cloning. These topics will give students the opportunity to evaluate techniques as well as to consider the different attitudes that people may have to these developing technologies.

Starting points

The Student Book provides a 'section opener', a double page spread that sets the scene for the students (see pages 320–321). It is structured in this way:

- An overview providing details of the areas of study
- Seven questions, presented in the same order as key areas of learning within the section, which can be used to introduce each key area
- A list of section contents.

The questions are intended to provide a structure for introducing the section.

1. Plants grow best under certain conditions. What are the best conditions for plant growth and how can we manipulate the environment to create them?

2. Pests reduce the yield of crops. What methods can be used to control crop pests and what are the advantages and disadvantages of each method?

3. We use microorganisms to make many foods. What conditions do microorganisms need for growth, and what foods can we produce using them?

4. We are increasingly farming fish in order to provide the food we need. What conditions do fish farms need to provide to maximise the growth of the fish?

5. Most of our animal breeds and crop plant varieties have been developed through selective breeding. How is this done?

6. Genetic modification is a technique that we hear about frequently in the media. What is it and what are its advantages and problems?

7. Cloning is another technique that is being used to develop plants and animals with the characteristics we need. How is cloning done, and what could it be used for?

The section opener has two main purposes:

- To acknowledge students' prior learning and to value it
- To provide a benchmark against which future learning can be compared.

You may use the seven questions or 'starting points' in the Student Book in a number of different ways to introduce the section:

- You could ask students to consider the questions as an introductory homework task.
- Students could divide into groups to share their own ideas and understanding and then report back to the whole class.
- Students access the Internet, preferably with a time limit, to find out the information required.

You could use a spider chart or other form of wall chart to summarise the ideas of all the students or groups.

The advantage of recording these initial ideas in this way is that you can retain them for reference as the individual topics are developed. In this way, you can readily acknowledge your students' progress in learning.

Introduction

In this topic, students learn about the conditions needed for maximising growth rates of crop plants, microorganisms used in producing food, and farmed fish.

Links to other topics

Sections	Essential background knowledge	Useful links
1 The nature and variety of living organisms	1a Characteristics of living organisms 1b Variety of living organisms	
2 Structures and functions in living organisms	2c Biological molecules 2d Movement of substances into and out of cells 2e Nutrition 2f Respiration	
4 Ecology and the environment	4b Feeding relationships 4c Cycles within ecosystems 4d Human influences on the environment	
5 Use of biological resources		5b Selective breeding 5c Genetic modification (genetic engineering)

Topic overview

B5a.1	**Crop plants**
	This activity builds on what students learned about factors affecting the rate of photosynthesis in Topic 2e Nutrition, to explain how to maximise the rate of growth of crops. This follows with a study of methods to control pest damage on crop plants.
B5a.2	**Growing microorganisms**
	In this activity students have the opportunity to investigate the effect of conditions on the growth of microorganisms, and learn about the applications of this to the growth of microorganisms on a large scale in fermenters.
B5a.3	**Farming fish (B)**
	In this activity students learn about the conditions needed to grow farmed fish as successfully as possible.
B5a.4	**Consolidation and summary**
	This activity provides an opportunity for a quick recap on the ideas encountered in the topic as well as time for the students to answer the End of topic questions in the Student Book.

Activity B5a.1 Crop plants

Specification reference: B5a.5.1; B5a.5.2; B5a.5.3; B5a.5.4

Learning objectives

- Describe how glasshouses and polythene tunnels can be used to increase the yield of certain crops.
- Understand the effects on crop yield of increased carbon dioxide and increased temperature in glasshouses.
- Understand how the use of fertiliser can increase crop yield.
- Understand the reasons for pest control and the advantages and disadvantages of using pesticides and biological control with crop plants.

Learning outcomes

- Explain how the conditions under which crop plants are grown in glasshouses and in fields can be manipulated to increase plant growth and yield of crop.
- Understand the reasons for pest control and the advantages and disadvantages of using pesticides and biological control with crop plants.

Common misconceptions

Increasing the concentration of carbon dioxide in the air in a glasshouse does not always increase the rate of plant growth. This is because carbon dioxide is acidic, and some plants are very pH-sensitive. So, increasing CO_2 levels can be harmful to some plants.

Resources

Student Book pages 322–329

Worksheet B5a.1a The problems with crop pests

Approach

1. Introduction

Give students a minute or so to revise the conditions that affect the rate of photosynthesis, then take answers from around the class. Their responses should include: light intensity, carbon dioxide concentration and temperature.

Ask students to sketch graphs to show how changes in these factors affect the rate of photosynthesis. Alternatively, ask a student to come to the board and draw a graph for one of the factors, and then ask a second student to come up and explain the shape of the graph, or amend it if they feel it is incorrect.

2. Maximising photosynthesis

The Introduction can lead directly into considering how these factors, and the supply of plant nutrients (mineral ions), could be adjusted to maximise the rate of growth in crop plants. Students should read about protected cultivation on page 323 of the Student Book, and use what they learn to explain why it is much easier to improve these conditions within sheltered surroundings, such as glasshouses and polytunnels, than in open fields.

If not done earlier, Worksheets B2e.1c, B2e.1d and B2e.2a would be appropriate to do here.

3. Crop fertilisers

Students could carry out research in books or on the internet to compare the use of organic fertilisers (such as manure), crop rotation and artificial fertilisers to maximise the rate of crop growth. They should draw up a table to show the relative advantages and disadvantages of each technique.

If necessary, remind students of their work on the nitrogen cycle in Topic 4c before they begin, to help them understand the importance of nitrates in soil water.

4. The problems with pests

Worksheet B5a.1a provides a range of examples of crop pests and the damage they do, and asks students to explain why, in each case, this reduces the harvest yield for humans. This will give them the opportunity to apply knowledge from earlier topics on plant nutrition, structure and growth.

They should understand that damage reduces the plant's ability to grow rapidly. This will reduce the amount of energy that can be converted into substances stored in the parts of the plant that we harvest.

5. Controlling pests

Introduce the use of pesticides, both chemical and biological, using pages 326–329 of the Student Book. Then ask students to carry out further research on both methods, using books or the internet.

They should use their findings to draw up a table to display the advantages and disadvantages of using chemical and biological methods of control.

Note that students may come across the term *integrated pest management* in their research. This uses a combination of strategies, including chemical and biological, to control pest numbers in a way that maximises impact on the crop but also minimises damage to the ecosystem.

If appropriate and there is enough time, students could extend their study to find out how this method works for a particular species and how it achieves its aims.

6. Consolidation: essay notes

Gives students a few minutes to write headings for paragraphs in an essay on *Managing crop growth for a successful harvest*. Take examples from around the class and encourage discussion to cover all the main points of this activity.

Answers

Page 323

1. Any four of the following: temperature, carbon dioxide, light, water, pests.

2. For each of the factors mentioned in Q1:

   - optimum temperature allows enzymes to work at fastest rate so maximising rate of growth

   - carbon dioxide is usually a limiting factor in photosynthesis, so increasing carbon dioxide concentration in the air around the plants should increase the rate of photosynthesis and therefore growth

   - light is needed for photosynthesis, so by keeping light levels high enough for photosynthesis throughout the day and night will increase the amount of growth of the plants

   - plants need water for photosynthesis and for the transport of soluble materials, so having the right amount of water all the time will increase the rate of growth

   - pests damage plants, limiting the rate of growth, so removing pests should increase the rate of growth.

3. Polytunnels help to protect a crop from the environment, because conditions inside them can be more controlled. So, using polytunnels can make it possible to grow crops when it may be too cold at night or in cooler seasons, or when it gets dark early in the evening, etc.

Page 325

1. To add nutrients to the soil so that the plants grow bigger and produce more yield to harvest.

2. Planting different crops in the same field at different times, to use different nutrients and to add nitrogen back to the soil when legumes are planted.

3. Natural fertilisers include manure, guano and dried sludge from sewage treatment. Artificial fertilisers are made from chemicals in industrial processes.

Page 328

1. They damage the plants so that they do not grow as quickly, so they do not produce as much yield.

2. It will keep the predator/parasite in the same place as the pest and so maximise predation/parasitisation of the pest. It will also reduce the chance of new pests getting to the crop.

3.

	Advantages	Disadvantages
Pesticides	removes large proportion of pests quickly easy to apply	pests may develop resistance may damage other species may result in greater numbers of pests (if predators killed)
Biological control	less likely for pest to develop resistance usually better targeted at pest so less damaging to other species (except for introduced species) very good within closed spaces, such as glasshouses	slower to act than chemicals introduced predators/parasites may cause more problems to the environment and be difficult to control may not work well in open areas as they may move away

Page 329

1. Pesticide use increased greatly from about 1000 tonnes per year in 1980 to over 25 000 tonnes in 1995.

2. Yield generally increased from about 350 kg/ha in 1980 to a maximum of nearly 800 kg/ha in 1991. After this it fell to between 500 and 600 kg/ha.

3. Yield may have increased between 1980 to 1991 as pesticide use increased and controlled the whitefly. However, increasing pesticide use after that did not prevent a decrease in yield, suggesting that the whitefly were becoming resistant to the pesticide.

4. As the prey numbers increase, the predators have more food and so can produce more young.

5. Increasing pesticide use killed predators as well as pests. So, as pest numbers increased after the pesticide had lost effect, there were too few predators to control them.

6. As whitefly become resistant to the pesticide, they are unaffected by it. But their predators are still killed by its use. So, the whitefly numbers can increase even further, which will increase the transmission of the virus that damages the cotton.

7. Using pesticides specific for whitefly will not kill the predators, so a combination of predators and chemicals can be used to keep the whitefly numbers under control so that damage to cotton is reduced and yield increases.

B5a.1a The problems with crop pests

Pests can damage crop plants in different ways. Here are some examples:

- The maize (corn) stalk borer is a caterpillar of a moth. It may burrow into crop plants at soil level and tunnel upward through the plant, eating plant tissue as it goes. Alternatively, it climbs up the outside of the plant and chews through leaves and buds to get into the plant. The damage can stunt the plant's growth, with top parts breaking at weak points in the stem.

- Aphids (such as greenfly, cotton scale) have tube-like mouthparts. They insert the mouthparts into a soft leaf or stem of the plant, until they penetrate the phloem. The pressure of flow of substances in the phloem pushes some of the liquid into the mouthparts and into the aphid. Aphids are small, but they reproduce asexually during the summer, rapidly increasing in numbers. Some aphids also carry viruses that do not affect them but can infect and damage the plant even further, such as the tobacco mosaic virus.

- Many crops are attacked by leaf eaters. Some eat large parts of the leaves, such as caterpillars, leaf-cutting ants and large herbivores such as pigeons, rabbits and deer. In the US, damage caused by white-tailed deer to crops is estimated to cost over US$100 million each year. Other leaf-eaters actually live inside the leaf, and just eat the cells between the upper and lower epidermis.

- Some soil organisms, such as cutworm caterpillars, eat the outside of the stems of plants just above soil level. The tissues they eat include the vascular bundles, with the xylem and phloem. Eating part way round the stem reduces plant growth, but if they eat all the way round the stem, the plant rapidly dies. Other soil pests, such as nematodes and cranefly larvae, eat the roots of plants underground. This reduces the rate of plant growth and may kill the plant.

For each of the examples given, explain why the damage caused by the pest results in a reduction of crop yield (the size of the harvest of the food we use from the plant). Use your knowledge of photosynthesis, plant nutrition, plant structure and growth to answer as fully as possible.

Activity B5a.2 Growing microorganisms

Specification reference: B5a.5.5; B5a.5.6; B5a.5.7; B5a.5.8

Learning objectives

- Understand the role of yeast in the production of food including bread.
- Practical: Investigate the role of anaerobic respiration by yeast in different conditions.
- Understand the role of bacteria (*Lactobacillus*) in the production of yoghurt.
- Understand the use of an industrial fermenter, and explain the need to provide suitable conditions in the fermenter, for the growth of microorganisms.

Learning outcomes

- Understand the role of yeast in the production of food such as bread.
- Describe a simple experiment to investigate anaerobic respiration by yeast, in different conditions.
- Understand the role of bacteria (*Lactobacillus*) in the production of yoghurt.
- Interpret and label a diagram of an industrial fermenter and explain the need to provide suitable conditions in the fermenter, including aseptic precautions, nutrients, optimum temperature and pH, oxygenation and agitation, for the growth of microorganisms.

Common misconceptions

Some people have difficulty believing that living things cause the changes in foods produced by microorganisms, but see these changes as chemical changes. If students are unsure of this, reinforce the fact that a living organism is involved by asking what would happen if the temperatures used to produce the food were too high – high enough to kill the microorganism involved.

Resources

Student Book pages 329–334

Worksheet B5a.2a Practical: Investigate the role of anaerobic respiration by yeast in different conditions (1) – The effect of temperature

Worksheet B5a.2b Practical: Investigate the role of anaerobic respiration by yeast in different conditions (2) – The effect of glucose concentration

Worksheet B5a.2c Constructing a fermenter

Resources for class practicals and demonstration (see Technician's notes, following)

Approach

1. Introduction

Show students a collection of foods that are made using microorganisms and give them a minute or so to work in pairs or small groups to guess the connection. The foods could include cheese, yoghurt, bread and yeast extract spread. Take examples from around the class, and use the answers to assess what they already know on the subject.

2. Effect of different conditions on anaerobic respiration by yeast

Worksheets B5a.2a and B5a.2b provide two practical methods for investigating anaerobic respiration by yeast. They include alternative methods for estimating the amount of carbon dioxide produced.

If there is not enough time for students to carry out both practicals, consider splitting the class into two groups and assigning one practical to each group. The two methods could then be compared for the repeatability of their results.

Worksheet B5a.2a gives students the opportunity to carry out a simple investigation into the effect of temperature on anaerobic respiration by yeast.

Students should find that the optimum temperature for carbon dioxide production is about 35 °C, though this will vary if using yeast species other than *Saccharomyces cerevisiae.* This should be related to the effect of temperature on the enzymes in yeast.

Worksheet B5a.2b gives students the opportunity to carry out the investigation described in the Developing investigative skills box on page 332 of the Student Book, investigating the effect of glucose concentration on anaerobic respiration by yeast.

3. Making yoghurt

If there is time, you could prepare milk as described in the Technician's notes below to make yoghurt. Note that any yoghurt produced can only be eaten if prepared in fully hygienic conditions in a food preparation area and not in a laboratory at all. If this is the case, allow students to compare the flavour of the milk and yoghurt (be aware of any students who are lactose-intolerant or allergic to milk).

Alternatively, ask students to read page 330 in the Student Book on the production of yoghurt. Students should then try to answer the following questions:

- Why does the milk need to be pasteurised before being used to make yoghurt?

- Why does the milk/yoghurt mix need to be kept at about 45 °C for several hours?

- What is happening in the milk/yoghurt mix over the time it takes for the milk to become yoghurt?

- How do milk and yoghurt differ, and why?

Note that another bacterium – *Streptococcus thermophilus* – plays an important role in yoghurt production, but students are not required to know about this.

4. Constructing a fermenter

Worksheet B5a.2c contains an unlabelled diagram of a fermenter for students to label and annotate. This can be used with page 333 of the Student Book to help students remember the conditions required for producing microorganisms on a large scale.

Note that examples of genetically engineered microorganisms grown this way are covered in Topic 5c.

5. Consolidation: guidelines

Gives students a minute or so to write key guidelines for a manufacturer that uses microorganisms to make food.

Then take examples from around the class to make sure that students have included the essential points (e.g. that conditions must be sterile/aseptic to exclude other microorganisms; conditions for culture must take into account if microorganism respires anaerobically or aerobically; all nutrients that are needed by microorganism are supplied; optimum temperature and pH; agitation).

Technician's notes

You will need the following resources for the class practicals.

Be sure to check the latest safety notes on these resources before proceeding.

B5a.2a Practical: Investigate the role of anaerobic respiration by yeast in different

conditions (1) – The effect of temperature

Ideally use fresh yeast made up into solution with a small amount of sugar and left for a few hours to activate. Alternatively use a fresh packet of dried yeast, made up according to the manufacturer's instructions. Old yeast will not work as well.

Class practical, per group:

yeast solution (5–10 g/litre of fresh yeast, or 2–5 g/litre of dried yeast)
sugar solution (50 g/litre)
4 water baths at different temperatures, e.g. 20 °C, 30 °C, 40 °C, 50 °C
4 test tubes and racks
4 balloons
10 cm^3 measuring pipettes or cylinders
vegetable oil
marker pen
long strip of paper, long enough to wrap round an inflated balloon and overlap
ruler

B5a.2b Practical: Investigate the role of anaerobic respiration by yeast in different conditions (2) – The effect of glucose concentration

See above for notes on using fresh yeast.

Class practical, per group:

5 boiling tubes
5 small test tubes
water bath, set at 30–35 °C
boiling tube rack
10 cm^3 measuring pipette
yeast solution (5–10 g/litre of fresh yeast, or 2–5 g/litre of dried yeast)
glucose
balance
vegetable oil
ruler

Making yoghurt

Note that all preparations must be made in fully hygienic conditions if the yoghurt is to be tasted.

1. Sterilise the pot or Thermos flask in which the yoghurt is to be made by pouring in boiling water and leaving for 10 minutes. Then pour out the water.

2. The milk needs to be at about 45 °C. If using the pot, add the milk and place it in the water bath until it reaches the correct temperature; if using the Thermos flask, heat the milk in a sterile pan on a cooker hob until it reaches temperature, then pour it into the flask. Milk that has been heated to 85 °C needs to be left for 5–10 minutes to cool to 45 °C before adding to the container.

3. Stir a large spoonful of live yoghurt into the warm milk. Cover the pot or flask. If using the pot, place it into the water bath for 5–6 hours. If using the Thermos flask, wrap it in warm towels and leave overnight.

4. After this time, the milk should have thickened to form yoghurt.

Demonstration:

milk, preferably pasteurised and kept chilled, alternatively heated to about 85 °C for 2 or 3 minutes to kill any microorganisms
small pot of live yoghurt
water bath set at about 35 °C, alternatively a Thermos flask
thermometer (0–100 °C range)
spoon, sterilised in boiling water for a few minutes
heatproof pot in which to make yoghurt (if not using Thermos flask)

Answers

Page 331

1. Any four suitable foods, such as bread, cheese, yoghurt, single-cell protein.

2. Milk → pasteurised to kill microorganisms → inoculated with *Lactobacillus* → bacteria convert lactose to lactic acid → lactic acid causes milk proteins to coagulate and form yoghurt.

Developing investigative skills, page 332

1. To prevent air getting into the mixture, because it is anaerobic respiration that is being investigated.

2. Reactions are carried out faster in warm conditions. So, respiration will be faster than if at room temperature.

3. Carbon dioxide released during anaerobic respiration.

4. As more glucose was added, the height that the tube rose increased.

5. The yeast is using glucose to produce carbon dioxide by anaerobic respiration, so an increase in glucose means an increase in the carbon dioxide produced and the higher the tube rises.

6. The more glucose there is in the solution, the more anaerobic respiration takes place.

7. Repeat the experiment so that average heights can be calculated, and any anomalous results identified.

Page 334

1. A large vessel in which microorganisms are grown in large numbers under controlled conditions.

2. a) Temperature, pH, oxygenation, nutrient concentration.

   b) Temperature will increase due to the reactions of respiration and other reactions of the microorganisms. If temperature rises too high, it may reduce rate of growth or kill the microorganisms.

   pH may change because of substances released by the microorganisms into the solution. This may reduce rate of growth.

   Oxygen concentration might fall as oxygen is used for respiration. Microorganisms are aerobic, so rate of growth will reduce if oxygen concentration falls.

   Nutrient concentration will fall as microorganisms use nutrients to make new cells. Rate of growth will fall if nutrients are not added to replace what is used.

3. a) Keeping things sterile.

   b) It prevents other microorganisms growing rapidly in the fermenter which could be harmful or compete with the added microorganisms.

B5a.2a Practical: Investigate the role of anaerobic respiration by yeast in different conditions (1) – The effect of temperature

Yeast is a single-celled fungus that respires anaerobically, releasing carbon dioxide from the breakdown of sugars. The reactions of respiration are affected by temperature because they are controlled by enzymes.

To measure the effect of temperature on the rate of respiration, we can measure the volume of carbon dioxide produced over time by yeast kept at different temperatures.

Apparatus

yeast solution

sugar solution

4 water baths at different temperatures

4 test tubes and racks

4 balloons

10 cm^3 measuring pipettes or cylinders

vegetable oil

marker pen

long strip of paper

ruler

SAFETY INFORMATION

Be careful when working with the hottest water bath.

Do not allow balloons to become over-inflated.

Method

1. Mark each of the tubes with your initials.

2. Measure 10 cm^3 of the yeast solution into each test tube. Then work quickly through steps 3 and 4.

3. With a clean pipette or cylinder, measure 10 cm^3 sugar solution into one of the tubes and mix it with the yeast using a long spoon or stick.

4. Carefully pour in about 1–2 cm^3 oil so that it sits on top of the solution. Immediately attach a balloon to the top of the tube, so that it will catch any gas produced and inflate. Place the tube in a tube rack.

5. Repeat step 2 as quickly as possible for each of the other tubes, placing each one in a different rack.

6. Place each rack in a different water bath, again being careful when interacting with the hottest bath.

7. Leave the tubes for 20 minutes, but being careful not to let the balloons over-inflate.

8. Measure the circumference of each balloon as follows:

    - Wrap a strip of paper around the widest point and mark the point where the strips overlap.

    - Take the strip of paper off the balloon.

    - Measure the length of the paper strip up to that point that you have marked.

9. Draw up a suitable table to record your results.

Analyse and interpret data

1. Use your table to draw a suitable chart or graph.

2. Describe any pattern shown in the graph.

3. Explain any pattern using your knowledge of the effect of temperature on living organisms.

Evaluate data and methods

1. This apparatus only gives an approximate measure of the carbon dioxide produced. Explain how you could adjust the apparatus to get a more accurate result. Do you think this would change your results? Explain your answer.

B5a.2b Practical: Investigate the role of anaerobic respiration by yeast in different conditions (2) – The effect of glucose concentration

This practical investigates the effect of glucose concentration on anaerobic respiration by yeast.

Apparatus

5 boiling tubes

5 small test tubes

bowl or sink of water

water bath

boiling tube rack

10 cm^3 measuring pipette

yeast solution

glucose

balance

vegetable oil

ruler

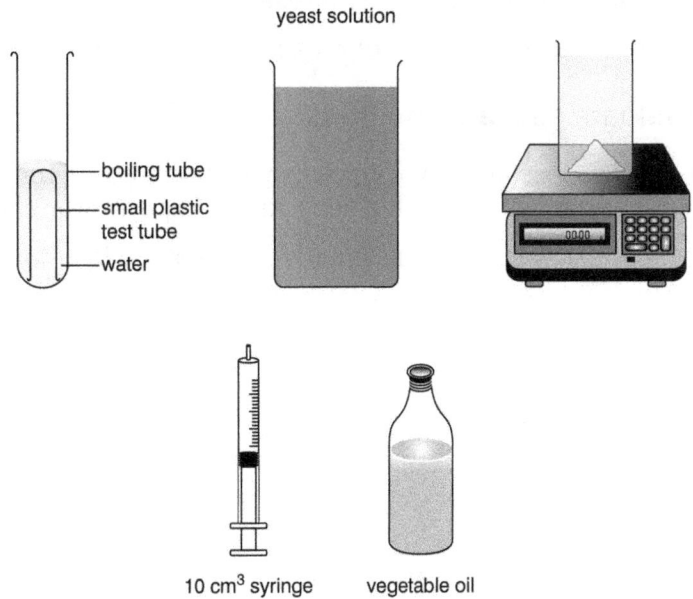

yeast solution

boiling tube

small plastic test tube

water

10 cm^3 syringe   vegetable oil

SAFETY INFORMATION

Be careful when working with the water bath.

Method

1. Prepare all the tubes as follows:

   - Submerge one boiling tube and one small tube completely in water, so all the air comes out of the tubes.

   - While underwater, push the small tube into the boiling tube, so that its top end faces downwards in the boiling tube.

   - Remove the tubes from the water, and carefully pour off water until the rounded end of the small tube is just submerged, as shown in the diagram, and stand the boiling tube in the tube rack.

   - Repeat with the other pairs of tubes, until you have five sets of prepared tubes.

2. Add 2 cm^3 of the yeast solution to each of the tubes.

3. Add the following amount of glucose to each of the tubes:

   - tube 1, 0.0 g
   - tube 2, 0.5 g
   - tube 3, 1.0 g
   - tube 4, 1.5 g
   - tube 5, 2.0 g

4. Carefully float a little oil on the top of the solution in each tube to exclude air.

5. Place the tubes in the rack in the water bath and leave for 30 minutes.

6. After 30 minutes, measure the height of the small tube above the solution level in the boiling tube.

7. Record your results in a suitable table.

Analyse and interpret data

1. Use your results to draw a suitable chart or graph.

2. Describe any pattern in your results.

3. Explain any pattern in your results using your knowledge of anaerobic respiration and cell reactions.

Evaluate data and methods

1. How successful do you think this method was in producing results that reliably estimate the amount of anaerobic respiration in the yeast cells? Explain your answer.

2. Suggest how you would improve the method to produce more reliable results.

B5a.2c Constructing a fermenter

The diagram below shows the structure of a large fermenter, used for growing microorganisms to produce products made by the microorganisms, such as the antibiotic penicillin.

Label the parts of the fermenter, then annotate the parts to explain why they are needed to make sure as much product is formed as quickly as possible.

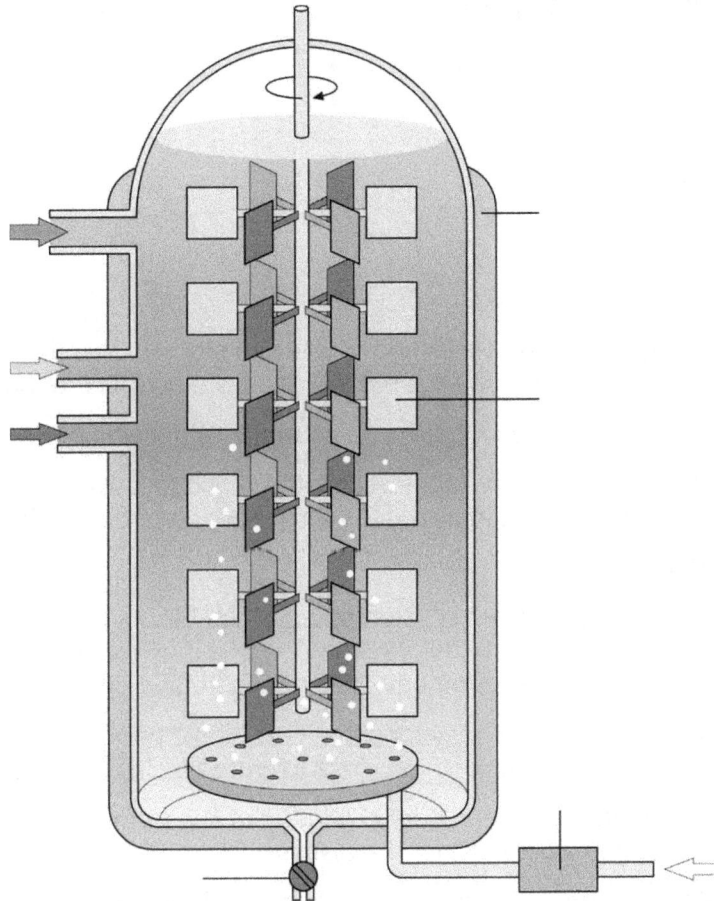

Activity B5a.3 Farming fish (B)

Specification reference: B5a.5.9**B**

Learning objectives

- Understand the methods used to farm large numbers of fish to provide a source of protein. **(B)**

Learning outcomes

- Explain the methods that are used to farm large numbers of fish to provide a source of protein, including maintenance of water quality, control of intraspecific and interspecific predation, control of disease, removal of waste products, quality and frequency of feeding and use of selective breeding. **(B)**

Resources

Student Book pages 335–337

Approach

1. Introduction (B)

Show students a news item related to the overfishing of wild fish stocks. Give them a few minutes to suggest what problems this will cause, both for the natural ecosystems and the food supply for humans.

Take examples from around the class and encourage discussion about which are most practical.

Note that selective breeding is covered more fully in Topic 5b, which follows. In this activity, keep the description to a minimum, such as to breed individuals with the best characteristics.

2. Setting up a fish farm (B)

Tell students that one solution to the problem of overfishing is fish farming, the cultivation of fish by humans specifically for the food market. Ask them to imagine that they have been asked to provide guidance and recommendations to a small company considering setting up a fish farm.

Give them a minute or so to write down the questions that they would need to answer in order to set up a successful venture. Take examples from around the class to create a class list of key questions.

If possible, invite a speaker who has experience or knowledge of fish farming to come and speak to the class. Use the class list of questions as a basis for the discussion.

Alternatively, students could research the setting up of a fish farm for a particular species. This can work well in small groups, each student looking at one aspect of cultivating that species.

They should present their findings in a short report, as a poster, or verbally in class, giving other students the opportunity to ask questions. If appropriate, at the end, students could vote for the best suggestion.

3. Consolidation: bullet point notes (B)

Give students the following titles and, for each, ask them to write one bullet point note about how it should be managed in order to maximise the rate of growth of farmed fish:

- water quality
- intraspecific predation
- interspecific predation
- disease
- waste products
- feeding
- selective breeding.

Take examples from around the class to discuss. Make sure students have learned the key points.

Answers

Page 337

1. Keeping fish in contained areas, improving growing conditions to increase the rate of growth, and harvesting the fish.

2. Any three from the following: quality of water, food supply, predators, stocking limit, pests and diseases.

3. For each factor given in Q2:

- to prevent build-up of fish waste and uneaten food, and to provide as clean a water supply as possible

- to provide food of the right sort at a high enough rate to maximise growth

- to prevent predators killing fish

- to prevent intraspecific predation in farmed fish that are carnivorous

- to prevent pests and diseases from harming fish and so reducing the rate of growth or killing them.

Activity B5a.4 Consolidation and summary

Learning objectives

- To review the learning points of the topic.
- To test understanding through answering questions.

Learning outcomes

- Be familiar with the knowledge and understanding summarised in the End of topic checklist.
- Be able to apply this knowledge and understanding by answering the End of topic questions.

Resources

Student Book pages 338–341

Approach

Ask students to answer the End of topic questions in the Student Book.

Answers

End of topic questions mark scheme

Question	Correct answer	Marks
1 a)	Carbon dioxide concentration in the air.	1
1 b)	The weight of lettuces and plants is greater with additional carbon dioxide than without.	1
1 c)	Carbon dioxide is used in photosynthesis,	1
	to make sugars, which are used in the plant to make new plant tissues.	1
1 d)	Temperature,	1
	because plants grow faster when it is warmer but more slowly if the temperature is too high.	1
	Water,	1
	because plants need water for photosynthesis.	1
	Mineral ions,	1
	because plants grow faster with enough mineral ions than without.	1
1 e)	Farmers must consider the cost of setting up and using glasshouses,	1
	including extra watering, control of temperature, etc., compared with growing crops in open fields where water comes from the environment.	1
	They need to compare the costs with the extra money made by the greater yield from glasshouse crops, and decide if the difference is worth the money and extra effort.	1
2 a)	Leaves photosynthesise and make sugars, some of which are converted to other substances that are needed to make new cells.	1
	So, if large amounts of leaf are removed from a plant it cannot make as much sugars and cannot make as many new cells including the part we harvest (the yield).	1

Question	Correct answer	Marks
2 b)	The stem contains the xylem, which takes water up to the leaves for photosynthesis, so damaging the xylem would reduce photosynthesis and the food available for making new cells.	1
	The stem also contains the phloem, which transports the sugars from the leaves to other parts of the plant, so damaging the phloem would prevent sugars being transported to other parts of the plant where they can be used to make more cells.	1
3 a)	Benefits: probably only needs one introduction as predator numbers will increase until they control the pest numbers.	1
	So, there is potentially less effort and less cost than with pesticides, which need to be applied more than once.	1
3 b)	Risks: if introduced predator prefers other species, it will not control the pest and instead causes damage to the food web.	1
	If predator does not have its own predator to control its numbers, it will be difficult to control if its numbers increase too high.	1
4 a)	glucose → ethanol + carbon dioxide	1
4 b)	It makes the dough rise / become soft and fluffy.	1
4 c)	Because bubbles of carbon dioxide produced by respiration	1
	are trapped in the sticky dough.	1
4 d)	Any one suitable answer, such as: cheese; yoghurt; single cell protein.	1
5 a)	i) Any two answers from: can be done in a smaller space;	2
	fish produce more protein for food eaten because they are 'cold-blooded';	
	conditions for maximum rate of growth are easier to control;	
	fewer greenhouse gases (such as methane from digestion) produced.	
	ii) May damage the local environment;	1
	predator fish still need food produced from wild fish, so does not reduce damage to wild food stocks as much as hoped.	1
5 b)	i) Antibiotics kill or stop bacteria growing;	1
	pathogenic bacteria can harm the fish and so reduce their growth rate.	1
	ii) Using antibiotics increases the chance of developing resistance of bacteria to the antibiotics;	1
	this increases the problem of trying to control bacterial infections with antibiotics and increases the risk of fish/people dying from these infections.	1
5 c)	Fish farming is not sustainable at present because pollution from tanks damages the local environment,	1
	and wild fish stocks are still being depleted to provide food for farmed fish such as salmon and seabass.	1
	Keeping herbivorous fish in specially built tanks is more sustainable because damage to the environment is much easier to limit.	1
	Total:	37

Introduction

In this topic, students learn about selective breeding in plants and animals for particular characteristics.

Links to other topics

Sections	Essential background knowledge	Useful links
1 The nature and variety of living organisms	1a Characteristics of living organisms	
3 Reproduction and inheritance	3a Reproduction 3b Inheritance	
5 Use of biological resources	5a Food production	5c Genetic modification (genetic engineering) 5d Cloning

Topic overview

B5b.1	Selective breeding in plants and animals
	This activity gives students the opportunity to learn about the process of selective breeding, and about examples of varieties of crop plants, and breeds of animals that have been selectively bred for particular characteristics.
B5b.2	Consolidation and summary
	This activity provides an opportunity for a quick recap on the ideas encountered in the topic as well as time for the students to answer the End of topic questions in the Student Book.

Activity B5b.1 Selective breeding in plants and animals

Learning objectives: B5b.5.10; B5b.5.11

Learning objectives

- Understand how selective breeding can develop plants with desired characteristics.
- Understand how selective breeding can develop animals with desired characteristics.

Learning outcomes

- Understand that plants with desired characteristics can be developed by selective breeding.
- Understand that animals with desired characteristics can be developed by selective breeding.

Common misconceptions

Some students may think that different varieties of plants, and different breeds of animals (such as dogs) are actually different species. It is important they understand that the breeds and varieties show how great the variation can be within a species, and that individuals are still capable of interbreeding.

Resources

Student Book pages 342–347

Worksheet B5b.1a The process of selective breeding

Worksheet B5b.1b Selective breeding in chickens

Approach

1. Introduction

Show students photographs of different breeds of animal, such as a range of different dog breeds. Ask them to describe the differences among them and to suggest how these differences were achieved. (Make sure they realise that different varieties/breeds still belong to the same species.)

Students should refer back to their work in Topic 3a Reproduction and 3b Inheritance to reply in terms of variation between individuals of a species and inheritance of parental characteristics as a result of sexual reproduction.

2. The process of selective breeding

Worksheet B5b.1a provides a set of cards that students can cut out and put in order, to help them explain the process of selective breeding. They need to become aware of the length of the process that is needed to develop a new variety/breed, and that this process relates to the time between generations to reach sexual maturity and the number of offspring produced.

In general, it is easier to produce a new variety/breed of a fast-breeding species with many offspring in a generation than a slow-breeding species. This is particularly relevant to breeding species of large mammals, such as cows, for characteristics that supply humans with food.

Students are asked to select an example of selective breeding of their choice to illustrate the correct sequence of statements. If possible, give them access to books or the internet to research a suitable example.

With more able students, you could discuss the impact of selective breeding on the variety in the offspring.

Encourage students to realise that the selection of one particular variation of one characteristic may also reduce the variety in other characteristics. This can lead to an increase in occurrence of negative traits, both physically (such as an increased risk of cancer in some breeds of dog) or mentally (as in an increased chance of unpredictable behaviour in some very inbred dog varieties). They may come across reference to this in their research.

3. Selective breeding in plants

Using what they learned about the problems of producing food from crop plants in Topic 5a, ask students to note down five characteristics in crop plants that selective breeding might be used for to improve crop yield. They should be able to suggest examples such as the following:

- more energy in the plant channelled into producing the part that we eat and less to other parts
- increased drought tolerance
- increased pest and disease resistance
- earlier maturing crop (so that it can be grown in different places).

Research on a suitable website, such as the British Society of Plant Breeders, would be helpful in supporting this.

Alternatively, invite a local farmer who grows crops to come and talk to the class about the advantages and disadvantages of using crop varieties that have been selectively bred. You could link this to the similar task in Topic 5c on Genetic modification (genetic engineering). This will give students the opportunity to learn about real examples of crop varieties produced by the different methods, and their relative advantages and disadvantages.

4. Selective breeding in animals

Worksheet B5b.1b offers a data analysis exercise on the effect of selective breeding in chickens, for a breed that is grown for meat and another grown for egg production. After completing the questions, students should appreciate how selective breeding can change characteristics in different ways in an animal species.

5. Consolidation: red, yellow, green notes

Give each student three cards, one red, one yellow and one green. Then ask students questions based on all parts of this activity and ask them to hold up a card depending on how certain they are of the answer: red = not sure, yellow = fairly sure, green = certain.

Suitable questions include:

- Are crop plants selectively bred for disease resistance?
- Does it take one or many generations to produce a new breed of animal by selective breeding?

Answers

Page 345 (top)

1. a) Characteristics that can be bred for in selective breeding programmes are those that are controlled by genes.

   b) If the desired characteristic is not controlled by a gene, it cannot be selectively bred for.

2. Any three from: increasing size of part that we eat; decreasing size of parts we do not eat; improving pest and disease resistance; improved growth in adverse conditions.

3. For each of the factors included in Q2:

- the part of the plant we eat is what is measured as the yield
- decreasing other parts means the plant has more energy to grow the part we do eat
- diseases and pests damage the plant so it does not grow as well as it could, so making plants resistant will help them to grow faster
- adverse conditions (such as heat or drought) slow the rate of growth, so improving growth in these conditions will help to improve yield where these conditions happen.

4. Because people like different plants, and new varieties of plants are often considered more attractive than old varieties.

Page 345 (bottom)

1. In sexual reproduction, the offspring inherit half their alleles from one parent and half from the other. In selective breeding, only a few parent types are used for breeding. So, this limits the range of variation in the alleles in the parents. So, the offspring can only inherit from this limited range.

2. This means that when they cross-breed, the seed produced is more likely to contain the characteristics that they have been bred for. Some of that seed planted in the following year will produce plants that still show the required characteristics.

3. The environment is continually changing, and may change a lot over the next century or so as a result of climate change. This means that characteristics that are useful now, may be less important than others in the future, such as the ability to withstand drought (if the climate gets hotter and drier in some places), or resistance to particular pests or diseases that are not common now may become more common as climate changes. If the varieties we are growing do not have these characteristics, then crop yield will be reduced as growth of the crop plants is reduced.

4. Any suitable answer with appropriate justification, such as: in the short term this does not seem to make sense because we need to grow enough food for everyone to eat, but in the long term it does make sense because the environment changes and we cannot predict how it will change and what characteristics we will need for crops in the future.

Page 347

1. Choose male and female animals with characteristics that are nearest to the desired characteristic and breed them. From the offspring, select individuals with characteristics that are nearest to the desired characteristic and breed them together. Repeat this for enough generations until you have individuals with the desired characteristic.

2. a) Muscle is the meat that we eat. So, this is increased yield.

   b) Disease harms the animal so that it grows more slowly, or may even die. Resistant animals will grow better and need less treatment for infections with chemicals such as antibiotics.

   c) Docile animals are easier to handle and move around, which makes them easier to work with.

3. Different breeds of sheep have different characteristics that are often linked to their local environment, or whether they are farmed for meat or milk, so there cannot be one breed that is suited to all environments and is equally good for meat and milk.

Worksheet B5b.1b

1. Both show an increase in growth/weight over time, but the meat chicken grows faster, with a mass of nearly 2400 g in 45 days, while the layer chicken only reaches a mass of about 600 g in the same time.

2. So, that the only difference in the experiment was breed, and any variation in results would be the result of breed only.

3. The meat chicken breed puts more of the energy from its food into producing new muscle tissue. The layer breed puts less energy into muscle tissue and more into producing eggs.

4. The graph shows that the increase in size of meat chickens is just the result of selective breeding, not additional chemicals.

5. a) Growing a meat chicken that produces more meat faster means the farmer will get more money for the animals when he sells them to a supermarket.

   b) Growing a layer chicken that puts less energy into making new body tissue and more into the eggs it produces, means that it will lay more eggs and the farmer will get more money for them.

6. The farmer would select a cockerel from an egg laid by a hen that lays large eggs and mate it with a different female that lays large eggs. He would select the hens from the offspring that lay the largest eggs and mate them with a different cockerel that came from an egg laid by a large-egg female. This would be repeated for many generations until the farmer could reliably produce larger eggs from the chickens that he is breeding.

B5b.1a The process of selective breeding

Cut out the statements below and then arrange them in the correct order to explain how selective breeding can result in a new variety of plant or new breed of animal.

Use an example of your choice to illustrate the process.

After many generations, individuals that match the required characteristics are produced in the offspring.	Offspring with the closest variation to the required characteristics are selected and grown to adulthood.
Parent organisms are chosen that show the closest variation to the required characteristics.	Sexual reproduction of the parent organisms produces offspring that show variety.
These individuals then form the new variety (plants) or breed (animals).	This stage is repeated again and again with each generation of offspring, each time with individuals whose characteristics are closer to the required characteristics.
When the offspring are fully grown, they are bred with each other to produce more offspring.	

B5b.1b Selective breeding in chickens

Different breeds of chicken are bred to produce different products for humans to eat. Some are grown for their meat, and some are grown to produce eggs (layer chicken). Selective breeding over many generations has produced distinct breeds for each purpose.

Some students investigated the effect of selective breeding in two breeds of chicken. They bought day-old chicks of both breeds and kept them in the same conditions, including feeding them the same food. They weighed the chickens at several times during their growth, and averaged the weight for individuals of the same breed. The graph shows their results.

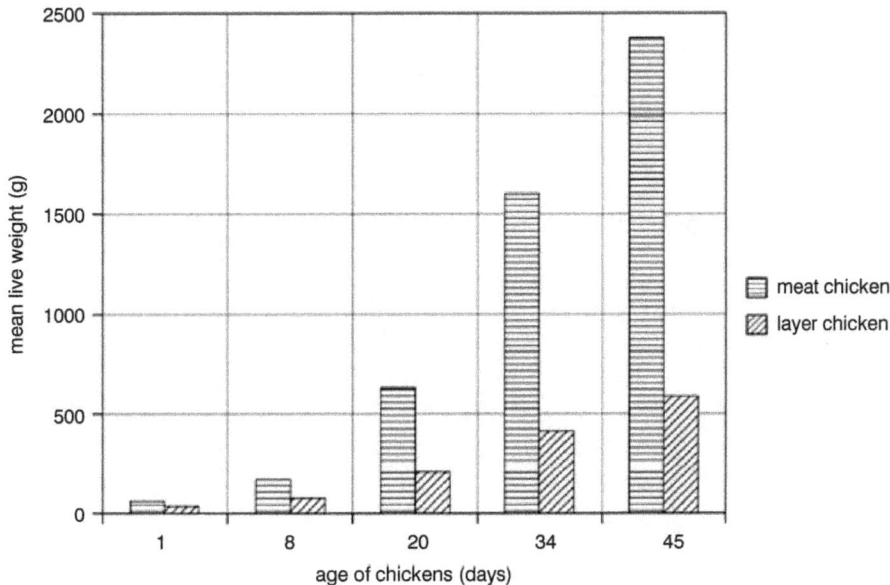

Graph source: http://www.chicken.org.au/page.php?id=205

1. Describe the patterns of results shown in the graph.

2. Explain why the students kept the chickens in the same conditions.

3. Suggest why there is such a difference in the two breeds after 45 days.

4. Many people think that chickens grown for meat become especially large because of additional chemicals in their feed. What does the graph suggest about this?

5. Explain the advantage to a farmer of growing selectively bred:

   a) breeds of meat chicken

   b) breeds of layer chicken.

6. Explain how a farmer could selectively breed chickens to produce a breed that lays larger eggs.

Activity B5b.2 Consolidation and summary

Learning objectives

- To review the learning points of the topic.
- To test understanding through answering questions.

Learning outcomes

- Be familiar with the knowledge and understanding summarised in the End of topic checklist.
- Be able to apply this knowledge and understanding by answering the End of topic questions.

Resources

Student Book pages 348–349

Approach

Ask students to answer the End of topic questions in the Student Book.

Answers

End of topic questions mark scheme

Question	Correct answer	Marks
1 a)	It can improve crop yield, or taste, or some other characteristic that makes it more valuable.	1
1 b)	It can take a long time (because it can take many generations to produce a new variety).	1
	It may produce new varieties that have the desired characteristic but are more susceptible to other problems.	1
2	She could take the pollen from one plant and use it to pollinate the other plant.	1
	She should then plant the seed that is produced and wait until the new plants have grown and produced flowers, and from the new plants select those that have flowers nearest to her desired characteristic.	1
	Then she will need to repeat the process, possibly many times, of selecting for breeding those plants that each generation have the largest, most red flowers, until she gets several plants with large red flowers so that she can guarantee producing plants that only have large red flowers when she breeds them together.	1
3 a)	So that they produce more meat (or another characteristic that is useful, such as milk or wool).	1
3 b)	Because the European or Australian breeds are not adapted to the conditions in India,	1
	so they will not grow as well.	1
3 c)	Selectively breed from individuals of the European breed, which produce the most meat, with individuals from the Indian breed that are best able to withstand the local conditions.	1
	Grow the lambs that are produced, then breed individuals that show the best combination of meat production and hardiness.	1
	Repeat the selection and breeding until there is a flock of sheep that show good meat production and tolerance of heat.	1
4 a)	They can reproduce together to produce offspring.	1
4 b)	By a mutation of a colour allele.	1
4 c)	The fish are kept for display,	1
	so breeds that look very different from others could be more desirable for showing off.	1
	Total:	16

Introduction

In this topic, students will learn how bacteria and crop plants can be modified genetically, by inserting specific genes, so that they produce new characteristics.

Links to other topics

Sections	Essential background knowledge	Useful links
1 The nature and variety of living organisms	1b Variety of living organisms	
2 Structures and functions in living organisms	2c Biological molecules	
3 Reproduction and inheritance	3b Inheritance	
5 Use of biological resources	5a Food production 5b Selective breeding	5d Cloning

Topic overview

B5c.1	The process of genetic modification (genetic engineering)
	In this short activity, students learn about the basic process of genetic modification, and about different kinds of vectors.
B5c.2	Genetically modified organisms
	This activity focuses on examples of transgenic organisms, including bacteria and plants, and looks at how to evaluate their usefulness.
B5c.3	Consolidation and summary
	This activity provides an opportunity for a quick recap on the ideas encountered in the topic as well as time for the students to answer the End of topic questions in the Student Book.

Activity B5c.1 The process of genetic modification (genetic engineering)

Specification reference: B5c.5.12; B5c.5.13; B5c.5.16

Learning objectives

- Understand how restriction enzymes are used to cut DNA at specific sites and ligase enzymes are used to join pieces of DNA together.
- Understand how plasmids and viruses can act as vectors, which take up pieces of DNA, and then insert this recombinant DNA into other cells.
- Understand that the term transgenic means the transfer of genetic material from one species to a different species.

Learning outcomes

- Describe the use of restriction enzymes to cut DNA at specific sites and ligase enzymes to join pieces of DNA together.
- Describe how plasmids and viruses can act as vectors, which take up pieces of DNA, then insert this recombinant DNA into other cells.
- Understand that the term *transgenic* means the transfer of genetic material from one species to a different species.

Common misconceptions

The discussion of genetically modified organisms can produce some very polarised debates among politicians, industry and the general public. These organisms are commonly presented as dangerous in the media and by environmental activists, with descriptions such as 'Frankenstein foods', which aim to scare. Similarly, companies who produce genetically modified organisms for profit will make obvious the advantages of their products and mention little of any problems.

It is essential that students develop a balanced understanding of the process of genetic modification (genetic engineering), and what potential benefits and risks it poses in different cases, so that they can see both sides of the argument and offer scientific evidence for their own point of view.

Resources

Student Book pages 350–353

Worksheet B5c.1a Genetic modification of bacteria

Approach

1. Introduction

Write the terms *genetic modification* and *genetic engineering* on the board. Ask students to suggest related words and how they could be added to build a mind map on the topic. Be prepared to accept a range of emotive words, which may come from knowledge built on what is reported in the media. Explain to students that after they have completed this topic they will be expected to use scientific evidence to support any claims that they make about genetic modification.

If not mentioned, introduce the term *transgenic*, meaning the transfer of genetic material from one species to a different one.

2. The process of genetic modification

Worksheet B5c.1a offers a cut-and-paste activity that builds a diagram of the process of genetic modification. Students cut out cards, arrange them in the correct order, stick them into their books and annotate them to explain the process.

If students are having difficulty with the order, ask them to read pages 350–351of the Student Book on the tools of genetic engineering to help them, and to help with annotation of their diagram.

The annotations should include reference to restriction enzymes, ligases and vectors. Make sure students understand why the transgenic cell produces the characteristic (because the genetic material in the inserted gene is within the chromosome or plasmid of the transgenic cell and will be used to produce its protein/characteristic in the same way as any other genes in the chromosome).

Note that this diagram can be added to in the next activity to show how insulin is produced from transgenic bacteria.

With more able students, you could discuss the difference between inserting a gene into a bacterium or early stage of a multicellular organism (so that all the cells produced from division of that cell contain the inserted gene), and inserting the gene into a body cell of a multicellular organism so that only cells formed by mitosis of that cell contain the inserted gene. (The latter is called gene therapy and is being trialled for conditions such as SCID, severe combined immunodeficiency disease.) This has implications for the use of genetic modification in humans, such as to treat genetic diseases. It creates an ethical debate about the rights of individuals, including those who have not yet been conceived.

3. Vectors

Ask students to read the section on vectors on page 351 of the Student Book and then carry out research into different kinds of vectors using books or the internet. Currently vectors include bacterial plasmids, viruses and liposomes.

Ask students to give examples of organisms that have been genetically modified with each kind of vector, and to describe the advantages and disadvantages of each kind of vector.

4. Consolidation: key word definitions

Ask students to write definitions for a web dictionary for the key words in this activity, including *genetic modification / genetic engineering, recombinant DNA, transgenic organism, restriction enzyme, ligase enzyme* and *vector*. Take examples from around the class and encourage discussion where students have different definitions in order to produce the best definition.

Answers

Page 353

1. a) An enzyme that cuts DNA at a specific site.

   b) An enzyme that joins two pieces of DNA.

   c) Something that carries genetic material into another cell.

2. Required gene extracted from DNA of organism using a restriction enzyme → bacterial plasmid removed from bacterium and cut open with same restriction enzyme → required gene and plasmid mixed together with ligase enzyme → ligase enzyme joins inserted gene and plasmid together → plasmid inserted into another bacterium → inserted gene produces new characteristic (such as production of human insulin) in bacteria.

3. Because the human insulin gene has been inserted into the bacterial DNA, and is decoded by the bacterial cell exactly as it would be in a human cell, producing human insulin.

B5c.1a Genetic modification of bacteria

The diagrams below, arranged together in the right order, show the process used to genetically modify bacteria.

Cut out the boxes and arrange them in the correct order to show the stages in the process. When you are happy with the order, stick them into your workbook.

Add any labels and annotations, such as which enzyme is used in which stages and which part is the vector, to explain clearly how the process is carried out.

Then explain why the transgenic bacterium will produce the characteristic coded for by the inserted gene.

required gene extracted

transgenic bacterium with genetically modified plasmid

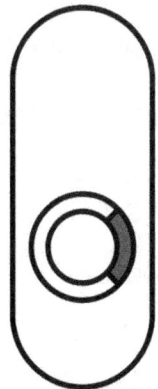

required gene in plasmid

required gene identified in a host cell (e.g. human insulin gene)

bacterium with plasmid

bacterial plasmid cut open

Activity B5c.2 Genetically modified organisms

Specification reference: B5c.5.14; B5c.5.15

Learning objectives

- Understand how large amounts of human insulin can be manufactured from genetically modified bacteria that are grown in a fermenter.
- Understand how genetically modified plants can be used to improve food production.

Learning outcomes

- Explain how large amounts of human insulin can be manufactured from genetically modified bacteria that are grown in a fermenter.
- Explain how genetically modified plants can be used to improve food production.

Common misconceptions

See the note in Activity B5c.1. It is important that students are able to give a range of points of view about genetic modification of organisms, and to support their own view with scientific evidence.

Resources

Student Book pages 354–355

Worksheet B5c.2a Growing GM crops

Approach

1. Introduction

To revise the last activity, ask students to think of a characteristic that would be useful to transfer from one organism to another, to help solve a current problem for agriculture or ecosystems.

Give them a few minutes to work out how they would produce the transgenic organism. Take examples from around the class and discuss the practicality and usefulness of each idea.

It is worth pointing out at this stage that the process of producing transgenic organisms is expensive, because only a few cells successfully take up the new gene, and sometimes in the wrong part of a chromosome (either a part that is not copied much normally, or within another essential gene so destroying a process that the cell needs for survival). So, producing a transgenic organism is only worthwhile if it is *economically viable* (it generates more money from its use than it took to produce it).

2. Insulin from genetically modified bacteria

Remind students of their work on growing bacteria in fermenters in Topic 5a Food production. Then, using the diagram they produced using Worksheet B5c.1a, give them a few minutes to add drawings and notes to explain how transgenic bacteria are made in order to produce large quantities of human insulin.

You could then ask them to read the Science in Context box on page 353 of the Student Book and to explain why most human insulin used by diabetics is produced this way rather than from animals.

3. Growing GM crops

Worksheet B5c.2a provides a series of statements on growing and using GM crops. Students should cut out the cards and use them first to distinguish opinion and evidence, and then to identify statements for and against the growing of GM crops. They should choose one group of statements to prepare for a class debate on growing GM crops.

If possible (as suggested in Topic 5b Selective breeding) ask a professional who has experience with selectively bred and genetically engineered crop varieties to talk to the class about the advantages and disadvantages of both techniques. Students could use these examples to help prepare their own discussion. Alternatively, you could allow time for research to produce graphs and statements that support their argument.

Ask students who are preparing the same viewpoint to work together to produce a set of key arguments. They should then choose two or three speakers to present their case.

Allow each viewpoint to be presented, then give other students the chance to ask questions. Make sure each viewpoint is allowed the same time for presentation. At the end, take a class vote.

4. Consolidation: pros and cons

Give students a few minutes to write down benefits and risks of producing and using transgenic organisms. Take examples from around the class to get a reasonable mix of both.

Answers

Page 355

1. Required gene inserted into bacterial plasmid → plasmid inserted into bacterium → bacterium 'infects' plant cell and inserts plasmid into cell → required gene inserted into plant DNA → plant cell cultured to divide to produce new plant → cells in new plant produced by mitotic division of original cell are genetically identical and contain a copy of the inserted gene.

2. Insertion of a gene for pest resistance, to kill caterpillars that try to eat the plant.

3. Any one of each of the following:

Advantage: reduces need for pesticide (so less damage to environment), reduces time needed to look after crop (so reduces cost), farmer does not risk health from spraying pesticides.

Disadvantage: seed is more expensive, gene may transfer to wild plants and potentially affect the food web, there may be health concerns with the food produced from the crop.

B5c.2a Growing GM crops

In some parts of the world, such as the US, parts of South America, India, China and Africa, the proportion of crops grown that are genetically modified (GM crops) compared with unmodified varieties has risen rapidly. Examples of these crops include cotton, maize and soybean. Genes that have been added to GM crops include resistance to particular pests (by the addition of the gene from *Bacillus thuringiensis* that produces toxins that kill caterpillars) and herbicide resistance.

Here are some statements about growing and using GM crops. Cut out the cards and sort them into opinions and evidence (or both) about GM crops.

You can also sort them into arguments for or against growing GM crops. Then choose either the 'for' or 'against' group and use them to prepare for a class debate on 'Should we grow more GM crops than we do now?'. If there is time, use research to find examples to support your argument.

Using herbicide-resistant crops reduces the amount of herbicide needed to kill weeds, meaning less damage to other organisms in the environment.	Adding genes to organisms is tampering with nature. This is dangerous and bound to cause problems.
Producing a greater yield is not always helpful. In years when the harvest is large, the market price for the crop (how much it sells for) is lower.	We cannot be certain that there will be no risk to health of eating food from GM crops over a human lifetime.
Food made from GM crops has so far proved no less safe for humans to eat than the same crops that are non-GM.	Seed for transgenic plants is more expensive than seed for similar varieties that are not modified.
Increasing the amount of food that we produce has to be a good thing, because it will prevent starvation as the human population continues to grow.	Some caterpillars are already showing resistance to the Bt gene in transgenic cotton and soybean. So, damage caused by caterpillars is increasing in the transgenic varieties.
What's the difference between selective breeding for better characteristics, which humans have been doing for centuries, and genetic modification? It's just quicker to do the GM way.	Many GM crops show greater yield than the equivalent varieties grown nearby. In developing countries, this could mean the difference between starvation and good health for farmers with small farms.
Herbicide-resistant genes added to crops have been transferred to closely related wild plants by pollination. This may make it difficult to control weeds in the future.	Independent trials of some GM crops show that they produce a smaller yield when grown in exactly the same conditions as non-GM equivalent varieties. This is because insertion of the gene has damaged some of the plant function. Only by adding extra fertiliser can the yield be increased.
Seeds collected from GM crops will not grow 'true' to the variety and farmers have to buy new, expensive seed every season.	GM crops such as 'golden rice' may be able to cure nutrient deficiency diseases that affect millions of people.
GM crops that are frost-resistant will extend the growing season of economically important plants.	Salt-resistant GM crops will help low-lying countries that often get flooded by the sea to increase their yields.

Activity B5c.3 Consolidation and summary

Learning objectives

- To review the learning points of the topic.
- To test understanding through answering questions.

Learning outcomes

- Be familiar with the knowledge and understanding summarised in the End of topic checklist.
- Be able to apply this knowledge and understanding by answering the End of topic questions.

Resources

Student Book pages 356–358

Approach

Ask students to answer the End of topic questions in the Student Book.

Answers

End of topic questions mark scheme

Question	Correct answer	Marks
1 a)	This means that if the virus contains a gene that has been inserted from another organism, it should insert that gene into the cell in a way that means the cell will decode that gene and produce the characteristic.	1
1 b)	Any viral genes that cause illness must be removed, so that they do not harm the transgenic organism.	1
2 a)	A sheep that contains a gene from another species.	1
2 b)	A vector.	1
2 c)	Restriction enzymes are used to cut the gene out of the human DNA,	1
	and to cut the vector open.	1
	Ligase enzyme joins the human gene to the vector DNA.	1
2 d)	It can be produced in much larger quantities.	1
	It is not at risk of carrying blood-borne human pathogens.	1
3 a)	To make people take notice – people are less likely to read something that looks boring.	1
3 b)	The headline is suggesting that transgenic plants are dangerous.	1
	This could be as a result of eating food produced from the plants, although there is no clear evidence of this yet.	1
	They could also be dangerous as a result of damaging the environment by gene transfer through pollination to wild plants. Again, there is little evidence of this at the moment.	1
	Although there is no evidence for either of these possible dangers it could happen, so we need to be cautious.	1
4 a)	Answer that includes reference to crossing two varieties, one with high yield and one with disease resistance,	1
	selecting individuals with the best characteristics and cross-breeding them, and repeating this until you have individuals with the right characteristics.	1
4 b)	Insert a gene for disease resistance from another organism,	1
	into a high-yielding crop variety. (Or vice versa.)	1
4 c)	Takes a long time to produce a new variety by selective breeding, much slower than using GM techniques.	1
4 d)	Any suitable answer with appropriate explanation, such as:	
	gene for resistance might be transferred to other wild plants,	1
	as a result of pollination.	1
	Total:	21

Introduction

In this topic, students will learn the techniques used to produce clones of plants and mammals, and to evaluate the usefulness of cloned organisms.

Links to other topics

Sections	Essential background knowledge	Useful links
1 The nature and variety of living organisms	1b Variety of living organisms	
3 Reproduction and inheritance	3a Reproduction 3b Inheritance	
5 Use of biological resources	5a Food production 5b Selective breeding 5c Genetic modification (genetic engineering)	

Topic overview

B5d.1	Micropropagation (B)
	In this activity students have the opportunity to carry out tissue culture (note this needs at least two months to produce plants that can be placed outside), and to learn how micropropagation differs from taking cuttings.
B5d.2	Cloning mammals (B)
	This activity describes the process of cloning of mammals from a mature diploid cell, and evaluates the usefulness of producing cloned mammals.
B5d.3	Consolidation and summary
	This activity provides an opportunity for a quick recap on the ideas encountered in the topic as well as time for the students to answer the End of topic questions in the Student Book.

Activity B5d.1 Micropropagation (B)

Learning objectives: B5d.5.17**B**; B5d.5.18**B**

Learning objectives

- Describe the process of micropropagation (tissue culture) in which explants are grown *in vitro.* **(B)**
- Understand how micropropagation can be used to produce commercial quantities of genetically identical plants with desirable characteristics. **(B)**

Learning outcomes

- Describe the process of micropropagation (tissue culture) in which small pieces of plants (explants) are grown *in vitro* using nutrient media. **(B)**
- Understand how micropropagation can be used to produce commercial quantities of genetically identical plants (clones) with desirable characteristics. **(B)**

Common misconceptions

Many students forget about the environmental contribution to variation between individuals and therefore consider clones to be totally identical. A comparison of identical twins should help to remind them that the genotype is not the only factor controlling characteristics.

Resources

Student Book pages 359–361

Worksheet B5d.1a Micropropagation **(B)**

Resources for class practical (see below)

Approach

1. Introduction (B)

Revise the work on taking cuttings in Topic 3b by asking students how they would go about producing lots of identical plants. Give them a minute or so to write down notes, then take examples from around the class to build up a flow chart on the board showing how to take cuttings and produce new plants. Encourage discussion to make sure no important stage is missed.

2. Explaining micropropagation (B)

Introduce micropropagation (tissue culture) by showing students the photograph on page 361 of the Student Book of large numbers of commercially produced identical plants, or a similar photo from the internet. Tell them that these plants were produced using a similar procedure to taking cuttings, but that much smaller numbers of cells were used to start each plant. Ask students to suggest what advantages and disadvantages this procedure might have in comparison with taking cuttings. They should be able to suggest that many more plants can be produced from the original one, but that special techniques and facilities might be needed for handling such small amounts of tissue.

3. Carrying out micropropagation (B)

Worksheet B5d1.1 provides a method for the micropropagation of explants from cauliflower. Note that this is a challenging method because it requires students to maintain aseptic conditions throughout the procedure. However, it is satisfying for students to see their work producing new plants. The roots take 6–8 weeks to develop, and the shoots another 2–3 weeks before the tiny plants can be potted into compost. So, this is a long-term project.

You should demonstrate a safe cutting technique before students carry out the practical.

Alternatively, ask students to work through the method on the worksheet and to compare it with the method they used for taking cuttings. They should identify any similarities and differences and explain them.

4. Examples of micropropagation (B)

Ask students to research examples and uses of micropropagation to produce plants on a commercial scale. Examples could include producing plants that are difficult to grow from seed, such as banana (a food crop) or orchid (for the horticultural market), or those where the initial sample is small, such as in propagating endangered plants (see the Kew, Botanic Gardens website for examples).

They should prepare a short report or poster on their findings, making clear why the technique is used and what advantages and problems there are with the technique.

5. Consolidation: true or false (B)

Give students two scraps of paper and ask them to write *true* on one and *false* on the other. Then give a series of statements related to this activity, some of which are true and others false, and ask students to hold up the correct piece of paper. Suitable statements include:

- Micropropagation produces clones of plants. (true)
- Micropropagation is a simpler method for producing new plants than tissue culture. (false)

Technician's notes

You will need the following resources for the class practical.

Be sure to check the latest safety notes on these resources before proceeding.

B5d.1a Micropropagation

All materials should be sterilised by autoclaving before and after use.

The tissue culture medium can be prepared as follows – this makes enough for 10 boiling tubes.

You will need:

Murashige and Skoog (M&S) salts
kinetin (0.215 g dm^{-3}) solution
sucrose
agar
250 cm^3 beaker
spatula
balance and weighing boat
boiling tubes
aluminium foil
hot plate or boiling water bath or microwave oven
autoclave or pressure cooker

1. To approximately 70 cm^3 of distilled water in the beaker add:

- 2.0 g sucrose
- 0.44 g M&S basal medium
- 1.25 cm^3 kinetin solution
- 1 g agar

Make up to 100 cm^3 with distilled water.

2. Mix well and heat on a hotplate (stirring constantly) until the solution becomes clear. If you do not have a hotplate, heat in a boiling water bath or a microwave oven. Do not overheat the medium; darkening indicates caramelisation of sugars, which can reduce cell growth.

3. Measure 10 cm^3 into each boiling tube or bottle.

4. Seal the tops of the tubes/bottles with tin foil 'lids'.

5. Autoclave for 15 minutes at 121 °C.

If a hotplate is not available the medium can be made up, autoclaved and then the 10 cm^3 volumes dispensed into sterile boiling tubes.

The same medium without kinetin can be used to root any shoots formed.

Class practical, per group:

knife
white tile or chopping board
forceps
scalpel with sharp blade
sterile Petri dish
fresh piece of cauliflower head
1% Virkon solution or 0.5% Milton® (sodium dichloroisocyanurate) solution
sterile water plus beaker of sterile water
3 sterile glass jars with screw cap
bottles of sterile tissue culture medium containing growth hormone, see notes above on preparation the bottles could be McCartney bottles or boiling tubes with metal foil caps.
stopwatch or clock
Bunsen burner
eye protection

Answers

Developing investigative skills, page 361

1. Plan should include the following:

- taking tiny pieces of plant material from shoot tips
- sterilising of explants and of all equipment used
- producing nutrient medium with correct balance of nutrients and hormones to stimulate growth and differentiation of cells to form tiny plants
- placing explants on nutrient medium, keeping sterile, then growing in ideal conditions of light and humidity to encourage rapid growth
- when tiny plants large enough, moving into small compost pots, and looking after them until fully established.

2. Sterilisation kills microorganisms that would grow well on the nutrients and in the humidity needed for the plants. They could quickly overgrow the explants or infect them, so the project would fail.

3. a) They will be identical.

b) Because they have the same genes in their cells.

Page 361

1. Micropropagation: the cultivation of explants (small pieces of plant tissue) in the laboratory to create many clones of the original plant.

2. Explants taken from parent plant and sterilised → explants placed on nutrient medium containing chemicals for growth as well as hormones → hormones stimulate growth and differentiation to produce roots, stems and leaves → when large enough to handle, the tiny plants are moved onto different nutrient media → when large enough, moved into pots of compost.

3. They are all produced by the mitotic division of the cells from the original plant so they all contain the same genes.

B5d.1a Micropropagation (B)

Micropropagation (tissue culture) of plants uses small numbers of cells (explants) taken from the parent plant to produce new plants. As microorganisms can grow and divide much faster than plant cells, it is essential that *aseptic techniques* are used throughout this practical. This means treating all equipment to make it sterile and keeping it as free as possible from microorganisms in the air and on surfaces while preparing and culturing the explants.

Apparatus

knife
white tile or chopping board
forceps
scalpel with sharp blade
sterile Petri dish
fresh piece of cauliflower head
sterilising solution and beaker of sterilising solution
sterile water and beaker of sterile water
3 sterile glass jars with screw cap
bottles of sterile tissue culture medium containing growth hormone
stopwatch or clock
Bunsen burner
goggles

SAFETY INFORMATION

Goggles should be worn when handling sterilising solution.

Handle sharp knives and scalpels carefully.

Method

1. Put on goggles.

2. Prepare the working area by wiping the bench and tile (or chopping board) with sterilising solution.

3. Sterilise the forceps and scalpel by dipping them in a beaker of sterilising solution then the beaker of sterile water. (You will need to repeat this every time you use these items.)

4. Using sterile forceps (not your hand), place the cauliflower floret on the tile and use the knife to cut a 'minifloret', about 10–15 mm^3.

5. Use the forceps to place the minifloret into one of the glass jars and cover it with sterilising solution. Replace the lid firmly, then gently shake the jar for five seconds. Repeat the shaking for five seconds of every minute for exactly 10 minutes.

6. Using sterile forceps, remove the minifloret from the jar and place it in another sterile glass jar. Cover the explant with sterile water, and swirl it gently for 10 seconds.

7. Repeat step 5 with the third sterile glass jar, to wash the minifloret again. Leave the minifloret in the water.

8. Using sterile forceps, remove the minifloret and place it in the sterile Petri dish. Holding the cauliflower tissue with the forceps, use a sterile scalpel to trim about 2 mm off the bottom/stalk end to remove cells damaged by sterilising solution. Cut the rest of the 'minifloret' up into tiny pieces about 3–5 mm^3 – these are the explants. Cover the Petri dish with a sterile lid until ready for the next step.

9. Using sterile forceps, and working quickly, remove the lid of the bottle of sterile medium and flame the neck of the bottle in the Bunsen flame. Then place an explant into the bottle, pressing the stalk gently down into the culture medium. Then quickly replace the lid of the bottle. Repeat this, putting one explant into each bottle, sterilising the forceps in between each time.

10. Place the tubes in a warm, light place. Check for signs of contamination every day, and give any that are looking mouldy to your teacher for disposal.

11. Shoots should form within 6–8 weeks. When the shoots are 1–2 cm long, they can be transferred to a dish or jar of rooting medium. Aseptic techniques are needed during this stage also.

12. Roots should develop within 2–3 weeks, after which the new plants can be transferred to small pots of sterile potting compost and covered with plastic bags for a few days until they have settled and started to grow.

Activity B5d.2 Cloning mammals (B)

Specification reference: B5d.5.19**B**; B5d.5.20**B**

Learning objectives

- Describe the stages in the production of cloned mammals by nuclear transfer. **(B)**
- Understand how cloned transgenic animals can be used to produce human proteins. **(B)**

Learning outcomes

- Describe the stages in the production of cloned mammals involving the introduction of a diploid nucleus from a mature cell into an enucleated egg cell, illustrated by Dolly the sheep. **(B)**
- Explain how cloned transgenic animals can be used to produce human proteins. **(B)**

Common misconceptions

Students are often confused by which sheep was the 'real' (biological) mother of Dolly. If this is the case, remind them to think of which part of a cell codes for characteristics and to 'follow the nucleus'.

Note that the method described in this specification is not the only way to produce cloned mammals. Another method is to divide an embryo at an early stage (4-cell or 8-cell) into separate cells that then develop into separate embryos. Each embryo is then placed in the uterus of a different female where it develops until birth. Students may find mention of this if they carry out their own research.

Resources

Student Book pages 362–364

Worksheet B5d.2a Creating Dolly **(B)**

Worksheet B5d.2b Is cloning mammals worth it? **(B)**

Approach

1. Introduction (B)

Remind students that in the last activity they were cloning plants. Then ask them to consider how they might go about cloning a large mammal, such as a cow or sheep. Give them a few moments to think about this, then take answers.

Some students may suggest using methods that they have learned can be used with plants: that is, cuttings and micropropagation. Explain that plant and animal cells differ in that most differentiated plant tissue retains the ability to form any type of cell or tissue after cell division, but animal tissue does not. Students should discuss the implications of this.

2. Creating Dolly (B)

Worksheet B5d.2a provides a simple cut-and-paste activity to help students learn the sequence of the process by which Dolly the sheep was made. It also includes some questions to help students identify the key points to remember.

3. Is cloning mammals worth it? (B)

Ask students to read pages 363–364 of the Student Book on the uses of transgenic mammals. Although students need to learn about cloned transgenic animals being used to produce human proteins, they should also be aware that they may get questions in their examination about unfamiliar examples where they are given information and then asked questions on the basis of that information. As an example of this, give them Worksheet B5d.2b, which provides facts about using cloned mammals to produce 'human' organs for transplant as well as to produce human antibodies in commercial quantities.

The questions at the end of the worksheet could be answered by students individually, or in small groups to encourage discussion, or used as the basis for a class discussion to help students develop their evaluation skills and see more than one point of view.

4. Consolidation: biotechnology concept map (B)

Give students the following words: *selective breeding*, *genetic engineering* and *cloning*. Ask them to use the words as the basis for a concept map on the production of food and other products for human use.

They should use what they have learned in this and Topics 5b and 5c to construct their map, including aspects of the arguments for and against some of the methods used to produce new varieties or breeds of organism for human use.

Give them a few minutes to do this, then ask them to compare their map with that of a neighbour and to work together to improve their maps. Take examples from around the class to make sure all the key points have been covered.

Answers

Page 364

1. A diploid cell taken from an adult sheep → nucleus removed and placed in an enucleated egg cell from another sheep → cell stimulated to start dividing to produce embryo → embryo placed in the uterus of another sheep to develop ready for birth.

2. Sheep B, as the diploid nucleus contains the genes that code for the characteristics of Dolly.

3. They can produce chemicals (e.g. antibodies) to treat human diseases.

B5d.2a Creating Dolly (B)

The pictures below, when arranged correctly, will show the process of cloning that produced Dolly the sheep.

Cut out the pictures and arrange them in the right order to show the process. When you have the right order, stick them into your workbook.

Add any labels or annotations to help explain the process as clearly as possible. Then answer these questions.

1. Why was the egg cell enucleated (nucleus removed)?

2. An egg cell is haploid. Were Dolly's body cells haploid or diploid? Explain your answer.

3. Which sheep was Dolly a clone of? Explain your answer.

egg cell taken from ovary of adult female sheep	embryo
nucleus from body cell placed in enucleated egg cell and the combined cell stimulated to start dividing	body cell taken from the udder of an adult female sheep
embryo placed in uterus of foster (surrogate) mother sheep	nucleus removed from egg cell and thrown away
nucleus taken from body cell, rest of cell thrown away	Dolly the lamb with her surrogate mother

B5d.2b Is cloning mammals worth it? (B)

Facts about organ transplants

More than 10 000 people in the UK need an organ transplant (such as kidney, liver, heart), and each year about 1000 of these people will die because there are not enough organs available from humans to treat them.	By combining genetic modification (to replace some 'pig' characteristics with 'human' ones) with animal cloning, scientists can produce pigs with organs that human bodies would accept more easily (though this is still not proving easy). Each pig could produce enough organs for two human kidney transplants, one liver transplant, one heart transplant, as well as transplants of other tissues.

Facts about antibody production

Human antibodies can be used to treat diseases such as cancer and heart disease, which kill thousands of people each year. We can't use humans to produce large quantities of antibodies, and it is difficult to produce some human proteins (such as antibodies) using microorganisms in a fermenter.	To make many cells that produce a particular human antibody, we start with a mouse that is genetically engineered to produce a human antibody instead of a mouse one. The mouse is injected with the chemical (antigen) that stimulates its body to make cells that produce the antibody. The mouse is killed and the cells extracted and treated to make them grow and divide continually. The cells are then grown in a fermenter, and large quantities of antibody can be extracted and purified from the solution.

Read each of the fact boxes and then answer the questions below. If you have time, carry out further research to add more facts to support your argument.

1. What are the advantages of using cloned mammals in this way?

2. What are the disadvantages of using cloned mammals in this way?

Some people are concerned that we should be thinking not only about human needs, but also the needs of the animals.

3. What problems does this cause? Explain your answer.

4. Is it right to grow animals to 'harvest' organs for organ transplants? Is this any different from growing animals to eat?

5. Is cloning mammals justified? Explain your answer as fully as you can.

Activity B5d.3 Consolidation and summary

Learning objectives

- To review the learning points of the topic.
- To test understanding through answering questions.

Learning outcomes

- Be familiar with the knowledge and understanding summarised in the End of topic checklist.
- Be able to apply this knowledge and understanding by answering the End of topic questions.

Resources

Student Book pages 365–366

Approach

Ask students to answer the End of topic questions in the Student Book.

Answers

End of topic questions mark scheme

Question	Correct answer	Marks
1 a)	Sexual reproduction of disease-resistant plant with plants of the same species with flowers of different colours.	1
	This should produce variation in the offspring.	1
1 b)	Cloning by micropropagation,	1
	as all the many offspring will be clones of the parent plant and have the blue flowers.	1
2 a)	Goats naturally produce milk (containing antithrombin),	1
	so it is easier to obtain/extract the antithrombin.	1
2 b)	Goat antithrombin is not exactly the same as human antithrombin	1
	so it will not act in exactly the same way.	1
3 a)	They grow from the old plant, in the same soil, so if the soil and old plant are infected, it is very likely that the new plant will be too.	1
3 b)	As infection spreads through plantations, more plants are diseased and produce fewer fruit.	1
3 c)	Take cells from the growing tip of a banana plant, and sterilise them.	1
	Place the cells on a sterile nutrient medium that contains plant hormones to encourage the cells to grow.	1
	Place the explants on a nutrient medium containing plant hormones that encourage the cells to differentiate and produce roots, shoots and leaves.	1
	Grow the tiny plants until large enough to handle for transplanting into pots.	1
3 d)	By taking only a few cells from the tip of the plant for tissue culture, it is easier to take cells that are uninfected by pests and diseases.	1
	If plants are uninfected, they will grow better and produce a greater yield of fruit.	1
3 e)	All the cells in the transgenic plant will contain the resistant gene,	1
	so plants grown by tissue culture will all contain the resistant gene in all their cells,	1
	because this is a form of asexual reproduction so all cells are identical.	1
	Total:	19

Question	Correct answer	Marks
2 a)	i) glucose → ethanol + carbon dioxide	3
	ii) Carbon dioxide makes the bread rise.	1
2 b)	i) Prepare a mixture of yeast, glucose and water and place in a boiling tube.	1
	Connect the bung in the boiling tube to a gas syringe using a delivery tube.	1
	Place the mixture in a water bath at 20 °C.	1
	Record the volume of carbon dioxide produced in a given time, e.g. 30 minutes.	1
	Repeat the investigation at different temperatures, e.g. 30 °C, 40 °C, 50 °C.	1
	5 marks for any other suitable method.	
	ii) Any two of the following:	1 mark for each point (maximum 2 marks)
	Concentration of sugar	
	Concentration of oxygen	
	pH	
	Type of sugar	
2 c)	Soy sauce / pizza dough	1
3 a)	i) Food web as shown	1 mark for each correct arrow up to a maximum 6 marks

Question	Correct answer	Marks
	ii) To meet its energy/food needs, each organism eats many individual organisms on the trophic level below.	1
	DDT is retained by each organism in the food web (and not excreted, respired or broken down).	1
	So the DDT becomes concentrated as it moves up the trophic levels.	1
3 b)	The reproduction of the birds is reduced, so there will be a reduction in the populations of cormorants and terns,	1
	the population of needlefish will increase,	1
	so, as they eat the minnows, the minnow populations will fall,	1
	numbers of needlefish will then fall,	1
	numbers of plankton increase.	1
4 a)	Fish are: high in protein,	1
	low in fat / high in essential fatty acids.	1
4 b)	**Water quality**: in open systems:	1
	maintained by moving water through the pond, lake or sea tank / location chosen so water quality can be relied on throughout the year to contain sufficient oxygen and to be clear of silt and chemicals	
	or in closed systems:	
	waste products from the fish and left-over food are removed on a continual basis / ponds need to be emptied on a regular basis and cleaned out.	
	Control of pests and diseases: pesticides to control pests and antibiotics to control disease.	1
	Control of predation: Interspecific predation must be prevented by protecting the fish from birds and mammals, e.g. otters, by placing netted or metal cages over the ponds	1
	or intraspecific predation prevented by keeping the fish at lower density.	
4 c)	i) In 1985: 34 600 tonnes	1
	Working out: nitrogen waste per fish = 77.5 kg = 0.0775 tonnes	1
	2683 tonnes of waste are produced,	
	therefore, number of fish that produce this mass of waste = 2683/0.0775 = 34 600 (3 sig. fig.)	
	In 2007: 814 000 tonnes	1
	Working out: nitrogen waste per fish = 50.2 kg = 0.0502 tonnes	1
	40 877 tonnes of waste are produced,	
	therefore, number of fish that produce this mass of waste = 40 877/0.0502 = 814 000 (3 sig. fig.)	
	ii) Nitrates/nitrogen compounds cause eutrophication of water,	1
	resulting in a population growth of algae,	1
	algae below surface die because they are shaded by those above,	1

Question	Correct answer	Marks
	the death of the algae further deprives the water of oxygen as bacteria feed on them and respire,	1
	the organisms in the water will die.	1
5 a)	*Lactobacillus*	1
	Accept also *Streptococcus thermophiles*	
5 b)	i) There is a rapid fall over the first five hours from a pH of 6.6 to 4.7,	1
	then a slow fall/fairly constant pH from five hours to 15 hours to a pH of 4.4	1
	ii) Lactic acid is produced by the bacteria.	1
5 c)	Warm temperature / temperature of 45 °C.	1
6	plasmids	1
	restriction	1
	ligase	1
	recombinant	1
	vectors	1
7 a)	In the soil.	1
7 b)	The insecticide may also kill beneficial butterflies and moths as well as those that are harmful to crops,	1
	and these insects are important pollinators.	1
7 c)	A gene gun.	1
7 d)	Wind-pollinated,	1
	as the pollen is sufficiently light to be blown in the wind.	1
7 e)	In principle, the GM maize should be an effective way of controlling insect pests of maize as the Insecticidal Crystal Proteins (ICP) are internal, and not sprayed onto the outside of the plant,	1
	where they could kill other butterflies and moths.	1
	Being internal, the ICPs will only kill insects that eat the plant,	1
	but there is concern that pollen may also carry the ICP.	1
	If the pollen is blown onto other plants, it may kill butterflies and moths eating these plants.	1
7 f)	Any one of the following (or any other suitable suggestion)	1
	Is pollen from other or all GM plants toxic?	
	Is GM pollen equally toxic to all butterflies and moths?	
	What distance can GM pollen travel?	
	Can insects develop a resistance to the *Bt* GM crop?	
	Total:	62

Activity number and name	Learning outcomes and objectives	Specification reference	Student Book pages	Practical
B1a.1 The eight characteristics of living organisms	**Learning objectives** • Name the eight characteristics shown by living organisms. • Describe each of the characteristics of living organisms. • Explain that not all living organisms show every characteristic all of the time. **Learning outcomes** • Revise what 'living' means. • Identify and give examples of the eight characteristics of living organisms.	1.1	10–12	
B1a.2 Consolidation and summary	**Learning objectives** • To review the learning points of the topic. • To test understanding through answering questions. **Learning outcomes** • Be familiar with the knowledge and understanding summarised in the End of topic checklist. • Be able to apply this knowledge and understanding by answering End of topic questions.	1.1	13–14	
B1b.1 Classifying organisms	**Learning objectives** • Describe the common features shown by eukaryotic organisms: plants, animals, fungi and protoctists. • Describe the common features shown by prokaryotic organisms such as bacteria. • Understand the term pathogen and know that pathogens may include fungi, bacteria, protoctists or viruses. **Learning outcomes** • To understand that living organisms can be classified by their features into the following groups: plants, animals, fungi, bacteria, protoctists, viruses. • To give examples of pathogens from fungi, bacteria, protoctists and viruses. • To understand that pathogenic organisms cause disease in other organisms.	1.2, 1.3, 1.4	15–22	

Activity number and name	Learning outcomes and objectives	Specification reference	Student Book pages	Practical
B1b.2 Consolidation and summary	**Learning objectives** • To review the learning points of the topic. • To test understanding through answering questions. **Learning outcomes** • Be familiar with the knowledge and understanding summarised in the End of topic checklist. • Be able to apply this knowledge and understanding by answering End of topic questions.	1.1–1.4	23–24	
B2a.1 Level of organisation within organisms	**Learning objectives** • Describe the levels of organisation in organisms: organelles, cells, tissues, organs and systems. **Learning outcomes** • Write definitions of the terms organelle, cell, tissue, organ, organ system. • Explain how the levels of organisation in a body contribute to effective functioning.	2.1	30–33	
B2a.2 Consolidation and summary	**Learning objectives** • To review the learning points of the topic. • To test understanding through answering questions. **Learning outcomes** • Be familiar with the knowledge and understanding summarised in the End of topic checklist. • Be able to apply this knowledge and understanding by answering End of topic questions.	2.1	34–35	
B2b.1 Plant and animal cells	**Learning objectives** • Describe cell structures, including the nucleus, cytoplasm, cell membrane, cell wall, mitochondria, chloroplasts, ribosomes and vacuole. • Describe the functions of the nucleus, cytoplasm, cell membrane, cell wall, mitochondria, chloroplasts, ribosomes and vacuole. • Know the similarities and differences in the structure of plant and animal cells. • Explain the importance of cell differentiation in the development of specialised cells. **(B)** • Understand the advantages and disadvantages of using stem cells in medicine. **(B)**	2.2–2.4; 2.5B; 2.6B	36–40	Using a light microscope

Activity number and name	Learning outcomes and objectives	Specification reference	Student Book pages	Practical
	Learning outcomes • Describe that plant and animal cells have a cell membrane, cytoplasm and nucleus. • Describe that plant cells also have a cell wall, chloroplasts and often a large central vacuole. • Describe how each type of cell structure has a specific purpose in the cell. • Explain how cell differentiation leads to the development of specialised cells. **(B)** • Describe the advantages and disadvantages of using stem cells in medicine. **(B)**			Making a microscope slide
B2b.2 Consolidation and summary	**Learning objectives** • To review the learning points of the topic. • To test understanding through answering questions. **Learning outcomes** • Be familiar with the knowledge and understanding summarised in the End of topic checklist. • Be able to apply this knowledge and understanding by answering End of topic questions.	2.2–2.4; 2.5B; 2.6B	41–42	

Edexcel International GCSE Biology Teacher Pack

383

© HarperCollins*Publishers* Ltd 2017

Activity number and name	Learning outcomes and objectives	Specification reference	Student Book pages	Practical
B2c.1 Food molecules	Learning objectives • Identify the chemical elements present in carbohydrates, proteins and lipids (fats and oils). • Describe the structure of carbohydrates, proteins and lipids, and name the basic units from which they are formed. • Practical: Investigate food samples for the presence of glucose, starch, protein and fat. Learning outcomes • Identify the chemical elements present in carbohydrates, proteins and lipids (fats or oils). • Describe the carbohydrates starch and glycogen as being large molecules made from simple sugars. • Describe proteins as being large molecules made from amino acids. • Describe lipids as being large molecules commonly made from fatty acids and glycerol. • Describe how to test foods for glucose, starch, protein and fat.	2.7–2.9	43–47	Food tests
B2c.2 Enzymes	Learning objectives • Understand the role of enzymes as biological catalysts in metabolic reactions. • Understand how temperature changes can affect enzyme function, including changes to the shape of active site. • Practical: Investigate how enzyme activity can be affected by changes in temperature. • Understand how enzyme function can be affected by changes in pH altering the active site. • Practical: Investigate how enzyme activity can be affected by changes in pH. **(B)**	2.10–2.13; 2.14B	48–51	Gelatin, enzymes and temperature

Activity number and name	Learning outcomes and objectives	Specification reference	Student Book pages	Practical
	Learning outcomes • Describe enzymes as biological catalysts that control reactions. • Describe and explain how temperature and pH affect the rate of enzyme-controlled reactions, including changes to the active site. • Describe simple experiments that show how enzyme activity is affected by changes in temperature and pH.			Trypsin, milk and temperature The effect of pH on amylase
B2c.3 Consolidation and summary	**Learning objectives** • To review the learning points of the topic. • To test understanding through answering questions. **Learning outcomes** • Be familiar with the knowledge and understanding summarised in the End of topic checklist. • Be able to apply this knowledge and understanding by answering End of topic questions.	2.7–2.13; 2.14B	52–54	
B2d.1 Diffusion	**Learning objectives** • Understand the process of diffusion by which substances move in and out of cells. • Understand how factors affect the rate of movement of substances into and out of cells, including the effects of surface area to volume ratio, distance, temperature and concentration gradient. • Practical: Investigate diffusion using living and non-living systems. **Learning outcomes** • Write a definition of the term *diffusion*. • Explain how diffusion can occur across cell membranes. • Describe factors that affect the rate of diffusion across cell membranes. • Carry out simple experiments to investigate diffusion.	2.15–2.17	55–60	Diffusion in a non-living system Temperature and the rate of diffusion Surface area and the rate of diffusion

Activity number and name	Learning outcomes and objectives	Specification reference	Student Book pages	Practical
B2d.2 Osmosis	**Learning objectives** • Understand the process of osmosis by which substances move into and out of cells. • Understand how factors affect the rate of movement of substances into and out of cells, including the effects of surface area to volume ratio, distance, temperature and concentration gradient. • Practical: Investigate osmosis using living and non-living systems. **Learning outcomes** • Write a definition of the term *osmosis.* • Explain how osmosis can occur across cell membranes. • Describe factors that affect the rate of osmosis across cell membranes. • Carry out simple experiments showing osmosis.	2.15–2.17	60–64	Osmosis in a non-living system Measuring osmosis by change in weight Osmosis and change in shape
B2d.3 Active transport	**Learning objectives** • Explain the importance of active transport for cells. • Understand the process of active transport by which substances move into and out of cells. • Understand how factors affect the rate of movement of substances into and out of cells, including the effects of surface area to volume ratio, distance, temperature and concentration gradient. **Learning outcomes** • Write a definition of the term *active transport.* • Explain how active transport can occur across cell membranes. • Give examples of active transport in animals and plants.	2.15, 2.16	64–65	

Activity number and name	Learning outcomes and objectives	Specification reference	Student Book pages	Practical
B2d.4 Consolidation and summary	**Learning objectives** • To review the learning points of the topic. • To test understanding through answering questions. **Learning outcomes** • Be familiar with the knowledge and understanding summarised in the End of topic checklist. • Be able to apply this knowledge and understanding by answering End of topic questions.	2.15–2.17	66–67	

Edexcel International GCSE Biology Teacher Pack

Activity number and name	Learning outcomes and objectives	Specification reference	Student Book pages	Practical
B2e.1 Photosynthesis	Learning objectives • Understand the process of photosynthesis and its importance in the conversion of light energy to chemical energy. • Know the word equation and balanced chemical symbol equation for photosynthesis. • Understand how varying carbon dioxide concentration, light intensity and temperature affect the rate of photosynthesis. • Describe the structure of the leaf and explain how it is adapted for photosynthesis. • Practical: Investigate photosynthesis, showing the evolution of oxygen from a water plant, the production of starch and the requirements of light, carbon dioxide and chlorophyll. Learning outcomes • Describe photosynthesis, and write word and symbol equations for the process. • Explain the role of photosynthesis in the nutrition of plants. • Describe how different factors affect the rate of photosynthesis. • Explain how the leaf is adapted for photosynthesis.	2.18–2.21, 2.23	68–77	Testing leaves for starch Chlorophyll and photosynthesis Carbon dioxide and photosynthesis Light and the rate of photosynthesis
B2e.2 Mineral ions in plants	Learning objectives • Understand that plants require mineral ions for growth, and that magnesium ions are needed for chlorophyll and nitrate ions are needed for amino acids. Learning outcomes • Describe the importance of some mineral ions in plant growth.	2.22	77–78	Plants and mineral nutrients

Activity number and name	Learning outcomes and objectives	Specification reference	Student Book pages	Practical
B2e.3 Human nutrition	**Learning objectives** • Understand what is meant by a balanced diet. • Identify the sources and describe the functions of nutrients in human nutrition. • Understand how energy requirements vary with activity levels, age and pregnancy. • Describe the structure and function of organs in the human alimentary canal. • Understand how food is moved through the gut by peristalsis. • Understand the role of digestive enzymes. • Understand that bile is produced by the liver and stored in the gall bladder. • Understand the role of bile in neutralising stomach acid and emulsifying lipids. • Understand how the small intestine is adapted for absorption, including the structure of a villus. • Practical: Investigate the energy content in a food sample. **(B)** **Learning outcomes** • Explain that a balanced diet should include appropriate amounts of carbohydrate, protein, lipid, vitamins, minerals, water and dietary fibre. • Describe the sources and functions of carbohydrate, protein, lipid (fats and oils), vitamins A, C and D, the mineral ions calcium and iron, water and dietary fibre as components of the diet. • Describe the structures and functions of organs in the human alimentary canal, including the mouth, oesophagus, stomach, small intestine (duodenum and ileum), large intestine (colon and rectum) and pancreas. • Describe the role of digestive enzymes, including the digestion of starch to glucose by amylase and maltase; the digestion of proteins to amino acids by proteases; and the digestion of lipids to fatty acids and glycerol by lipases. • Describe the role of bile indigestion. • Explain the importance of the structure of a villus. • Be able to describe an experiment to work out the energy content in a sample of food. **(B)**	2.24–2.32; 2.33B	78–90	The energy in foods The digestion and absorption of carbohydrates

Activity number and name	Learning outcomes and objectives	Specification reference	Student Book pages	Practical
B2e.4 Consolidation and summary	**Learning objectives** • To review the learning points of the topic. • To test understanding through answering questions. **Learning outcomes** • Be familiar with the knowledge and understanding summarised in the End of topic checklist. • Be able to apply this knowledge and understanding by answering End of topic questions.	2.18–2.32; 2.33B	91–96	

Activity number and name	Learning outcomes and objectives	Specification reference	Student Book pages	Practical
B2f.1 Respiration	**Learning objectives** • Understand how the process of respiration produces ATP in living organisms. • Know that ATP provides energy for cells. • Describe the differences between aerobic and anaerobic respiration. • Know the word equation and the balanced chemical symbol equation for aerobic respiration in living organisms. • Know the word equation for anaerobic respiration in plants and in animals. • Practical: Investigate the evolution of carbon dioxide and heat from respiring seeds or other suitable living organisms. **Learning outcomes** • Know that respiration releases energy in living organisms. • Understand aerobic respiration uses oxygen from the air to release energy from glucose. • Write the word and balanced symbol equations for aerobic respiration: glucose + oxygen $\rightarrow$ carbon dioxide + water (+ energy) $C_6H_{12}O_6 + 6O_2 \rightarrow 6CO_2 + 6H_2O$ (+ energy). • Describe how anaerobic respiration releases energy from glucose without oxygen. • In animals, the equation for the reaction is: glucose $\rightarrow$ lactic acid (+ energy). • In some plants and fungi, the equation for the reaction is: glucose $\rightarrow$ ethanol + carbon dioxide (+ energy).	2.34–2.39	97–102	Respiration in germinating seeds

Activity number and name	Learning outcomes and objectives	Specification reference	Student Book pages	Practical
B2f.2 Consolidation and summary	**Learning objectives** • To review the learning points of the topic. • To test understanding through answering questions. **Learning outcomes** • Be familiar with the knowledge and understanding summarised in the End of topic checklist. • Be able to apply this knowledge and understanding by answering End of topic questions.	2.34–2.39	103–104	
B2g.1 Gas exchange in flowering plants	**Learning objectives** • Understand the role of diffusion in gas exchange. **(B)** • Understand gas exchange (of carbon dioxide and oxygen) in relation to respiration and photosynthesis. **(B)** • Understand how the structure of the leaf is adapted for gas exchange. **(B)** • Describe the role of stomata in gas exchange. **(B)** • Understand that respiration continues during the day and night, but that the net exchange of carbon dioxide and oxygen depends on the intensity of light. **(B)** • Practical: Investigate the effect of light on net gas exchange from a leaf, using hydrogen-carbonate indicator. **(B)** **Learning outcomes** • Understand plants exchange gases with the environment to support cellular respiration. **(B)** • Understand plants also exchange gases with the environment to support photosynthesis. **(B)** • Explain how the net exchange of oxygen and carbon dioxide between a plant and the environment depends on light intensity. **(B)** • Describe how leaf structure is adapted for efficient gas exchange. **(B)** • Describe how stomata allow gases to enter and leave the leaf. **(B)**	2.40B–2.45B	105–109	Net gas exchange in plants Leaf peels

Activity number and name	Learning outcomes and objectives	Specification reference	Student Book pages	Practical
B2g.2 Gas exchange in humans	**Learning objectives** • Describe the structure of the human thorax, including the ribs, intercostal muscles, diaphragm, trachea, bronchi, bronchioles, alveoli and pleural membranes. Understand the role of the intercostal muscles and the diaphragm in ventilation. • Explain how alveoli are adapted for gas exchange by diffusion between air in the lungs and blood in capillaries. • Understand the biological consequences of smoking in relation to the lungs and the circulatory system, including coronary heart disease. • Practical: Investigate breathing in humans, including the release of carbon dioxide and the effect of exercise. **Learning outcomes** • Know that the human thorax contains the ribs, intercostal muscles, diaphragm, trachea, bronchi, bronchioles, alveoli and pleural membranes. • Describe how the diaphragm and intercostal membranes are used in ventilation. • Explain how the alveoli are adapted for efficient exchange of gases by diffusion between the blood and the air in the lungs. • Understand the damaging effects that smoking has on the lungs and circulatory system.	2.46–2.50	110–119	The effect of exercise on breathing Structure of the human gas exchange system
B2g.3 Consolidation and summary	**Learning objectives** • To review the learning points of the topic. • To test understanding through answering questions. **Learning outcomes** • Be familiar with the knowledge and understanding summarised in the End of topic checklist. • Be able to apply this knowledge and understanding by answering End of topic questions.	2.40B–2.45B; 2.46–2.50	120–123	

Activity number and name	Learning outcomes and objectives	Specification reference	Student Book pages	Practical
B2h.1 Transport in flowering plants	**Learning objectives** • Understand why simple, unicellular organisms can rely on diffusion for movement of substances in and out of the cell. • Understand the neec for a transport system in multicellular organisms. • Describe the role of phloem in transporting sucrose and amino acids between the leaves and other parts of the plant. • Describe the role of xylem in transporting water and mineral ions from the roots to other parts of the plant. • Understand how water is absorbed by root hair cells. **(B)** • Understand that transpiration is the evaporation of water from the surface of a plant. **(B)** • Understand how the rate of transpiration is affected by changes in humidity, wind speed, temperature and light intensity. **(B)** • Practical: Investigate the role of environmental factors in determining the rate of transpiration from a leafy shoot. **(B)** **Learning outcomes** • Understand that large organisms need a transport system to carry materials around the body. • Describe how xylem tissue transports water and mineral salts from the roots to other parts of the plant. • Describe how phloem tissue transports sucrose and amino acids around the plant. • Understand how water enters plants through root hair cells. **(B)** • Understand that transpiration is the evaporation of water from a leaf, and the rate of transp ration is affected by several environmental conditions. **(B)**	2.51–2.54; 2.55B–2.58B	124–131	The rate of transpiration

Not applicable.

Activity number and name	Learning outcomes and objectives	Specification reference	Student Book pages	Practical
B2h.2 Blood	Learning objectives • Describe the composition of the blood: red blood cells, white blood cells, platelets and plasma. • Understand the role of plasma in the transport of carbon dioxide, digested food, urea, hormones and heat energy. • Understand how adaptations of red blood cells make them suitable for the transport of oxygen, including shape, the absence of a nucleus and the presence of haemoglobin. • Understand how the immune system responds to disease using white blood cells, illustrated by phagocytes ingesting pathogens and lymphocytes releasing antibodies specific to the pathogen. • Understand how vaccination results in the manufacture of memory cells, which enable future antibody production to the pathogen to occur sooner, faster and in greater quantity. **(B)** • Understand how platelets are involved in blood clotting, which prevents blood loss and the entry of microorganisms. **(B)** Learning outcomes • Explain that human blood is formed from plasma carrying red blood cells, white blood cells and platelets. • Explain how plasma is important in the transport of carbon dioxide, digested food molecules, urea, hormones and heat energy around the body. • Describe how red blood cells have special adaptations for carrying oxygen, including haemoglobin. • Understand how white blood cells are part of the immune system that responds to infection by pathogens. • Understand how vaccination results in the production of memory cells and how they respond to infection. **(B)** • Understand the role of platelets in blood clotting. **(B)**	2.59–2.62; 2.63B; 2.64B	131–135	

Activity number and name	Learning outcomes and objectives	Specification reference	Student Book pages	Practical
B2h.3 The human circulatory system	**Learning objectives** • Describe the structure of the heart and how it functions. • Explain how the heart rate changes during exercise and under the influence of adrenaline. • Understand how factors may increase the risk of developing coronary heart disease. • Understand how the structure of arteries, veins and capillaries relate to their function. • Understand the general structure of the circulation system, including the blood vessels to and from the heart and lungs, liver and kidneys. **Learning outcomes** • Describe the structure of the heart and be able to link this to its function in pumping blood to the lungs and other parts of the body. • Understand heart rate is affected by exercise and adrenaline. • Understand the factors that may increase the risk of coronary heart disease. • Explain how the structure of arteries, veins and capillaries is related to their different roles in transporting blood around the body. • Describe the human circulatory system and know that it includes the heart and blood vessels that support all the organs of the body.	2.65–2.69	135–142	
B2h.4 Consolidation and summary	**Learning objectives** • To review the learning points of the topic. • To test understanding through answering questions. **Learning outcomes** • Be familiar with the knowledge and understanding summarised in the End of topic checklist. • Be able to apply this knowledge and understanding by answering End of topic questions.	2.51–2.69	143–147	

Activity number and name	Learning outcomes and objectives	Specification reference	Student Book pages	Practical
B2i.1 Excretion in organisms	**Learning objectives** • In plants, understand the origin of carbon dioxide and oxygen as waste products of metabolism and their loss from the stomata of a leaf. • In humans, know the excretory products of the lungs, kidneys and skin (organs of excretion). • Describe the structure of the urinary system, including the kidneys, ureters, bladder and urethra. **(B)** **Learning outcomes** • Understand that plants lose excess carbon dioxide and oxygen to the environment through stomata in their leaves. • Understand that in humans, the organs of excretion are the lungs, kidneys and skin. • Describe the human urinary system and know that it includes the kidneys, ureters, bladder and urethra. **(B)**	2.70; 2.71; 2.73B	148–149	

397

© HarperCollins*Publishers* Ltd 2017

Activity number and name	Learning outcomes and objectives	Specification reference	Student Book pages	Practical
B2i.2 Producing urine	**Learning objectives** • Understand how the kidney carries out its roles of excretion and osmoregulation. **(B)** • Describe the structure of a nephron, including the Bowman's capsule and glomerulus, convoluted tubules, loop of Henle and collecting duct. **(B)** • Describe ultrafiltration in the Bowman's capsule and the composition of the glomerular filtrate. **(B)** • Understand how water is reabsorbed into the blood from the collecting duct. **(B)** • Understand why selective reabsorption of glucose occurs at the proximal convoluted tubule. **(B)** • Understand that urine contains water, urea and ions. **(B)** **Learning outcomes** • Describe the structure of a nephron including a Bowman's capsule, glomerulus, convoluted tubules, loop of Henle and collecting duct. **(B)** • Describe how ultrafiltration takes place in the Bowman's capsule and glomerulus, producing the glomerular filtrate. **(B)** • Describe how water is reabsorbed from the kidney tubule in the collecting duct. **(B)** • Describe how selective reabsorption of glucose occurs in the proximal convoluted tubule. **(B)** • Understand that excreted urine contains water, urea and salts. **(B)**	2.72B; 2.74B–2.77B; 2.79B	149–152	Kidney dissection

Edexcel International GCSE Biology Teacher Pack

Activity number and name	Learning outcomes and objectives	Specification reference	Student Book pages	Practical
B2i.3 Osmoregulation	Learning objectives • Understand how the kidney carries out its roles of excretion and osmoregulation. **(B)** • Understand how water is reabsorbed into the blood from the collecting duct. **(B)** • Describe the role of ADH in regulating the water content of the blood. **(B)** Learning outcomes • Describe the role of the kidneys in osmoregulation. **(B)** • Understand that water is reabsorbed from the kidney tubule in the collecting duct. **(B)** • Understand that ADH is the hormone that is involved in regulation of the water content of the blood. **(B)**	2.72B; 2.76B; 2.78B	152–153	
B2i.4 Consolidation and summary	Learning objectives • To review the learning points of the topic. • To test understanding through answering questions. Learning outcomes • Be familiar with the knowledge and understanding summarised in the End of topic checklist. • Be able to apply this knowledge and understanding by answering End of topic questions.	2.70–2.79B	154–156	

Edexcel International GCSE Biology Teacher Pack

399

© HarperCollins*Publishers* Ltd 2017

Activity number and name	Learning outcomes and objectives	Specification reference	Student Book pages	Practical
B2j.1 Plant tropisms	**Learning objectives** • Understand how organisms are able to respond to changes in their environment. • Understand that plants respond to stimuli. • Describe the geotropic and phototropic responses of roots and stems. • Understand the role of auxin in the phototropic response of stems. **Learning outcomes** • Describe how plants respond to stimuli with tropic responses, such as geotropism in response to gravity and phototropism in response to light. • Explain the role of auxin in the phototropic response of stems.	2.80; 2.83–2.85	157–160	Investigating geotropism Investigating phototropism
B2j.2 Human nervous system	**Learning objectives** • Understand how organisms are able to respond to changes in their environment. • Understand that a coordinated response requires a stimulus, a receptor and an effector. • Understand that the central nervous system consists of the brain and spinal cord and is linked to sense organs by nerves. • Understand that stimulation of receptors in the sense organs sends electrical impulses along nerves into and out of the central nervous system, resulting in rapid responses. • Understand the role of neurotransmitters at synapses. • Describe the structure and functioning of a simple reflex arc illustrated by the withdrawal of a finger from a hot object. • Describe the structure and function of the eye as a receptor. • Understand the function of the eye in focusing on near and distant objects, and in responding to changes in light intensity.	2.80; 2.82;2.87–2.92	160–167	Speed of reaction

Activity number and name	Learning outcomes and objectives	Specification reference	Student Book pages	Practical
	Learning outcomes • Know that a coordinated response requires a stimulus, receptor and effector. • Understand the human central nervous system consists of the brain and spinal cord, which are linked to the sense organs of the body by nerves. • Describe how stimulation of a sense organ produces electrical impulses in nerves, leading to a rapid response. • Describe the role of neurotransmitters in a synapse. • Know that an example of a simple reflex arc is the withdrawing of a finger from a hot object. • Describe the structure of the eye as an organ specialised for the reception of light stimuli. • Understand how the eye can change focus between near and far objects, and can respond to changes in light intensity.			
B2j.3 Homeostasis	Learning objectives • Understand that homeostasis is the maintenance of a constant internal environment, and that body water content and body temperature are both examples of homeostasis. • Describe the role of the skin in temperature regulation, with reference to sweating, vasoconstriction and vasodilation. Learning outcomes • Understand that homeostasis is the maintenance of a constant internal environment, such as body water content and body temperature. • Describe how the skin regulates internal body temperature by sweating, vasoconstriction and vasodilation.	2.81; 2.93	167–169	Investigating a model for sweating

Activity number and name	Learning outcomes and objectives	Specification reference	Student Book pages	Practical
B2j.4 Human hormonal system	**Learning objectives** • Describe how nervous and hormonal communication control responses and understand the differences between the two systems. • Understand the sources, roles and effects of the following hormones: adrenaline, insulin, testosterone, progesterone and oestrogen. • Understand the sources, roles and effects of the following hormones: ADH, FSH and LH. **(B)** **Learning outcomes** • Describe how, in humans, the nervous system produces rapid responses to stimuli by a particular effector, while the hormonal system usually produces slower responses that last longer and may involve more than one effector. • Understand the sources, roles and effects of adrenaline, insulin, testosterone, progesterone, oestrogen, ADH, FSH and LH.	2.86; 2.94; 2.95B	169–171	

Activity number and name	Learning outcomes and objectives	Specification reference	Student Book pages	Practical
B2j.5 Consolidation and summary	**Learning objectives** • To review the learning points of the topic. • To test understanding through answering questions. **Learning outcomes** • Be familiar with the knowledge and understanding summarised in the End of topic checklist. • Be able to apply this knowledge and understanding by answering the End of topic questions.	2.80–2.95B	172–176	
B3a.1 Sexual and asexual reproduction	**Learning objectives** • Understand the differences between sexual and asexual reproduction. • Understand that fertilisation involves the fusion of a male and female gamete to produce a zygote that undergoes cell division and develops into an embryo. • Understand that plants can reproduce asexually by natural methods (illustrated by runners) and by artificial methods (illustrated by cuttings). **Learning outcomes** • Explain that sexual reproduction is the production of new individuals by the fertilisation of a female gamete by a male gamete to produce a zygote that develops into an embryo. • Explain that asexual reproduction is the production of new genetically identical individuals from the body cells of a parent organism. • Describe natural and artificial methods for producing new individuals in plants by asexual reproduction.	3.1; 3.2; 3.7	190–195	Taking plant cuttings

Activity number and name	Learning outcomes and objectives	Specification reference	Student Book pages	Practical
B3a.2 Pollination in plants	**Learning objectives** • Describe the structures of an insect-pollinated and a wind-pollinated flower and explain how each is adapted for pollination. • Understand that the growth of the pollen tube followed by fertilisation leads to seed and fruit formation. **Learning outcomes** • Describe the structures of an insect-pollinated and a wind-pollinated flower. • Explain how the structures of an insect-pollinated and a wind-pollinated flower are adapted for pollination. • Explain how growth of the pollen tube leads to fertilisation, which leads to seed and fruit formation.	3.3; 3.4	195–197	Flower dissection
B3a.3 Fertilisation and seed formation	**Learning objectives** • Understand that fertilisation involves the fusion of a male and female gamete to produce a zygote that undergoes cell division and develops into an embryo. • Understand that the growth of the pollen tube followed by fertilisation leads to seed and fruit formation. **Learning outcomes** • Explain that fertilisation involves the fusion of a male and a female gamete to produce a zygote that undergoes cell division and develops into an embryo. • Describe how growth of the pollen tube followed by fertilisation leads to seed and fruit formation.	3.2; 3.4	197–199	Looking at seeds

Edexcel International GCSE Biology Teacher Pack

Activity number and name	Learning outcomes and objectives	Specification reference	Student Book pages	Practical
B3a.4 Seed germination	Learning objectives • Practical: Investigate the conditions needed for seed germination. • Understand how germinating seeds utilise food reserves until the seedling can carry out photosynthesis. Learning outcomes • Explain that seeds need particular conditions for germination. • Describe how germinating seeds use their food reserves until the seedling can carry out photosynthesis.	3.5; 3.6	199–202	Conditions for germination
B3a.5 Human reproductive system	Learning objectives • Understand how the structure and function of the male and female reproductive systems are adapted for their functions. • Understand the roles of oestrogen and testosterone in the development of secondary sexual characteristics. Learning outcomes • Explain that the organs, tissues and cells in the male and female human reproductive systems are adapted for their role in reproduction. • Describe how oestrogen and testosterone control the development of secondary sexual characteristics.	3.8; 3.13	202–203	

Activity number and name	Learning outcomes and objectives	Specification reference	Student Book pages	Practical
B3a.6 Human menstrual cycle	Learning objectives • Understand the roles of oestrogen and progesterone in the menstrual cycle. • Understand the roles of FSH and LH in the menstrual cycle. **(B)** Learning outcomes • Understand how the hormones oestrogen and progesterone control the menstrual cycle. • Understand how FSH and LH control the menstrual cycle. **(B)**	3.9; 3.10B	204–205	
B3a.7 Development of the human fetus	Learning objectives • Describe the role of the placenta in the nutrition of the developing embryo. • Understand how the developing embryo is protected by amniotic fluid. Learning outcomes • Be able to describe the role of the placenta in providing nutrition for the developing embryo. • Explain how structures in the uterus support the developing embryo.	3.11; 3.12	205–208	
B3a.8 Consolidation and summary	Learning objectives • To review the learning points of the topic. • To test understanding through answering questions. Learning outcomes • Be familiar with the knowledge and understanding summarised in the End of topic checklist. • Be able to apply this knowledge and understanding by answering End of topic questions.	3.1–3.13	209–213	

Activity number and name	Learning outcomes and objectives	Specification reference	Student Book pages	Practical
B3b.1 The structure of DNA and protein synthesis	Learning objectives • Understand that the genome is the entire DNA of an organism and that a gene is a section of a molecule of DNA that codes for a specific protein. • Understand that the nucleus of a cell contains chromosomes on which genes are located. • Describe a DNA molecule as two strands coiled to form a double helix, the strands being linked by a series of paired bases: adenine (A) with thymine (T), and cytosine (C) with guanine (G). **(B)** • Understand that an RNA molecule is single stranded and contains uracil (U) instead of thymine (T). **(B)** • Describe the stages of protein synthesis including transcription and translation, including the role of mRNA, ribosomes, tRNA, codons and anticodons. **(B)** • Understand how genes exist in alternative forms called alleles which give rise to differences in inherited characteristics. • Know that in human cells the diploid number of chromosomes is 46 and the haploid number is 23. Learning outcomes • Explain that a nucleus contains chromosomes, on which genes are located. • Describe a gene as a small portion of DNA coding for a specific protein, and the genome comprises all the DNA of an organism. • Describe a DNA molecule as two strands coiled to form a double helix, the strands being linked by a series of paired bases: adenine (A) with thymine (T), and cytosine (C) with guanine (G). **(B)** • Explain that RNA differs from DNA in being single stranded and containing uracil (U) instead of thymine (T). **(B)** • Describe the stages of protein synthesis i.e. transcription and translation, including the role of mRNA, ribosomes, tRNA, codons and anticodons. **(B)** • Explain that genes exist in alternative forms called alleles, which give rise to differences in inherited characteristics. • Explain that human diploid body cells contain 46 chromosomes, and human haploid gamete cells contain 23 chromosomes.	3.14–3.19; 3.32	214–219	

Activity number and name	Learning outcomes and objectives	Specification reference	Student Book pages	Practical
B3b.2 Inheriting characteristics	**Learning objectives** • Understand the meaning of the terms: dominant, recessive, homozygous, heterozygous, phenotype and genotype. • Understand the meaning of the term codominance. **(B)** • Understand that most phenotypic features are the result of polygenic inheritance rather than single genes. • Describe patterns of monohybrid inheritance using a genetic diagram. • Understand how to interpret family pedigrees. • Predict probabilities of outcomes from monohybrid crosses. • Understand how the sex of a person is controlled by one pair of chromosomes, XX in a female and XY in a male. • Describe the determination of sex of the offspring at fertilisation, using a genetic diagram. **Learning outcomes** • Write a definition for important terms in genetics include: dominant, recessive, homozygous, heterozygous, phenotype, genotype and codominance. • Understand that most phenotypic features are the result of polygenic inheritance. • Describe patterns of monohybrid inheritance using genetic diagrams, which can be used to predict probabilities of outcomes. • Understand how to interpret family pedigrees. • Describe how the sex of a person is controlled by one pair of chromosomes: XX in a female and XY in a male. • Describe the determination of the sex of offspring at fertilisation, using a genetic diagram.	3.20–3.27	219–230	Investigating monohybrid inheritance

Activity number and name	Learning outcomes and objectives	Specification reference	Student Book pages	Practical
B3b.3 Cell division	**Learning objectives** • Understand how division of a diploid cell by mitosis produces two cells that contain identical sets of chromosomes. • Understand that mitosis occurs during growth, repair, cloning and asexual reproduction. • Understand how division of a cell by meiosis produces four cells, each with half the number of chromosomes, and that this results in the formation of genetically different haploid gametes. **Learning outcomes** • Explain how division of a diploid cell by mitosis produces two cells that contain identical sets of chromosomes. • Explain that mitosis occurs during growth, repair, cloning and asexual reproduction. • Explain that division of a cell by meiosis produces four cells, each with half the number of chromosomes, and that this results in the formation of genetically different haploid gametes.	3.28–3.30	231–233	

Edexcel International GCSE Biology Teacher Pack

© HarperCollins*Publishers* Ltd 2017

Activity number and name	Learning outcomes and objectives	Specification reference	Student Book pages	Practical
B3b.4 Variation and mutation	**Learning objectives** • Understand how random fertilisation produces genetic variation of offspring. • Understand that variation within a species can be genetic, environmental, or a combination of both. • Understand that mutation is a rare, random change in genetic material that can be inherited. • Understand how a change in DNA can affect the phenotype by altering the sequence of amino acids in a protein. **(B)** • Understand how most genetic mutations have no effect on the phenotype, some have a small effect and rarely do they have a significant effect. **(B)** • Understand that the incidence of mutations can be increased by exposure to ionising radiation (for example gamma rays, X-rays and ultraviolet rays) and some chemical mutagens (for example chemicals in tobacco). **(B)** **Learning outcomes** • Explain that random fertilisation produces genetic variation of offspring. • Explain that variation within a species can be genetic, environmental, or a combination of both. • Explain that mutation is a rare, random change in genetic material that can be inherited. • Describe how a change in DNA can affect the phenotype by altering the sequence of amino acids in a protein. **(B)** • Explain that most genetic mutations have no effect on the phenotype, some have a small effect and rarely do they have a significant effect. **(B)** • Describe how the incidence of mutations can be increased by exposure to ionising radiation (for example gamma rays, X-rays and ultraviolet rays) and some chemical mutagens (for example chemicals in tobacco). **(B)**	3.31; 3.33; 3.34; 3.35B–3.37B	234–236	

Edexcel International GCSE Biology Teacher Pack   410   © HarperCollins*Publishers* Ltd 2017

Activity number and name	Learning outcomes and objectives	Specification reference	Student Book pages	Practical
B3b.5 Evolution by natural selection	**Learning objectives** • Explain Darwin's theory of evolution by natural selection. • Understand how resistance to antibiotics can increase in bacterial populations, and appreciate how such an increase can lead to infections being difficult to control. **Learning outcomes** • Describe the process of evolution by means of natural selection. • Explain how resistance to antibiotics can cause an increase in the size of bacterial populations.	3.38; 3.39	236–239	A model of natural selection
B3b.6 Consolidation and summary	**Learning objectives** • To review the learning points of the topic. • To test understanding through answering questions. **Learning outcomes** • Be familiar with the knowledge and understanding summarised in the End of topic checklist. • Be able to apply this knowledge and understanding by answering End of topic questions.	3.14–3.39	240–247	

Activity number and name	Learning outcomes and objectives	Specification reference	Student Book pages	Practical
B4a.1 Ecology and organisms	**Learning objectives** • Understand the terms population, community, habitat and ecosystem. • Practical: Investigate the population size of an organism in two different areas using quadrats. • Understand the term biodiversity. **(B)** • Practical: Investigate the distribution of organisms in their habitats and measure biodiversity using quadrats. **(B)** • Understand how abiotic and biotic factors affect the population size and distribution of organisms. **Learning outcomes** • Write definitions for the terms *population, community, habitat, ecosystem and biodiversity*. • Describe how to use quadrats to measure the population size of an organism. • Describe how to use quadrats to measure the distribution of organisms in a habitat, and measure biodiversity. **(B)** • Explain how abiotic and biotic factors affect the population size and distribution of organisms.	4.1–4.5	256–264	Measuring environmental factors Random sampling with a quadrat Sampling along a transect
B4a.2 Consolidation and summary	**Learning objectives** • To review the learning points of the topic. • To test understanding through answering questions. **Learning outcomes** • Be familiar with the knowledge and understanding summarised in the End of topic checklist. • Be able to apply this knowledge and understanding by answering End of topic questions.	4.1–4.5	265–268	

412

Activity number and name	Learning outcomes and objectives	Specification reference	Student Book pages	Practical
B4b.1 Trophic levels and food webs	Learning objectives • Understand the names given to different trophic levels, including producers, primary, secondary and tertiary consumers and decomposers. • Understand the concepts of food chains and food webs. • Understand the transfer of substances and energy along a food chain. Learning outcomes • Identify and explain the names given to the different trophic levels. • Write definitions for the terms *food chain* and *food web*. • Explain how substances and energy are transferred along a food chain.	4.6–4.8	268–271	
B4b.2 Using pyramid diagrams	Learning objectives • Understand the concepts of pyramids of number, pyramids of biomass and pyramids of energy. Learning outcomes • Write definitions of the terms *pyramid of number*, *pyramid of biomass*, *pyramid of energy*.	4.7	272–276	
B4b.3 Energy losses in food chains	Learning objectives • Understand the transfer of energy along a food chain. • Explain why only about 10% of energy is transferred from one trophic level to the next. Learning outcomes • Explain how energy is transferred along a food chain. • Explain why there are limits to the proportion of energy in one trophic level that is transferred to the next trophic level in a food chain.	4.8, 4.9	276–279	

Edexcel International GCSE Biology Teacher Pack

Activity number and name	Learning outcomes and objectives	Specification reference	Student Book pages	Practical
B4b.4 Consolidation and summary	**Learning objectives** • To review the learning points of the topic. • To test understanding through answering questions. **Learning outcomes** • Be familiar with the knowledge and understanding summarised in the End of topic checklist. • Be able to apply this knowledge and understanding by answering End of topic questions.	4.6–4.9	280–283	
B4c.1 Carbon cycle	**Learning objectives** • Describe the stages in the carbon cycle, including respiration, photosynthesis, decomposition and combustion. **Learning outcomes** • Describe stages in the carbon cycle, including respiration, photosynthesis, decomposition and combustion.	4.10	283–286	
B4c.2 Nitrogen cycle	**Learning objectives** • Describe the stages in the nitrogen cycle, including the roles of bacteria and decomposers. **(B)** **Learning outcomes** • Describe the stages in the nitrogen cycle, including the roles of nitrogen fixing bacteria, decomposers, nitrifying bacteria and denitrifying bacteria. **(B)**	4.11B	286–282	
B4c.3 Consolidation and summary	**Learning objectives** • To review the learning points of the topic. • To test understanding through answering questions. **Learning outcomes** • Be familiar with the knowledge and understanding summarised in the End of topic checklist. • Be able to apply this knowledge and understanding by answering End of topic questions.	4.10; 4.11B	290–293	

Activity number and name	Learning outcomes and objectives	Specification reference	Student Book pages	Practical
B4d.1 Air pollution	Learning objectives • Understand the biological consequences of pollution of air by sulfur dioxide and carbon monoxide. Learning outcomes • Describe the biological consequences of pollution of air by sulfur dioxide and by carbon monoxide.	4.12	293–298	Acidity and germination
B4d.2 The greenhouse effect	Learning objectives • Understand that water vapour, carbon dioxide, nitrous oxide, methane and CFCs are greenhouse gases. • Understand how human activities contribute to greenhouse gases. • Understand how an increase in greenhouse gases results in an enhanced greenhouse effect and that this may lead to global warming and its consequences. Learning outcomes • Name the greenhouse gases and explain how human activities are contributing to their release. • Explain how an increase in greenhouse gases may lead to an enhanced greenhouse effect and global warming, and discuss the effects this may have.	4.13–4.15	298–301	
B4d.3 Eutrophication	Learning objectives • Understand the biological consequences of pollution of water by sewage. • Understand the biological consequences of eutrophication caused by leached minerals from fertiliser. Learning outcomes • Explain the biological consequences of pollution of water by sewage, including increases in the number of microorganisms causing depletion of oxygen. • Explain how eutrophication and water pollution can result from fertiliser leaching into water.	4.16; 4.17	301–305	

Activity number and name	Learning outcomes and objectives	Specification reference	Student Book pages	Practical
B4d.4 Deforestation	**Learning objectives** • Understand the effects of deforestation, including leaching, soil erosion, disturbance of evapotranspiration and the carbon cycle, and the balance of atmospheric gases. **(B)** **Learning outcomes** • Describe the effects of deforestation, including leaching, soil erosion, disturbance of evapotranspiration, and the balance of atmospheric oxygen and carbon dioxide. **(B)**	4.18B	305–306	
B4d.5 Consolidation and summary	**Learning objectives** • To review the learning points of the topic. • To test understanding through answering questions. **Learning outcomes** • Be familiar with the knowledge and understanding summarised in the End of topic checklist. • Be able to apply this knowledge and understanding by answering End of topic questions.	4.12–4.18B	307–310	

Activity number and name	Learning outcomes and objectives	Specification reference	Student Book pages	Practical
B5a.1 Crop plants	**Learning objectives** • Describe how glasshouses and polythene tunnels can be used to increase the yield of certain crops. • Understand the effects on crop yield of increased carbon dioxide and increased temperature in glasshouses. • Understand how the use of fertiliser can increase crop yield. • Understand the reasons for pest control and the advantages and disadvantages of using pesticides and biological control with crop plants. **Learning outcomes** • Explain how the conditions under which crop plants are grown in glasshouses and in fields can be manipulated to increase plant growth and yield of crop. • Understand the reasons for pest control and the advantages and disadvantages of using pesticides and biological control with crop plants.	5.1–5.4	322–329	

Activity number and name	Learning outcomes and objectives	Specification reference	Student Book pages	Practical
B5a.2 Growing microorganisms	Learning objectives • Understand the role of yeast in the production of food including bread. • Practical: Investigate the role of anaerobic respiration by yeast in different conditions. • Understand the role of bacteria (*Lactobacillus*) in the production of yoghurt. • Understand the use of an industrial fermenter, and explain the need to provide suitable conditions in the fermenter, for the growth of microorganisms. Learning outcomes • Understand the role of yeast in the production of food such as bread. • Describe a simple experiment to investigate anaerobic respiration by yeast, in different conditions. • Understand the role of bacteria (*Lactobacillus*) in the production of yoghurt. • Interpret and label a diagram of an industrial fermenter and explain the need to provide suitable conditions in the fermenter, including aseptic precautions, nutrients, optimum temperature and pH, oxygenation and agitation, for the growth of microorganisms.	5.5–5.8	329–334	The effect of temperature on yeast The effect of glucose concentration on yeast Making yoghurt
B5a.3 Farming fish	Learning objectives • Understand the methods used to farm large numbers of fish to provide a source of protein. (B) Learning outcomes • Explain the methods which are used to farm large numbers of fish to provide a source of protein, including maintenance of water quality, control of intraspecific and interspecific predation, control of disease, removal of waste products, quality and frequency of feeding and the use of selective breeding. (B)	5.9B	335–337	

Activity number and name	Learning outcomes and objectives	Specification reference	Student Book pages	Practical
B5a.4 Consolidation and summary	Learning objectives • To review the learning points of the topic. • To test understanding through answering questions. Learning outcomes • Be familiar with the knowledge and understanding summarised in the End of topic checklist. • Be able to apply this knowledge and understanding by answering the End of topic questions.	5.1–5.9B	338–341	
B5b.1 Selective breeding in plants and animals	Learning objectives • Understand how selective breeding can develop plants with desired characteristics. • Understand how selective breeding can develop animals with desired characteristics. Learning outcomes • Understand that plants with desired characteristics can be developed by selective breeding. • Understand that animals with desired characteristics can be developed by selective breeding.	5.10; 5.11	342–347	
B5b.2 Consolidation and summary	Learning objectives • To review the learning points of the topic. • To test understanding through answering questions. Learning outcomes • Be familiar with the knowledge and understanding summarised in the End of topic checklist. • Be able to apply this knowledge and understanding by answering End of topic questions.	5.10; 5.11	348–349	

Activity number and name	Learning outcomes and objectives	Specification reference	Student Book pages	Practical
B5c.1 The process of genetic modification (genetic engineering)	**Learning objectives** • Understand how restriction enzymes are used to cut DNA at specific sites and ligase enzymes are used to join pieces of DNA together. • Understand how plasmids and viruses can act as vectors, which take up pieces of DNA, and then insert this recombinant DNA into other cells. • Understand that the term transgenic means the transfer of genetic material from one species to a different species. **Learning outcomes** • Describe the use of restriction enzymes to cut DNA at specific sites and ligase enzymes to join pieces of DNA together. • Describe how plasmids and viruses can act as vectors, which take up pieces of DNA, then insert this recombinant DNA into other cells. • Understand that the term *transgenic* means the transfer of genetic material from one species to a different species.	5.12; 5.13; 5.16	350–352	
B5c.2 Genetically modified organisms	**Learning objectives** • Understand how large amounts of human insulin can be manufactured from genetically modified bacteria that are grown in a fermenter. • Understand how genetically modified plants can be used to improve food production. **Learning outcomes** • Explain how large amounts of human insulin can be manufactured from genetically modified bacteria that are grown in a fermenter. • Explain how genetically modified plants can be used to improve food production.	5.14; 5.15	352–355	

Edexcel International GCSE Biology Teacher Pack

© HarperCollins*Publishers* Ltd 2017

Activity number and name	Learning outcomes and objectives	Specification reference	Student Book pages	Practical
B5c.3 Consolidation and summary	**Learning objectives** • To review the learning points of the topic. • To test understanding through answering questions. **Learning outcomes** • Be familiar with the knowledge and understanding summarised in the End of topic checklist. • Be able to apply this knowledge and understanding by answering End of topic questions.	5.12–5.16	356–358	
B5d.1 Micropropagation	**Learning objectives** • Describe the process of micropropagation (tissue culture) in which explants are grown *in vitro*. **(B)** • Understand how micropropagation can be used to produce commercial quantities of genetically identical plants with desirable characteristics. **(B)** **Learning outcomes** • Describe the process of micropropagation (tissue culture) in which small pieces of plants (explants) are grown *in vitro* using nutrient media. **(B)** • Understand how micropropagation can be used to produce commercial quantities of genetically identical plants (clones) with desirable characteristics. **(B)**	5.17B; 5.18B	359–361	Micropropagation

Edexcel International GCSE Biology Teacher Pack

Activity number and name	Learning outcomes and objectives	Specification reference	Student Book pages	Practical
B5d.2 Cloning mammals	**Learning objectives** • Describe the stages in the production of cloned mammals by nuclear transfer. **(B)** • Understand how cloned transgenic animals can be used to produce human proteins. **(B)** **Learning outcomes** • Describe the stages in the production of cloned mammals involving the introduction of a diploid nucleus from a mature cell into an enucleated egg cell, illustrated by Dolly the sheep. **(B)** • Explain how cloned transgenic animals can be used to produce human proteins. **(B)**	5.19B; 5.20B	362–364	
B5d.3 Consolidation and summary	**Learning objectives** • To review the learning points of the topic. • To test understanding through answering questions. **Learning outcomes** • Be familiar with the knowledge and understanding summarised in the End of topic checklist. • Be able to apply this knowledge and understanding by answering End of topic questions.	5.17B–5.20B	365–366	

Notes

Notes